KATHERINE MANSFIELD

Selected Letters

Katherine Mansfield *c.*1920. Reproduced by permission of the
Turnbull Library, Wellington, New Zealand.

KATHERINE MANSFIELD

Selected Letters

Edited by
VINCENT O'SULLIVAN

Drawn from
The Collected Letters of Katherine Mansfield, edited by
Vincent O'Sullivan and Margaret Scott

CLARENDON PRESS · OXFORD
1989

Oxford University Press, Walton Street, Oxford OX2 6DP
Oxford New York Toronto
Delhi Bombay Calcutta Madras Karachi
Petaling Jaya Singapore Hong Kong Tokyo
Nairobi Dar es Salaam Cape Town
Melbourne Auckland

and associated companies in
Berlin Ibadan

Oxford is a trade mark of Oxford University Press

Published in the United States
by Oxford University Press, New York

British Library Cataloguing in Publication Data
Mansfield, Katherine, 1888–1923
Katherine Mansfield : selected letters.
1. Fiction in English. New Zealand writers.
Mansfield, Katherine 1888–1923
I. Title II. O'Sullivan, Vincent, 1937–
823
ISBN 0-19-818592-8

Library of Congress Cataloging in Publication Data
Mansfield, Katherine, 1888–1923.
[Correspondence. Selections]
Katherine Mansfield selected letters / edited by Vincent O'Sullivan.
p. cm.
"Drawn from The collected letters of Katherine Mansfield, edited
by Vincent O'Sullivan and Margaret Scott."
Bibliography: p. Includes index.
1. Mansfield, Katherine, 1888–1923—Correspondence. 2. Authors. New Zealand—
20th century—Correspondence. I. O'Sullivan, Vincent. II. Title.
823'.912—dc19 PR9639.3.M258Z48 1989 [B] 88-26576
ISBN 0-19-818592-8

Set by Latimer Trend & Company Ltd, Plymouth
Printed in Great Britain by
The Alden Press, Oxford

CONTENTS

INTRODUCTION   vii

LIST OF LETTERS   xv

CHRONOLOGY   xxi

BIOGRAPHICAL REGISTER   xxv

THE LETTERS   I

NOTES   287

INDEX   315

INTRODUCTION

PEOPLE write letters with the assumption that absence can be atoned for. The closer the correspondents or the more important their communication, the greater the skills they must find if the fiction of direct contact is to be maintained. The strong personal letter, with its intimacies and frank exchanges and shared concerns, its sense of thought being generated as though in conversation, is perhaps the kind we now value most. Keats and Byron in the last century, and Woolf and Lawrence in this, seem the obvious examples. Katherine Mansfield might be offered as another. Her letters carry the same conviction that how others hear her is for the moment her primary concern; she strives to have them receive her as directly as they would through her spoken word. Even her punctuation is turned to that end, so often refusing the conventions of comma and point for the breaks and dashes that keep a sense of connection alive. For energy, as much as wit or encouragement, may be read as an extension of courtesy. In print as in speech, she will earn attention rather than simply assume it.

In any selection the quality of single letters builds towards something else; the immediacies of each day form a life whose contours only gradually emerge. Each letter is read within this double perspective, the business of here and now taken into a pattern which can never quite be available to the writer herself. A subsequent clarity, however, is one of the reasons why we continue to be held—by the figure on the skyline, as it were, at the same time as she talks about moving towards it.

When the seventeen-year-old Kathleen Beauchamp, still undecided about her name but already certain of her calling, confided to a schoolfriend that to try '*all* sorts of lives' (p. 5) was both irresponsible and fascinating, she might have been setting the terms by which later she was so often judged. 'Enigmatic' is the term most often implied by those who knew her. An even wilful indeterminacy is what acquaintances remarked on, reminding them of masks and attitudes. They found her witty yet secretive, at times cynical and calculating, and variously charming, affectionate or remote. D. H. Lawrence put his finger on her colonialism as a defining mark, her tendency to be at odds with wherever she happened to be, yet for all that making the claims of the banker's privileged daughter (*Collected Letters*, I, p. xv). There was a duality about her that could seem theatrical and troubling, as though her tendency to elude expectations was something she must account for.

Where others asked for markers of permanence, Mansfield preferred to view life as a process, a matter of trial and error from which one's reality emerged — 'one must be ... continually ... shedding & renewing, & examining & trying to place' (p. 168). The young girl in Wellington had copied into her notebooks Wilde's advice that we are here to realize our natures perfectly, that to be final is to be limited. In her stand against her parents, she flaunted Art as her vocation and personality as its splendidly drifting accòmplice. For Walter Pater was a presence too in her thinking. His fine discriminations would shade into her own life of glimpses, as she later regarded with some misgivings her grasping at a world in which the impressionist's vivid moments took precedence over consistency. But that general sense of the adventitious that can be taken from Mansfield's writing in any genre is to be balanced by the clear-eyed, unsentimental appraisals of herself. Among daily events and ordinary exchanges, increasingly poor health and divergent moods, one picks up her dissatisfaction with those 'many selves'. Over several years there is a push towards an alternative, towards what one might call a centre of self-acceptance that she found difficult to talk about, but essential to her before she knew quite where to look. Part of Mansfield's modernity is precisely this sense throughout her correspondence of wanting to be settled, of needing some point of emotional or religious stability, yet accepting that to want it implied neither the right nor the likelihood of attaining it.

Mansfield's letters, then, are so often reports from a front whose position is seldom fixed. She has become perhaps the representative voice for a certain kind of twentieth-century woman and a certain cast of thought. She speaks for the *femme seule* of her fiction, the mind that finds itself on the edge of things, its expectations already tinged with anticipated regret. It is the voice of the invalid and the stranger, of railway stations and temporary lodgings, brief acquaintances and altered plans, waiting rooms and cafés in which one could 'watch the pattern people make among tables & bottles and glasses, to watch women when they are off their guard. . . . To air oneself among these things, to seek them, to explore them and then to go apart and detach oneself from them—and to write—after the ferment has quite subsided' (p. 54). Her restlessness expanded into that delight in detail and observation which bad health and loneliness both fretted at and was consoled by at the same time. Her will to control minutely suggested a larger mastery than was usually the case. As she had told her first lover, 'I like always to have a great grip on Life, so that I intensify the so-called small things—so that truly everything is significant' (p. 19). Yet it could be an almost febrile excitement that she brought to whatever held her attention, with a recording sometimes as painful as it was intense.

There were occasions when Mansfield spoke of life as being like a cinema, a stream of images passing before one that increased the sense of the surrounding dark. She spoke quite differently of painting, as a fixing of specific values. Her letters as much as her stories extend both ideas. The feeling of performance present at times in her correspondence, as it was also in her friendships, is in part a wariness of any standpoint sustained for too long. It is an impatience, too, for something to oppose the belief that she was not yet quite where she belonged or where she was content to be. And at the centre of that restlessness, as much as her health and its unpredictable demands, was her love for Middleton Murry; that 'utterly INTENSE love', as she called it, (p. 97) which was both exhausting and necessary.

Against the evidence, Murry later embalmed that love in a perfection it was far too interesting ever to have possessed. Their correspondence in fact points up how infrequently their lives were either predictable or steady. They seldom experienced the domestic certainties Mansfield so envied in her mother and in Virginia Woolf. There was never the child she hoped for, nor the permanent home, nor quite the money. Yet whatever went wrong or failed to measure up, there was the assumption that their love was robust enough to survive.

That faith echoed at the end of her informal will: 'I feel no
other lovers have walked the earth so joyfully—in spite of all'
(p. 267).

Mansfield's letters to Murry worked with tact as well as great
warmth to make up for their separations. They flatter and
amuse and assure, they direct with practicalities while also
continuing the game of gifted children in their secret and
untainted world. And their tart exasperations are a real part of
the exchange. Mansfield quite understood that Murry was less
resilient than herself. The thing to do was to ease him from the
gloom he was easily given to, to advise him when she could, and
at times to joke about it. Murry was no more spared her
sharpness than Gurdjieff would be, when she sat at the guru's
feet and yet referred to him off-handedly as 'the rug merchant'. As a friend remembered, 'she would tell how Murry
stood in the bus looking so *gone*—"like a pair of moleskin
trousers hung out to dry." Someone said "*give* the poor old
soldier a seat", but Katherine said "He was like that *before* the
war." (Mantz papers, Texas). But if the slurs came from
elsewhere she was quick in his defence. 'If you get past the
knocker & open the door you'd find an extraordinarily simple
eager passionate boy, very sensitive, *desperately* loyal, full of
tweaks and twirls of <u>fun</u>' (p. 110). The word 'boy' is to the
point. The diminutives were numerous in a relationship that
frequently insisted it would walk its own enchanted path
without being impinged on by the crudities of others. She was
to be big sister and little mate as well as lover and wife. At the
same time Mansfield was more aware than Murry of what the
relationship didn't have, and what stood in their way. She
would put much down to her having no desire to be simply an
intellectual, while Murry's inclination was to be little else.

The seventy letters in this selection are less than a fifth of
those that passed between them. They do, though, fairly
represent their years together and the feelings those years took
in. The months October 1919 to February 1920 are given more
fully than any others, as an example of those almost daily
exchanges during one of several troubled times between them.
The letters to other correspondents are also chosen with an eye
to a balanced proportion from each of the five volumes of the
Collected Letters, and from the kinds of letters she wrote.

The number of people Mansfield corresponded with was never large, and contracted over the years. This may reflect an increasing caution in committing herself to new friendships, as it may the fact that when the telephone was installed at Portland Villas, the Hampstead home she lived in longer than anywhere else, the need to write to London friends at least would have been reduced. Whenever she was apart from Murry he dominated her correspondence as he did her thoughts, and at such times there are comparatively few letters to anyone else. For only a handful of friends mattered very much—Koteliansky perhaps most of all, Ottoline Morrell at times, Dorothy Brett in the last two years especially, and Lawrence intermittently (although he did not keep what she wrote to him). They sustained her links with a world going on apart from her, apart from her declining health and her work and her anxieties with Murry. Other exchanges kept her in touch with a small number of painters and writers, as seen in letters of spontaneous kindness to young Richard Murry or to strangers like the South African novelist Sarah Gertrude Millin. There were letters too which were less sincere, which pressed the Schiffs to false intimacies or Sydney Waterlow to assume greater concern than she felt. Of course, some communications have been lost, and others Mansfield deliberately got rid of, including the hundreds of pages she instructed Ida Baker to burn. The most important of her friendships accordingly has been assessed by what she wrote of it to Murry, a version true for the day with its rages and irritations, but without the extended affection that only a few letters and Baker's own memoirs preserve. Most too of what she wrote to her New Zealand family has not survived, although enough remains to catch both the warmth and the uneasiness, and the massive presence of her father in her life. For all her guying of him in her stories, he was a parent whose approval she anxiously courted.

It has been claimed with a certain facile plausibility that illness and nothing else took Mansfield at the end of her life to the Gurdjieff Institute for the Harmonious Development of Man at Fontainebleau, a kind of last hope once medical possibilities ran out. The later letters show something far less simple taking place, a deliberate conclusion to twelve years of living with a brilliant but cautiously limited man of letters, and sixteen of putting on fronts, dodging and equivocating—judgements she passed on herself. Mansfield was not after miracles so much as good luck, and there was no attempted 'mysticism' about it. When her reading and the information she picked up from friends led her to ask if she might join Gurdjieff's community, it was useful and logical that she take that step. She could think of nowhere else that might relieve her of the divorce between mind and ordinary living that increasingly disturbed her. There was nowhere else that held out the ideal of shared community she no longer expected from her marriage. She felt too that she had reached an impasse with her stories, and the restrictions her own fastidiousness placed on her. She experienced more acutely than ever 'how isolated we each of us are— at the last' (p. 218). Fontainebleau was her chance of getting through. And as Antony Alpers' biography has pointed out, it was also a kind of coming home to that family ambience she had written about many times yet felt excluded from. In a sense Gurdjieff was even Father in another guise, wiser and more tolerant. His programme of eastern music and physical work and dismantling the ego was an antidote to her long disenchantment with Europe and its war, and with what she seemed to herself in their context. Where she stood finally, with that collection of Russian émigrés and eccentrics, displaced persons and spiritual adventurers, she stood utterly by an act of will. Her long friendship with Koteliansky, her longer admiration for Slavic writing and life, allowed her a rare sense of rapport. 'They are', as she had never said of the English or the French, 'my own people at last' (p. 275).

All the letters in this selection are unabridged. The text is that prepared by Margaret Scott for the *Collected Letters* and reproduces Mansfield's distinctive punctuation, the underlinings and capitalization that seem an extension of her spoken emphases, her sometimes erratic spelling and paragraphing, and her occasional grammatical awkwardness. Addresses and closures have been standardized, with a vertical line indicating a line break in the manuscript. When addresses, dates or other material are supplied by the present editor, these are placed in square brackets.[1] A degree sign ° indicates that a note may be found at the end of the book.[2]

The reader may find problems with two aspects of Mansfield's language. One is the hypocoristic distortion sometimes used in letters to Murry. Usually this is transparent enough—'fack' for 'fact', for example—but occasionally elucidation seems called for. A greater difficulty occurs with her use of foreign languages. Although she spoke French with ease, and German to a lesser extent, her written use of both was imperfect. At times she sits somewhere between English and the other language, carrying the expression of one into the structure of the other, or guessing at a foreign idiom based on an English one, quite aware that what she writes is a quirky *mélange*. Usually there is no problem in catching the drift of what she intends, but there may be a considerable one in offering a translation. Often the version in square brackets must be hedged with reservations. In a few cases her choice of words defies even an approximation (e.g. p. 65). I am grateful to Lauris Edmond and Jacqui Matthews for advice on these tricky patches, as I am more generally to Antony Alpers, the finest of Mansfield's biographers, and to her eminent bibliographer, Brownlee Kirkpatrick. I also thank Stephanie Pride for her energetic research.

Mansfield's letters are widely dispersed and a number of institutions kindly gave permission for their use: the Alexander Turnbull Library, Wellington; the University of Birmingham; the British Library, London; Dartmouth College Library, Hanover, New Hampshire; the Mitchell Library, Sydney; McMaster University, Hamilton, Ontario; the Newberry Library, Chicago; Stanford University, Stanford, California; the University of Sussex, Brighton; the Humanities Research Center, the University of Texas at Austin; the University of Windsor, Windsor, Ontario; the University of Witwatersrand, Johannesburg.

[1] My own words in the text are in square brackets. Angle brackets < > enclose material written and crossed out by Mansfield.

[2] Many people are referred to in the letters. Where their identitites are known, they are provided either in the notes or in the Biographical Register.

LIST OF LETTERS

Correspondent

Sylvia Payne	23 Dec. 1903	1
Sylvia Payne	24 Jan. 1904	2
Sylvia Payne	24 Apr. 1906	3
Sylvia Payne	8 Jan. 1907	5
E. J. Brady	23 Sept. 1907	6
Annie Burnell Beauchamp	20 Nov. 1907	7
Sylvia Payne	4 Mar. 1908	10
Vera Beauchamp	19 June 1908	12
Garnet Trowell	23 Sept. 1908	15
Garnet Trowell	13 Oct. 1908	17
Garnet Trowell	8 Nov. 1908	18
Ida Baker?	before Apr.? 1909	20
J. M. Murry	Early May 1913	21
J. M. Murry	May–June? 1913	22
Ida Baker	24 Feb. 1914	23
Frieda Lawrence	20 Feb. 1915	24
S. S. Koteliansky	8 Mar. 1915	25
J. M. Murry	21 Mar. 1915	25
J. M. Murry	25 Mar. 1915	28
J. M. Murry	28 Mar. 1915	29
J. M. Murry	15 May 1915	32
S. S. Koteliansky	17 May 1915	34
Leslie Beauchamp	25 Aug. 1915	36
S. S. Koteliansky	19 Nov. 1915	37
J. M. Murry	11 Dec. 1915	38
J. M. Murry	14–15 Dec. 1915	40
J. M. Murry	25 Dec. 1915	42
Frederick Goodyear	4 Mar. 1916	46
S. S. Koteliansky	11 May 1916	48
Beatrice Campbell	14 May 1916	51
Bertrand Russell	7 Dec. 1916	53
Bertrand Russell	17 Dec. 1916	53

Correspondent

Ottoline Morrell	24 June? 1917	54
Virginia Woolf	24 June? 1917	55
Ottoline Morrell	13 July 1917	56
J. M. Murry	late July 1917	58
Dorothy Brett	11 Oct. 1917	59
J. D. Fergusson	15 Jan. 1918	61
J. M. Murry	21 Jan. 1918	63
J. M. Murry	23 Jan. 1918	65
J. M. Murry	30–31 Jan. 1918	67
J. M. Murry	3 Feb. 1918	69
J. M. Murry	3–4 Feb. 1918	71
J. M. Murry	19 Feb. 1918	72
J. M. Murry	3 Mar. 1918	74
J. M. Murry	18 Mar. 1918	77
J. M. Murry	23 Mar. 1918	79
J. M. Murry	30 Mar. 1918	80
J. M. Murry	1 Apr. 1918	82
J. M. Murry	6 Apr. 1918	83
Ida Baker	12 Apr. 1918	85
Ida Baker	18 Apr. 1918	86
Ottoline Morrell	12 May 1918	87
J. M. Murry	19 May 1918	88
Dorothy Brett	22 May 1918	89
J. M. Murry	23 May 1918	91
Ottoline Morrell	24 May 1918	93
J. M. Murry	26 May 1918	95
J. M. Murry	27 May 1918	97
J. M. Murry	5 June 1918	100
J. M. Murry	6 June 1918	102
J. M. Murry	9 June 1918	104
Ottoline Morrell	16 July 1918	106
Virginia Woolf	23 July 1918	107
Dorothy Brett	26 July 1918	109
Ida Baker	1 Aug. 1918	111
Dorothy Brett	14 Aug. 1918	112
Ottoline Morrell	8 Oct. 1918	113

Correspondent
Ottoline Morrell	22 Oct. 1918	114
Anne Estelle Drey	13 Jan. 1919	116
S. S. Koteliansky	7 Apr. 1919	118
Virginia Woolf	c.10 Apr. 1919	119
Ottoline Morrell	c.12 June 1919	121
Ottoline Morrell	c.13 July 1919	123
Ottoline Morrell	17 Aug. 1919	125
J. M. Murry	12 Oct. 1919	127
J. M. Murry	13 Oct. 1919	128
J. M. Murry	20 Oct. 1919	131
J. M. Murry	27 Oct. 1919	132
J. M. Murry	29 Oct. 1919	134
J. M. Murry	30 Oct. 1919	135
J. M. Murry	1 Nov. 1919	137
J. M. Murry	2 Nov. 1919	138
J. M. Murry	3 Nov. 1919	140
J. M. Murry	7 Nov. 1919	143
J. M. Murry	7 Nov. 1919	144
J. M. Murry	8 Nov. 1919	145
J. M. Murry	10 Nov. 1919	147
J. M. Murry	12 Nov. 1919	148
J. M. Murry	16 Nov. 1919	150
J. M. Murry	20 Nov. 1919	151
J. M. Murry	21 Nov. 1919	153
J. M. Murry	4 Dec. 1919	155
J. M. Murry	12 Dec. 1919	158
S. S. Koteliansky	13 Dec. 1919	161
J. M. Murry	13 Jan. 1920	162
J. M. Murry	21 Jan. 1920	165
J. M. Murry	23 Jan. 1920	166
J. M. Murry	7 Feb. 1920	170
Sydney and Violet Schiff	4 May 1920	173
Sydney and Violet Schiff	14 May 1920	174
J. M. Murry	19–21 Sept. 1920	175
J. M. Murry	4 Oct. 1920	178
J. M. Murry	18 Oct. 1920	180

Correspondent

J. M. Murry	1 Nov. 1920	182
J. M. Murry	10 Nov. 1920	185
J. M. Murry	10 Nov. 1920	187
J. M. Murry	c.8 Dec. 1920	189
J. M. Murry	12 Dec. 1920	191
Anne Drey	26 Dec. 1920	192
Richard Murry	17 Jan. 1921	194
Richard Murry	3 Feb. 1921	196
Sydney Waterlow	9 Feb. 1921	198
S. S. Koteliansky	19 Feb. 1921	200
Dorothy Brett	1 Mar. 1921	201
Ida Baker	8 Mar. 1921	202
Ida Baker	13 Mar. 1921	203
Sydney Waterlow	16 Mar. 1921	204
Ida Baker	20 Mar. 1921	206
Princess Bibesco	24 Mar. 1921	208
J. M. Murry	7 May 1921	209
Anne Drey	12 May 1921	211
J. M. Murry	23 May? 1921	213
Ottoline Morrell	c.23 June 1921	214
Ottoline Morrell	24 July 1921	217
Ida Baker	29 Aug. 1921	219
Dorothy Brett	29 Aug. 1921	220
Ida Baker	7 Sept. 1921	223
Dorothy Brett	12 Sept. 1921	224
Ida Baker	24 Sept. 1921	227
Jeanne Renshaw	14 Oct. 1921	229
John Galsworthy	25 Oct. 1921	230
Harold Beauchamp	1 Nov. 1921	231
Dorothy Brett	5 Dec. 1921	232
S. S. Koteliansky	c.20 Dec. 1921	234
Dorothy Brett	21 Jan. 1922	235
S. S. Koteliansky	3 Feb. 1922	237
J. M. Murry	3 Feb. 1922	238
J. M. Murry	7 Feb. 1922	240
J. M. Murry	7 Feb. 1922	241

Correspondent

Elizabeth Russell	8 Feb. 1922	243
Dorothy Brett	26 Feb. 1922	245
William Gerhardi	13 Mar. 1922	249
Ida Baker	14 Mar. 1922	250
Ida Baker	29 Mar. 1922	253
Dorothy Brett	30 Mar. 1922	254
Sarah Gertrude Millin	March 1922	257
Ida Baker	24 Apr. 1922	259
Richard Murry	28 May 1922	260
Elizabeth Russell	5 June 1922	262
S. S. Koteliansky	17 June 1922	264
S. S. Koteliansky	17 July 1922	265
J. M. Murry	7 Aug. 1922	267
Sydney Schiff	26 Aug. 1922	268
J. M. Murry	11 Oct. 1922	269
J. M. Murry	15 Oct. 1922	270
S. S. Koteliansky	19 Oct. 1922	272
J. M. Murry	23 Oct. 1922	273
J. M. Murry	25 Oct. 1922	275
J. M. Murry	10 Nov. 1922	276
J. M. Murry	17 Dec. 1922	278
Ida Baker	24 Dec. 1922	280
J. M. Murry	26 Dec. 1922	282
Harold Beauchamp	31 Dec. 1922	283

CHRONOLOGY

1888   Kathleen Mansfield Beauchamp (KM), third daughter of Harold and Annie Burnell Beauchamp, born at 11 Tinakori Road, Wellington, 14 October.

1893   Beauchamps move to Karori, small village six miles from Wellington, where KM attends local school.

1898   Harold Beauchamp appointed a director of the Bank of New Zealand. Family move to 75 Tinakori Road, Wellington. KM attends Wellington Girls' High School.

1899–1902   At Miss Swainson's School, Wellington.

1903–6   Family sails for London, where KM and two sisters enrol at Queen's College, Harley Street; meets Ida Baker (LM). Returns to New Zealand (October 1906); begins keeping 'journal', and writing fiction.

1907   Publishes first stories in the *Native Companion* (Melbourne); travels with camping party through North Island (November–December).

1908   Sails for London alone (6 July), with annual allowance from father of £100. Resident at Beauchamp Lodge, hostel for music students; love affair with Garnet Trowell terminated by his parents.

1909   Marries George Bowden at Paddington Register Office (2 March), but leaves him the same day. Resumes affair with Garnet Trowell and becomes pregnant. In Brussels briefly, alone, during April. Her mother takes her to Bad Wörishofen, Bavaria in early June; loses child soon after.

1910   Returns briefly to Bowden. Begins her Bavarian sketches in the *New Age*. Spends time at Rottingdean with LM after appendicitis. In autumn takes a flat at 131 Cheyne Walk, Chelsea.

1911   Moves to 69 Clovelley Mansions, Gray's Inn Road (January). Family on visit to England for George V's coronation. In December meets John Middleton Murry (JMM), Oxford undergraduate and editor of *Rhythm*. *In a German Pension* published.

1912   JMM becomes her lodger (April), and soon her lover; she becomes assistant editor of *Rhythm*. They move to Runcton Cottage, near Chichester (September) until magazine's publisher absconds leaving JMM responsible for debts. Move to office-cum-flat at 57 Chancery Lane.

1913   Move to The Gables, Cholesbury, Bucks. (March); last three issues of *Rhythm* renamed the *Blue Review*; meets D. H. Lawrence (June). In July move to Chaucer Mansions, Barons Court; in December to Paris, taking flat at 31 rue de Tournon. Meeting with Francis Carco.

1914   Return to various addresses in Chelsea after JMM declared bankrupt in February; in October to Rose Tree Cottage, The Lee, Great Missenden. Meeting with S. S. Koteliansky.

1915   KM to France 15–25 February, to join Carco at Gray (Saône-et-Loire) for four days, in Paris en route; returns to Paris twice during March–May; moves with JMM in June to 5 Acacia Road, St. John's Wood. Brother Leslie killed in France 7 October. With JMM to Bandol (November), Murry returning and KM alone at Hôtel Beau Rivage. Her allowance now £120 a year.

1916   January–March with JMM at the Villa Pauline, Bandol. They then join the Lawrences at Higher Tregerthen, near Zennor, Cornwall, and in June move to Sunnyside Cottage, Mylor, near Penryn. KM first visits Lady Ottoline Morrell at Garsington near Oxford during summer. When JMM begins work as a translator at War Office in September, they share a house at 3 Gower Street, Bloomsbury. KM meets Virginia Woolf, and at end of year is meeting and corresponding with Bertrand Russell.

1917   KM's allowance increased to £156 a year. Moves in February to a studio at 141A Old Church Street, Chelsea; JMM nearby at 47 Redcliffe Road. Returns to writing for the *New Age*. At end of year falls ill with pleurisy; TB diagnosed, and advised to winter abroad.

1918   Leaves alone in early January for Bandol, where LM joins her in mid-February; first lung haemorrhage 21 March. KM and LM detained for three weeks by military conditions in Paris. Joins Murry at 47 Redcliffe Road on 11 April. Divorce from Bowden finalized, so they marry on 3 May at South Kensington Register Office. KM at Headland Hotel, Looe, Cornwall, May–June, still in poor health. *Prelude* published by Hogarth Press in July; mother dies in Wellington on 8 August. In

September KM and JMM move to 2 Portland Villas, East Heath Road, Hampstead, and KM first consults Dr Sorapure.

1919   JMM takes over editorship of the *Athenaeum* in February and KM begins her weekly fiction reviews. In September leaves with JMM and LM for San Remo, Italy. JMM returns to England until mid-December, KM with LM at the Casetta Deerholm, Ospedaletti. Her father increases her allowance to £300, and Murry earns £800 a year for his editing.

1920   JMM back to England early January, and KM goes to Menton to stay with her cousin Connie Beauchamp. Back at Portland Villas May-August, and then returns to Menton, staying with LM at Villa Isola Bella. *Bliss and Other Stories* published by Constable in December, when she concludes reviewing for the *Athenaeum*.

1921   JMM joins her at Menton mid-February, giving up his editorship. In May they move to Montreux, then Sierre, and late June rent the Chalet des Sapins, Montana-sur-Sierre, with LM boarding nearby.

1922   30 January to Paris with LM, to begin Manoukhin treatment. *The Garden Party and Other Stories* published in London. In Paris with JMM from February to early June, then together at Randogne-sur-Sierre. Makes her will, and returns to London in August to stay with Dorothy Brett at 6 Pond Street, Hampstead. Crosses to Paris with LM at the beginning of October, and two weeks later enters Gurdjieff's Institute for the Harmonious Development of Man at Avon, Fontainebleau. She withdraws from both JMM and LM, although corresponds with both.

1923   9 January JMM arrives at Fontainebleau to visit KM. She dies that evening.

BIOGRAPHICAL REGISTER OF CORRESPONDENTS AND PERSONS FREQUENTLY CITED

BAKER, IDA CONSTANCE (1888–1978). The daughter of an Indian Army doctor, she spent her childhood in Burma, and was a student at Queen's College, Harley Street, when KM and her sisters arrived in 1903. Often referred to as 'LM', 'Leslie Moore', and a range of belittling nicknames, she was KM's closest woman friend for almost twenty years. KM depended on her as confidante, companion, household help, and scapegoat. Ida Baker wrote of their relationship in *Katherine Mansfield: The Memories of LM* (1971).

BEAUCHAMP, ANNIE BURNELL, née DYER (1864–1918). Married Harold Beauchamp at the age of twenty. KM was the third of her daughters, and felt she disappointed her parents in not being a son. Annie is portrayed in several stories as delicate, witty, and detached, although KM came to admire her 'high courage'.

BEAUCHAMP, CHARLOTTE MARY ('CHADDIE') (1887–1966), often called 'Marie' because of her likeness to the actress Marie Tempest. She married Lieut.-Col. John Campbell Perkins in 1913, lived in India, and was widowed in 1916. After the First World War she lived at Wood Hay, the New Forest, in a house bought for her and her sister Jeanne by their father.

BEAUCHAMP, CONNIE (b. 1849). Harold Beauchamp's first cousin, she and her close friend Jinnie Fullerton owned a nursing home in London, and wintered at the Villa Flora, Menton. It was their invitation that took KM to Menton in early 1920, although their kindness would prove too ardently Catholic for her taste.

BEAUCHAMP, HAROLD (1858–1938). Leaving school at thirteen, he pursued an energetic and highly successful business career as importing merchant, company director, member of several boards, and director of the Bank of New Zealand. He married Annie Burnell Dyer in 1884, and his relationship with his wife and children is referred to constantly in KM's writing. He remarried in 1920, and was knighted in 1923.

BEAUCHAMP, JEANNE WORTHINGTON (b. 1892). The youngest of the Beauchamp sisters, she settled in England after the First World War, and married Capt. Charles Renshaw in 1922.

BEAUCHAMP, LESLIE HERON (1894–1915). Referred to always as 'Chummie', he was KM's only brother, and her favourite in the family. He saw her intermittently during his training as an officer for the British Army, and stayed with her briefly at 5 Acacia Road. Commissioned as a lieutenant in the South Lancashire Regiment, he crossed to France as a bombing instructor in September 1915. He was killed in a hand-grenade accident during training at Ploegsteert Wood, near Armentières, on 7 October 1915.

BEAUCHAMP, VERA MARGARET (1885–1977). KM's eldest sister, she attended Queen's College in London at the same time, and married James Mackintosh Bell ('Mac') (1877–1934), a Canadian geologist, in Wellington in 1909. She spent her married life in Canada, and did not meet KM after 1908.

BOWDEN, GEORGE (1877–1975). A choral scholar at King's College, Cambridge, he was a professional singer and teacher when they met through musical circles. They were married on 2 March 1909 at Paddington Register Office. KM left her husband on the same day, but was officially Mrs. G. Bowden until their divorce in April 1918.

BRADY, EDWARD JAMES (1869–1952). An Australian journalist and biographer, he edited the Melbourne periodical the *Native Companion*, where he published several of KM's early sketches in 1908.

BRETT, THE HON. DOROTHY (1883–1977). Elder daughter of 2nd Viscount Esher, she had been an art student at the Slade and later a close friend of Lady Ottoline Morrell and D. H. Lawrence. She and KM grew close through meetings at Garsington, and for several months in 1916–17 they shared a house at 3 Gower Street, Bloomsbury. KM also stayed with her during her last visit to England in 1922.

CAMPBELL, BEATRICE (LADY GLENAVY) (1885–1970). A student at the Dublin Metropolitan School of Art, then at the

Slade School in London, she became a friend of KM's in 1912, and recorded her memories of her in *Today We Will Only Gossip* (1964).

CAMPBELL, HENRY GORDON (LORD GLENAVY) (1885–1963). An Irish barrister and close friend of Murry's, he later became 2nd Baron Glenavy of Milltown, and Director of the Bank of Ireland.

CARCO, FRANCIS (1886–1958). Born Francis Carcopino-Tusoli in New Caledonia. A poet and novelist, and a friend of Murry's since his student days, he became friendly with KM during her stay in Paris in the winter of 1913–14. She visited him in the War Zone for a brief affair in February 1915, and had the use of his flat at 13 Quai aux Fleurs over the following months. He wrote of her in his novel *Les Innocents* in 1915, while she placed him as Raoul Duquette in *Je ne parle pas français*.

DREY, ANNE ESTELLE, née RICE (1879–1959). Born near Philadelphia, she was associated with J. D. Fergusson when KM first knew her in Paris. She contributed to *Rhythm*, and became a considerable painter. Her portrait of KM, done during their time together in Looe in 1918, hangs in the National Gallery, Wellington. She married the journalist and art critic O. Raymond Drey (1885–1976) in 1913, and proved to be one of KM's most enduring friends.

'ELIZABETH'. KM's second cousin Mary Annette Beauchamp (1866–1941), married Count Henning von Arnim in 1891, and became a celebrity on publishing *Elizabeth and her German Garden* (1898). She continued to write novels as 'Elizabeth', was widowed in 1910, and six years later married John Francis Stanley, 2nd Earl Russell. When the marriage failed, she made her home in Sierre, Switzerland, where she was KM's neighbour in 1921.

FERGUSSON, JOHN DUNCAN (1874–1961). A Scottish painter strongly influenced by the Fauves, whose painting 'Rhythm' provided the title and cover design for Murry's magazine in 1911. A warm and close friend of KM's, he was a witness at her marriage to Murry in 1918.

GALSWORTHY, JOHN (1867–1933). Best known for his series of novels in The Forsyte Saga, he corresponded with KM after her reviewing his work in the *Athenaeum*.

GERHARDI, WILLIAM (1895–1977). Novelist and critic, he was born in St Petersburg of English parents, and served as military attaché to the British Embassy in Petrograd during the First World War. He had returned to Oxford as an undergraduate when he and KM corresponded in 1922. They in fact never met.

GOODYEAR, FREDERICK (1887–1917). A friend of Murry's from Oxford, and a contributor to *Rhythm*, he was serving with the Essex Regiment when he died of wounds near Arras in May 1917. KM was particularly fond of him, and he perhaps in love with her.

GURDJIEFF, GEORGE IVANOVICH (1872–1949). Born on the border of Armenian Russia, Gurdjieff claimed a range of esoteric experience in Eastern monasteries, among Sufis and dervishes, and combined spiritual teaching with business acumen. He had first established his Institute for the Harmonious Development of Man in Moscow, but after the Russian Revolution travelled for some years before resettling the Institute, and many of his followers, at La Prieuré des Basses Loges at Fontainebleau, forty miles from Paris, in 1922. Encouraged by Koteliansky and A. R. Orage, as well as her general disposition towards Russian life, Mansfield joined Gurdjieff in October 1922. His behaviour towards her in the last months of her life was both understanding and kindly.

HASTINGS, BEATRICE (1879–1943). A South African-born journalist, she was living with A. R. Orage, editor of *New Age*, when KM first wrote for the paper in 1910. For a time Hastings exercised a strong influence on her, but their intimacy soured after KM took up with Murry. Their later meetings in Paris were unhappy, and Hastings bore her ill-will for many years. Their correspondence was destroyed shortly before Hastings's suicide.

KOTELIANSKY, SAMUEL SOLOMONOVITCH (1882–1955). A Ukrainian Jew who came to England from Kiev University in 1911, he remained in London for the rest of his life, earning a living mainly as a translator of Russian. He became KM's closest male friend, a man of severe probity who encouraged her interest in Russian literature, and worked closely with her in translating Chekhov's letters for the *Athenaeum*. He is sometimes referred to as 'Kot' in her letters.

LAWRENCE, DAVID HERBERT (1885–1930). Novelist, poet, essayist, for a time he greatly influenced Murry's views, and encouraged KM and Murry to live as close neighbours to him in Cornwall in 1916. Their failure as disciples led to bitter disagreements, although KM continued to admire Lawrence as both man and writer.

LAWRENCE, FRIEDA (1879–1956). Born Frieda von Richthofen, she had three children with Ernest Weekley, professor of French at Nottingham University; she eloped with Lawrence in 1912. For a time KM was close to her, and with Murry was witness to the Lawrence's marriage in 1914.

MANOUKHIN, IVAN. A Russian doctor who supervised the Red Cross Hospital at Kiev during the First World War, and then returned to Paris where he had previously worked at the Pasteur Institute. He claimed wide success with tuberculosis patients by treating the spleen with X-rays, and set up a clinic in Passy. The three-month treatment which KM began at the beginning of February 1922 was painful, expensive, and medically useless.

MILLIN, SARAH GERTRUDE (1888–1968). A South African novelist and historian, whose novel *The Dark River* KM praised in the *Athenaeum*, and whom she advised privately to avoid the glitter of metropolitan literary life.

MORRELL, LADY OTTOLINE (1873–1938). Half-sister of 6th Duke of Portland, she was educated privately, spending her girlhood at her father's estate at Welbeck Abbey. In 1902 she married Philip Morrell, Liberal Member of Parliament 1906–18, and heir to Morrell's Brewery. After they moved to Garsington Manor, near Oxford, in 1915, she made her home a centre for artists and intellectuals, her generosity frequently satirized by her guests. For a time KM regarded her as 'my dearest woman friend'.

MURRY, JOHN MIDDLETON (1889–1957). A scholarship boy to Christ's Hospital, then a classics scholar at Brasenose College, Oxford, Murry was editor of *Rhythm*, although still an undergraduate, when he met KM in late 1911. They began living together in April 1912, and married on 3 May 1918. Throughout the war he worked as a translator for MI7, becoming head of his section, and was awarded the OBE for his services. He took up the editorship of the *Athenaeum* in

February 1919. A prolific and energetic journalist, a remarkable editor, and a fine critic, his later selective nurturing of KM's reputation shaped the misleading view of her that survived until Alpers's biographies.

MURRY, RICHARD (1903–1982). John Middleton Murry's younger brother. KM expressed dislike of his given name Arthur, and he officially adopted Richard at her suggestion. She regarded him as something of a mascot because he had suffered from tuberculosis and recovered. He was both designer and operator of the Heron Press at Portland Villas, Hampstead, and KM encouraged him in deciding on design and art as a career.

PAYNE, SYLVIA (1887–1949). The daughter of Joseph Frank Payne (1840–1910), medical historian and Emeritus Harveian Librarian at the Royal College of Physicians, whose mother was the sister of Joseph Dyer, KM's maternal grandfather. Sylvia and her sister Evelyn were both students at Queen's College when KM arrived.

RENSHAW, JEANNE. *See* BEAUCHAMP, JEANNE

RUSSELL, THE HON. BERTRAND (1872–1970). Philosopher, mathematician, and radical social commentator, had been a Fellow of Trinity College, Cambridge, since 1895 when KM met him during the First World War, and interested him for 'her very good mind, and I like her boundless curiosity' (Ronald W. Clarke, *The Life of Bertrand Russell* (1973), p. 314).

ELIZABETH RUSSELL. *See* 'ELIZABETH'

SCHIFF, SYDNEY (1868–1944). An aristocratic patron of the arts and artists, who published largely autobiographical novels under the pseudonym of Stephen Hudson. He was the publisher of *Art and Letters*, which printed stories by KM, and she had praised his novel *Richard Kurt* (1919) in the *Athenaeum* before they met in the south of France in April 1920. He and his wife VIOLET (1876–1962) were considerate and generous friends.

SULLIVAN, JOHN WILLIAM NAVIN (1886–1937), a science graduate and journalist who worked with Murry in Intelligence during the war, and then as his assistant on the *Athenaeum*. Remembered for his *Beethoven: His Spiritual Development* (1927), he wrote widely on both music and science. His first wife had been a friend of KM's at Queen's College.

TROWELL, GARNET (1889–1947). He and Thomas Trowell (1889–1966) were the twin sons of a Wellington musician, and studied together at the Hoch Conservatorium in Frankfurt. KM was in love with Tom before she returned to New Zealand from Queen's College, and with Garnet when she went back to London. She miscarried Garnet's child in Bad Wörishofen in 1909.

WATERLOW, SYDNEY (1878–1944). Related to KM through his mother Charlotte Beauchamp, the sister of 'Elizabeth', Waterlow was educated at Eton and Trinity College, Cambridge. A friend of the Woolfs and the Bloomsbury circle, he combined scholarship with an intermittent diplomatic career. In 1920 he attended the Paris Peace Conference for the Foreign Office, and retired in 1939 as British Minister in Athens.

WOOLF, VIRGINIA (1882–1941). Novelist and critic, whom KM met towards the end of 1916. There followed a cautious but genuine friendship. With her husband Leonard Woolf (1880–1969), scholar and social commentator, she published KM's *Prelude* from the Hogarth Press in 1919.

To Sylvia Payne

The Retreat°|Bexley—Kent,|23/xii/03

Dearest Sylvia—

I want to write to you this afternoon, so here I am—I am not at all surprised at myself, I knew that I would not wait till you had written. Why should we lose any time in knowing each other, when we have lost so much already.

I cannot tell you how sorry I am that I shall not see you again. I like you much more than any other girl I have met in England & I seem to see less of you. We just stand upon the threshold of each other's heart and never get right in. What I mean by 'heart' is just this. My heart is a place where everything I love (whether it be in imagination or in truth) has a free entrance. It is where I store my memories, all my happiness and my sorrow and there is a large compartment in it labelled '*Dreams*.' There are many many people that I like very much, but they generally view my public rooms, and they call me false, and mad, and changeable. I would not show them what I was really like for worlds. They would think me madder I suppose—

I wish we could know each other, so that I might be able to say 'Sylvia is one of my *best* friends.' Don't think that I mean half I look and say to other people. I cannot think why I so seldom am myself. I think I rather hug myself to myself, too much. Don't you? Not that it is beautiful or precious. It is a very shapeless, bare, undecorated thing just yet. I have been fearfully cross this morning—It was about my music. Yesterday I got a concerto from Tom° for a Xmas present and I tried it over with Vera [Beauchamp] this morning. She *counted aloud* and said *wrong wrong*, called me a pig, and then said she would go and tell Aunt Louie° I was swearing at her. I laugh as I read this now. At the time I felt *ill* with anger. So much for my excellent temper!!

It is quiet here now. I am alone in my bedroom. O don't you just thank God for quiet. I do. If only it could last though. Something always disturbs it. There is a bird somewhere outside crying ♪♫ , yet for all this, I am sorry, very sorry, to have left London. I like it so very much. Next term I really shall work hard. I MUST—I am so fearfully idle & conceited.

Why I have written this letter, I do not know. Forgive me dear. I do not dare to read it through. I should burn it if I did. Goodbye for the present. I beg of you write soon to

Your very loving Friend
Kathleen

[*On back of last page*]
Private.
If you fell absurd or jolly don't read this.
Private.

To Sylvia Payne

[Queen's College] 41 Harley Street | W. | 24/i/04.

Dearest Sylvia—

It was ripping of you to write to me such a long letter! I was very pleased to receive it. I certainly do *hate* fogs. They are abominable. Yesterday I did nothing but practise and I wrote to Gladys° and to Tom [Trowell]. I heard from G. yesterday morning. It was a perfectly lovely letter, but *so* queer. Just exactly like her. I do wish that people did not think her fast, or empty. She has more in her than almost anyone else I know. She has the most glorious ideas about things, and is wonderfully clever—Her letters are just full of keen originality, and *power*. Do you understand? Perhaps other people would think them foolish. I don't. O, how thankful I am to be back at College, but, Sylvia, I am *ashamed* at the way in which I long for German.° I simply can't help it. It is dreadful. And when I go into class, I feel I must just stare at him the whole time. I never liked anyone so much. Every day I like him more. Yet on Thursday he was like *ice*! By the way, is not this *heavenly*:—'To every man, there come noble thoughts which flash across his heart like great white birds.'°(Maeterlinck.)

O, that is wonderful. Great white birds. Is not that perfect?!
I wish there was not a night before College. O, I wish you were
a boarder!!! What times we would have together. I do love you
so, much more each time I see you. So little goes on here. All
the girls are so very dull.

Is not the condition of the Poor just now awful. Miss Wood
told us all about [it] the other afternoon, so I have arranged a
Celebrity Evening for next Thursday night. Admission sixpence. Gwen Rouse° is going to help me, and the money is to be
sent to a poor parish—On Friday afternoon I went to
Mudie's.° What a fascinating place it is!! I had some peeps into
most lovely books, & the *bindings* were exquisite. I always think
that it is so sinful to publish 'Bloody Hands', by Augusta St.
John, in green leather, & Bleak House, in, paper for 6d. 'Tout
marche de travers [Everything goes wrong].' That is very true!

My writing this afternoon is most erratic. I do not know
why. You know you always say that you are not *17*, well,
pardon me, I think you *are quite*. I mean to *work* specially hard,
this term. I am taking *19* hours. Dear, I must finish this 'ego'.
You must be tired of it

With my love from | Your loving Friend
Kathleen—

To Sylvia Payne

30 Manchester Street | W.° | 24.iv.06

My dearest Cousin,

I was so delighted to get your letter yesterday—and to hear
what a fine time you are having. Truth to tell—I am just
longing for the country—and especially for pine woods—they
have a mystical fascination for me—but all trees have. Woods
and the sea—both are perfect.

We have been staying here since last Friday with Father and
Mother, and have had a very good time. I don't think I have
ever laughed more. They are both just the same *and* we leave
for New Zealand in October. Strange thought—for some
things I am very glad, now—but I feel as though all my

English life was over, already. Do you know—I have a fancy that when I am there, we shall write far more often and know each other far better than we do now. I do hope it will be so—dear—because I have always wanted us to be friends—and we never seem to pass a certain point—once a Term, perhaps, I feel 'Sylvia & I really know each other now', and next time we meet—the feeling is gone.

A great change has come into my life since I saw you last. Father is greatly opposed to my wish to be a professional 'cellist or to take up the 'cello to any great extent—so my hope for a musical career is absolutely gone. It was a fearful disappointment—I could not tell you what I have felt like—and do now when I think of it—but I suppose it is no earthly use warring with the Inevitable—so in the future I shall give *all* my time to writing.° There are great opportunities for a girl in New Zealand—she has so much time and quiet—and we have an ideal little 'cottage by the sea'° where I mean to spend a good deal of my time. Do you *love* solitude as I do—especially if I am in a writing mood—and will you do so—too. Write, I mean, in the Future. I feel sure that you would be splendidly success-ful—

I am so keen upon all women having a *definite* future—are not you? The idea of sitting still and waiting for a husband is absolutely revolting—and it really is the attitude of a great many girls. Do you know I have read none of the books that you mentioned. Is not that shocking—but—Sylvia—you know that little 'Harold Brown' shop in Wimpole Shop [*for* Street]—I picked up a small collection of poems entitled 'The Silver Net' by Louis Vintras°—and I liked some of them immensely. The atmosphere is so *intense*. He seems to me to belong to that school which flourished just a few years ago—but which now has not a single representative—a kind of impressionist litera-ture school. Don't think that I even approve of them—but they interest me—Dowson—Sherard—School.° It rather made me smile to read of you wishing you could create your fate—O, how many times I have felt just the same. I just long for power over circumstances—& always feel as though I could do such a great deal more good than is done—& give such a lot of pleasure—aber [but] — — — — — — —

We have not seen a great deal of the Bakers,° but they are

flourishing. Mother asks me if you know a house suitable for a lady two wee children and two maids anywhere near? It is just by the way. I am enjoying this Hotel life. There is a kind of feeling of irresponsibility about it that is fascinating. Would you not like to try *all* sorts of lives—one is so very small—but that is the satisfaction of writing—one can impersonate so many people—

Au revoir—dear friend.

Will you give my love to Cousin Ellie & Marjory°

I send you a great deal.

Your friend
K.

To Sylvia Payne

75 Tinakori Rd° | 8.1.07.

My dearest Sylvia—

I have to thank you for really charming letters—Please believe that I appreciate your letters really more than I can say—And your life sounds so desirable—also you gave me a sudden illuminating glimpse of chrysanthemums at that moment you might have [been] R L S.° The New Year has come—I cannot really allow myself to think of it yet. I feel absolutely *ill* with grief and sadness—here—it is a nightmare—I feel that sooner or later I must wake up—& find myself in the heart of it all again—and look back upon the past months as —
— — — cobwebs—a hideous dream. Life here's impossible—I can't see how it can drag on—I have not one friend—and no prospect of one. My dear—I know nobody—and nobody cares to know me—There is nothing on earth to do—nothing to see—and my heart keeps flying off—Oxford Circus—Westminster Bridge at the Whistler hour°—London by hansom—my old room—the meetings of the Swans°—and a corner in the Library. It haunts me all so much—and I feel it must come back soon—How people ever wish to live here I cannot think—

Dear—I can't write anything—Tonight I feel too utterly hopelessly full of Heimweh [homesickness]. If you knew how I

hunger for it all—and for my friends—this absence of com-
panionship—this starvation—that is what it is—I had better
stop—hadn't I—because I can think of nothing joyous. I have
been living too—in the atmosphere of Death. My Grand-
mother° died on New Year's Eve—my first experience of a
personal loss—it horrified me—the whole thing—Death never
seemed revolting before—This place—steals your Youth—that
is just what it does—I feel years and years older and sadder.

But I shall come back because here I should die—

Goodnight. It is almost frightening to say goodnight across
such a waste of waters—but dear—please—think of me
always—in silence—or when our letters speak as

Ever your loving friend
Kass.

To E.J. Brady

4 Fitzherbert Terrace.|Wellington|23.ix.07.

E.J. Brady Esq

Dear Sir—

Thank you for your letter—I liked the peremptory tone—

With regard to the 'Vignettes'° I am sorry that [they]
resemble their illustrious relatives° to so marked an extent—
and assure you—they feel very much my own—This style of
work absorbs me, at present—but—well—it *cannot* be said that
anything you have of mine is 'cribbed' — — — Frankly—I
hate plagiarism.

I send you some more work—practically there is nothing
local—except the 'Botanical Garden' Vignette—The reason is
that for the last few years London has held me—very tightly
indeed—and I've not yet escaped. You ask for some details as
to myself. I am poor—obscure—just eighteen years of age—
with a rapacious appetite for everything and principles as light
as my purse — —

If this pleases you—this MSS please know that there is a
great deal more where this comes from—

I am very grateful to you and very interested in your Magazine.

Sincerely
K. M. Beauchamp.

To Annie Burnell Beauchamp

Waipunga Riverside.°|Wednesday
[20 November 1907]

Dear my Mother—

I wrote you my last letter on Monday—and posted it at Pohui° in the afternoon. I continue my doings. We drove on through sheep country—to Pohui that night—past Maori 'pahs'° and nothing else—and pitched our camp at the top of a bare hill above the Pohui Accommodation House—kept by a certain Mr. Bodley°—a *great* pa-man° with 14 daughters who sit & shell peas all day! Below the hill there was a great valley—and the bush I cannot describe. It is the entrance to the Ahurakura Station—and though we were tired & hungry Millie, Mrs. Webber° & I dived down a bridle track—and followed the bush. The tuis really sounded like rivers running—everywhere the trees hung wreathed with clematis and rata and mistletoe. It was very cool & we washed in a creek—the sides all smothered in daisies—the ferns everywhere, and eventually came to the homestead. It is a queer spot—ramshackle & hideous, but the garden is gorgeous—A Maori girl with her hair in two long braids, sat at the doorstep—shelling peas—& while we were talking to her—the owner came & offered to show us the shearing sheds. You know the sheep sound like a wave of the sea—you can hardly hear yourself speak. He took us through it all—they had only two white men working—and the Maoris have a most strange bird like call as they hustle the sheep—When we came home it was quite dark & *how* I slept.

Next morning at five we were up & working—and really looking back at yesterday I cannot believe that I have not been to a prodigious biograph° show. We drove down the Titi-o

'Kura°—and the road is one series of turns—a great abyss each side of you—and ruts so deep that you rise three feet in the air—scream & descend as though learning to trot. It poured with rain early—but then the weather was very clear & light—with a fierce wind in the mountains. We got great sprays of clematis—and konini,° and drove first through a bush path—But the greatest sight I have seen was the view from the top of Taranga-kuma. You draw rein at the top of the mountains & round you everywhere are other mountains—bush covered—& far below in the valley little Tarawera° & a silver ribbon of river—I could do nothing but laugh—it must have been the air—& the danger.

We reached the Tarawera Hotel in the evening—& camped in a little bush hollow.

Grubby, my dear—I felt dreadful—my clothes were white with dust—we had accomplished 8 miles of hill climbing—so after dinner (broad beans cooked over a camp fire and tongue & cake and tea,) we prowled round and found an 'aged aged man'° who had the key of the mineral baths. I wrapt clean clothes in my towel—& the old man rushed home to seize a candle in a tin—He guided us through the bush track by the river—& my dear I've never met such a cure—I don't think he ever had possessed a tooth & he never ceased talking—you know the effect?

The Bath House is a shed—three of us bathed in a great pool—waist high—and we of course—in our nakeds—The water was very hot—& like oil—most delicious. We swam—& soaped & swam & soaked & floated—& when we came out each drank a great mug of mineral water—luke warm & tasting like Miss Wood's eggs° at their worst stage—But you feel—inwardly & outwardly like velvet—This morning we walked most of the journey—and in one place met a most fascinating Maori—an old splendid man. He took Mrs. Webber & me to see his 'wahine' & child—It is a tropical day—the woman squatted in front of the whare—she, too, was very beautiful—strongly Maori—& when we had shaken hands she unwrapped her offspring from under two mats—& held it on her knee. The child wore a little red frock & a tight bonnet—such a darling thing—I wanted it for a doll—but in a perfect

bath of perspiration. Mother couldn't speak a word of English
& I had a great pantomime.

Kathleen—pointing to her own teeth & then to the baby's—
'*Ah*!'

Mother—very appreciative—'*Ai*!?'

Kathleen—pointing to the baby's long curling eyelashes '*Oh*!'

Mother—most delighted '*Aii*!'

And so on.

I jumped the baby up & down in the air—and it crowed
with laughter—& the Mother & Father—beaming—shook
hands with me again—Then we drove off—waving until out of
sight—all the Maoris do that—Just before pulling up for lunch
we came to the Waipunga Falls—my first experience of great
waterfalls. They are indescribably beautiful—three—one beside the other—& a ravine of bush either side. The noise is like
thunder & the sun shone full on the water. I am sitting now, on
the bank of the river—just a few bends away—the water is
flowing past—and the manuka flax & fern line the banks.

Must go on. Goodbye, dear—Tell Jeanne I saw families of
wild pigs & horses here—& that we have five horses—such
dear old things. They nearly ate my head through the tent last
night.

I am still bitten & burnt, but oil of campher, Solomon
solution,° glycerine & cucumber, rose water—are curing me, &
I keep wrapt in a motor veil. This is *the* way to travel—it is so
slow & so absolutely free, and I'm quite fond of all the
people—they are ultraColonial but thoroughly kind & good
hearted & generous—and always more than good to me. We
sleep tonight at the Rangitaiki° & then the plains & the back
blocks.

Love to everybody. I am *very* happy—

Your daughter
Kathleen

Later. Posting at country shed. Can't buy envelopes. Had
wonderful dinner of tomatoes—Ah! he's found me an hotel
envelope.   K.

To Sylvia Payne

By the Sea°|March 4th [1908]

My dear Cousin—

I am—you see, at last writing you a letter—because I must tell you—here tonight Sylvia—that I love you—far more than I loved you in England—that I would [like]—such an immeasurable great deal—to open wide this door—and welcome you in to the fire—and to the raging sea which breaks & foams against the yard fence.

Summer is over with us—there are briar berries in a green jar on the table—and an autumn storm is raging—The sea has never seemed so high—so fierce—It dashes against the rocks with a sound like thunder. Last night I was lying in my bunk. I could not sleep—I was thinking of you. Do you realise—I wonder—Cousin—how your voice charmed me at the Swanick meetings. I cannot exactly define what I mean—but it always made me feel I was very near you indeed—When I slept I dreamed that I came back to visit College—the only girl I knew in the Library was Marjory—she was not at all surprised to see me—I see her now—pushing back the ribbon in her hair—you know the way she had—and I asked for you—She said you were with Tudge°—and then I saw you standing by the window in the Waiting room—My dear—I felt I must run and put my arms round you and just say '*Sylvia*' but you nodded & then walked away—and I did not move—

It was a terrible dream.

How much has happened since we two walked together to the New Barnet Station.° My life has been so strange—full of either *sorrow*—or excitement—or disgust or happiness. In a year to have lived so much! And I have not made a friend. It is no good I can have men friends—they persist in asking for something else. Do you know Sylvia *five* men has asked me to marry them. And now you will put down this letter and say 'Kass is a second Sylvia Gifford',° but it is the stupid truth—I have been reading—French & English—writing and lately have seen a great many Balls—and loved them—and dinners and receptions. They have such a different meaning for me now—and here. I have finished My First Book.° If it never gets

published—you shall laugh with me over its absurdities. Also I
hope to leave for London next month—It is not unwise of
me—it is the only thing to be done. I cannot live with Father—
and I must get back because I know I shall be successful—look
at the splendid tragic optimism of youth! One day—you must
please know my brother. He knows you very well indeed—and
he and I mean to live together—later on. I have never dreamed
of loving a child as I love this boy. Do not laugh at me when I
tell you I feel so maternal towards him. He is intensely
affectionate and sensitive—he reads a great deal—draws with
the most delicate sympathetic touch—and yet is a thoroughly
brave healthy boy. Do not let me write of him—he is away at
school—and if I go back next month we may not meet for
years—

I hear, constantly, from Ida [Baker]. You know I love her
very much indeed—I am—Sylvia—the most completely unsatisfactory disappointing—*dull* friend it is possible to conceive—and when we meet again you will think—that is
enough—cela suffit—Chaddie & I—with our maid—are living
alone at this little cottage built on the rocks. It has only three
rooms—two bedrooms fitted with bunks—and a wide living
room—We had both been feeling wretchedly ill—and bored
with Wellington—oh, the tedium vitae of 19 years! so have
come here—where we bathe and row and walk in the bush or
by the sea—and read—and I write—while she pursues the
gentle art of fashioning camisoles. One could not be lonesome
here—I seem to love it more each day—and the sea is a
continually new sensation with me. Our life is absolutely free—
absolutely happy—and our maid is—Sylvia—we just die
laughing—She is reading Marie Corelli° now—needless to
remark Miss Corelli is her Messiah—and she treats Chaddie
and me like slightly troublesome babies—Oh, do come—my
Friend & spend a week with me—Have you received one tenth
of my wireless messages? I do not feel that I have been away
from you one day. Now I can feel your hand clasping mine—
but the *wasted* years when we might have been friends. But I
was always afraid then—& I am now—that you do not know
me—& when you do—you will hate me.

Still—Sylvia—I love you—very dearly—and I shall do so
always.

                                                    Kass

To Vera Beauchamp

[4 Fitzherbert Terrace] In the Smoking Room|
June 19th [1908]

Liebe Schwesterchen [Dear little sister]—

I was so exceedingly glad to receive a special letter from you
by the last mail; I love your Family letters—you know, but they
do not breathe of the Inner You, which I prise and delight in—
as you know—

So, after all, the cable came, and I sail today fortnight—
incredibly delightful Thought! The Papanui leaves from Lyttelton on July 4th. I leave here by the Maori° July 2nd—the
cable came on Wednesday morning—I was at The Technical
School° & when I came home the family were all out—laying
in large and varied stocks of machine needles! Nelly told me the
news—I rang up Trix—who declared 'God bless my soul—
pretty nice—dear—*come* & see me'—and then popped round to
Fan.° Do you know before I saw her I did not feel one ounce of
excitement—but when she heard the whistle of Carennos
Staccatto Etudes°—she came to the door—and we literally fell
into each other's arms—I know I had tears of joy. We sat in
Fan's little room—and talked it all over again—the joy—the
freedom—the bonhomie—the cheapness of the laundry—the
Beauchamp Lodge knock—which is the two opening bars of
Lohengrin's Wedding March—then I came home and descen-
ded unto vests and stockings—

Vera, it is really hard to realise—I am so afraid that I shall
wake up and hear the bath tap running—why are we always so
much more chary to recognise grief than joy—isn't it absurd—
and distinctly shows a great lack of that mental fineness of
poise—which will one day be the joyful lot of every one of us—
(Here I am going to digress & describe clothes, because I want
your opinion.)

I've nothing fashionable *at all*—simplicity and art shades
reign supreme—A black flop hat with a wide wreath of mauve
chrysanthemums round the crown—a little evening frock of
satin—soft satin—made exactly after the pattern of Grandmother Dyer's wedding dress—a green straw Home Journal

travelling hat with wide black wings—and everything in like
manner—Chad & Mother have been yearning, I know to
blossom into empire frocks and créations de la moment—but I
haven't one—Clothes ought to be a joy to the artistic eye—a
silent reflex of the soul—so I'm training my amenable little soul
accordingly—Do you like it — — — — — — —

Digression *no 2*—I had to leave this letter—go into the
kitchen & cut myself an entire round of bread & bloater
paste—tin loaf—because the body refuses to consider itself
dined on one piece of flounder & an orange—I didn't know
that Life held anything so ineffably delicious as this bread—
was für Warheit [that's the truth!] Simple pleasures are the
refuge of the complex, nicht?

Oh, Vera, and while I am on the subject of eating—for I am
convinced E. F. Benson wrote the book on an empty, healthy
tummy, do please read 'Sheaves'—It is delightful—and also it
is, in parts Simpson Hayward° incarnate. If you asked me for
Benson in a nutshell I would quote:—'Ah, I *must* speak', said
Hughie, taking fish and bacon on his plate at the same time,
and eating very fast, . . .° The book is by no means a menu,
don't think that—Oh, in a way it is—it creates a wonderful
appetite—but *do* ménus do that—for many things. If you read
it—*do* talk to me about it.

They have been making havoc of our pine avenue—cutting
down some of the trees—sawing the branches off others—a
horrible, crashing, tearing sound, then the clinging roots
scattered on the yellow clay—The whole sight—the men in
their rough clothes—the toiling horses—patches of sunshine
lacing through the silver point boughs—on to the emerald
grass—makes me think of a modern Belgian painting—do you
see it—full of suggested sound—and strangely—death!

Chaddie has gone to a Ball at the Masonic Hall — — — to
what base uses! It is after twelve o'clock so I shall sit up for
her—as I feel—Eastbourne like—fresher than ever—I am glad
that you will see Aunt Lil.° She is really, what Mac° would call
'one of the best', and, between you & me, she worships you, my
dear—endows you with all the virtues—respects you, and loves
you very whole heartedly. Writing to you, I live again, very
vividly, certain charming experiences. Giggleamus et Viandem—the 'Admiral's Broom'°—at Macs—and hair soup &

raisins on the wild sea. Now I know I am going on to a ship—I
feel almost hypernautical; the shipboard life—which is such an
utterly different existence—another plane of existence—suddenly predominates. I can hear & smell & feel and see—
nothing but ships—do you know that?

I pray you—marry an Englishman & come live in London—
and take your Poor Relation to an Art Gallery with an
Entrance Fee once a month—Ida & May have been down at
Ridge Cap.° Easter time & heavy snow—Will you ever forget
that time & Cousin Lou, and our poor little shocked souls when
Aunt Belle & Uncle Harry° performed a charade in kimonos!
Have you forgotten Ralph's° Easter egg, or his nice, Grecian
mouth—how often the Gods endow a man with a perfect
profile and no brains to live up to it! Now *you* live up to your
eyebrows—do you realise that fact—Talking about you I
inst[inct]ively think of enamal work—perhaps—You know
that charming remark of Dante Gabriel Rossetti:—'I am
trying to live up to my blue china'°—that is by no means
absurd—To whom shall I send your love, my dear? And of
course you know if ever you want anything from a Watts
Original to a Dying Pig—I am yours to command—Oh,
Vera—the first time I stand on those College steps—dear
sister—I shall send you a wireless of the most pregnant order—
& when Henry Wood° stands in his place & lifts his hand—
silently—for one moment—I['ll] send you another.

Do write to me—I feel I never can stop—Oh, that—face to
face—we two could talk, I wonder when and how she [for we]
shall again—and what will have happened in the meantime—

Do you know Theodore Watts Duntan's work—in the main,
intensely artistic critical essays—but it was he brought into
being that constantly recurring expression:—the renascence of
wonder—I admire the man very much indeed; he lives with
Swinburne, was a friend of George Borrow, William Morris—
all that 'set'°—Isn't it extraordinary how one can never tire of
these people—they are my very good friends—and I know
them immeasurably better than the people I meet here—There
is a fascination almost unequalled in collecting all the details of
a man's life—studying his portrait—his work—bringing him,
splendidly willing, to one's own fireside—I have R.L.S. and
Dante Gabriel Richard Wagner & Jimmy Whistler—*all* the

Brontës—countless others—haven't you? One day let us give a
dream party—invite those in the flesh who are attune to meet
those in the spirit. 'Oh, Alice, allow me to introduce you to Mr
Stuart Mill' — — —

It is bitterly cold; I hope that you are wrapped in a nice piece
of dog—and have a fire in your bedroom—that is the epitome
of quiet, fastidious, charming luxury—Aunt Li° is giving me
pour souvenir an opal ring—Do you know a large, uncut opal
[*drawing of oval stone, with* natural size *written beside it*]—which
she possesses—and she is having it set in a thin wide silver
setting—I am so pleased because—as you know *opals* are my
aura, & any jewellry which I do possess is mounted in silver. I
don't wish for gold—It is to fit the second finger—Doesn't it
sound beautiful—My black box is up in my bedroom—there is
a vast amount of sorting to be done—steamer clothes &
otherwise. Clara° is giving me a red leather manuscript book
stamped with a black tiki° & my name—I'm taking only half a
dozen books and my photographs and the W.F.C.A.° green
candlestick—Your jewel case sticketh unto me more closely
than a brother—thank you again for it.

My dear—this is all—Write me *reams*, please. I do want to
have you again—before I sail—Vera—It is a lovely moonlight
morning—

Bon Jour—Yours as ever
K.

'Meine Seele sucht nach Dir [My soul longs for thee].'

To Garnet Trowell

[Beauchamp Lodge, Warwick Crescent]
Wednesday Night. [23 September 1908]

Heart's Dearest—

I dreamed last night, most vividly, that I was with you. It
was so sweet that I trembled to wake, and yet *when* I woke there
was a letter from you—So reality was as good as dreaming. All
that you say to me seems almost curiously familiar, for

beloved—I feel it so strongly—Know that I shall love you eternally. When I think for one moment of what the Future holds for us together, what days, and oh, my Husband, *what nights,* I feel really that I do not belong to this earth—it's too small to hold so much. You and I we are surely universal. Other husbands and wives seem to me to be sitting in corners, you and I—*we* are exploring the whole house—from cellar to garret—nicht? If *all* the world left me and you remained then Life would be full—if *all* the world came to me and you were not here, in my soul, then Life would be empty ... Oh, I could lock you in a prison of my arms and hold you there—until you killed me. Then, perhaps, I would be satisfied. I love you, Garnet, I love you. There is one comfort—every moment that we are parted brings us a moment nearer.

This afternoon I went to the Palace Music Hall & saw Maud Allen,° the danseuse—she was wonderful. As she dances, under the changing lights, coming and going to the sound of a thin, heady music which marks the rhythm of her movements like a kind of clinging drapery, she seems to sum up the appeal of everything that is passing, and coloured and to be enjoyed. Dance music is wonderfully fascinating in its way. The rhythm of a walze, slow, insinuating, gathering impetus which is held back, creeping into the blood; and it is possession and abandonment, the very symbol of love—tu comprends? [you understand?]

It is a clear, still night. I think I shall go down to the Victoria Hall° & wait for the Opera to be over, then walk home with you, arm-in-arm. Are you tired, dearest. Would you like me to cut you some sandwitches, and I promise not to forget the mustard!

Above me a woman is practising the drum—not an inspiring instrument. It sounds like the growling of some colossal dog, and I know I shall have dreadful nightmares. She is working to play next year at Westgate in a chef d'oeuvre called 'The Policeman's Chorus'. Bien, mon cher, there is surely nothing like aiming high—I wish her success! Oh, the people here would make you laugh. Three months ago I would have rather scoffed at them, now I feel that I can't help loving them all— Beloved, I do so feel I can afford to be generous. Oh, dear, next door someone has started scales on the trombone—curiously like a Strauss Tone Poem of Domestic Snoring.°

I read & reread your precious letters—I'm still terribly busy, but over and above everything there is *you—you—you*.

I am yours for ever. You know that—yet I can't help but tell you over & over.

Goodnight darling
Kass.

To Garnet Trowell

[Beauchamp Lodge, Warwick Crescent] |
Tuesday Morning [13 October 1908]

Beloved—though I do not see you, *know* that I am yours. Every thought, every feeling in me belongs to you—I wake in the morning and have been dreaming of you—and all through the day, while my outer life goes on steadily, my inner life, I live with you, in leaps and bounds. I go through with you every phase of emotion that is possible—*loving* you—*that* life pulsates with sunshine and Happiness, unlimited, vast unfathomable wells of Happiness—and *you*. Oh, would that I could once express in words all the passionate, heavenly thoughts that break in tumultuous waves over my heart at the thought of you.

I wonder if you have ever swum in a very rough sea. I have—You plunge into the breakers—the waves break right over you—but you shake the water out of your eyes and hair—and there is a sensation of extraordinary strength. Something gigantic has you in its power—you are laughing, intoxicated—half wild with laughter and excitement. So I feel when I am tossed upon the very sea of passionate bliss. I love you—I *love* you.

Today London is muffled in a wrapper of grey fog. It is cold and raw. There is a heavy, rumbling sound of carts passing . . . You know such a day in a city?

Last night I went to the theatre—with some New Zealand people—and came right back here from Trafalgar Square in a hansom. It was close upon twelve o'clock. The sky was flushed with faint fires—hollowed into a perfect pearl. Dim men and women were clustering in broken groups round the doors of the public houses. From some of the bars came the sound of horrible laughter. And all the streets stretching out on every side like the black web of some monstrous spider. In the Edgeware Road we passed a great procession of the unemployed.° They carried a scarlet banner. You cannot think how horrible and sinister they looked—tramping along—hundreds of them—monotonously, insistently—like a grey procession of dead hours.

I came back into my room here and made some tea—& drank it, sitting curled up in my chair—a little heap of your letters on my lap. I read them slowly, my darling, and seemed to be living with you as I read—your wonderful satisfying letters. Were you, I wonder in bed and asleep, while I sat, still, and thought of you so vividly that I feel you would have been waked from the deepest slumber.

Garnet, this is the last day of my nineteenth year. Just think when we are both *over thirty*. I think we will be very young indeed. I must work.

My Beloved—dearest of all the World I kiss you. I kiss you—I am so happy today that I would like to wave a flag out of my window—you know that feeling? Ah, dearest—*I love you*

I am yours for ever—
Kass.

To Garnet Trowell

44, KEYHAM TERRACE, | H.M. DOCKYARD, |
DEVONPORT. | Sunday Morning.
[8 November 1908]

My dearest—
I am alone in the house; a cold day & everybody has gone to church—but here there is a brilliant fire and I am far happier.

Since writing to you yesterday—a great deal seems to have happened—that is always the case — — — — — Yesterday afternoon I saw the launching of a great battle-ship—one of the most splendid, impressive sights possible, I think. There were thousands of people—from the ultra smart to the poorest workmen and their wives—all gathered together—And the ship was held in place by iron girders and supports. She towered above everybody. On a flag enveloped platform—Mrs Asquith—a very large section of the Naval world°—and a chaplain and choir assembled. We were all you see down below. It was a brilliant day, but a fierce wind rushed down and about. The crowd was silent, while the choir & sailors sang a hymn. You see the dramatic effect—it caught me. Strange visions of the victories and defeats—death—storms—their voices seemed crying in the wind. And all the builders of the ships—the rough men who had toiled at her—stood silently on her deck, waiting for the moment to come — — — And all the time we heard inside the ship a terrible—knocking—they were breaking down the supports, but it seemed to me almost symbolical as tho' the great heart of the creature pulsated— And suddenly a silence so tremendous that the very wind seemed to cease—then a sharp, wrenching sound, and all the great bulk of her swept down its inclined plank into the sun— and the sky was full of gold—into the sea—which waited for her. The crowd cheered, screamed—the men on board, their rough faces—their windblown hair—cheered back—In front of me an old woman and a young girl—the little old woman, whose grand uncle had been in the fighting Temeraire°— trembled & shook and cried—but the girl—her flushed face lifted—was laughing, and I seemed to read in her tense, young body, anticipation, realisation—comprends tu? . . .

Oh, Garnet, why is it we so love the strong emotions? I think because they give us such a keen sense of *Life*—a violent belief in our Existence. One thing I cannot bear and that is the mediocre—I like always to have a great grip of Life, so that I intensify the so-called small things—so that truly everything is significant. In Winter—to look out over a silent garden—I like first, to get that sense of loneliness, so [*for*? that] simplicity of barrenness—and *then* always—I like to be able to see the flowers pushing their way up through the brown earth. It is the superficial attitude which kills Art, always. Give Life a little attention, a little enthusiasm—and 'Fair Exchange is no robbery', she says, & heaps our arms with treasures. Why, it is the same with Love. The more you give me, the more I feel that you enrich my nature so I can give you more.

I dreamed last night that we were at a Tchaikovsky concert together last night. And in a violin passage, swift & terrible—I saw to my horror, a great flock of black, wide winged birds—fly screaming over the orchestra—it's rather strange—waking I can see that—too, in much of his music—can't you? Oh, Music, Music—Oh, my Beloved—the *worlds* that are ours—the *universes* that we have to explore—we two, my dearest, shall find the heart of Life hidden under its wrappings—like the gold seeds of a rose under a thousand crimson petals. I love you. I love you. It is like this. I have been wandering through a castle with barred windows, locked doors, helplessly. At last I come to the gates—and you have unlocked them and you are there. I give you the keys—and you say 'It is so simple, it is like this.' Unlocking one door of my castle—all the others fly open to you. Keep my keys. What use are they to me—they are yours. I belong to you.

Loving you
Kass.

To Ida Baker?

[London, before April ?1909°]

Did you ever read the life of Oscar Wilde—not only read it but think of Wilde—picture his exact decadence? And wherein lay his extraordinary weakness and failure? In New Zealand Wilde acted so strongly and terribly upon me that I was constantly subject to exactly the same fits of madness as those which caused his ruin and his mental decay.° When I am miserable now—these recur. Sometimes I forget all about it—then with awful recurrence it bursts upon me again and I am quite powerless to prevent it—This is my secret from the world and from you—Another shares it with me, and that other is Kitty Mackenzie° for she, too is afflicted with the same terror—We used to talk of it knowing that it wd eventually kill us, render us insane or paralytic—all to no purpose—

It's funny that you and I have never shared this—and I know you will understand why. Nobody can help—it has been going on now since I was 18 and it was the reason for Rudolf's death.

I read it in his face today.°

I think my mind is morally unhinged and that is the reason—I know it is a degradation so unspeakable that — — one perceives the dignity in pistols.

Your
Katie Mansfield '09

To J. M. Murry

['The Gables', Cholesbury, early May 1913]

Jack dear.

Yes Friday *will* be fun. I am beginning to 'pretend' that you are a sailor—trading with all sorts of savages from Monday until Friday—& that the Blue Review° is your schooner & Secker° the Fish Eyed Pilot. Couldnt you write a long-compli-cated-extremely-insulting-symbolical-serial round that idea with minute, obscene descriptions of the savage tribes ...? Thank you for Pa's letter. He was cheerful and poetic, a trifle puffed up but very loving. I feel towards my Pa man like a little girl. I want to jump and stamp on his chest and cry 'youve *got* to love me'. When he says he does, I feel quite confident that God is on my side.

It is raining again today, and last night the wind howled and I gloomed and shivered—and heard locks being filed and ladders balanced against windows & footsteps padding up-stairs — — — all the old properties jigged in the old way—Im a lion all day, darling, but with the last point of daylight I begin to turn into a lamb and by midnight—mon Dieu! by midnight the whole world has turned into a butcher!

Yes, I like Boulestin° very much. There's something very sympathetic about him.

Goodbye for today, darling
Tig.°

To J. M. Murry

Am I such a tyrant—Jack dear—or do you say it mainly to tease me? I suppose Im a bad manager & the house seems to take up so much time if it isn't looked after with some sort of method. I mean ... when I have to clean up twice over or wash up extra unnecessary things I get frightfully impatient and want to be working. So often, this week, Ive heard you and Gordon [Campbell] talking while I washed dishes. Well, someone's got to wash dishes & get food. Otherwise—'there's nothing in the house but eggs to eat.' Yes, I hate hate HATE doing these things that you accept just as all men accept of their women. I can only play the servant with very bad grace indeed. Its all very well for females who have nothing else to do ... & then you say I am a tyrant & wonder because I get tired at night! The trouble with women like me is—they cant keep their nerves out of the job in hand—& Monday after you & Gordon & Lesley [Ida Baker] have gone I walk about with a mind full of ghosts of saucepans & primus stoveses & 'will there be enough to go round' ... & you calling (whatever I am doing *Tig*—isn't there going to be tea. Its five o'clock.) As though I were a dilatory housemaid! I loathe myself, today. I detest this woman who 'superintends' you and rushes about, slamming doors & slopping water—all untidy with her blouse out & her nails grimed. I am disgusted & repelled by the creature who shouts at you 'you might at least empty the pail & wash out the tea leaves!' Yes, no wonder you 'come over silent'.

Oh, Jack, I wish a miracle would happen—that you would take me in your arms & kiss my hands & my face & every bit of me & say 'its alright—you darling thing. I quite understand.'

All the fault of money, I suppose.

But I love you & I feel humiliated & proud at the same time. That you *dont* see—that you *dont* understand and yet love me puzzles me — — —

Will you meet me on Wednesday evening at the Café Royale° at about 10.30. If you cant be there let me know by

Wednesday morning . . . Ill come back & sleep at '57'° if I may even though I *don't* live there.

Jack—Jack—Jack.

Your wife
Tig.

To Ida Baker

31 RUE DE TOURNON (6ème) | Last moments.
[24 February 1914]

Dear Ida—

Everything is packed of ours—the book packer is here now & we are waiting for the man to come & take away the furniture. Grimy and draughty and smelling of dust, tea leaves and senna leaves and match ends in the sink—cigaret ash on the floor—you never saw an uglier place—now, nor more desolate. The clock (sold, too) is ticking desperately—& doesn't believe it's going yet & yet is hopeless. Jack, in a moment of desperation yesterday sold even the bedding . . . Yes I *am* tired, my dear a little—but its mostly mental. I'm tired of this disgusting atmosphere & of eating hardboiled eggs out of my hand & drinking milk out of a bottle—Its a gay day outside. What we shall do until the train goes I can't think— Very little money and we both don't want cafés. Oh, how I love Jack. There is something wonderfully sustaining & comforting to have another person with you—who goes to bed when you do & is there when you wake up—who turns to you & to whom you turn. The dear little toilet set is on the same table with me—all packed into the basin. I have been talking to the book packer. He is tall & more graceful than anyone Ive ever seen. He wears light blue woollen shoes & has never worn boots since he was 'tout petit—that's why he walks so—doesn't seem to put his feet *down* at all but he has a delightful sort of swaying stride. I have given Carco a few souvenirs—the egg timer which *charmed* him and some odd little pieces like that. The guitar has gone—& the candlesticks—except the dragons. I have an idea I shall find the femme de ménage [housekeeper] has taken something really important before I go. She was a little too gushing and grateful to be innocent, I'm afraid. (Katie, you are really revolting.) I wonder they are [*illegible*] going down to Canterbury . . .!

[*No signature*]

To Frieda Lawrence

[Gray, Haute-Saône, 20 February 1915]

England is like a dream. I am sitting at the window of a little square room furnished with a bed, a wax apple and an immense flowery clock. Outside the window there is a garden full of wall flowers and blue enamel saucepans. The clocks are striking five and the last rays of sun pour under the swinging blind. It is very hot—the kind of heat that makes one cheek burn in infancy. But I am so happy I must just send you a word on a spare page of my diary, dear.

I have had some dreadful adventures on my way here because the place is within the zone of the armies and not allowed to women. The last old pa-man who saw my passport, 'M le Colonel'—very grand with a black tea cosy and gold tassel on his head and smoking what lady novelists call a 'heavy Egyptian cigarette' nearly sent me back. But Frieda, its such wonderful country—all rivers and woods and large birds that look blue in the sunlight. I keep thinking of you and Lawrence. The French soldiers are 'pour rire [a scream]'. Even when they are wounded they seem to lean out of their sheds and wave their bandages at the train. But I saw some prisoners today— not at all funny—Oh I have so much to tell you. I had better not begin. We shall see each other again some day, won't we, darling.

'Voila le petit soldat° joyeux et jeune [There's the young and happy little soldier]' he has been delivering letters. It is hot as summer—one only sits and laughs.

Your loving
Katherine.

To S. S. Koteliansky

[Rose Tree Cottage, The Lee, Great
Missenden] Monday. [8 March 1915]

My dear Kotiliansky.

I have wanted to write to you; you have been in my mind several days. Thank you for doing those things for me—the english money does not really matter. I am in bed. I am not at all well. Some mysterious pains° seem to like me so well that they will not leave me. All the same I am grateful to your Ancestral Grandfathers—for—for some curious reason I can work. Im writing quite quickly—and its good. Send me a little letter when you have the time. I have an idea that Lawrence will be in London today. It is very cold here. It is winter and the sky from my window looks like ashes. I hear my little maid go thumping about in the kitchen and when she is quiet I listen to the wind. My God, what poverty! So I write about hot weather and happy love and broad bands of sunlight and cafés—all the things that make life to me. Yes, you are quite right. I *am* wicked. Would it be very rude if I asked you to send me a few cigarettes? If it would—do not send them.

Today I had a most lovely postcard sent me from my concierge in Paris—hand painted roses as big as cabbages—and so many of them they simply fall out of the vase!

Always your friend
Kissienka.

To J. M. Murry

[13 quai aux Fleurs,° Paris IVᵉ] Sunday early afternoon.
[21 March 1915]

My darling one,

Still no letter—perhaps I can be certain of one tomorrow. I walked to the post this morning and then finding neither light nor murmur there I went to the Luxemburg gardens. About 3 of the biggest chestnut trees are really in leaf today—you never

saw anything lovelier with pigeons & babies adoring. I walked
and walked until at last I came to a green plot with the back
view of the head and shoulders of a pa-man rising out of an
enormous stone urn—d'une forme d'une carotte [in the shape
of a carrot]. Laughing with my muff as is my solitary habit I
sped to see his face & found that it was a statue of Verlaine.°
What extraordinary irony! The head seemed to me to be very
lovely in its way bashed in but dignified as I always imagine
Verlaine. I stayed a long time looking at that & then sunned
myself off on a prowl. Every soul carried a newspaper—
L'Information came out on orange sails—La Patrie lifted up
its voice at the metro stations. Nothing was talked of but the
raid last night.° (Im dying to tell you about this raid but Im
sure I shant be able to.) Oh, Jaggle, it was really rather fine. I
came home late—I had been dining with B.° at the Lilas.° It
was a lovely night. I came in, made some tea—put out the
lamp and opened the shutters for a while to watch the river.
Then I worked until about one. I had just got into bed and was
reading Kipling's 'Simple Contes des Collines,'° Bogey,° when
there was a sharp quick sound of running and then the
trumpets from all sides flaring 'garde à vous [Attention!]'. This
went on—accompanied by the heavy groaning noise of the
shutters opening and then a chirrup of voices. I jumped up &
did likewise. In a minute every light went out except one point
on the bridges. The night was bright with stars. If you had seen
the house stretching up & the people leaning out — — & then
there came a loud noise like doo-da-doo-da repeated hundreds
of times. I never thought of zeppelins until I saw the rush of
heads & bodies turning upwards as the Ultimate Fish (see *The
Critic in Judgement*°) passed by, flying high with fins of silky grey.
It is absurd to say that romance is dead when things like this
happen—& the noise it made—almost soothing you know—
steady—and clear doo-da-doo-da—like a horn. I longed to go
out & follow it but instead I waited and still the trumpets
blared—and finally when it was over I made some more tea &
felt that a great danger was past—& longed to throw my arms
round someone—it gave one a feeling of boundless physical
relief like the aftermath of an earthquake. Beatrice [Hast-
ings]'s flat is really very jolly. She only takes it by the quarter at
900 francs a year—four rooms & a kitchen—a big hall a

cabinet and a conversatory. [*sic*] Two rooms open on to the garden. A big china stove in the salle à manger [dining room] heats the place. All her furniture is second hand & rather nice. The faithful Max Jacobs° conducts her shopping. Her own room with a grey self colour carpet—lamps in bowls with Chinese shades—a piano—2 divans 2 armchairs—books— flowers a bright fire was very unlike Paris—really very charm- ing. But the house I think detestable—one *creeps* up and down the stairs. She has dismissed Dado° & transferred her virgin heart to Picasso°—who lives close by. Strange and really beautiful though she is still with the fairy air about her & her pretty little head still so fine—she is ruined. There is no doubt of it—I love her, but I take an intense, cold interest in noting the signs. She says—'it's no good me having a crowd of people. If there are more than four I go to the cupboard & nip cognacs until its all over for me, my dear.'—or 'Last Sunday I had a fearful crise—I got drunk on rhum by myself at the Rotonde & ran up & down this street crying and ringing bells & saying "save me from this man". There wasn't anybody there at all.' And then she says with a fairish show of importance—'of course the people here simply love me for it. There hasn't been a real woman of feeling here—since the war—but now I am going to be careful—'

Myself, I am dead off drink—I mean the idea of being drunk revolts me horribly. Last time I was drunk was with Beatrice here and the memory stays and shames me even now. We were drunk with the wrong people. Not that I committed any sottise [foolishness] but I hate to think of their faces and— ugh! no—I shall not drink again—like that—never—never. As I write to you the concierge is doing the flat and she will persist in talking. Do I like flowers? Cold or heat? Birds or beasts? She is one of those women who can't lift or replace a thing without giving it its *ticket*—but she's a good soul and looks after me and fills the lamp without being told. Of course everybody she ever knew has died a grisly death in this war—& the fact that Carco is going to Turkey° seems to delight her beyond measure. Il ne reviendra jamais! [He'll never come back!]

Today everywhere they are crying voici les jolies violettes de Parme [here are pretty violets] & the day is like that. Under the bridges floats a purple shadow—I must start working. (I believe now she is dusting simply to spite me—& to keep me off my work. What a bore these women are—) How are you managing? dearest? Does the house-keeper come up—oh, Jack write often. I am *lost lost* without letters from you—things haven't got their real flavour—Keep me very close to your heart in my own place. Dearest of all I love you utterly—

I am your
Tig.

To J. M. Murry

[13 quai aux Fleurs] Thursday morning.
[25 March 1915]

My own Bogey—

Yesterday I had your letters at last. But first I *never* got a cross postcard about the sofa: you never mentioned it until this letter. Here are the directions. Take a bus to Blandford Street which is off Baker Street. Walk down it and turn into South Street. King has got a filthy little shop with a sewing machine in the window and some fly blown cards which say 'Loose Covers'. More than that I can't tell you myself. Have you written to him and enclosed a stamped envelope? If not, I would do that *at once*.

You seem to have done perfect wonders with the rooms—the carpentering job I saw and heard as plain as if Id been there—to the very sand papering. All the things are floating in my brain on a sea of blue ripolin.° I feel those rooms will be lovely. If Frieda is there ask her about the curtains. She can sew even though I don't think shed have ideas. I saw such jolly low stools yesterday—very firm with rush seats 1.75. I wish I could send you 2 or 3. They are nice.

I had a great day yesterday. The Muses descended in a ring like the angels on the Botticelli Nativity roof°—or so it seemed to 'humble' little Tig and I fell into the open arms of my first novel° I have finished a huge chunk but I shall have to copy it on thin paper for you. I expect you will think I am a dotty when you read it—but—tell me what you think—won't you?

Its queer stuff. Its the spring makes me write like this. Yesterday I had a fair wallow in it and then I shut up shop & went for a long walk along the quai—very far. It was dusk when I started—but dark when I got home. The lights came out as I walked—& the boats danced by. Leaning over the bridge I suddenly discovered that one of those boats was exactly what I want my novel to be—Not big, almost 'grotesque' in shape I mean perhaps *heavy*——with people rather dark and seen strangely as they move in the sharp light and shadow and I want bright shivering lights in it and the sound of water. (This, my lad, by way of uplift) But I *think* the novel will be alright. Of course it is not what you could call serious—but then I cant be just at this time of year & Ive always felt a spring novel would be lovely to write.

Today I must go to Cooks° with my last goldin sovereign in my hand to be changed—I am getting on alright as regards money & being very careful. Cooked vegetables for supper at 20 the demi livre [half-pound] are a great find and I drink trois sous de lait [three sous' worth of milk] a day. This place is perfect for working.

I read your letter yesterday in the Luxembourg gardens. An old gentleman seeing my tender smiles offered me half his umbrella & I found that it was raining but as he had on a pair of tangerine coloured eye glasses I declined. I thought he was a Conrad spy. My own dear darling—what are you doing about a bed? Surely not that vile sofa all these nights!

I have adopted Stendhal. Every night I read him now & first thing in the morning. This is a vague letter but it carries love and love and kisses from your

Tig.

To J. M. Murry

[13 quai aux Fleurs] Saturday.
[28 March 1915]

Dearest one,

I am really worried about money for you. Will you have got another cheque by now? I do hope to heaven that you have. I always feel you become wicked and don't spend enough on food if you're hard up & you are really rather dependent on good meals—if you only knew it. I shall be eating chestnut buds if Kay° doesn't send me my money sometime next week. I don't know how money goes—I keep a strict account (one of those amazing fourfold affairs in which we are so expert) and every penny is reckoned—and yet, Bogey, it seems to fly. A franc in Paris is really 8d in England just now. But don't think I am complaining, because I am not—merely stating my case—& I know my money *will* come next week. I have asked Kay to send it through Cooks. It is the simplest way and really the post offices are merely a collection of stools and stamp paper. Yesterday, after I had nearly cried through a grating about my lost letter, the man suggested brightly, cleaning his nails on an old nib, 'perhaps the postman *threw it away*' . . .

I wanted to tell you about a nice time I had on Thursday night. At about seven I left the house buttoned up in my black & white coat & went for a walk behind the Hotel de Ville. I found most curious places—and I found at last a little market where every third body was either frying or eating polish pancakes. The air smelled of them and of 'petis gris'—tiny snails which you bought by the shovelful. It began to rain— Under an old stone arch 3 hags wrapped in black shawls were standing—their hands crossed over their bellies. At their feet there lay three little baskets of herbs—Dry twigs—withered bundles and tiny packets. Their heads were raised, watching the drizzle and the green light from a lantern fell on their faces. All of them were talking—whether to each other or to them-selves you could not tell, for their voices did not pause. It sounded like a song. It was one of the most ancient things I have ever seen or heard. Having a besoin to faire mon service [need to relieve myself] I went into one of those little 10c places. In the passage stood an immense fat and rosy old market woman, her skirts breast high, tucking her chemise into her flannel drawers and talking to an equally fat old ouvrier [workman]—who began to help her arrange her affairs, saying as he tugged and buttoned 'mais tu sais, *ma petite* tu ne peux pas sortir comme ça [but you know, little one, you can't go out like that].' I went on much further, then down an alley on to a quai—There was a bird shop there. The window was flying

with canaries and java sparrows and green love birds and white
doves and parrots. Outside the shop two little girls were
standing, their arms round each others necks. One had rings in
her ears and the other wore a bangle—They were watching the
birds and eating an orange between them quarter by quarter—
The birdseller was a dark young man with long black mous-
taches and narrow eyes ... I don't know why but I had a
curious sensation that I was in a dream and that I had seen all
this years and ages ago.

Finally it poured so with rain that I hunted and hollered and
found a café—very poor—the people eating—chauffeurs and
rag-bags of people. But a woman came in—skinny, enceinte
[pregnant], but very alive—and a curious enough boy followed
her. They were so wet that the woman said 'faut danser [we
must dance]'. And they danced—As far as I could make out
this is what they sang as they turned round and round—the
people who ate banged with the bread on the table and the
plates clattered—

> Si'l en reste un bout ce sera pour la servante
> Si'l en reste pas d'tout elle se tapera sur l'ventre
> Et zon zon zon Lisette, ma Lisette
> Et zon zon zon Lisette, ma Lison.
>
> [If there's a crust over leave it for the maid.
> If there isn't any, she'll have to pat her tum,
> so pom pom pom Lisette, my Lisette,
> pom tiddly pom Lisette, my Lison.]

All the while my hat dripped over the table. I kept taking it off
and shaking it on the floor but when the boy was greeted by a
very smart young friend who came to my table and said 'je
veux manger une belle fricassee avec vous, ma fleur [I would
like to have a nice meal with you, my flower], I paid and ran
away.

The concierge has brought me another letter, written on
Wednesay night. My darling, if you write me letters like that Ill
not be able to bear my love. I simply adore you. But that old
beast° upstairs must be poisoned, Jaggle. Don't give him
another crumb. I *implore* you. I think you were very brave all
the same. Im glad about the curtains & glad Kot° came.
Floryan° is rather a hateful idea. No, you won't find anything
of mine in the New Age because I won't send them a line. I

think Orage is too ugly°. No, *don't send me any money*—I haven't
the need of it.

Heres a confession. I cannot write if all is not well with us—
not a line. I do write in my own way through you. After all it is
love of you now that makes me write & absolutely deep down
when I write well it is love of you that makes me see and feel.
You darling—you darling. Je te veux. [I want you.]

Tig.

To J. M. Murry

[13 quai aux Fleurs] Saturday afternoon.
[15 May 1915]

I got very sane after I had written to you yesterday—I wish
something in you didn't make me feel a 'silly' when I want to
write at full tilt. Its because you never do; you're such a
guarded and careful little Bogey—and so frightened I shall
'make a scene'. I won't, dear. I promise you. Im not *at* all sure
this afternoon whether Ill come on Wednesday or whether Ill
wait a week. Perhaps Id better wait a week. If I *do* come I *won't*
wire if I *dont* come I *will* wire. Its a fair toss up. Yesterday
evening I sat in a little parc and played with the idea with a *sou*.
The sou said every time 'Yes, go—' but that was yesterday.
And this morning again your calm letter as though we were
'seule pour la vie [apart for life]' shook up against the apple
cart.

You sent me a letter from Lesley—which was simply marvellous. She wrote, as she can, you know of all sorts of things, grass
and birds and little animals and herself and our friendship with
that kind of careless, very intimate joy—There is something
quite absolute in Lesley—She said at the end of a page—
'Katie, dearie—what is *Eternity*?' She's about the nearest thing
to 'eternal' that I could ever imagine. I wish she were not so far
away.° Things are so changed now. You and I still love each
other, but you haven't the need of me you had then and
somehow I do always have to be '*needed*' to be happy. Ive
expressed that abominably—and its not even quite true, for

what I call your need of me was more or less an illusion on my part. Youre an amazing person in the way you can accept just so much and no more—No, Im beating about the bush and not really saying what I want to—*and* it really doesn't matter—But I do wish my tall, pale friend were here to walk with and sit with. Youre not the slightest use—for it doesn't come natural for you to desire to do such things with me. Its I who plead like 'une petite pensionnaire [a little boarding-school girl]' to be taken out on a Saturday afternoon or to a music hall—

A lovely woman sits in here with me. She's got a fool of a man with her that she hates beyond words. So would I. She wears a big rose under her chin—her eyes are lovely but very shadowed with a purple ring. She is not *only* bored: she is trying not to cry. Three fat jossers at a table nearby are vastly amused. Two dirty little froggies smoking pipes 'a l'anglaise' & ragging each other are next to me. They occasionally sing at me—or snap their fingers. They are the most hideous little touts—Blast them! Now, I might have known it, my lovely woman is playing a game of cards with her cavalier—Mon dieu! She does look lovely with the fan of cards in her hand, the other hand hovering over and her lips just pouting. I must go. This is a fool of a letter. What makes you disgruntled? Is your book° worrying you? No, I can't send any of mine because Im too dependent on it as a whole under my hand. The BUGS are still flourishing in the kitchen. One violated me last night.

Pretty business this german chasing°—and a pity they have to photograph such decent, honest looking wretches as the belles proies [great catch]. Its a filthy trick; there's no dif-ference between England and Germany when the mob gets a hand in things—No difference between any nation on earth—They are all equally loathsome.

Goodbye for now, my dear. *Hanged* if I know whether I'll see you on Wednesday or not—If I do wire that I am not coming you might send me that £1; just to reassure me—will you—Oh, Bogey—dearest—

                                        Tig.

To S. S. Koteliansky

[13 quai aux Fleurs] Monday night.
[17 May 1915]

Kotiliansky, dear friend, I will not wait any longer for a letter from you. Jack tells me about you, but that is not enough; it is too remote. I had wanted a letter from you to say that you 'understood'—not to reassure me, you understand, but just because—I always want you to understand. It is a rainy evening—not at all cold, rather warm, but rainy, rainy. Everything is wet; the river is sopping, and if you stand still a moment you hear the myriad little voices of the rain. As you walk the air lifts just enough to blow on your cheeks. Ah! How delicious that is! It is not only leaves you smell when you stand under the trees today; you smell the black wet boughs and stems—the 'forest' smell. This evening I went walking in a park. Big drops splashed from the leaves and on the paths there lay a drift of pink and white chestnut flowers. In the fountain basin there was a great deal of mixed bathing going on among some sparrows. A little boy stood just outside the park. He thrust one hand through the railing among the ivy leaves and pulled out some tiny snails, arranging them in a neat row on the stone wall. 'V'la! Mes escargots! [Look! My snails!]' But *I* was rather frightened, that, being french, he'd take a pin out of his jacket and begin eating them! And then they locked the park up. An old caretaker in a black cape with a hood to it locked it up with a whole bunch of keys. There is a wharf not far from here where the sand barges unload. Do you know the smell of wet sand? Does it make you think of going down to the beach in the evening light after a rainy day and gathering the damp drift wood (it will dry on top of the stove) and picking up for a moment the long branches of seaweed that the waves have tossed and listening to the gulls who stand reflected in the gleaming sand, and just fly a little way off as you come and then—settle again.

This evening a mist rose up from the river and everything looks far away. Down below, two nuns went by, their ample skirts gathered in one hand, the other holding an umbrella over their white hoods. And *just below*—there is a court where the market men take their barrows for the night—their palms, and their rose trees and china blue hydrangea bushes. You see the barrows with waving shining leaves float by like miraculous islands. Very few people are out. Two lovers came and hid behind a tree and put up an umbrella. Then they walked away, pressed against each other. It made me think of a poem that our german professor° used to read us in class.

> Ja, das war zum letzenmal
> Das, wir beide, arm in arme
> Unter einem Schirm gebogen. — —
> Alles war zum letzenmal.°

> [Yes, that was the last time
> as arm in arm we walked
> together under an umbrella
> the very last time.]

And I heard again his 'sad' voice (so beautiful it seemed, you know) and I saw again his white hand with a ring on it, press open the page! But *now* I know the perfect thing to do on a night like this. It is to ride in a little closed cab. You may have the windows open but you cannot keep out the smell of leather and the smell of *upholstered buttons*. The horse makes an idle klipperty klopperting. When we arrive at the house there is a big bush of lilac in flower growing over the gate and it is so dark that you do not stoop low enough and drops and petals fall on you. The light from the hall streams down the steps.

Scene II

K: 'Tell me frankly. Does it *not* feel damp to you?'

Visionary Caretaker: 'Ive had fires in all the rooms, m'm. Beautiful fires they were too. It seemed a pity to let them out; they burned that lovely.'

M. or N: 'It feels as dry as bone to me, I *must* say.'

The Visionary Caretaker beams at 'M or N'. Her little girl puts her head round the door. In her pinafore she has rather a wet kitten.

Visionary C: 'And if you *should* like a chicken at any time, m'm, or a few greens I'm sure my husband and I would be only too pleased etc etc etc etc ...

I am laughing, are you? The queer thing is that, dreaming like that I can't help living it all, down to the smallest details— down to the very dampness of the salt at supper that night and the way it came out on your plate, the exact shape of the salt spoon . . .

Do you, too feel an infinite delight and value in *detail*—not for the sake of detail but for the life *in* the life of it. I never can express myself (and you can laugh as much as you please.) But do you ever feel as though the Lord threw you into eternity— into the very exact centre of eternity, and even as you plunged you felt every ripple that flowed out from your plunging— every single ripple floating away and touching and drawing into its circle every slightest thing it touched. No, I shan't write any more. I see you, my wise one, putting down this letter and saying—'no. I must go to Barbara° to explain this . . .'

I feel a little bit drunk. Its the air, and the noise the real waves make as the boats, with long fans of light, go dancing by.

We shall see each other again soon. But I can't deny that I feel a little neglected. I had *counted* on a reply to my letter, after all. Don't forget me—don't go far away. As I write I hear your voice and I see you swing out into the hall of the bureau as though you were going to beat to death the person who had dared to come in.

With this letter I send you big handfuls of very 'good' love.

Kissienka.

To Leslie Beauchamp

SELFRIDGE & CO. LTD. | OXFORD
STREET | LONDON—W, | THE LOUNGE,
READING AND WRITING ROOMS, | Wednesday
[25 August] 1915

Dearest,

I have an odd moment to spare & I'll use it in sending you a line—Ever since last Sunday you are close in my thoughts. It meant a tremendous lot, seeing you and being with you again and I was so frightfully proud of you—you know that—but I like saying it. But the worst of it is I want always to be far *more* with you and for a long enough time for us to get over the 'preliminaries' and live together a little.

I heard from Mother this mail. She was very cheerful & says she has such happy letters from you. Again she wanted first hand news of you so I have written this mail & told her just what I would want to hear if I were she. She is a darling and her personality simply enchants me in her letters.

Do you know a day when your heart feels much too big? Today if I see a flag or a little child or an old beggar my heart expands and I would cry for joy. Very absurd—Im 26 you know—This is not a letter. It is only my arms round you for a quick minute.

Your
Katie.

To S. S. Koteliansky

GRAND BAR DE LA SAMARITAINE | I RUE
DE LA REPUBLIQUE, | & QUAI DU PORT, 2 |
MARSEILLE | 19ième Novembre 1915

Koteliansky dear,

I have been on the point of writing to you several times but—just not had the time or the place or something. *Business first.* I left one of my brother's caps in a drawer upstairs in his room. Would you get it and keep it safely for me. Also, I meant to give you for your room the *fur rug* in my sitting room—you know the one. I don't want the Farbmans° to use it and I do want you to keep it for me. Put it on your bed. It is so warm and it looks and feels so lovely. Tell Sarah that I have written to you and asked you to send it to me— PLEASE do this. That is all—except that our address is c/o Thomas Cook + Sons, Tourist Agency, Rue de Noailles, Marseille—We shall call there for letters under the name of *either* Bowden (when Ill get them) or Murry, for Jack. If I started to tell you about all that has happened I never would end. Indeed, I have been gathering a big bouquet for you, but it has become too big to hold and it has dropped out of my arms. You will have to believe me, darling, that the flowers *were* there and *were* for you—I am glad that I came. Many times I have realised that Acacia Road and all that it implied is over—for ever.

This is a confused and extraordinary place—It is full of
troops—french, african, indian, english—In fact there are
'types' from all over the world and all walking together down
narrow streets choked with tiny carriages painted yellow, white
mules with red fringes over their eyes — — — All those kinds
of things you know. The port is extremely beautiful. But Ive
really nothing to say about the place until I write to you for
weeks, for all my observation is so *detailed* as it always is when I
get to France. On the mantelpiece in my room stands my
brother's photograph. I never see anything that I like, or hear
anything, without the longing that he should see and hear,
too—I had a letter from his friend again. He told me that after
it happened° he said over and over—'God forgive me for all I
have done' and just before he died he said 'Lift my head, Katy
I can't breathe—'

To tell you the truth these things that I have heard about
him blind me to all that is happening here—All this is like a
long uneasy ripple—nothing else—and below—in the still pool
there is my little brother.

So I shall not write any more just now, darling. But I think
of you often and always with love.

                                                        Katy.

To J. M. Murry

[Hôtel Beau Rivage, Bandol] | Saturday.
                              [11 December 1915]

My dear one,
    No letters today. I cannot hope to hear from you before
Monday, I think. So I am not disappointed. The weather has
changed. Last night a wind sprang up—one of the lesser
winds—a forlorn, piping creature that I don't remember
having heard on land before—a wind I always connect with
the open sea & night in the cabin—and a hollow dread that the
land has gone for ever. I dreamed that I had a baby (Virtue
always rewards me with this elfin child) and Grandmother was
alive. I had been to sleep after it was born & when I woke it

was night & I saw all the people in the house lying on their backs asleep too. And I was sure my baby was dead. For a long time I was too frightened to call anyone—but finally called to Grandmother & she came in and said nonsense, child he's getting on beautifully (as though 'he' were a cake in the oven.) She brought him in to reassure me—a charming little creature in a flannel gown with a tuft of hair. So I got up and kissed Grandmother who handed me the baby and I went downstairs & met you in the street. The moon was shining—you looked lovely; it shone paticularly on your grey felt hat which you wore à l'espagnole—But we were very poor; we lived in a tenement & you had put a banana box across 2 chairs for the baby. 'The only *brick* is,' you said, 'how the hell can we go to a music hall?' Then I woke up, switched on the light & began to read Venus & Adonis. It's pretty stuff—rather like the Death of Procris.°

Yesterday I had de la veine [struck it lucky] & wrote in the afternoon & then went for a short walk along that bar that encloses the harbour. It was sunset. Its a good place to walk—the sea on either side rushes up & the town—just showing a glimmer of light here and there looked marvellous. I sat on a stone & began thinking 'I believe it is perfectly necessary to one's *spiritual balance* to be somewhere where you can see the sun both rise & set' etc etc—& such like nonsense—très serieuse [very serious]—when I remarked a gazelle like military form approaching—in blue with a braided cap. This ensemble, thought I, is exactly like the cover of a 95 centimes novel. Myself on a rock—a red sunset behind—this graceful form approaching — — — It came near—& then a blithe, cheerful dead sure voice positively *hailed* me. Vous promenez seule, Madame? [You walk by yourself, Madame?] I had a good look at the upstart—olive skin, silky eyebrows & silky moustache—*Vain*—there is no word for it. I said 'oui, Monsieur seule [yes, by myself].' Vous demeurez à l'hotel Beau Rivage, n'est-ce pas? [You're staying at the Hotel Beau Rivage, isn't that so?] Silence. Je vous ai déja remarqué plusieurs fois [I've already noticed you several times]. (His French was right—Mine isn't.) Then I looked at him like Frank Harris° would look at Dan Ryder° quoting Shakespear & he drew himself up, saluted, said 'Ah, pardon je suis très indiscret [Excuse me, I'm being very indiscreet].' I said *exactly* like Harris—*très* indiscret Monsieur [*Very*, Monsieur], & walked home. Scarcely had I gained the road when a gentleman in a cape approached. Vous promenez seule, Madame? But that was a bit too steep. I said 'Non Monsieur, avec une canne [No, Monsieur, with a stick]—' What a race! They're like german commercial travellers! Send me a bulldog in your next letter, sweetheart. The sea is very choppy today. Far as you can see the waves break—like a school of fishes—I love you—I am your own girl

Wig.

To J. M. Murry

[Hôtel Beau Rivage, Bandol] Tuesday.
[14–15 December 1915]

Dearest of all

Don't you worry about me. My femme de chambre [chambermaid], when she goes off duty leaves me in her 'friends' charge & her 'friend' is a little spry creature with a pale blue nose who is very gentille [kind] indeed to me. 'Il ne faut pas vous gêner [You mustn't put yourself out]'—she keeps saying to me—'Je veux faire tout ce que je peux pour vous [I would like to do everything I can for you].' In fact the servants here seem to think Im a *dear* little thing! *And* after midday that Englishman,° terribly shy, knocked at my door. It appears he has a most marvellous cure for just my kind of rheumatism. Would I try it? All this was explained in the most preposterous rigmarole, in an attempt to appear off hand and at his poor unfortunate ease. I never saw a man so shy! Finally he says that if the pharmacien [chemist] can't make it up here he will take the first train to Toulon this afternoon & get it for me. It is a rubbing mixture which he got off a german doctor one year when he was at Switzerland for winter sports & had an attack of sciatic rheumatism. It sounds to me—very hopeful—but I'd catch any straw! So I thanked him and bowing and humming and hawing he went off. I cant think what frightened him so. I shall have to put on a hat and a pair of gloves when he brings me back the unguent. Oh, that postman is a tortoise, a detestable tortoise—half a tortoise—for I am hot and he is slow. (Bogey I am an awful little cod. My bed is going to my brain. Now I'll wait for your letter before I go on.)

Later. I did wait with a vengeance. At half past 3 I rang the bell. 'Le courier—a-t il déja passé? [The postman—has he been yet?] '*Ah oui*, Madame—une *bonne* demi heure! [Oh *yes*, Madame—a *good* half-hour ago!]' 'Merci bien [Thank you]' But when she had gone I confess I turned to the wall & cried bitterly ... I think mostly from rage. Then I began to think how my Father always always had time to write every single day to my Mother etc etc etc. Then in despair I climbed out of bed, found a piece of ribbon and sat up & made myself a hat. Once before, I remember when I was ill at Rottingdean° and alone & waiting for a letter that didn't come I made myself a hat out of pins and fury & it was the hat of my life. So is this. But I am desperately disappointed, I must confess. And I think it is awfully awfully cruel. Once I get better I'll forgive you if you don't write but Oh—to lie in this silent room & know the postman has *been*. You wouldn't like it, Bogey. Now I've had dinner, an omelette, some cauliflower & stewed apple. I am getting thin. There are 2 hollows in my cheeks but no little love kisses them. My Englishman has arrived with his pot of ointment & refuses to take even a pin or a bead in payment. How kind he is. Its easy to see *he* hasn't lived with me 3 years.

I am very angry, but not really with you—you couldn't help your letter missing the post I suppose—or perhaps you were handing cups & saucers for that quiet lady with the cast eye.°

I should like to be at a large circus tonight, in a box—very luxurious, you know, very warm, very gay with a smell of sawdust & elephants. A superb clown called Pistachio—white poneys, little blue monkeys drinking tea out of Chinese cups—I should like to be dressed beautifully, beautifully down [to] the last fragment of my chemise, & I should like Colette Willy to be dressed just exactly like me° & to be in the same box. And during the entr'actes while the orchestra blared Pot Pourri from The Toreador we would eat tiny little jujubes out of a much too big bag & tell each other all about our childhood. A demain [Till tomorrow], then. *Are* you a darling? Oh, I forgive you. I love you. I hug your blessed little head against my breast

& kiss you—I love you you bad wicked precious adorable and enchanting boge. I am

Wig Tig

Wednesday

Dear Jack I have opened my letter to say that now another day has come & again I have no news. I am sending the maid with a wire this morning, for I cannot but believe there is something terribly wrong. I do not deny that today I am *dreadfully anxious*.

Oh, Jack, I appeal even to your imagination as a novelist—do not leave me like this without news. It is so cruel—cruel—I weep bitterly as I write but if you do not answer my wire I shall weep no more but face the fact that—no I can't write it. Ever since Sunday my hope has been for letters & Ive not had one—Your silence makes me ashamed to so let you see my heart—and its need of you. I am still in bed.

[*Very heavily scored line*]

To J. M. Murry

[Hôtel Beau Rivage, Bandol] It is Xmas
Morning. [25 December 1915]

My Little King,

The rain is pouring down & the sea is roaring out the Psalms—Even in the harbour the boats are rocking—but I am so happy and there are so many candles and angels burning on the tree that you have planted in my heart that I can hardly write to you. I want to come flying into your arms and I want us to stay close—close kissing each other because we are in love. There is a large pine cone on the fire. I put it on just before I began this letter—to be a kind of celebration. And do you remember that black headed pin you stuck in my curtain to make it 'hang'. Its still there—it has got to look very like you. I am going to write a fearfully long letter this morning for if I do not I shant be able to keep my heart from going off like a Xmas cracker.

Dear love—my own beloved, precious marvellous and ador-

able little Boge. If I live to be the age of those first and original
Pa men in the Bible I shall never be able to love you enough. I
quite understand God making eternity—Catch hold of me
Bogey—stop me. Oh, dearest hold me close. My body trembles
for love of you today—I can feel you in every minutest part of
me.

Before I write any more I must tell you something. I hope
you don't kiss anybody at Lady Ottolines. After all I have
said—it does sound absurd! But I minded you kissing even
Anne [Drey] 'seriously'. I minded you *really* kissing. For this
reason. If I wished to—I could not. There is no question of will
or reason, but I have to be physically faithful to you because
my body wouldn't admit anyone else—even to kiss *really* you
know. That was why I wrote so stiffy about your going there
for Xmas. Is this jealousy? I suppose it is. But you're mine—
you're mine and when we have not been lovers for so long I feel
I could not bear anyone else to touch even the threshold of
your lips. But tell me *all* that happens at Lady Ottolines and if
you have kissed somebody—(I'm laughing a little, precious, as
I write that because it is a little absurd.) Tell me and I'll bear it
and understand and not take it to heart. Only, *tell me* always.
Now you'll say 'good God, my goblin is changing into a
dragon.' I'm not.

Two letters came from you today. One you had been to see
Lawrence (but I explained that away—didn't I?) and in the
other, thank God, you had got my telegram° at [last] Ah, dear
heart, really our stormy passage is over. Then just as I had
brushed my hair 100 times I had your telegram. You couldn't
have sent me a lovelier present—I keep on reading it and it
looks so awfully funny and sweet because its so written
wrong—by the man here and scratched over. Tenderest *lion* (I
read that *love*) wonderful LITTERS received perfectly haRPy and
your name is MErcy!! It is even nicer like this. I feel as though
fate did it on purpose to show that she really does love us and
we really are her funny little children . . .

Although it is damp and raining I have not even a touch of
rheumatism. That cure is wonderful.

When I went out to put your letter in the Palais D'Azur
yesterday I found out why the boats had come in—for there
was a procession of dark young sailors, barelegged, their bright

blue trousers rolled to the thigh in big full blouses & with their [hair] cropped 'en pudding' carrying on their shoulders little red kegs & filling them at the fountain. A great dispute went on because it was midday & the women had come to draw water too—& the sailors would not take the kegs away and only laughed—They had a tiny boat rocking at the steps of the quai—On deck, three sailors hung over a rail plucking three ducks. The feathers floated on the water. The boat is called the *Felicina* and she comes from Verragia. The other boat hasn't got a name. Today they are dressed & flying five or six snippets of flags.

Yesterday afternoon I went off by myself into the woods & spent all the afternoon exploring little tracks and 'chemins de chamois [goat paths]'. I picked such lovely daisies too, with pink tips—It got very faery after the sun went down, and when I go to the road to come home, still deep in the woods there came a tinkle and round the corner came an old man with a herd of brindled goats. As I came into the town all the babies were flocking in the streets looking at the Xmas toys. Heaven knows they are a sorry little show, but you should have heard the screams of joy. 'Ah, ah, le beau chemin de fer. Dis! Dis! Qu'il est mignon le p'tit chien! Ah, la grande—la belle! [Oh, look at the lovely toy railway. Look! How sweet the little dog is! Oh, the big one—it's beautiful!] I began to look too & I nearly bought an elephant or a dog with one ear standing up, or a *lovely* tea set with roses painted on it & a sugar basin with a tiny strawberry for the handle on the lid. Then the captain of the Felicina landed & came marching up the street—very grand— all gold braid—little clipped beard—stiff linen. He was followed by 2 sailors and he disappeared behind the bead curtain of the butcher's shop. Then another ship came sailing in. Which makes *five*. Can you feel how thrilling they are in this tiny place? And how one longs to go on board and walk up and down little ladders?

There is a crêche in the church. It has been all made by the children. It is simply beautiful. A landscape with painted cardboard houses—even shutters to the windows. A windmill—little bridges of twigs—fountains made of falling silver paper cut in strips, the roads all of fresh sand the hills and the valleys all of moss that they gathered in the woods. Trees are planted in the moss & hung with silver stars (far too big for them). There are sheep under the trees—shepherds, holy men—the three kings—one with a black face and awful whites to his eyes. Fat little angels perch in all sorts of places and in a neat cardboard grotto is Mary, St. Joseph (a very old Dotty) and a naked 'p'tit *Ch*esau [baby Jesus]' as they say, who can open & shut his eyes. The priest was showing this Marvel to a baby when I was there but she could say nothing except in a very hushed voice 'il est tout nu [he's got no clothes on].' The dove is also perched on a tree—a drunken fowl bigger than the ox & the ass—& out of one house there is the head of the innkeeper in a night cap with a tassel on it telling Mary he hasn't got a room ...

My love. I have only time to run to the post with this. I love you—*love* you. I am always your own

Tig.

Plus tard [*Later*]. Colette has come—thank you love.

I have opened my letter (I am always doing that—its like popping just ones head in again) to say that when I ran to the post it was shut for all today & I am afraid this letter will not go until tomorrow, love. But I am glad I opened it for I want to ask you something.

Do you want me to come back? Do you think you will work better at your Dosty Book° alone? Shall I stay here until it is finished or until the Spring, or when? I am willing to come back today if you want me—you know that, my heart. But speak to me frankly about this, will you? And when you DO want me back write me a note saying that Hara° is ill and you would be very relieved if I would come to England immediately etc. just so that I will have a definite something to show the consuls and the passportiers. (We are still quite babies enough to play with dolls and I'd much rather pretend about Hara than about a real person. I would so see her, with her little hands in her kimono sleeves, very pale & wanting her hair brushed.)

I have just had a Xmas dinner—very dreadful and indecent to be partaken of alone. The 'belle famille [good family]' had an *enormous* feed. I left the little tiny ones leaning back in their chairs with their legs stretched out utterly helpless—& slightly the worse for wine. For even the baby who is not yet three

drank until her glass rested on her nose, where she left it and
blew into it & stared at me through the top. Now I am going
for a walk with the Englishman who leaves definitely the day
after tomorrow.

Later. It was a long walk through the woods & then we left the
paths and he taught me *how* to climb as taught by the guides in
Norway. It was boring beyond words but absolutely successful—We scaled dreadful precipices & got wonderful views.
Then I had to learn *how* to descend—and how to balance if the
stones roll when you put your foot on them. What a pa man!
All this of course he takes deadly seriously—and I find myself
doing so too and I don't get one bit tired. I wish you could see
my room. Even the blue glass vases we put away have had to
come out for the big bouquets of yellow and pink roses.
Tonight I have promised to dine with this pa man.° I don't
doubt I shall get a lecture on touring in Spain. I already know
more about how to travel in Italy than any living being, I
should think—

I am going to try to send you a nutshell in this letter for a
little hat. Its dark now and the waves are beating right up the
road among the palms.

Do you feel my love?

Always & toujours [always]
Tig

To Frederick Goodyear

Villa Pauline | Bandol | (Var) | Sunday.
[4 March 1916]

Mr F.G.

Never did cowcumber lie more heavy on a female's buzzum
than your curdling effugion° which I have read twice and wont
again if horses drag me. But I keep wondering, and cant for the
life of me think, whatever there was in mine to so importantly
disturb you. (Henry James is dead.° Did you know?) I did not,
swayed by a resistless passion say that I loved you. Nevertheless
I'm prepared to say it again looking at this pound of onions

that hangs in a string kit from a saucepan nail. But, Betsy love, what has that got to do with the Kilner Idea?° I recognise the Kilner Idea, I acknowledge it and even understand it, but whats it got to do with me? Nothing. I don't want to rob you of it ... And why should you write to me as though I'd got into the family way with H.G.W.[ells] and driven round to you in a hansom cab to ask you to make a respectable woman of me? Yes, youre bad tempered, suspicious and surly. And if you think I flung my bonnet over you as a possible mill, my lad, you're mistook. So shut up about your Fire Whorls *and* a Hedgehog,° and send me no more inventories of those marbil halls wherein of aforetime they did delight to wander.

In fact, now I come to ponder on your last letter I don't believe you want to write to me at all and Im hanged if Ill shoot arrows in the air. But perhaps that is temper on my part; it is certainly pure stomach. Im so hungry, simply empty, and seeing in my minds eye just now a surloin of beef, well browned with plenty of gravy *and* horseradish sauce and baked potatoes I nearly sobbed. There's nothing here to eat except omelettes and oranges and onions. Its a cold, sunny windy day—the kind of day when you want a tremendous feed for lunch & an armchair in front of the fire to boaconstrict in afterwards. I feel sentimental about England now—English food, *decent* English *waste!* How much better than these thrifty french whose flower gardens are nothing but potential salad bowls. There's not a leaf in France that you cant 'faire une infusion avec [make tea with]', not a blade that isn't bon pour la cuisine [good for cooking]. By God, Id like to buy a pound of the best butter, put it on the window sill and watch it melt to spite em. They are a stingy uncomfortable crew for all their lively scrapings ... For instance, in their houses—what appalling furniture—and never one comfortable chair. If you want to talk the only possible thing to do is go to bed. Its a case of either standing on your feet or lying in comfort under a puffed up eiderdown. I quite understand the reason for what is called french moral laxity—you're simply forced into bed—no matter with whom—there's no other place for you ... Supposing a *young* man comes to see about the electric light & will go on talking and pointing to the ceiling, or a friend drops in to tea and asks you if you believe in Absolute Evil. How can you give your mind to these things when youre sitting on four knobs and a square inch of cane. How much better to lie snug and *give yourself up to it.*

Later.

Now I've eaten one of the omelettes and one of the oranges. The sun has gone in; its beginning to thunder. There's a little bird on a tree outside this window not so much singing as sharpening a note—He's getting a very fine point on it; I expect you would know his name ... Write to me again when everything is not *too* bunkum.°

Goodbye for now

With my 'strictly relative' love
'K.M.'

To S. S. Koteliansky

[Higher Tregerthen, Zennor, Cornwall]
Thursday. [11 May 1916]

I am quite alone for all the day so I shall write to you. I have not written before because everything has been so 'unsettled'; now it is much more definite. I wish I could come and see you instead of writing; next month I shall come to London probably for a little time and then we shall be able to meet and to talk.

You may laugh as much as you like at this letter, darling, all about the COMMUNITY. It *is* rather funny.

Frieda and I do not even speak to each other at present. Lawrence is about one million miles away, although he lives next door. He and I still speak but his very voice is faint like a voice coming over a telephone wire. It is all because I cannot stand the situation between those two, for one thing. It is degrading—it offends ones soul beyond words. I don't know which disgusts one worse—when they are very loving and playing with each other or when they are roaring at each other and he is pulling out Frieda's hair and saying 'I'll cut your bloody throat, you bitch' and Frieda is running up and down the road screaming for 'Jack' to save her!! This is only a half of what literally happened last Friday night. You know, Catalina, Lawrence isn't healthy any more; he has gone a little bit out of his mind. If he is contradicted about *anything* he gets into a frenzy, quite beside himself and it goes on until he is so exhausted that he cannot stand and has to go to bed and stay there until he has recovered. And whatever your disagreement is about he says it is because you have gone wrong in your sex and belong to an obscene spirit. These rages occur whenever I see him for more than a casual moment for if ever I say anything that isn't quite 'safe' off he goes! It is like sitting on a railway station with Lawrence's temper like a big black engine puffing and snorting. I can think of nothing, I am blind to everything, waiting for the moment when with a final shriek— off it will go! When he is in a rage with Frieda he says it is she who has done this to him and that she is 'a bug who has fed on my life'. I think that is true. I think he is suffering from quite genuine monomania at present, through having endured so much from her. Let me tell you what happened on Friday. I went across to them for tea. Frieda said Shelleys Ode to a Skylark was false. Lawrence said: 'You are showing off; you don't know anything about it.' Then she began. '*Now* I have had enough. Out of my house—you little God Almighty you. Ive had enough of you. Are you going to keep your mouth shut or aren't you.' Said Lawrence: 'I'll give you a dab on the cheek to quiet you, you dirty hussy'. Etc. Etc. So I left the house. At dinner time Frieda appeared. 'I have finally done with him. It is all over for ever.' She then went out of the kitchen & began to walk round and round the house in the dark. Suddenly Lawrence appeared and made a kind of horrible blind rush at her and they began to scream and scuffle. He beat her—he beat her to death—her head and face and breast and pulled out her hair. All the while she screamed for Murry to help her. Finally they dashed into the kitchen and round and round the table. I shall never forget how L. looked. He was so white—almost green and he just hit—thumped the big soft woman. Then he fell into one chair and she into another. No one said a word. A silence fell except for Frieda's sobs and sniffs. In a way I felt almost glad that the tension between them was over for ever— and that they had made an end of their 'intimacy'. L. sat staring at the floor, biting his nails. Frieda sobbed. Suddenly, after a long time—about a quarter of an hour—L. looked up and asked Murry a question about French literature. Murry replied. Little by little, the three drew up to the table. Then F. poured herself out some coffee. Then she and L. glided into talk, began to discuss some 'very rich but very good macaroni cheese.' And next day, whipped himself, and far more thoroughly than he had ever beaten Frieda, he was running about taking her up her breakfast to her bed and trimming her a hat.

Am I wrong in not being able to accept these people just as they are—laughing when they laugh and going away from them when they fight? *Tell me*. For I cannot. It seems to me so *degraded*—so horrible to see I cant stand it. And I feel so furiously angry: I *hate* them for it. F. is such a liar, too. To my face she is all sweetness. She used to bring me in flowers, tell me how 'exquisite' I was—how my clothes suited me—that I had never been so 'really beautiful'. Ugh! how humiliating! Thank Heaven it is over. I must be the real enemy of such a person. And what is hardest of all to bear is Lawrence's 'hang doggedness'. He is so completely in her power and yet I am sure that in his heart he loathes his slavery. She is not even a good natured person really; she is evil hearted and her mind is simply riddled with what she calls 'sexual symbols'. Its an ugly position for Lawrence but I cant be sorry for him just now. The sight of his humiliating dependence makes me too furious.

Except for these two, nothing has happened here. A policeman came to arrest Murry° the other day, & though M. staved him off he will have to go, I think.

I am very much alone here. It is not a really nice place. It is so full of huge stones, but now that I am writing I do not care for the time. It is so very temporary. It may all be over next month; in fact it will be. I don't belong to anybody here. In fact I have no being, but I am making preparations for changing everything. Write to me when you can and scold me.

Goodbye for now. Dont forget me.

I am always
Kissienka.

To Beatrice Campbell

[Higher Tregerthen, Zennor, Cornwall]
Sunday Night. [14 May 1916]

Ma très chère [My very dear one]:

I have been waiting for the time and the place to answer you in—& they both seem here. So first of all 'thank you' for the prescription (which you shall have back) and for your letter and the 2 papers. Nor must I forget Marjory's° account *NOR* Gordon's comment upon her reason for not being a S.F.° We have just been talking about you and G[ordon]. I hope your four ears kept up a pleasant burning for we are awfully fond of you always. G. is quite sincerely and for ever Murrys only love but G. knows that . . .

It is still awfully difficult to credit what has happened and what is happening in Ireland. One cant get round it—This shooting, Beatrice, this incredible shooting of people! I keep wondering if Ireland really minds—I mean really won't be pacified and cajoled and content with a few fresh martyrs and heroes. I can understand how it must fill your thoughts—for if Ireland were New Zealand and such a thing had happened there . . . it would mean the same for me—It would really (as *un*fortunately George-Out-of-Wells° would say) Matter Tremendously . . .

Dear woman, I am a little afraid of jarring you by writing about the whole affair—for I know so little (except what you've told me) and I've heard no discussion or talk.

Gracie Gifford's story° was spoilt by her having broken down before the jeweller in Grafton Street when she bought the ring and confided in him. Otherwise it was almost an Irish On The Eve of Turgeniev° . . . Poor Plunket's picture too—a cross between Jack Squire and Willie Yeats.° There is a strange passionate cynicism about Orpen's drawing° of women's hands. Even the Daily Mirror couldn't suppress it.

It is Sunday evening. Sometimes I feel I'd like to write a whole book of short stories and call each one Sunday. Women are far more 'sensitive' to Sundays than to the moon or their monthly period—Does Sunday mean to you something vivid and strange and remembered with longing — — The description sounds rather like the habits contracted by Jean Jacques Rousseau when his blood was inflamed by his youth°—or like G[ordon] C[ampbell] lying on his bed reading the Police Court News—but I don't mean that—Sunday is what these talking people call a rare state of consciousness—and what *I* would call—the feeling that sweeps me away when I *hear* an *unseen* piano. Yes, that's just it—and now I come to think of it—isn't it extraordinary how many pianos seem to come into being only on Sunday. Lord! someone heaven knows where—starts playing something like Mendelssohn's Melodie in F—or miles away—some other one plays a funny little gavotte by Beethoven that you—simply can't bear—I feel about an unknown piano, my dear what certain men feel about unknown women — — No question of love—but simply 'an uncontrollable desire to stalk them' (as the Crown Prince on Big Game Shooting says). Not that there is even the ghost of a pianner here. Nothing but the clock and the fire and sometimes a gust of wind breaking over the house. This house is very like a house left high and dry. It has the same 'hollow' feeling—the same big beams and narrow doors & passages that only a fish could swim through without touching. And the little round windows at the back are just like port holes—Which reminds me—there has been a calf lying under the dining room window all day. Has anyone taken it in? It has been another misty Highland-Cattle-Crossing-the-Stream-by-Leader day & the little calf has lain shivering and wondering what to do with its far too big head all the day long. What time its Mother has guzzled and chewed away and looked into the distance and wondered if she were too fat to wear a tussore coat like any Christian woman. Oh, Lord, why didst Thou not provide a tucking away place for the heads of Thy Beasts as Thou Didst for Thy Birds—If the calf were only something smaller I could send my soul out wrapped in a nonexistent shawl and carrying a nonexistent basked lined with non-existent flannel and bring it in to the dead out kitchen fire to get warm and dry ...

I must stop this letter. Write to me again very soon, Bici love.

[*No signature*]

To Bertrand Russell

[3 Gower Street, Bloomsbury] Thursday
Evening. [7 December 1916]

I have just re-read your letter and now my head aches with a kind of sweet excitement. Do you know what I mean? It is what a little girl feels when she has been put to bed at the end of a long sunny day and still sees upon her closed eyelids the image of dancing boughs and flowery bushes. To work—to work! It is such infinite delight to know that we still have the best things to do and that we shall be comrades in the doing of them. But on Tuesday night I am going to ask you a great many questions. I want to know more about your life—ever so many things ... There is time enough, perhaps, but I feel devilishly impatient at this moment.

You have already, in this little time, given me so much—more than I have given you, and that does not satisfy me. But at present, my work simply springs from the wonderful fact that you *do* stand for Life—

Adieu until Tuesday—I shall not read your letter again—It 'troubles' me too greatly—but thank you—Thank you for it.

                                        Katherine.

To Bertrand Russell

[3 Gower Street, Bloomsbury] Sunday
evening. [17 December 1916]

I meant to write to you immediately after you left me on Friday night to say how sorry I was to have been such cold comfort and so useless to lift even ever so little the cloud of your fatigue. For a long time I sat before the fire after you had gone feeling that your goodbye had been quite final—was it? And I did not explain myself as I wished to—I left unsaid so much that perhaps you were misled. Its true that my desire is to bring all that I see and feel into harmony with that rare 'vision' of

life of which we spoke, and that if I do not achieve this I shall
feel that my life has been a fault at last, and its my God terribly
true that I dont see the means yet—I dont in the least know
definitely *how* to live. But its equally true that life never bores
me. It is such strange delight to observe people and to try to
understand them, to walk over the mountains and into the
valleys of the world, and fields and road and to move on rivers
and seas, to arrive late at night in strange cities or to come into
little harbours just at pink dawn when its cold with a high wind
blowing somewhere *up* in the air, to push through the heavy
door into little cafés and to watch the pattern people make
among tables & bottles and glasses, to watch women when they
are off their guard, and to get them to talk then, to smell
flowers and leaves and fruit and grass—all this—and all this is
nothing—for there is so much more. When I am overcome by
one of the fits of despair all this is ashes—and so intolerably
bitter that I feel it never can be sweet again—But it is—To air
oneself among these things, to seek them, to explore them and
then to go apart and detach oneself from them—and to
write—after the ferment has quite subsided — — — —

After all youll cry me very vague & dismiss me perhaps as a
woman with an ill regulated mind ... But—

> Goodnight
> Katherine.

To Ottoline Morrell

[141A Church Street, Chelsea] Sunday.
[24 June? 1917]

Dearest Ottoline

'They' tell me that you are coming to town this week. I do
hope that you are, so that we shall have a laugh and a frisk
together. Of course I longed to tell you of my meeting with
Greaves—Mary Hutch° gave a dinner party at her new
house—Robby Ross, Roger Fry, Greaves, Eliot,° Jack [St.
John] Hutch[inson], she and I ... Oh God! Those parties.
They are all very well in retrospect but while they are going on

they are too infernally boring. Mary, of course went all out for Roger Fry and Robby Ross with an *eye* on Greaves and an *eyebrow* on Eliot. From Marys end of the table whiffs of George Moore and Max Beerbohm and Lord Curzon and Duhamel floated°—while Jack tied a white apron round himself and cut up, trimmed and smacked into shape the whole of America and the Americans. *So* nice for poor Eliot who grew paler and paler and more and more silent. In the middle sat Greaves chat chatting incessantly of what I told my sergeant and what my men said to me and how I brought them back at the point of my revolver etc. etc. I did not like that young man at *all*. In fact I longed to snub him and to tell him that one does not talk unless one has something to say. He seemed to me, too, to be so stupidly callous about the war and he was so frightfully boring about how the beer was diluted at La Bassée.° Roger Fry looked like an undiscovered unauthentic portrait by Jimmy Whistler and Robby Ross' teeth rang so false. And in and out among us all Mary moved like a spilt liqueur. I came away with Eliot and we walked past rows of little ugly houses hiding behind bitter smelling privet hedges; a great number of amorous black cats looped across the road and high up in the sky there was a battered old moon.° I liked him very much and did not feel he was an enemy.

Its so late: I must continue this tomorrow. Goodnight, my dearest friend. Always your

Katherine

To Virginia Woolf

141A, CHURCH STREET, | CHELSEA, S.W.
[24 June? 1917]

Virginia dear

I shall love to come and dine on Wednesday night with you alone: I cant manage Friday. Ever since I read your letter I have been writing to you and a bit 'haunted' by you: I long to see you again. The memory of that last evening is so curious: your voice & Vanessa's° voice in the dark, as it were—white

rings of plates floating in the air—a smell of strawberries &
coffee—Murry telling Woolf that you worked it with a handle
& it had a cylinder° & then M. and W. disappearing—and a
feeling that outside the window floated a deep dark stream full
of a silent rushing of little eels with pointed ears going to
Norway & coming back . .

My God I love to think of you, Virginia, as my friend. Dont
cry me an ardent creature or say, with your head a little on one
side, smiling as though you knew some enchanting secret:
'Well, Katherine, we shall see' . . . But pray consider how rare is
it to find some one with the same passion for writing that you
have, who desires to be scrupulously truthful with you—and to
give you the freedom of the city without any reserves at all.

Curse it! Here is the laundry boy snatching at my flying feet.
Ill tell you about Garnett° on Wednesday.

(Come in, little boy and sit down. I won't be two shakes of a
lambs tail) and we'll talk about Asheham,° please & lots & lots
of other things.

Yours ever
K M

To Ottoline Morrell

[141A Church Street, Chelsea] Friday
[13 July 1917]

. . . I am thankful to know that you are better and that we
shall soon be able to see each other again. What a dreadful
time you have had, I had no idea that the measles were so
formidable and over-whelming. I envy you going to the sea—
even for a few days. Oh, I have such a longing for the sea as I
write, at this moment. To stand on the shore long enough to
feel the land behind one withdrawn into silence and the loud
tumbling of the waves rise and break over one's whole
being. . . .

But the English summer sea is not what I mean. I mean that
wild untamed water that beats about my own forlorn island.
Why on earth do I call it 'forlorn'. My bank Manager assures

me that it's a perfect little gold mine and whenever I go down to the Bank of New Zealand I turn over a heap of illustrated papers full of pictures of electric trains and American buildings and fashionable ladies and gentlemen who might have walked out of the Piccadilly Grill . . . But all that sham and vulgarity is hard to believe in: I don't believe in it all. There is another side that you would believe in too. Ah, my dear, I know the most heavenly places that cannot be spoiled—and that I shall go back to as surely as if they were 'Dixie'.° And I shall think of you, and wish to God I expect that I were sitting opposite you at the Maison Lyons!° Life is a queer, a damn queer business!

It's a golden day. The blinds are down. I have some big yellow lilies in the studio. The garden door is open and the fig tree throws a wavy pattern on the floor and walls among big soft spots of sunlight. Four o'clock in the afternoon. I've been sitting at this table since morning, writing and smoking. And somewhere quite near someone is playing very old-fashioned dance tunes on a cheap piano, things like the Lancers,° you know. Some minute part of me not only dances to them but goes faithfully through, Ladies in the Centre, Visiting, Set to Corners, and I can even feel the sensation of clasping young warm hands in white silk gloves, and shrinking from Maggie Owen's° hand in Ladies Chain because she wore no gloves at all—

Talking about dancing reminds me of last Saturday night, when I really 'saw' [Augustus John]° for the first time. It was at a show at Margaret Morris's theatre.° He was there with two very worn and chipped looking ladies—the saddest looking remnants of ladies—in fact they reminded me of those cups without saucers that you sometimes see outside a china shop— all-on-this-tray-one-penny. But [John] was really impressive looking. I seem to see his mind, his haggard mind, like a strange forbidding country, full of lean sharp peaks and pools lit with a gloomy glow, and trees bent with the wind and vagrant muffled creatures tramping their vagrant way. Everything exhausted and finished—great black rings where the fires had been, and not a single fire even left to smoulder. And then he reminded me of that man in Crime and Punishment° who finds a little girl in his bed in that awful hotel the night before he shoots himself, in that appalling hotel. But I expect this is all rubbish, and he's really a happy man and fond of his bottle and a goo-goo eye. But I don't think so.

[*No signature*]

To J. M. Murry

[141A Church Street, Chelsea, late July 1917]
Private

My dear Jack,

I got up at that moment to re-read your article on Leon Bloy.° The memory of it suddenly *rose* in my mind, like a scent. I don't like it. I don't see its use at all, even artistically. It's a 'Signature' style of writing° and its *appeal* is in some obscure way—to me—mind me—I suppose only to me—indecent. I feel that you are going to uncover yourself and quiver. Sometimes when you write you seem to abase yourself like Dostoievsky did. Its *perfectly* natural to you I know, but oh my God, dont do it. Its just the same when you say—talking to Fergusson and me—if I am not killed—if *they don't kill* me. I always laugh at you then because I am ashamed that you should speak so.

What is it? Is it your desire to torture yourself or to pity yourself or something far subtler? I only know that its tremendously important because its your way of damnation.

I feel (forgive fanciful me) that when certain winds blow across your soul they bring the smell from that dark pit & the uneasy sound from those hollow caverns—& you long to lean over the dark driving danger & just not fall in—But letting us all see meanwhile how low you lean—

Even your style of writing changes then—little short sentences—a hand lifted above the waves—the toss of a curly head above the swirling tumble—Its a terrible thing to be alone—yes it is—it is—but dont lower your mask until you have another mask prepared beneath—As terrible as you like—but a *mask*.

K.M.

Forgive me for not telling you frankly when you read it to me—what I felt. I was wrong.

To Dorothy Brett

[141A Church Street, Chelsea] Thursday
[11 October 1917]

My dear Brett,

It is a cold sharp day—I can see the sun flying in the sky like a faint far-away flag—My Japanese doll has gone into boots for the winter and the studio smells of quinces. I have to write all day with my feet in the fringe of the fire—and Oh Alas! it is sad to think that I shall be warm in front and cold behind from now until next June. It seems to me so extraordinarily right that you should be painting Still Lives just now. What can one do, faced with this wonderful tumble of round bright fruits, but gather them and play with them—and *become them*, as it were. When I pass the apple stalls I cannot help stopping and staring until I feel that I, myself, am changing into an apple, too—and that at any moment I may produce an apple, miraculously, out of my own being like the conjuror produces the egg. When you paint apples do you feel that your breasts and your knees become apples, too? Or do you think this the greatest nonsense. I don't. I am *sure* it is not. When I write about ducks I swear that I am a white duck with a round eye, floating in a pond fringed with yellow blobs and taking an occasional dart at the other duck with the round eye, which floats upside down beneath me. In fact this whole process of becoming the duck (what Lawrence would, perhaps, call this 'consummation with the duck or the apple') is so thrilling that I can hardly breathe, only to think about it. For although that is as far as most people can get, it is really only the 'prelude'.° There follows the moment when you are *more* duck, *more* apple or *more* Natasha than any of these objects could ever possibly be, and so you *create* them anew. Brett (switching off the instrument°): 'Katherine I *beg* of you to stop. You must tell us all about it at the Brotherhood Church° one Sunday evening.' K: Forgive me. But that is why I believe in technique, too (you asked me if I did.) I do, just because I don't see how art is going to make that divine *spring* into the bounding outlines of things if it hasn't passed through the process of trying to *become* these things before recreating them.

I have left your letter unanswered for more days than I could have wished. But don't think it was just because I am so careless & faithless. No, really not. I enjoyed keeping silent with the letter just as one enjoys walking about in silence with another until a moment comes when one turns and puts out a hand and speaks.

I threw my darling to the wolves° and they ate it and served me up so much praise in such a golden bowl that I couldn't help feeling gratified. I did not think they would like it at all and I am still astounded that they do. What form is it? you ask. Ah. Brett, its so difficult to say. As far as I know its more or less my own invention. And how have I shaped it? This is about as much as I can say about it. You know, if the truth were known I have a perfect passion for the island where I was born. Oh, I out-Chili Chili° any day! Well, in the early morning there I always remember feeling that this little island has dipped back into the dark blue sea during the night only to rise again at beam of day, all hung with bright spangles and glittering drops—(When you ran over the dewy grass you positively felt that your feet tasted salt.) I tried to catch that moment—with something of its sparkle and its flavour. And just as on those mornings white milky mists rise and uncover some beauty, then smother it again and then again disclose it. I tried to lift that mist from my people and let them be seen and then to hide them again ... Its so difficult to describe all this and it sounds perhaps overambitious and vain. But I don't feel anything but intensely a longing to serve my subject as well as I can—But the unspeakable thrill of this art business. What is there to compare! And what more can one desire. Its not a case of keeping the home fire burning for me. Its a case of keeping the home fire down to a respectable blaze and little enough. If you don't come and see me soon there'll be nothing but a little heap of ash and two crossed pens upon it.

Are you coming to London soon—Let me know. Let us meet. Shall I see you float across my window upon a chariot of bright umbrellas?°

Venus Laughing From the Skies. Isn't it a beautiful title, when all is said and done—Goodbye goodbye goodbye. It is all *too* wonderful.

Katherine.

To J. D. Fergusson

My official name and address. |
Madame Bowden | Hôtel Beau Rivage |
Bandol | (Var.) | 15.1.1918.

Dear Fergusson,

Take the word of a 'sincere well wisher' and never attempt this journey during the War. When Murry and I came down here two years ago it was nothing of an ordeal, but this time . . . Well, a hundred Bill Nobles° crying Jesus Christ isn't your sofa pillows would not be enough. I would not do it again for all the oranges and lemons and lovely girls dans tout ce pays [in the whole of this country]. I would say: 'No! Leave me on the dear old Fulham Road,° let me hail the bus that none stop, go to the butcher who hasn't any meat, and get home to find the fire is out and the milkman hasn't come and doesn't intend coming . . .'

Just to mention one or two details. The train was not heated. There was no restaurant car. The windows of the corridor were broken and the floor was like a creek with melted snow. The cabinets did not open. There were no pillows for hire. We were hours late.

The French do not suffer as we do on these occasions. For one thing I think they obtain great relief by the *continual* expression of their feelings, by moaning, groaning, lashing themselves into their rugs, quietening their stomachs with various fluids out of bottles, and charming the long hours away with recitations of various internal diseases from which they and their friends have suffered . . .

We arrived at Marseilles to find no porters, of course. I was just *staggering* out when a pimp in white canvas shoes bent on reserving a place for a super pimp bounced up and gave me a blow on the chest which is still a very fine flat ripolion purple. 'This, thought I, is Johnnie's Marseilles'. And it was the harmonising motif of my stay there. You know the kind of thing. Waiting in a Q for one hour for a ticket and then being told I must have my passport viséd first, and finding myself after that at the end of the tail again, without even the excuse of the little woman in front of me who got on famously by tapping each man on the shoulder and saying 'Pardon Monsieur j'attends un Bébé [Excuse me, sir, I'm expecting a baby].' Even her ticket seemed to be punched ten times faster in consequence and the porter simply whisked her luggage away. It's quite an idea pour la prochaine fois [for next time].

When I did pass the barriers it was to discover that the train for Bandol was due to arrive at all four platforms and there was a terrific crowd on each. Every time a train came in it was thronged by people and even then not an official knew whether it was the right one or not. After two hours of this the real train did arrive, on the furthest platform of course. You picture me running on the railway lines with my rugs, suitcase, umbrella, muff, handbag, etc. and finally chucking them and myself into a 1ère [first class carriage] where I sat for the next ten minutes in a corner saying to muff 'Fool! do not cry. You can't begin crying like a baby at this stage'. However, there was suddenly an immense uproar and a body of soldiers rushed the train, commandeered it and began throwing out the civilians bag and baggage. They were not at all a 'I-tiddley-i-ty take me back to Blighty'° crowd either. They were bad tempered and very ugly. Happily I was in a carriage with 8 Serbian officers and they put up a fight. It was very unpleasant—the soldiers swarming at the windows, tugging at the doors—and threatening to throw you out. But these good chaps lashed the doors up with leather straps, pinned the curtains together and barricaded the door into the passage. They won, and I got here in the middle of the night, walked into a dark, smoky, wet-feeling hall, saw a strange woman come forward wiping her lips with a serviette and realised in a flash that the hotel had changed hands. If you will just add to all this 1 raging chill and fever which I caught on the journey I think you will agree that it's not a bad total . . . That was on Thursday.

Today is Tuesday. I have not even unpacked yet—it is cold. Wood costs 2.50 le panier [per box] and this hotel is much more expensive. But I shall have to stay here until I am well. At present I spend my time getting in and out of bed—and although there is a bud or two outside the windows and a lilac-coloured sea I feel what the charwomen call 'very *low*'. At night especially, my thoughts go by with black plumes on their heads

and silver tassels on their tails and I sit up making up my mind
not to look at my watch again for at least five minutes.
However all this will pass. To Hell with it.

I thought last night it is a bad thing during this war to be
apart from the one or two people who do count in one's life.
After all we are not solitary palm trees in deserts—thank
God—we are groups of two or three with a spring of sweet
water between us and a piece of grassy shade. At this time, to
go away alone to another country is a thoroughly bad idea.
(This of course is the precisely useful moment for me to make
this discovery).

Are you working? You know quite well what I thought of
those pictures, don't you. I knew in a way they would be *like
that* but that did not make them any less of a revelation. They
are unforgettable.

Write me a card when you feel inclined to, just to give me a
hail from your ship. Goodbye for now.

Yours ever,
Mansfield.

To J. M. Murry

[Hôtel Beau Rivage, Bandol] Monday
[21 January 1918]

My own Boge,

I am only going to write you a note today just to say that I
still feel better. The weather is 1000 times rougher. Never, not
even on shipboard or in my own little country or anywhere
have I heard such wind. And in the night, when one lay quiet
in bed & listened God knows how many Ancient Mariners
cried in it or how many lost souls whirled past. I thought then
what an agony it must be to be wife to a fisherman. How could
a poor soul comfort herself & to whom could she pray when
such a wind & such a sea fought against her ... I thought too,
it must have been just such a storm when Shelley died.° This
morning at red dawn a destroyer & a submarine tried to put
out to sea, but they were obliged to return. I despised them for

that & thought no english sails would not have mastered it. But you know, for all my big talk, I never believe the frenchies can sail a boat, or throw a ball, or do anything at all which is a patch upon the English ... If you could see this sea today heaving and smoking like a herd of monsters run mad ..

Last night my little maid brought me a present of rose buds. Two green jars full of them & some yellow *soleil d'or* [jonquils] beside. She had been for a walk in the country she said & a friend had made her a present. She came to the door with them—so pretty—wearing a black woollen cap and her cheeks were red—Shortly after the Madame came to ask if I would like some hot wine at night for my cough. 'Je ne savais pas que vous avez été si fatiguée [I did not know that you were so worn out]'. Well, though it is a bit tard [late] for remedy as I am such a much better girl I said Yes to the wine—& it was a rare fine posset. 3rd The submarine captain, having heard me try to get tobacco presented me with a whole packet of maryland—not cigarettes but tobacco—so I feel people have been unusually caring.

My precious heart, as I write the sun forced his head through a positive monks hood of a cloud & blesses you & me upon this page .. I thought this morning—in February I shall be able to say when I come back the month after next. And too February is a very tiny little month so that after it is gone & March has blown in there will only be a few weeks before April—Does this comfort you as it does me? I shall be awfully well—and all hung with presents for you with 2 candles that cant be put out—in my eyes—Youll have to discover me like a Christmas tree. Then we will wave & wave as the train carries us towards each other & then we'll be in each others arms. I fully expect Rib to be with you in your green overcoat cut down very small with a feltie on—

Does this letter make you feel that you are the most loved & cherished Bogey in all the world. If it dont—its none of mine—but it must. Now I am going to the post—then to have lunch then to come up here—light my fire & write.

I am always your own
Wig.

TAKE CARE OF YOURSELF—

To J. M. Murry

[Hôtel Beau Rivage, Bandol] Wednesday.
[23 January 1918]

My dear life,

Here is your letter of Friday night under my hand—the one in which Rib° rolled over and laughed. I have an idea that our children will use us just so. They will adore us but our love will make them *laugh at us*, in just his careless, infinitely confident way. Oh, dont let us ever forget Ribni. He must be always with us and our babies must only be allowed to sit next to him & perhaps stroke down his fringe with their tiny brown hands.

Last night, when I had finished capturing all I could of this wind, and rain and cold, it ceased, and this morning the sun came out. There is still a stiff breeze but its warm in the sun and indescribably lovely. Every mortal thing looks to be sheathed in a glittering beauty. It began, for me with your letter. There was a pulse in your letter that set my heart beating. I got up at about eleven and went out to buy myself une canne avec une frique.° The disagreeable shop has become aimable [likeable]. I bought a small stout one for 1.25. and then walked up the road behind the front past Ma'am Gamels, to the top of the hill and a little way further. The sky over the sea was like an immense canterbury bell, darkly transparently blue. Towards me came walking an old woman in a pleated black dress with a broad straw hat tied under her chin with a linen band and she carried a pack of jonquils. Then there came a butterfly, my little sister, weak in the wing, and staggering a little but *basking*. The cats lay on the windowsills. In a field against the sea a man and a woman were digging; the olive trees blew silver and the sea, very wild still, embraced the shore as though it loved it. As I came back I saw an old man sitting in a corner of a field, some wine & bread in a basket by him. He had a pair of breeches over his knees that he was carefully darning. They looked awfully forlorn as though he had just given them a beating.

But how can all this have happened in a night? Yesterday— midwinter. I walked to the post wearing your wadded coat, my woolen one, my great blue one over all & was perished. I staggered home, and decided that I must ask you to send me an anchor, a small one, shaped like a crab perhaps, with whiskers, that I could draw behind me on a string, to keep me from blowing (a) into the sea or (b) over le grand cerveau°—and here's today come to mock me. On a vraiment chaud [It's really warm]. By the way, my precious, my wadded coat has been and is a perfect treasure. It keeps out the draughts like nothing else. I wear it every day & sit up in bed in it and enfin—it is just what I ideally wanted.

Oh, the washer girl came today while I was in bed. You remember her? How fine she was, always so gauffré [got up] with frills over her hands & gold rings in her ears, and very expressive sparkling eyes. Now, poor wench shes so changed. There cant have been a soul in bandol with pyjame de laine [woollen pyjamas] 2.50 the washing since you left. She has shed all her brightness, jusqu'a ses pieds [right to her feet] which were covered in lovely red kid slippers. I hope it will *monte* [come back] again. She charged me 3.50 but it was not a 'swin' really.

I must tell you my little maid is becoming more and more friendly. She looks like the girl you read of who spreads the linen to dry in the orchard while the young boy up the ladder fills her apron with red pears. She was saying yesterday that she did not like the hotel to be so empty. We sit together, said she, there's nothing to do .. 'Alors, nous nous regardons—nous causons—mais, c'est triste, vous savez, ce n'est pas si gai que la service! [So we just look at each other, we chat, but it's sad, you know? It's not such fun as work!]' What do they talk about & where do they sit? I began to wonder ...

I am thankful that the studio is let° and off our hands. *No* don't send the £5. Put it in the bank. Ill cry when I am empty but being very well trained not before. I am doing all I can to live without spending, to wear my old clothes & shoes—We shall feast and array ourselves when we are together, and 'fleet the time carelessly as they did in the golden world'°

My adored one. Now that you know I am so much better you will tell me all about yourself & you will take care of yourself.

'And this is not a boon
'Tis as I should entreat you—wear your gloves
Or feed on nourishing dishes, or keep you warm
Or sue to you to do a peculiar profit
To your own person.'°

Warmly, warmly, passionately eternally I love you.
                                                    Wig.

[*Across top*]
Please can you send me my old mended shoes. I do need them
so and L.M says she gave them to you ... If its not a bother.

To J. M. Murry

[Hôtel Beau Rivage, Bandol] Late afternoon.
                          [30 and 31 January 1918]

My dearest
   I am not going to make a habit of writing to you deux fois
par jour [twice a day]—but just on these days when there is
something 'out of joint' I must—I must.
   I decided when I went out this afternoon to buy the little
coffee pot & the coffee. But first I walked in the direction of the
Hotel des Bains. Yes, it was beautiful, very—silver and gold
light—old men painting boats, old women winding wool or
mending nets—young girls making those gay wreaths of yellow
flowers—and a strange sweet smell came off the sea. But I was
homesick. I went to the paper shop to exchange a smile with
someone—& bought for 3 sous le Paris Daily Mail *and* a smile.
A commercial traveller with a wooden leg was in the shop
taking orders. 'Toujours pas de chocolat [There's never any
chocolate]' said Madame. 'Mon Dieu, Madame, if my poor leg
etait seulement de vrai menier, je serais millionaire! [Good
God, Madame, if my poor leg was only genuine chocolate, I'd
be a millionaire!]'
   Ha Ha! Very good. Very typical. Very french. But I am
faint with homesickness. Although it is so goldy warm the tips
of my fingers & my feet and lips and inside my mouth—all are
dead cold. And so I walk along until I come to the public wash

place and there are the women slipping about in the water in their clattering sabots, holding up those bright coloured things, laughing, shouting, & not far away from them a travelling tinker with his fat woman sits on the ground beside his mule and cart. He has a little fire to heat his solder pan & a ring of old pots round him. It makes a good 'ensemble'—the washer women bawl after me 't'as remarqué les bas! [look at your stockings!]' but I do not care at all—I would not care if I had no stockings on at all. And here are those villas built up the hillside. Here is the one whose garden is always full of oranges & babies clothes on a line. Still is. Also there is a dark woman in a wide hat holding a very tiny baby to her cheek & rocking it. The road is all glare & my shoes make a noise on it as though it were iron. I feel sick sick—as though I were bleeding to death. I sit down on a milestone & take out the Daily Mail. I turn my back to the shining sea & the fishers all out in their little boats spearing fish.

Air Raid in London.° Between 9–10 and again at 12.30. Still in Progress. Thats all — — He would have had his dinner and be on the way home—Or if he escaped that one he was in bed—Today is Wednesday. It happened on Monday. It is no use wiring. A cart comes up full of chunks of hay. An old man in a blue blouse with great bushy eyebrows holds up his hand & cries 'Il fait beau au soleil [It's beautifully sunny]' and I smile. When he passes I shut my eyes—This must be borne. This must be lived through. Back back again along the bright burnished road and all the way composing useless telegrams: 'Heard Raid Is all well' and so on and so on .. Varied with letters to the B[ritish] C[onsul] in Marseilles saying urgent family affairs compel me to return at once. Will there be any difficulty?

| | Shall I come back now and not wait? Answer this my own.

                                        Thursday.
My dear love
The facteur [postman] has just been and brought me a letter from Kay but there is again not a *line* from you. It is not as though the english post were delayed then; there must be another reason. I do most earnestly IMPLORE you to wire if all is not well. You know what this suspense is like. It is quite

dreadful. I cannot write any more until I hear again for I am too uneasy. *For Gods sake never spare me.* Always write at once or wire. You can think what I felt when that bloody postman came to my door & left me empty hearted—oh Jag!

Wig.

To J. M. Murry

[Hôtel Beau Rivage, Bandol] Sunday morning.|
February 3rd 1918. Sunday

Dearest,

It is early for me to be up, but I had such a longing for a cigarette, and as I sit here in my pyjamas smoking a very good one Ill begin your letter. There was nothing from you yesterday & the facteur [postman] hasn't been yet today—however — —

I really feel I *ought* to send you some boughs and songs, for never was there a place more suited, but to tell you the truth I am pretty well absorbed in what I am writing & walk the bloody countryside with a 2d ⟨envelope⟩ note book shutting out les amandiers [the almond trees]. But I don't want to discuss it in case it dont come off . . . . .

Ive two 'kick offs' in the writing game. *One* is joy—real joy—the thing that made me write when we lived at Pauline, and that sort of writing I could only do in just that state of being in some perfectly blissful way *at peace.* Then something delicate and lovely seems to open before my eyes, like a flower without thought of a frost or a cold breath—knowing that all about it is warm and tender and 'steady'. And *that* I try, ever so humbly to express.

The other 'kick off' is my old original one, and (had I not known love) it would have been my all. Not hate or destruction (both are beneath contempt as real motives) but an *extremely* deep sense of hopelessness—of everything doomed to disaster—almost wilfully, stupidly—like the almond tree and 'pas de nougat pour le noël'°—There! as I took out a cigarette paper I got it exactly—*a cry against corruption* that is *absolutely* the nail on the head. Not a protest—a *cry*,and I mean corruption in the widest sense of the word, of course—

I am at present fully launched, right out in the deep sea with this second state. I may not be able to 'make my passage'—I may have to put back & have another try, thats why I don't want to talk about it—& have breath for so little more than a hail. But I must say the boat feels to be driving along the deep water as though it smelt port—(no darling, better say 'harbour' or youll think I am rushing into a public house)

After lunch.

My Boge,

I have just read your Tuesday note, written after *another* raid.° You sound awfully tired, darling and awfully disenchanted. You are overworking ... its too plain. (Curse my old shoes.° Keep them for me. dont worry about them any more.)

Yes I agree with you—blow the old war. It is a toss up whether it dont get every one of us before its done. Except for the first warm days here when I really did seem to almost forget it its never out of my mind & everything is poisoned by it. Its *here in* me the whole time, eating me away—and I am simply terrified by it—Its at the root of my homesickness & anxiety & panic—I think. It took being alone here and unable to work to make me fully fully *accept* it. But now I don't think that even you would beat me. I have got the pull of you in a way because I am working but I solemnly assure [you] that every moment away from my work is MISERY. And the human contact—just the pass the time away chat distracts you—& that of course I dont have at all. I miss it very much. Birds & flowers and dreaming seas dont do it. Being a biped—I must have a two legged person to *talk* to—You cant imagine how I feel that I walk alone in a sort of black glittering case like a beetle — —

Queer business ...

By the way I dreamed the other night that Frieda [Lawrence] came to you & asked you for money. She 'knew you had some', she bullied you into giving her £5. I woke terrified lest this might happen. Never let it. Your money is really earned with your blood. Never give it away. You need it; you must have it. PLEASE please!

I wonder what you will say to my 'important' letter & if you agree will they let me through? Can they keep me out of my own country? These are a couple of refrains which are pretty persistent. They say here that after March this railway will probably be closed till June ...

My own precious I love you *eternally*

Your
Wig.

To J. M. Murry

[Hôtel Beau Rivage, Bandol] Sunday Night
[3 and 4 February 1918]

My precious

I dont dare to work any more tonight. I suffer so frightfully from insomnia here and from night terrors. That is why I asked for another Dickens; if I read him in bed he diverts my mind. My work excites me so tremendously that I almost feel *insane* at night and I have been at it with hardly a break all day. A great deal is copied and carefully addressed to you, in case any misfortune should happen to me. Cheerful! But there is a great black bird flying over me and I am so frightened he'll settle—so terrified. I dont know exactly what *kind* he is.

If I were not working here, with war and anxiety I should go mad, I think. My night terrors here are rather complicated by packs & packs of growling, roaring, ravening, prowl and prowl around dogs.

God! How tired I am! And Id love to curl up against you and sleep.

Goodnight, my blessed one. Dont forget me in your busy life.

Monday. February 4th.

Dearest

No letter from you today. I had one from Ida written on *Friday*—so the posts have got a real grudge against you & me ... I am posting you the first chapter of my new work today. I have been hard put to it to get it copied in time to send it off but I am so EXCEEDINGLY anxious for your opinion.

It needs perhaps some explanation. The subject I mean lui qui parle [the narrator] is of course taken from—Carco & Gertler° & God knows who. It has been more or less in my mind ever since I first felt strongly about the french. But I hope youll see (of course you will) that I am not writing with a sting. Im not, indeed!

I read the fair copy just now and couldn't think where the devil I had got the bloody thing from—I cant even now. Its a mystery. Theres so much much less taken from life than anybody would credit. The african laundress I had a bone of— but only a bone—Dick Harmon of course° is partly is

Oh God—is it good? I am frightened. For I stand or fall by it. Its as far as I can get at present and I have gone for it, bitten deeper & deeper & deeper than ever I have before. Youll laugh a bit about the song. I could see Goodyear grin as he read that .... But what is it like! Tell me—dont spare me. Is it the long breathe as I feel to my soul it is—or is it a false alarm? Youll give me your *dead honest opinion*—wont you Bogey?

If this gets lost I break my pen——

I am only at the moment a person who works comes up to read newspapers, AND to wait for postmen goes down again, drinks tea. Outside the window is the scenic railway—all complete & behind that pretty piece is the war—

Forgive an empty head. It rattled all night. I cant manage this sleeping business.

Goodbye for now my hearts treasure.

Yours yours only for ever
Wig.

To J. M. Murry

[Hôtel Beau Rivage, Bandol]
February 19th [1918]

(Your Thursday & Friday letters received)
Dearest

I want to tell you some things which are a bit awful—so hold me *hard*. I have not been so well these last few days. Today I

saw a doctor. There happens by an extraordinary chance to be
an english doctor here just now, & L.M. got him to come. Look
here! I cant leave this place till April—its no earthly go. I cant
& mustnt—see. Cant risk a draught or a chill & mustnt walk.
Ive got a bit of a temperature & I am not so fat as I was when I
came—& Bogey, this is NOT serious does NOT keep me in bed is
absolutely easily curable, but I have been spitting a bit of
blood. See? Of course I'll tell you? But if you worry—unless
you laugh like Rib does I can't tell you: you mustnt type it on
the typewriter or anything like that my precious—my own—
and after all Lawrence often used to—so did I think [Aunt]
Belle Trinder. But while it goes on Ive got to be most
enormously careful. See? Ive got this doctor & Ive got the
Slave—so I am provided for, & determined to stick it out till
April & not come back till the first week of *then*. Its agony to be
parted from you but it would be imbecile to get the March
winds as I am so parky—and everybody would be madly
cross—& I couldn't stick in bed in 47. Id only be a worry. So
here I stay & work—and try to bear it. Ive *ample* money for
everything & my journey money fastened up with a pin and
locked away.

   I can do all this and everything as long as I know you are taking care of
yourself and that you dont worry about me and do *feed* and dont
overwork too dreadfully. I am afraid it must be done. Before
[the] doctor came (you can imagine) I was so frightened. Now
Im confiding ... its not serious. But when I saw the bright
arterial blood I nearly had a fit. But he says its absolutely
curable—and if I sit in the sun till April Ill then come back &
see a specialist and Papa will pay for that—He can look at my
wings with his spyglass & decide. Of course this man says this
coast is my eye because its not bracing. Still now I am here—
here I must stay & he is looking after me & I am to have
injections of strichnine & other stuff—I don't know what, and
more food still. So its a good thing L.M. came (even though I
feel in some mysterious way *she has done it*. Thats because I *loathe*
her so—I do.) Still Ill use her as a slave. As I shall be here a
whole month longer I can get a lot of work done & that may
bring pennies. Oh, I can bear it—or anything as long as you
are well. And tell me when [you] feel a boiled haddock—don't
disguise anything because I wont disguise things from you. See

how I tell you *bang out* because our love will stand it. My money
is splendid—and I shall *work work work*. In April there can't be
the same chance of a snowstorm or a wind that might make
'pas de nougat pour le noël' for us both. I think it must be—
And then, please God we'll be married, & see how lucky I am I
can work! I had your letter about the 2nd part of Je ne parle
pas & I feel you are disappointed ... Is that true & if it is true
please tell me why—This is a silly old letter all about my wings.
Forgive it, my love, and answer it as soon as you can. Oh my
own precious don't work too hard—& love me love me till
April. Your own little

Wig.

To J. M. Murry

[Hôtel Beau Rivage, Bandol] Sunday morning.
[3 March 1918] (3 more Sundays only.)

My precious darling
Another jour glacé [freezing day]—so cold, indeed that the
country might be under deep deep snow. Its very quiet and
through the white curtains the sea shows white as milk. I am
still in my bye for I have just had mon petit déjeuner [my
breakfast]. It *was* good. I made it boiling in my tommy cooker.
I really think that Maman must have gone to see a fire-eater or
been frightened by one before I was born—why else should I
always demand of my boissons [drinks] that they be in a
'perfeck bladge'° before I drink em ... And now I am waiting
for the courier. Alas! the same light quick steps wont carry it to
me any more—for Juliette is gone. She came into my room last
evening, in an ugly stiff black dress without an apron. I noticed
she had her boots on and that she was very thickly powdered.
   She leaned against a chair looking at the floor & then
suddenly she said, with a fling of her arm: 'Alors je pars—pour
toujours ... J'ai reçu des mauvaises nouvelles—une dépêche—
mère gravement malade viens de suite. Alors! et ben—voila i'y
rien à faire [I have to go—for ever ... I've had bad news—a

telegram—mother seriously ill, come at once. Well—there's
nothing one can do]'—& then suddenly she took a deep
sobbing breath: 'J'ai bien de la peine! [I suffer so much!]' I was
so sorry that I wanted to put my arms round her. I could only
hold her warm soft hand and say 'ah ma fille je regrette, je
regrette de tout coeur [ah, I'm sorry my dear girl, sorry with all
my heart].' She lives on the coast of Corsica. The idea of the
journey of course *terrifies* her and then she was so happy—'si
bien-bien-bien-ici! [so very very happy here!]' And the beau
temps [good weather] is just coming and she did not know how
she could pack up her things—for she came here 'avec toutes
mes affaires enveloppées d'un grand mouchoir de maman
[with everything I owned wrapped up in a large handkerchief
of my mother's]', but she'd never saved and always spent 'il me
faut acheter un grand panier serieux pour les emballer [I'll
have to buy a big *proper* basket to carry them]'—Of course she
thinks she'll never come back here again—she's in the desperate state of mind that one would expect of her—and she wept
when we said 'goodbye'—'Qui vous donnerait les fleurs main-
ten-ant, Madame—vous qui les aimez tant—c'était mon grand
plaisir—mon grand plaisir! [Who will give you flowers now,
Madame—you who love them so. It was my great pleasure—
my great pleasure!]' I saw her in the hall before she left
wearing a hideous hat and clasping her umbrella and panier
serieux as though they had cried *To The Boats* already. I must
not write any more about her, darling Heart, for after all she
cant mean much to you. She *has* meant an enormous lot to me.
I have really loved her—and her songs, her ways—her kneeling
in front of the fire and gronding the bois vert [scolding the
green wood]—her rushes into the room with the big bouquets
and her way of greeting one in the morning as though she loved
the day and also the fact that she distinguished your letter from
others. 'Ce n'est pas *la* lettre—malheur! [It's not *the* letter,
alas!]' Goodbye Juliette, my charming double stock in flower.
Ill never forget you. You were a real being. You had *des racines*
[roots].
   (L.M. is seaweed if Juliette is double stock.)
   This morning it was Madeleine the laundrymaid, Juliettes
friend, promoted, who brought mon déjeuner. Très *fière* [very
proud], in consequence. With her fringe combed down into her

big eyes—a dark red blouse and a scalloped apron—I could write about these 2 girls for ever I feel today—Yes, I'll write just a bit of a story about them—& spare you any more—

You remember writing me in your criticism of *je ne sais pas* that Dick Harmon seemed to have roots. It struck me then & the sound of it has gone on echoing in me. It is really the one thing I ask of people and absolutely the one thing I cannot do without. I feel so immensely conscious of my own roots. You could pull and pull & pull at me—Ill not come out—You could cut off my flowers—others will grow—Now I feel that equally (it goes without saying my darling) of you—and *Johnny* has roots—Sullivan (I think)—Arthur Richard Murry, I am sure—Ottoline never—L.M. never. In fact I could divide up the people with or without them in a jiffy—and although one may be sometimes deceived—(sometimes they are so clever—the bad ones—they plant themselves and look so fair that those two little children we know so well stand hand in hand admiring and giving them drops of water out of the tin watering can—) they fade at the going down of the sun and the two little children are perfectly disgusted with them for being such cheats & they hurl them over the garden wall before going back to their house for the night.

Well well! The heap of dead ones that we have thrown over—but ah the ones that remain. All the English poets. I see Wordsworth, par exemple—so *honest* and *living* & *pure*.

(Heres the courier.)

Good God—Bogey—your Tuesday letter—and I read 'Wordsworth—so honest and so pure.' And remember my letter yesterday about our little house and here is yours in answer—just the same—We *are one*. Well I suppose I ought to accept this—but oh, the sweet sweet shock that goes through my heart each time it happens!

Yes, you are quite right, my precious shipmate. I *do* laugh at your preparations for this voyage of ours—I laugh so quietly that not even a harebell could hear—I laugh with every drop of my blood—and two tears laugh on my eyelids. You see—I am doing *just the same.* How many times have I lighted the lamp, wrapped up in my shawlet—sat down on the floor at your knees & said Boge—you read first—How many times has Cinnamon & Angelica° been published by us—have we leaned over each others shoulders looking at it—have you said in a rough soft voice 'it looks pretty good'. Now Ribni has begun walking all over the cushions with a walking stick & a broad hat on pretending he is fetching in our cow—What an *imp he* is.

Why Ive just remembered I did a drawing of our house yesterday.

Oh—our divine future—The mists of morning are still upon it but underneath it sparkles—ready—waiting just for the sunrise—and then we shall catch hold and *run* into its garden & I will put the key in the door & you will turn it but being small ones we'll walk in together—

I must get up darling Heart and make myself a pretty girl for Sunday. I feel *simply immensely well today*, skipping and hopping never never stopping°—dont cough at all—dont know how to—madly hungry and my hair in the most lovely little curls of bacon out of sheer crispness.

And its March 3rd and the next month Mrs J Middleton Murry will arrive—which *ought* to excite you—

How is your EYE?

You know you feel how I love you—How I am this moment as you read running into your arms & having a small lift up while I *hug* my darling Bogey until he cant breathe—Yes, underneath of course I am serious—but oh God! what a joyful thing it is to have a true love! I have given myself to you for keeps for ever.

Wig.

To J. M. Murry

Marseilles Monday. | [18 March 1918]
Café de Noailles

Dearest,

Everything seems changed—My whole life is *uprooted* and this calm of living in Bandol & even with the Gs° and L. M. feels like *calm* compared to this violent battle.° I arrived here, very late this evening, too late for the Consul or for Cooks: the train was 2 hours en retard [late]. And so I got a room at the

Hotel de Russie, had some food and here I am. I must bring you up to date with this Battle of the Wig. Last night after I wrote you I felt desperate & sent L. M. after Doctor Poached Eyes. Even though it really was rather late. He was at dinner— fatal time! but promised to turn up. Whereupon I set to— turned L. M. out of my room—dressed in my red frock & a black swanny round my neck, *made* up—drew chairs to the fire—& waited for this little toad. If you could have come in you would have been horribly shocked I think. I have not felt so cynical for years—I knew my man & I determined to get him by the only weapon I could—& that *he* could understand. He came, far more than 3 parts on—and I sat down & played the old game with him—listened—looked—smoked his cigar- ettes—and asked finally for a chit that would satisfy the consul. He gave me the chit but whether it will Ill not know till tomorrow. It could not be more urgent in its way—I dictated it & had to spell it <u>&</u> lean over him as he wrote <u>&</u> hear him say— what dirty hogs do say—I am sure he is here because he has killed some poor girl with a dirty buttonhook—He is a maniac on *venereal* diseases & *passion*—Ah, the filthy little brute! There I sat and smiled & let him talk. I was determined to get him for our purpose, any way that didn't involve letting him touch me. He could say what he liked: I laughed and spelled—and was so sweet and soft & so *obliged*. Even if this chit fails I think he can get me through in other ways—He has, for all this shadiness, a good deal of very useful influence in high quarters in Marseilles & Toulon—& its all at my disposal. So Ill use it.

Oh dear oh dear! I feel so strange. An old dead sad wretched self blows about—whirls about in my feverish brain—& I sit here in this cafe—drinking & looking at the mirrors & smoking and thinking how utterly corrupt life is—how hideous human beings are—how loathsome it was to catch this toad as I did— with *such* a weapon—I keep hearing him say, very thick 'any trouble is a pleasure for a lovely woman' & seeing my *soft smile* . . . I am very sick, Bogey.

Marseilles is so hot and loud—They scream the newspapers and all the shops seem full of caged birds—parrots & canar- ies—shrieking too—And old hags sell nuts & oranges—& I run up & down *on fire*—Anything—anything to get home!—It all spins like a feverish dream. I am not *un*happy or happy. I am just as it were in the thick of a bombardment—writing you, here, from a *front* line trench. I do remember that the fruit trees on the way were all in flower & there were such big daisies in the grass & a little baby smiled at me in the train—But nothing matters until I have seen the Consul. I am staying tonight at the Hotel de Russie. It is clean and good. I have Elle & Lui to read°—But this is all a dream you see. I want to come home— to come home—Tomorrow Ill wire you after Ive seen the man. Under it—above it—through it I am yours—fighting & tired but yours for ever

Wig.

To J. M. Murry

Select Hotel | 1 Place de la Sorbonne |
Paris | Saturday. [23 March 1918]

Tel. 'Selecotel'
My precious darling
I am afraid I shall have to wait until Monday before I hear from you. Ive never been so long without news. It is simply horrible, but it can't be helped and I must just go on—trusting that they will finally let me through ... I have written to Bedford Square, applied at the Police for permission to return & now there is nothing to do but wait. This place is in a queer frame of mind. I came out of the restaurant last night into plein noir [complete darkness]. All the cafés shut—all the houses—couldn't understand it. Looked up & saw a very lovely aeroplane with blue lights—'couleur d'espoir [the colour at hope]' said an old man pointing to it. And at the door of the hotel was met by the manager & made to descend to the caves [cellars]. There had been an alerte. About 50 people came & there we stayed more than long enough. It was a cold place & I was tired. At eight this morning as I lay in bed—bang, whizz— off they went again. I washed & dressed & just had time to get downstairs before the cannons started. Well *that* alerte n'est pas encore fini [isn't over yet]. Its now *3.45.* Most of the shops are shut—all the post offices—the shops that are not quite have a

hole in the shutters & you put your arms over your head & *dive* through—The *curse* is the post office as I have to register my letter to Bedford Square & now Ive lost a whole day. I have gone out, between the showers, to the police & fixed all *that* up, thank goodness—& now as soon as I can post this other—there will be rien de faire qu'attendre. C'est joliment assez! [nothing to do but wait. It's such fun!]

I look out at the lovely hot day and think—I might have been at Havre by now! Does this letter tinkle far away? I feel it does. It ought not to but oh Bogey it is so very long since I have heard from you—& tu sais comme je suis un enfant gaté [you know what a spoiled child I am]—*and* I hardly know where I am myself until I know that you know. I am not *found* until you have found me too & taken my hand & walked away with me — — If I had a letter. Yes, a letter. Thats what I *need so*. I am getting so very very impatient. Also I want to see a medicine man & ask if there is any divine reason why I have never seen Aunt Marthe *since that Sunday afternoon*°—I shant hope a bit till I have asked him. But I had to tell you: its on my mind, rather. This *waste* of life here—Why should the Lord treat us so: its not fair. Oh Bogey a letter a letter to revive a parched fainting little Wig.

[*No signature*]

To *J. M. Murry*

[Select Hôtel, 1 Place de la Sorbonne, Paris]
Saturday. [30 March 1918]

My darling Heart

I *should* have been home nearly a week by now—and Im still far away. But yes, this is better than that far distant South— for as soon as a train or a boat can go—I will be on it. I have been to the M[ilitary] P[ermit] O[ffice] this morning. They have not yet received our permission from Bedford Square. The whole office was in a vague state of unquiet and the official to whom I spoke seemed to think that, while this battle raged, civilians would be held up—i.e. that eight days was all

too hopeful an idea. L. M. is going off to the consul this
afternoon to try and get work.

I suppose the blockade has started for no post has come
today here or at Cooks. It is raining fast and the bombardment
is—frankly *intensely* severe. The firing takes place every 18
minutes as far as I can make out. I wont try & tell you where
the bombs fall—It is a very loud ominous sound—this super
Kanon°—I am not frightened by it even though I have been
extremely near the place where the explosions have taken place
but I *do* feel there is a pretty big risk that one may be killed by
it. You see there is no warning as to where the next shell will
fall—neither is it frequent enough to make one stay in the icy
cellars. Also one *must* go about to consuls etc & try & get away.
If it were not for you I should not care whether I were killed or
not. But as you *are* there I care passionately and will take all the
precautions you would have me take & I you in the same
straits. Today—people are frightened—quite otherwise to
what they have been before—and the ghastly massacre in the
church° has added very much to their feeling.

I tell you all this—I cant keep anything back from you. But I
am *not at all* frightened. And so I want to add—don't worry
about me, my own. But that is absurd. For I worry about you,
too. No rather—*think* about me & tell me in your next letter
that I shall at least be home for the 17th° and I shall believe
that. Ah, I cant say what store I set on that day—It seems to
mean such an infinite thing to us—a sort of blessing from on
high will be visited upon us when we walk out of the place into
the street—hand in hand—and telling everybody by our smile
that we have just come fresh from heaven. Rib must be there
too—I shall carry him & he shall have 1 grain of rice in one
hand shut up tight and one piece of pink confetti in the other.
Now you are smiling—are you—my own love? I want to put
my arms round your neck & pillow your head on my bosom. I
just want to hold you and kiss you & *never* let you go—After all,
I have fallen into this old war—I felt that one of us would—
but Bogey—oh—God—I thank Thee that it is *I* and not my
beloved who am here—That—from the bottom of my soul—
Goodbye my own for now—

I adore you and I am for eternity

                                        Your own Wig.

To J. M. Murry

[Select Hôtel, 1 Place de la Sorbonne, Paris]
Easter Monday. [1 April 1918]

My darling Heart

I wonder if your holiday has begun today—and if the weather is fine. Here is April—our longed for April—the month in which we mean to get married—I felt this year that April was simply made for us—and that it would be such a glory—such a spring as never never had been known before. And now—all I think is—when will the boats start again? When shall I be able to get through? It is idle to tell you again (yet I must tell you again) how simply boundless my longing for you is. I feel I *must* see you soon with my own eyes & hold you & be held. What perils we have gone through and are going through—& to think that those fruit trees are in flower in the Heron° orchard and all the flowers are open to the sun and our children walk about with handfuls of tired little violets . . .

There is no post today—I suppose that means there was no Good Friday post in England. Cooks is shut & the Consuls, so nothing can be done. Ill visit both tomorrow. I am thank God alone—as L. M. has gone to the cantine°—and won't be back till late night. It has just struck 3—so beautifully and calmly—with a kind of sunny langour—and my silly childish heart said—'Darling, shall we go for a small walk?' And away we went, going slowly, me on your arm, & talking very quietly, just for ourselves, you know. And occasionally you gave my hand a squeeze and said '*Wig*'. But no, these dreams are too sweet: I *cant* dream them while I am so far away. Shall I be home next Sunday? What do *you* think? Oh, Bogey I *must* be on my way home at least. The boats must start again and they cant keep all people away from their own country. If only we had influence. I asked for Sydneys man° at the M.P.O. [Military Permit Office] but was met with the coolest stare 'Dont know him. Major Knight is the head of this office'. So *that* was *not much good*!

At that moment a knock came at my door & the maid opened it pushing in front of her a tiny little boy in a white pinafore and white socks with red shoes. *Very* small just two years old. He was eating his goûter—a bit of bread and he staggered in & when he saw me turned his back—She said might she leave him a moment & when she had gone I remembered I had a little piece of chocolate in my despatch case. When I mentioned it he was so moved that he sort of— waded 100 miles over to me and about 200 more to the cupboard & there he stood—beating time with his toes as fast as possible while I got the chocolate out. He was so very nice. I held him up to the glass and he gave the other little baby first a crumb of bread & then a taste of the other. When the maid came for him—being anxious to kiss his hand, he kissed the bread instead & waved it at me. How fine and lovely little children can be. When he sat on my lap I felt a moment of almost *peace* as though the Sodom & Gomorrah world had stopped just for an instant. But now he's gone again — —

Every taxi that stops at this hotel stops at my heart, too. I know how utterly absurd that is. But I feel by some miracle — — — And I wonder—would they phone me from downstairs or should I just hear steps along the passage? — — — So far there has only been one shot today—but few people are out in the streets & it is not gay.

Goodbye my own darling—God keep us both.

Your own Wig

To J. M. Murry

[Select Hôtel, 1 Place de la Sorbonne, Paris]
Saturday Night. [6 April 1918]

Precious, dearest, darling Heart

I am so hopeful tonight. Two letters have come from you today—one written on Tuesday evening & one on Wednesday afternoon—& they bring you so . . . tremblingly near. I had a phone message from Sydneys man at the Embassy today, too, went to see him & he said that I would *definitely* get across on Wednesday—He gave me a card to the M.P.O. telling them that it was *urgent* I should go (he was a great ponce). And the

M.P.O. still say that a boat will go on Wednesday—though Cooks say it is most uncertain. I think it is absurd *not* to regard it as uncertain—for it is a race between Wednesday & this second battle—and those vile germans are still marching on. But everybody & every tree & every person & every breath seems now to *incline* towards Wednesday—If that again is just a big black hole & again there comes the uncertainty—and the waiting I don't know what I *shall do*. I am glad Kay was decent. Kiss your darling little Mummy for me—I am so glad that I am going to be her real daughter-in-law. & oh how I want to see the little brother [Richard Murry] again—the dear lad. But all these things come after.

First of all there is just YOU. L. M. has just lifted 150 off me: she cant help it & its alright of course—Ive plenty & shell pay me back but I wish she was not dead drunk as a result of one dubonnet. She is—& can only (as she says) 'giggle' . . . If you knew — — —

The bombardment has gone on again today & its 8.30. Ive had news. Id better get back as soon as possible—But there is still a good quarter of an hour. I havent had any *bread* since this new rule came in. I do want a crust—As to butter it dont exist.

Do you know IF I ever do get back it will be just a week before our wedding—& your mother must ask us to tea (we'll say its the anniversary for she must *never* know°) & we'll take her flowers—lovely ones—& be very gay children—Shall we?—Shall we? Is it all before us? Not all swept away?

I spend my nights now playing Demon patience. I sit up in bed & play & play. This morning at 3 oclock a mouse jumped into my waste paper basket & began to squeak—

But I can hardly tell you these things. Wednesday begins to more than loom—Again I think—I must take him back a peppermill—& another of those red & green cups & saucers. God! If ever I do get back then I feel our trial will be over for ever.

But the German army & the big gun & the raids and all this vast horror still rolls between.

Bogey—hope *for* me—Ive been so tortured that I must have someone to *help* me *hope*. Your letters are my salvation—but that—you know.

Your own Wig.

To Ida Baker

[47 Redcliffe Road, Fulham] Friday.
[12 April 1918]

Dearest Jones°

The little Messenger at the door sent me back years & years ... Thank you dearie for the 'goods'. I am glad the box has turned up. What is the next step to take & which of us takes it? I am also glad that Stella° was there as well. I'd like to know what the fights are—I have been wondering about you so — — —

'Home' looked lovely, & feels so lovely—I never want to go out again. I had to spend a long time casting up my eyes at all the 'surprises' and improvements. They really *were* many. Ribni was sitting in the window on the lookout on a little box which held my letters. When he saw the taxi you can imagine how he began to wave & tap his toes on the glass—& then when I *did* come there said he was only looking to see if the milkman was coming. He has got rather out of hand & bosses me up—if I so much as move a thing out of its place—

Johnny [Fergusson] came in last night—God!—He gave me such a welcome. Before I knew where I was we had hugged & kissed each other & Johnny kept saying 'this is a great success'. It really was! And you can imagine all the enjoyment he got out of a *fig* or two. We are dining with him tonight.

I feel horribly weak & rocky now that the strain is over—*blissfully* happy—incredibly happy—but really ill. I phoned Ainger.° He is away until next week—I'll wait if I can. I weighed myself. Curse it. 7 stone 6. Ive just lost a stone, alors. Isn't that annoying. But ever since I came HOME I have done nothing but eat. I am hungry all the time so perhaps my last state will be worse than my first & I will put on stones like I've thrown them off.

But Jones—ones OWN fire—and lighting the gas & making tea, and oh! the hot bath which really was hot—& Jack & Jack and Jack.

Does it gleam to you, too—like a little jewel beyond price— those hours on the boat when you sat on the floor in a draught

& I sat on the longue & we put the red on the black & wanted a seven? I was so happy — — — Were you? Try & forget that sad sick Katie whose back ached in her brain or whose brain ached in her back—Its such a lovely afternoon & very warm. I would like to turn to you & say 'Oh Jones we are quite all right, you know'—

About Saturday—Jack has got the afternoon off & we have to go & see his Mother—youll understand. Try & find a minute to write to me in—Do you want money?

Yours, dearie.
Katie

To Ida Baker

[47 Redcliffe Road, Fulham] Thursday.
[18 April 1918]

Dearest Jones

I am so glad of your little notes. Please keep on sending them when you can. I am *not* remarried yet as the court has not sat on the decree nisi but all the same, dearie, will you please address me as Mrs J. M. M.? If you hadn't asked me which you should do I should have asked you to, but you know how devilishly contrarywise Katie is!

I saw Ainger yesterday & discovered he was a New Zealand boy. That explains my feeling of confidence. But hes called away to France on Saturday—till the end of the war. What a bother! HE said: Yes there is no doubt I have definitely got consumption. He appreciated that a sanatorium would kill me *much* faster than cure me (Its a 2nd lunatic asylum to me) ∴ I am to try a 'cure' at home—Home is to be either Hampstead or Highgate or further afield. Must live in a summer house (*find* the summer) eat & drink milk and not get excited or run or leap or worry about anything—you know all the old wise saws. In fact repeat fortissimo with a good strong accent on the second note: 'she *must* lead the *life* of a *child* of *8*'. Cant you *now* hear the oboe taking it up & making it oh so plaintive with little shakes and twirls and half sobs? I must not borrow a

handkerchief (this is serious, Betsy, for you know how they fly
from me) or drink out of loving cups or eat the little bear's
porridge with his spoon. And so on. But you see I am ever so
gay—with long beams coming from my fingers & sparks flying
from my toes as I walk.

(As to money—well—I keep on taking taxis for the moment—I can't help it but I will draw in my horns the moment
my wings put forth). Tell me all about the coat & skirt
dearest—*Most* important. In fact tell me all you can about
everything. Belle & Chaddie called last night in a private
kerridge & brought me some oranges & dead roses. Fergusson
came to dinner & we talked strangely enough about 'this Art
business' & 'what is honesty'. But however often I wander in
that orchard I always find fresh fruits and bigger boughs &
loftier trees. So its an adventure.

Goodbye darling.
Katie.

To Ottoline Morrell

[47 Redcliffe Road, Fulham] Sunday.
[12 May 1918]

Dearest Ottoline

It never was a secret; and certainly not from you. It is true—
what you so perfectly say—I am always renewing a marriage
with Murry. This last and really 'funny' one was—more than
Id tell anyone—because I loathed and abominated my other
legal name. Whenever it smote up at me from a passport or a
police paper I hated it again. Now it's gone. But perhaps the
chief reason was my hatred of the Human Snigger—and in
fact, of human beings generally—of the 'Bloomsbury element'
in life—enfin. I do feel now more hidden from it somehow—
though perhaps that sounds far-fetched and absurd. But we
were a funny party. Brett, like some delightful bird who had
flown in, laughing through the bright anemone flowers—

I am so sorry—we cannot come down to Garsington. I am
leaving London again on Friday for—I don't know in the least

how long—and Murry is tied by every leg to his office stool. The country must be divine. I am going to *Looe* which is full of pigs and bluebells, cabbages & butterflies and fishermen's orange shirts flung out to dry on pink apricot trees. It sounds un printemps bien solide! [a *total* spring!]

Life feels to me so full at present—simply *charged* with marvellous exciting things. Is it the Spring that won't be denied even at my age?

Yes, I know that God is a monster and there are moments when one *realises* the war but there *are* other moments when one rebels in spite of oneself and then—the floodgates are open and one is swept away on this heavenly tide. Do you feel that—or do you think Im *too* heartless? But what is to be done? How can one remain *calm* when even the barrel organ seems to put forth new leaves and buds and laburnum is in full flower in the Redcliffe Road. It is all—as M. would say—*too difficult.*

Yours ever with Love
Katherine

To J. M. Murry

[Headland Hotel, Looe, Cornwall]
Sunday morning [19 May 1918]

Dear Love

Your wire came yesterday between two and three and made you feel near. Now I want a letter—of course—for I am un enfant trop gaté [a very spoilt child]—yes always—

When I got up yesterday I sat in my long chair in a kind of pleasant daze—never moved—*slept* and really did not wake until tea when I opened Dorothy Wordsworth and read on steadily for a long time. The air is heavenly—but don't imagine I walk or lift anything or even move more than I need. I cant even if I would—for the least effort makes me cough & coughing is such a fiendish devilish pain that Id lie like a mummy to avoid it. However—the divine sea is here, the haze & brightness mingled. I stare at that & wonder about the gulls—and wonder why I must be ill. All the people who pass are so well—so ruddy—They walk or run if they have a mind—or row past in little boats. Perhaps the curse will lift one day—

This place is very good for *just now*. You see I am going to stay in bed all day—not going to move—and all is done for me—so pleasantly by the old'un. She came in early & threw open my windows at the bottom—and said the air was better than medicine—which it is—and yesterday she patted my cushion & said I must try and gather up a little *harn*ful of strength. I am always *astonished amazed* that people should be kind. It makes me want to weep—you know—Its dreadfully upsetting, Bogey—What! can it be they have a *heart*! They are not playing a trick on me—not 'having me on' & ready to burst their sides at my innocence?

Anne & Drey came in last evening with an armful of those yellow irises that grew in the Marsh near Hockings Farm. They had been picnicking in the woods all day among the bluebells & were very burnt and happy—Anne must be doing *some* kind of good work, for I can feel her state of mind—a sort of *still* radiant joy which sits in her bosom—

There pipes a blackbird—& the waves chime. Would that you were here—yet, perhaps—better not. I try you too much— This is God's final joke—that even I should weigh you down— fall on you—like a dreadfully incredibly heavy sparrow—my darling, & take still more of your precious life & energy—

Try & take care of yourself & see Johnny [Fergusson] now & then. He, I know, loves you—

Yours for ever.
[*No signature*]

To Dorothy Brett

Headland Hotel,
Looe, | Cornwall. | Wednesday. [22 May 1918]

Dearest Brett

First there came a divine letter from you and then enough cowslips to make a chain from Garsington to London—with bluebells between. It is very lovely of you to do such things.

I wish I could have seen you again before you went to Scotland. BE SURE you see J.D.F.'s show° if you can. I popped in at the Private View and I thought it *wonderful*—I seem to spend nine-tenths of my life arriving at strange hotels, asking if I may go to bed, saying—'Would you mind filling my hot water bottle?' 'Thanks very much; that is delicious'—and then lying still growing gradually familiar, as the light fades, with the Ugliest Wallpaper of All ... This has been my programme since I arrived here last Friday with the tail-ends of another attack of pleurisy. However—its over again and I am up, sitting at *three* windows which positively hang over the sea, the sky and an infinite number of little ships—The sea is *real* sea— it rises and falls, makes a loud noise—has a long silky roll on it as though it purred—seems sometimes to climb half up into the sky—and you see the sail boats perched upon clouds like flying cherubs—and sometimes it is the colour of a greengage—and today it looks as though all the floor of it were covered with violets—If it weren't for the boats which are a distraction for the *drunken eye* I should become quite bedazzled and never turn my head from this 'vast expanse' as they say, again—I havent seen anything more of this place yet—Anne Rice, who is staying up in the village, says it is extremely beautiful—and 'full of the most lovely drawing'—As soon as my knees do not melt backwards I shall go forth again—But tell Ottoline—will you—I have at last found—he whom we have all looked for so long and so ardently—THE doctor. He appeared at 11.30 p.m. on Saturday night—I felt they had gone up into the hills to fetch him away from his flocks and herds—He is—or looks about 18—and is an irish peasant lad—very ardent—with curling hair—but, I suspect, a sort of natural genius. No nonsense about whispering '99'—or shouting '99'—He went over the old battlefield with his stethoscope—and said 'I can see whats wrong with ye and the kind of woman ye are'—and immediately began to cure me—You can imagine he made me feel like a very old worn Georges Sand, washed up by the tide, with a pen behind each ear—But after the London quack— quacks—its a great relief—

Our time with Ottoline was a failure. We were both so ready for her—spiritually, you know what I mean?—But then she brought Philip [Morrell]. And Philip was not only as she said '*grim*' he lay back and yawned so loudly that each gasp took a

little more of ones real self away—It was awfully silly—a waste
of time. He & Murry played politics and O. and I played
books—That was what I felt. After she had gone I lay down in
dismay and heard myself saying 'How awful! How awful!'
Perhaps it wasn't as bad as that but I felt it was—I feel it was
another ghastly failure between us—And yet I *still* feel there is
that between us—which if it were only *allowed* to flower—but it
isn't—at present—Curse Life!

I have been reading Dorothy Wordsworth's journals°—She
& 'William' & Coleridge had no end of a good time—but we
could have a better. If we went jaunting off in a little painted
cart or if we lay in the orchard & ate cherries—we should
laugh more—we should have far more *fun. Should*—indeed. I
mean *shall*.

Hallo! Here come two lovers, walking by the sea—she with a
pinched in waist—a hat like a saucer turned upside down and
4/11¾d. velvet shoes, he with a sham panama & hat guard—
cane—etc—his arm enfolding. Hideous—hideous beyond
words. Walking between the sea and the sky—and his voice
floats up to me: 'Of course *occasional* tinned meat does not
matter but a *perpetual* diet of tinned meat is bound to produce
. . .' I am sure that the Lord loves them and that their seed will
prosper & multiply for ever—

Send me darling Brett—if youve a mind a skirl of the
bagpipes frae bonnie Scotland—I presume you will call in on
Murry on your return in kilt, sporran, wee velvet jacket &
tartan bow & be discovered by him dancing the sword dance in
the waiting room—

I hereupon rise, and according to the Act of Parliament
declare that—I love thee—

                                                                Tig.

To J. M. Murry

[Headland Hotel, Looe, Cornwall]
Thursday—In bed. 11 am. [23 May 1918]

The old un has just brought your Monday night letter 'right
up'—Your letters all arrive perfectly now. My wire was sent

really—in a panic, because of that *cursed* raid—which you evidently in the 13th Corinth. manner 'winked at'°—the raid, I mean—

I dont worry. But for God's sake *dont* keep anything from me so that I shant worry—That is so appaling to think of.

Today I am going for a walk—down to the Surgery to be weighed. The weather has changed. It rained in the night & this morning the light is so uncertain—so exquisite—running silver over the sea.

An idea — — — —

Are you really only happy when I am not there? Can you conceive of yourself buying crimson roses and smiling at the flower woman° if I were within 50 miles? Isn't it true that, now, even though you are a prisoner, your time is your own. Even if you are 'lonely' you are not being 'driven distracted'—Do you remember when you put your handkerchief to your lips and turned away from me? And when you asked me if I still believed in the Heron? Is it true that if I were flourishing you would flourish ever so much more easily & abundantly without the strain & wear of my actual presence—We could write each other letters & send each other work & you would quite forget that I was 29 & brown—People would ask is she fair or dark & you'd answer in a kind of daze—'oh I think her hair's yellow.'

Well—well—its not quite a perfect scheme. For I should have to hack off my parent stem *such* a branch—oh, such a branch that spreads over you and delights to shade you & to see you in dappled light & to refresh you & to carry you a (quite unremarked) sweet perfume—But it is NŎT the same for you. You are always pale, exhausted, in a kind of anguish of set fatigue when I am by. Now I feel in your letters, this is lifting and you are breathing again—'She's away and she is famously "alright"—Now I can get on.'

Of course L. M. would keep us one remove from each other—She'd be a help that way—Did you reckon on that when you were so anxious to keep her. For of course, as you realised, Id have given her the chuck for ever after the Gwynne affair° if it hadn't been for your eagerness—

You are simply, incredibly perfect to me—You are always 'in advance' of ones most cherished hopes—dreams—of what a lover might be—

But whether I am not really *a curse* ... I wonder—
Mrs Maufe's letter° was most lovely—
                                    Goodbye for now, dearest Bogey.
                                                        Wig.

To Ottoline Morrell

                                    Headland House, | Looe, | Cornwall.
                                                    [24 May 1918]

Dearest Ottoline
    Yes, its you I want to write to—yes—you. For you alone will
not only 'keep my secret'—oh, I feel you will so beautifully, so
fully understand and respond — — —
    I have been walking up and down this huge, bright, bare
hotel bedroom, really, if one had looked through the 'spiritual'
keyhole—wringing my hands—quite overcome, for the nth
time by the *horror of life*—the sense that something is almost
hopelessly wrong. What might be so divine is out of tune—or
the instruments are all silent and nobody is going to play again.
There *is* no concert for us. Isn't there? Is it all over? Is our
desire and longing and eagerness—quite all that's left? Shall we
sit here for ever in this immense wretched hall—waiting for the
lights to go up—which will never go up?
    Heavens! the hysterical joy with which Id greet the first faint
squeakings of a tuning up—the lovely relief with which one
would lean back and give oneself up and up to it. But no—I
don't hear a sound—Its all very well to say like Koteliansky: 'I
am dead' but what the devil is the good of that with all this *fury*
of living burning away in my bosom—with God knows nothing
to feed it or fan it—just burning away—
    But the ugliness—the ugliness of life—the intolerable cor-
ruption of it all—Ottoline. How is it to be borne? Today for
the first time since I arrived, I went for a walk—Anne Rice has
been telling me of the beauty of the spring—all the hedges one
great flower, of the beauty of these little 'solid' white houses set
in their blazing gardens—and the lovely hale old fishermen.
But—the sea stank—great grey crabs scuttled over the rocks—

all the little private paths and nooks had been fouled by human cattle—there were rags of newspaper in the hedges—the village is paved with *concrete* and as you passed the 'tiny solid white houses' a female voice yells: 'you stop it or Ill lay a rope end across eë.'

And then—*hotels*, you know, strange hotels! The horror of them—the grimace for service rendered—the perpetual 'would you please bring up my letters as soon as the post arrives?'— another *strange bed*—and the mysterious people whom one always passes going to or coming from the lavatory . . .

Oh—how I *loathe* hotels. I know I shall die in one. I shall stand in front of a *crochet dressingtable cover*, pick up a long invisible hairpin left by the last 'lady' and die with disgust. Its almost funny—loving as I do, loving passionately, beautiful rooms, the shapes of furniture, colours, quiet, I find myself wandering eternally in rooms papered with birds, chrysanthemums in urns & bunches of ribbons, and furnished with fumed oak and lace curtains—and that *glare* from the windows—that dreadful gape which reaches to every corner—that sense of nowhere to hide! But all that is only part of the other, greater curse which is upon life—the curse of *loneliness*—I am quite certain that it is all wrong to live isolated and shut away as we do—never exchanging and renewing and giving AND receiving—There ought to be something fine and *gay* that we tossed about among us—and kept ever so thrillingly in the air, as it were, and never let fall—a *spirit*—But where is it. Ottoline, and who wants it? . . . I am in despair. In such despair that sometimes I begin weeping like a green girl—but that is no use, either. My tiny world tinkles: 'Of course with all that sea and air outside and all that butter, milk and cream *in* you'll be as fit as a fiddle in no time.' Which is altogether too simple.

Write to me—will you? I shall be here another week at any rate. Then I must wander somewhere else I think. This place is grotesquely expensive, too—But *write* to me—if you can—

I am always your very loving
Katherine—

To J. M. Murry

[Headland Hotel, Looe, Cornwall] Sunday
[26 May 1918]

Dearest Bogey

I had a wire from you yesterday—Funny french it was by
the time it reached here too—But it was awfully sweet of you to
send it & you are *not* to feel your coeur declinéd [heart
refused]. Now how can I prevent that? Prevent it I must. Look
here! Ill go on writing truthfully to you because I can't
'pretend' (you *do*, a bit) but if my truth is melancholy & you
feel gay just pretend it is all my I and pay it no serious
attention—But I can't dance s'il ne joue pas [if he doesn't
play]—and you wouldn't have me just keep silent. Or would
you? Tell me, darling—

Its true—the melancholy fit is on me, at present. But as I told
you when I was in the S. of F. (seemed to be always telling poor
you) that to be alone (i.e. without you) and to be utterly
homeless, just uprooted as it were and tossed about on any old
strange tide, is utterly horrible to me and always will be—even
though I were 12 stone & a prize fighter—though I own my
horror would be a bit ridiculous, then. However—I fully freely
acknowledge that *its got to be* for the present and my only
salvation lies in drowning my melancholy fit in a flood of work.
Which aint impossible. But what about Anne? you ask. Oh, yes,
of course I see Anne occasionally—as much as both of us want
to—for an hour at a time, perhaps, but you know its all on the
awfully jolly surface—I cant really talk to Anne, at all. Still its
nice to have her here and shes a distraction and 'too kind for
words' ... Passons outre [Let's talk of something else]. Its
Sunday. Cornwall in black with black thread gloves prome-
nades on the edge of the sea—little tin bells ring & the Midday
Joint is in the air. Pas de soleil [No sun]. Low tide & the sea
sounds to have got up very late & not found its voice yet.
Damned queer thing. I have dreamed for two nights in
succession of the name of a street *Rue Maidoc.* 'Not Rue Medoc'
says Chummie, but *Rue Maidoc.* There is an exhibition of
pictures there and Chummie is showing 3—two landscapes & a

portrait by Leslie H. Beauchamp. We idled down the street afterwards—arm in arm. It was very hot—He fanned himself with the catalogue. And he kept saying: 'Look, dear', and then we stopped, as one person, & looked for about 100 years and then went on again. I woke & heard the sea sounding in the dark—and my little watch raced round & round, & the watch was like a symbol of imbecile existence ...

There is a Circulating Library here. Not quite bare. Its got In a German Pension and Eve's Ransom by Gissing.° I took out the second yesterday—Although, like all poor Gissings books its written with cold wet feet under a wet umbrella—I do feel that if his feet had been dry & the umbrella furled it would have been extremely good. As it is, the woman of the book is quite a little creation. The whole is badly put together, & there is so much which is entirely irrelevant—Hes very clumsy—very stiff and alas! poor wretch! almost all his 'richness' is eaten up by fogs, catarrh, Gower street, landladies with a suspicious eye, wet doorsteps, Euston Station. He must have had an infernal time. Ill send you back D[orothy] W[ordsworth]'s journal in a day or two, just in case you have a moment to glance into them—to refresh yourself with the sight of W. sticking peas & D. lying in the orchard with the linnets fluttering round her. Oh, they *did* have a good life.

Well, I am going to work down till lunch. Goodbye, dearest.

Toujours
Wig.

[*Across top of letter*]
Boge. Please dont forget to tell the moment Harrison° sends my story back. Back it will come of course. But I want to know AT ONCE.

To J. M. Murry

[Headland Hotel, Looe, Cornwall]

While you read this feel that my arms are round you & your head is hidden—& Im telling you it all—with every part of me.

Monday. [27 May 1918]

My dearest own

I think, reading your three letters this morning I suffered every atom that you suffered.° Nay, more, because it was I who inflicted it on you—you who came crying to me & saying 'this is what you have done to me! This!' Even now I cant get calm & I am all torn to pieces by love and hideous remorse & regret. I must try & explain all this away & it is so difficult—so difficult—with these great clumsy words. I could do it were I to see you—in a moment—in a breath. Only *one thing*. Never never have I ever said to myself—'shut up shop take your love away'.° If you ever feel that dont tell me until you <u>do</u> take it away. It really nearly killed me. The sky—the whole world fell. Before I begin to speak—you must know that youre all life to me. God—havent all my letters said just that. Hasn't all my suffering & misery been just because of that, because of my terrible—exhausting—utterly INTENSE love. But you must have understood that? That was the whole why & wherefore—

You see, I was in the S. of F. from December till April. What was it like on the whole—just HELL. As you know it nearly killed me. Then I came back to rest with you. All my longings, all my desires, all my dreams & hopes had been just to be with you amen—to come back to my home. Bien! I came. Heard how ill I was, scarcely seem to have seen you—except through a mist of anxious—felt that ALL your idea was for me to get away into the country again—Well I understood that—although please try & realise the appaling blow it was to me to uproot again—& so soon—with hardly a word spoken—Please do try & realise that. Plus the knowledge that I was more ill than Id thought & that all my precious 'privacy', my love of 'self contained' life—doing all for myself in my own way—doing all—enfin [finally] for <u>you</u> was to be taken away from me— was 'bad' for me—enfin.

However it was only for a month or six weeks that I was to be alone. Then you came down for your holiday & we went back together—I arrived—& found I was to be here (without a word explaining why this change had been) at LEAST 4 months—until the *late* autumn—No word of your coming—no word of anything else. It was the sort of ultimate comble [last straw]. It knocked me back onto my own lonely self. I was in despair as you know, and I saw Life quite differently. I felt that if all I had oh so passionately pleaded & protested without shame or fear about my love—my longing for married life—as soon as possible—was to be just delayed—not understood—I could endure no more—& I fell into the dark hollow which waits for me always—the old one—& I wrote from there—I felt he has not this same great devouring need of me that I have of him—He *can* exist apart from me. I have been in the S. of F. nearly four months & here is another four—He will never realise that I am only WELL when we are 'together'—All else is a mockery of health. I depend on him as a woman depends on a man & a child on its little playfellow, but he, as long as he knows I am alright, he can play 'apart'—

Now do you see a little bit? Is it a little bit clearer? But there is more to say.

Our marriage—You cannot imagine what that was to have meant to me. Its fantastic—I suppose. It was to have shone—apart from all else in my life—And it really was only part of the nightmare, after all. You never once held me in your arms & called me your wife. In fact the whole affair was like my silly birthday. I had to keep on making you remember it — — — —

And then—all the L. M. complex is—taking the reins out of my hands. I am to sit quiet & look at the country—I cant—I cant. Dont you know that LIFE—married Life with you—co-equal—*partners*—jealously alone—jealous of every other creature near—is what I want—I am jealous—jealous of our privacy—just like an eagle. If I felt that you & she discussed me even for my own good—Id have to fly out of the nest & dash myself on the rocks below.

My little Boge-husband, you dont know me even yet. I adore you & you only—I shall not take my love away ever—not even long after I am dead. Silly little button flowers will grow on my very grave with Bogey written on the petals ... Do you understand now? (Maintenant, c'est moi qui pleure [Now I'm the one who's crying].) There is my answer for ever to you.

Now about the Elephant.° Get it if you can & we will make it a Singing Elephant with all our hearts—

As I wired you this morning I am not going to leave this hotel after all. I cannot explain to another landlady that my lungs is weak—Also the fag of wondering what I shall order to eat would mean Id order nothing. Here it comes—one eats it— & its over. And they know me here, now, & are more than kind to me. The old'un, Mrs Honey is 'pure Heron'—Bless her—I can always hear her & my Gran'ma talking as they put the linen away. So here I shall remain & I will take your money, please. Unless it leaves you short. I will take it from you—You must try & come here, as we did once arrange—even for a week & well have a sail boat and go 'whiffing for pollocks'.° I am working hard & Pagello° says I have made remarkable great strides.

So now, please God let us be calm again. *I will not be sad.* Let us be calm. Let our love keep us quiet & safe—like two children in a great big quiet field—sitting there hidden in the flowers & grasses.

Oh, thou who hast all of my heart. Accept me—

I am simply for ever & ever your own little

Wig.

I have told the manageress I am staying for the whole of June—*at least*.

The books came & the cigarettes—thank you, love. Tell me all the practical things. Dont spare me—Tell me all the worries. They are my RIGHT. I must have them & discuss them. You are NOT to have any worry *un*shared.

To J. M. Murry

[Headland Hotel, Looe, Cornwall,
5 June 1918]

Mittwoch. Die Hitze ist zurückgekommen [Wednesday. The heat has started again].

Dearest. Your Monday night letter & ½oz from Tuesday afternoon, & the Immensely Good Chinese poems°—(We ought to have that chap's book, you know. I think its notwendig [necessary] to the Heron.)

The oranges will be positively thrilling. It is very lovely of you to send them: I do only hope they are not shudderingly dear. One really sighs for fruit here & its not to be had. Strawbugs are on the market—but teuer [expensive] and they're no fun without sugar & cream—

Im much less depressed today, Bogey. Oh God I DO get black. I simply go dark as though I were a sort of landscape & the sun did not send one beam to me—only immense dark rolling clouds above that I am SURE will never lift. It is terrible—terrible. *How* terrible I could only 'put into writing'—& never say in a letter. This afternoon I am going to drive to Polperro with Anne—& we shall 'boire du thé sur l'herbe fraiche [drink tea on the cool grass]'. She came up to see me last night. She has quite the right idea about the country & living in it—I explained to her last night what I meant by *religion*. I feel awfully like a preacher sometimes—I really have a *gospel*—this seemed rather to startle her. Last night (this letter is like kalter Aufschnitt [coldcuts]—please forgive it), I read The Well Beloved by Thomas Hardy.° It really is *appalingly bad simply rotten*—withered, boring and pretentious. This is very distressing. I thought it was going to be such a find & hugged it home from the library as though I were a girl of fifteen. Of course I wouldnt say this about it to another human being but you—c'est entendu [that's understood]—The style is so PREPOSTEROUS too. Ive noticed that before in Hardy occasionally—a pretentious, snobbish, schoolmaster vein (Lawrence echoes it) an 'all about Berkely Square-ishness', too, and then to think as he does that it is the study of a temperament—I hope to God hes ashamed of it now at any rate. You wont like me writing like this about him—but dont you know the feeling. If a man is 'wonderful'—you want to fling up your arms & cry 'oh do *go on* being wonderful—don't be less wonderful.' (Which is unreasonable, of course.)

This happened yesterday.

Wig: (gets up from table & is followed by old white bearded monkey with bruised eyes & false teeth) Excuse me Modom, is thaat a New Zealand stone you are wearing.

W. yes.

O. M. Do you come from N.Z. may I ask.

W. Yes, I do.

O. M. Reely! From what part, may I enquire?

W. Wellington.

O. M. I know Wellington. (Shows false teeth) Do you know a Mr Charles William Smith a cousin of mine who was residing there in 1869.

W. — — —

O. M. But perhaps you were not born then.

W. (very faintly) No, I don't think I was.

Voilà for my grey hairs.

Oh how lovely these Chinese poems are. I shall carry them about with me as a sort of wavy branch all day—to hide behind—a fan—

I hope Ottoline turns up trumps.° I feel *fond* of her just now. Go down if you can—do, my precious & refresh yourself. Dear Brett will keep the bad things away—

Its good, I think that I didn't meet Massingham° who I am sure will not print Carnation—And please dont forget to tell me when Bliss comes back. I feel it is come. Thats why—

Goodbye for today my dear love—If you go to Garsington don't forget to let the Woolves know— + try & catch the Sunday post (if its not a bother) for then Ill get the letter on Monday—But if youd rather rest—I understand, my precious & will be happy to know it.

Your
Wig.

Was the review° alright?

To J. M. Murry

[Headland Hotel, Looe, Cornwall] Thursday
[6 June 1918]

Dearest and Best of All

(As I write that the 'worm' who hears everything my pen says takes a sort of little pinging guitar out of his sleeve & begins to play—striking an attitude, you know, and rolling his eyes at me. He is a ribald wanton Worm and badly wants a beating *by* you.) I have just eaten a juicy, meaty orange—an orange that *hasn't* riped among soup squares and blotting paper like the ones down here. And theyre not only food for the body—they positively *flash* in my room—a pyramid of them, with, on either side, attending, a jar of the brightest, biggest vividest marigolds Ive ever seen. (Yesterday on m'a fait un cadeau [I received a present] from Mr Pallisers° cliff garden— of spanish irises and marigolds—a boatload full.) Its *very* warm. I have a letter from you saying the Elephant seems to want us—as did your telegram. (God how I love telegrams—I could live on them supplementé par oranges and eggs.) But I have so much to say that I *cant* begin. Let me dance my way through the flowery mazes of your letter again—until I get to (what's the place called in the middle of a maze where you stand on a little platform & look round?) Well, Im there now & standing on the top.

(1) They say there are superb *sales* here. We might jingle bells off to one when you're here—chairs, par exemple. Eh?

(2) I saw Pagello yesterday who gave me more cod and iron. He's satisfied with me & he says Ill always be a Light Weight Champion so don't expect me, darling Boge, to be a Heavy One. Jimmy Wilde is more my size than Jack Johnson.°

(3) Rib is glad you liked his letter. He was very incommoded by a pen—He writes with a brush made of mouse's whiskers as rule—but you cant get them while the war's on.

(4) Nice lookout for Art when Billing is pelted with flowers and Lord A.D. our conquering Hero. I feel very very sorry for poor Maud Allen°—

(5)→Which is a very nice age. I LOVE you more than ever—

I am sending you some of my notebook today. Please let me
know what you think of it. Ive been keeping it since I was here.
Do you think the New Witness° might — — — ? Or am I
getting a little 'fresh'. Heres a letter I got from Virginia, too,
which is nice. We must try & find out who that man Edwards°
is. Useful.

Well, yesterday Anne & I went to Polperro. Its all my I, you
know to go to places like Etaples & so on while these spots are
here. Polperro is *amazing*—a bit spoiled by <u>artists</u> who have
pitched garden suburb tents in and out among the lovely little
black & white & gray houses—houses that might have been
built *by* seagulls *for* seagulls. But you must see this yourself.
Youll NOT believe it. I didn't & cant even now—It was a
divine afternoon—foxgloves out everywhere. *AND* we found
the most SUPERB fresh strawberries. Anne was a darling
yesterday. You can imagine both of us at finding these—our
excitement. We each bought a basket & had a basket put by for
us to bring home AND arranged for the carrier (for 2d) to bring
us fresh berries 3 times a week.
Wig: (feverishly) Will they last till 20th of this month.
Strawberry woman: 'Why bless eë they be just a coming on.'

They are grown there in gardens overhanging the sea. Anne
& I took ours & ate them on the cliffs—ate a basket each ($\frac{1}{2}$lb.
8d) & then each ate & drank our propre thé [own tea]—and
became 'quite hysterical' as she says—We could hardly move &
stayed much longer than we had meant to—The whole afternoon in my memory is hung with swags of strawberries. We
carried home our second baskets (just having 'one more
occasionally') & talked about raspberries and cherries and
plums—& tried not to say too often 'when Murry comes'. Looe
is much more beautiful than Polperro. Polperro smells—like
those Italian places do—& the people (families who have been
there since the time of the Armada—that's true) are dark
swarthy, rather sloven creatures. Looe is brilliantly clean—But
dearest—it really is—you know—a place to have in one's
inward eye. I saw Hugh W's cottage° but went no furder.

As I wrote that I have kept up a running fire with Mrs
Honey. *She* says I ought to have children. 'It might make eë a
deal stronger and they do be such taking little souls.' I agreed
& asked her to order me half a dozen—The other night her
husband 'waited' for her outside & she asked me to come &

look at him—on the bal-*cony*. A fine, neat old man, walking a
bit shaky—She said: 'He's dont look his age—do eë. He war a
rare *haandsome* lad.' There is still love between these two: thats
what attracts me to Mrs Honey.

Oh, dont forget to bring a bathing suit. The beach here—the
beaches in fact are perfect for bathing or you can take
Pengellys boat & bathe from that. At any rate you've got to
bathe—I must ask Pagello if I can, too—otherwise I will sit on
your cricket shirt under my parachute & wave a lily hand at
your darling sleek head—

I wonder if you *feel* how I love you just *here now*—I wonder if
you feel the *quality* of my love for you. I am carrying you with
me wherever I go—especially as I lean over & look at the new
boat—or read the names of the other boats. (There is one, pray
tell Johnnie [Fergusson], which is called *The Right Idea*. But
they have such lovely names: Harvest Home: A Ring of Bells.)

Tomorrow fortnight. It will be a real holiday—won't it?

(Dont tell L. M.) I eat marmalade puddings here—all kinds
of boiled puddings. They are delicious—and these people give
one *plenty* of sugar.

I ADORE YOU.

Oh what *can* I do—how *can* I tell you—Well here is your
Wigwife.

To J. M. Murry

[Headland Hotel, Looe, Cornwall] Sunday.
[9 June 1918°]

Precious darling

I have just been writing about Gus Bofa.° Now I want to
write to you. It all feels so different today; its been raining and
'tis loövely air as Mrs Honey says. No sun—rather cold—the
curtains blowing—very very desolate & far away from everybody—11500 miles° away at least . . . Oh dear! I wish I were in
London (but you'd be angry). I wish I could have some tea

(but you wouldn't let me go into the kitchen). In the middle of
last night I decided I couldn't stand—not another day—not
another hour—but I have decided that so often. In France *and*
in Looe. And have stood it. 'So *that* proves', as they would say
'it was a false alarm.' It doesnt. Each time I have decided that
I've died again—talk about a pussy's nine lives: I must have
900. Nearly every night at 11 o'clock I begin wishing it were 11
a m. I walk up & down—look at the bed—look at the writing
table—look in the glass & am frightened of that girl with
burning eyes—think 'will my candle last until its light?'° &
then sit for a long time *staring* at the carpet—*so* long that its
only a fluke that one ever looks up again. And oh God! this
terrifying idea that one must *die* & maybe *going* to die ... The
Clovelly Mansions,° S[outh] of F[rance] writing 'a few last
words' business ... This will sound like exaggeration but it
isn't. If you knew with what feelings I watch the last gleam of
light fade! ... If I could just stroll into your room—even if you
were asleep & BE with you a moment—'all would be well.' But
I really have suffered such AGONIES from loneliness and
illness combined that Ill never be quite whole again. I don't
think Ill ever believe that they wont recur—that some grinning
Fate wont suggest that I go away by myself to get well of
something!! Of course externally & during the day one smiles
and chats & says one has had a pretty rotten time, perhaps—
but God! God! Tchekhov would understand: Dostoevsky
wouldn't. Because he's never been in the same situation. Hes
been poor and ill & worried but enfin—the wife *has* been there
to sell her petticoat—or there has been a neighbour. He
wouldn't be alone. But Tchekhov has known just EXACTLY
this that I know. I discover it in his work—often.

I have discovered the ONLY TREATMENT for consumption It is NOT to cut the malade [invalid] off from life: neither
in a sanatorium nor in a land with milk rivers, butter mountains & cream valleys. One is just as bad as the other. Johnny
Keats anchovy° has more nourishment than both together.
<u>DONT YOU AGREE???</u>

However Ill cling to the rope & bob up & down until Friday
week but not a day later. Look here! dear. Do please give me
every bit of your attention just to hear this. I MUST NOT BE
LEFT ALONE. Its not a case of L. M. or a trained nurse you

know. Its different. But that really is a cry for help. So do remember.

Your Wigwife

This letter is not to make you sad. I expect my tomorrow's will appear to absolutely deny it. But it will not really. This *does* stand for all time & I *must* let you know.

To Ottoline Morrell

47 Redcliffe Road S.W.10. | Tuesday.
[16 July 1918]

Dearest Ottoline,

It was with infinite pleasure that I read your letter this morning. I had thought that my stupid cry from Cornwall° had really disgusted you and I was to be banished, but then I heard from Brett how ill you were and I realised only too well why you had not written to me.

It is simply dreadful that you should suffer so much & that doctors should be such useless fools. What can one say? I know so devilishly well the agony of feeling perpetually ill and the longing—the immense longing—just to have what everybody else takes so easily as their portion—health—a body that isn't an enemy—a body that isn't fiendishly engaged in the old, old 'necessary' torture of—breaking ones spirit — — — 'Why *wont* you consent to having your spirit broken?' it wonderingly asks. 'Everybody else yields without a murmur. And if you'd only realise the comfortable, boundless numbness that you would enjoy for ever after — — —' I wonder sometimes how it will end. One will never give in and so — — All the same, it would be more tolerable if only people understood—ever so little— but *subtly*—not with a sort of bread jelly sympathy—but with exquisite, rare friendship. (Oh, dear, I *still* believe in such a thing and *still* long for it.) You see, I cannot help it—My secret belief—the innermost 'credo' by which I live is that *although* Life is loathesomely ugly and people are terribly often vile and cruel and base, nevertheless there is something at the back of it all—which if only I were great enough to understand would

make *everything* everything indescribably beautiful. One just
has glimpses, divine warnings—signs—Do you remember the
day we cut the lavender? And do you remember when the
russian music sounded° in that half empty hall? Oh, those
memories compensate for more than I can say — —

This is all vaguely, stupidly written, but I want to be in
touch with you somehow: I would so have loved seeing you
today. I imagine we might have talked. There is always so
much to say—Dearest Ottoline, you are so real to me—always.
And now Ill confess. I was hurt a little bit that you didn't
answer my letter. But only for a moment. After all—I had
written and I have enough faith in you for ever to know that
you do—respond—There is my feeling for you—whatever you
may think of me—grown into my heart, as it were—and never
to be uprooted — — — But this you know.

Thank you dearest friend, for all that you so beautifully say
about my tiny book.°

And *do please* let me know when you are in town again.

With my love
Katherine.

To Virginia Woolf

47 Redcliffe Road | S.W.10. | Tuesday
[23 July 1918]

Dear Virginia

I am sorry I shall not see you this week and her laship
informs me that you are to be served hot-and-hot between two
plates this week*end* at Garsington. She asked me to be there,
too, but really after the great San Philip's arunning down of
the little Revenge in this weeks Nation° I don't think I *can*
break 'crumb' in their house again. I should lose control of
myself—I should do something dreadful—sin against very
Decency—commit some hideous crime—eat the clove out of a
stuffed orange or—or—God knows!

But it is only too plain from all this that Johnny Murry and I
are arrogant outcasts with cannon balls for eyes. Do not be

surprised, dear Virginia to see us arrive at Asheham, Murry en avance, with a knolled stick, fur cap, black eye, blue chin, me following with unbraided hair & a quilty shawl over my nonexisting bosom—a kind of Bill Sykes and Nancy,° with the bulldog tagging behind gripping a copy of Massingham's paper in his slobbering jaws. However, I 'note' as Dostoievsky is so fond of saying that Enid Bagnold has all too beautifully come to Sassoon's rescue° this week as well as Philip ... Generous creature! To have told us, too, so expressly that she hears with her ear! Now how could one have known a thing like that otherwise? I defy anyone to have guessed such a thing.

'And I hear
With my Ear'

Great stuff!! as Frank Harris used to say—'Oh Miss this is an Ewent at which Evings itself looks down'. But I wish to God she would sit up occasionally in her uncomfortably twanging bed and read her verses aloud to that intelligent organ at a moment when it is—as one might say en rapport ... Passons [Let's move on].

I love to hear of Lyttons success.° It seems quite measureless to man.° I put my head out of window at night and expect to find his name pricked upon the heavens in real stars. I feel he is become already, a sort of myth, a kind of legend. Modern princelings are hushed to sleep with tales of him and grave young duchesses disguise themselves at their Fairs and Pageants with — — the delicate beard, the moonlit hat, the shy, reluctant umbrella ...

Yes, I am very sorry that we shall not see each other this week. Your Pearl of a Letter made me realise what an infinite deal I want to talk about with you. But it will keep. I have spent the last two days lying on the sommier [mattress] with a temperature for doux ami [my intimate friend]. But writing seems a great labour and every book I want—out of reach— the topmost leaf of the tallest tree°—But I like to listen to this street. There is a piano in it, a parrot, and a man who cries feather brooms—all excellent in their way—

Yours ever
Katherine.

To Dorothy Brett

'47' [Redcliffe Road, Fulham] | Friday
[26 July 1918]

Dearest Brett,

Your long absorbingly interesting letter came yesterday. You
are as Kot [Koteliansky] would say a 'wonderful being'—and
if ever in a dark hour you feel that nobody loves you—deny the
feeling on the spot. For I do. I love you dearly. So does Johnny
[Murry]. You seem to me to have the most *exquisite* virtues. I
only hope that one day you will become a part of our life for a
time and we'll share a gorgeous existence somewhere painting
and writing and looking out of the window on to the sea
perhaps—with painted ships sailing on it & sailors playing ball
with oranges and little black niggers sitting in the bows playing
twing-twang-twing on guitars made of coconuts! This I fondly
dream while the rain pours down & the old lady in the
basement tells 'er friend across the way that 'er legs 'urt er
somethink 'orrible . . .

I am delighted to think you will be in London in September
and for a long time—long enough to really *talk* and *really* laugh
without the backs of our minds flying off to railway trains. If
you dont think our particular Elephant a King of Beasts I shall
be *very* disappointed. And now that I have fairly started and we
are sitting before a fire of friendship with our skirts turned
back comfortable & something hot with a nutmeg in it at our
elbows Ill really answer all your letter. But again—how the
dickens *can* I? The whole affair is so complicated and there is
poor young Sassoon tucked up in bed with a wound in the
head°—given him by Murry, perhaps, in a paper cap with a
carrot stuck in it . . . I have read Johnny's review 'time and
time again' as they say. I think it is severe—terribly straight but
to say that Sassoon would let himself be shot because of it, or
that if someone had said it about Prelude Murry would have
'stabbed them' is simply *fantastic* to me. I tried to talk it out
with O. the first afternoon she came here, but it was a failure.
In the first place I think she was astounded that I didn't agree
with her as against Johnny. In the second I simply couldn't get

on ground with her that didnt, after one minute, *rock* so that I
was off again. I do wish shed say—bang out—that she hated
Johnny. The picture she draws of him absolutely revolts me;
and though she said one moment she utterly believed in his
honesty & that he wouldn't attack S. S. personally, at the next
she wondered whether he didnt wish to seize the opportunity of
showing how much he disliked her—by wounding her through
the body of S's book. Well Brett, the second monster is greater
than the first. If that cad were Johnny Life would be a very
different affair to me. It made me blush deeply to hear her say
this. I could only murmur: 'Oh, no, he wouldn't do that kind of
thing'. And then the idea that Johnny is solely a black, morbid,
depressed, ill, melancholy object, like a crêpe knocker on the
handle of a house, closed for the duration of the war—that
isn't the case either. If you get past the knocker & open the
door you'd find an extraordinarily simple eager passionate boy,
very sensitive, *desperately* loyal, full of tweaks and twirls of
<u>fun</u>—and more shy and more modest than even I, who know
him pretty well, can remember. The great brick is that hes only
this self when he feels safe—when he is with people whom he
feels are after the same thing as he is. What is that? It is
'profoundly speaking'—to be honest—That sounds so bald
when I say it but perhaps you'll understand what I mean ...

(All my letter seems to be a defence of Johnny & I feel rather
like the poster of the young girl in Her Love Against the
World.)

And Oh—Oh!—*don't* lets quarrel! It isn't really 'like that'—
As Bill Noble says—'Jesus Christ! You folks just float around
with razors in your socks *all* the time!' <u>I</u> don't want to hate
people: I want to love them. If I *do* lose my faith in people I
want to run to them and to cry: 'Oh, please Ive lost my faith in
you: have you seen it about anywhere. Do give it back to me: I
wouldn't be without it for anything!' But perhaps that sounds
childish to you ...

Now it has stopped raining; the air feels lovely—I wish you
were here. (I have a teeny little study in the Nation° this week
or next—Its just a sort of glimpse of adolescent emotion: I am
full of work again.)

Write again, Brett, when you have a mind to—

Your loving
Tig.

To Ida Baker

47 Redcliffe Road|S.W.10. [1 August 1918]

Dear Jones

Come in tomorrow evening if you *can* manage, for I may be able to lend you something for your weekend—or a suitcase. Would you like Jack's small suitcase for instance? I thought of getting you some handkerchiefs—but then you are so particular about quality I get a bit frightened of buying you 'on the spec': you might despise 'em.

We are very unfortunate in our meetings. I dont *want* to quarrel, though I believe you think I do. The truth is that for the time being my nature is quite changed by illness. You see I am never one single hour without pain. If its not my lungs it is (far more painful) my back. And then my legs *ache* and I never can even change my position without such a creaking of all the joints as ever was. This, plus very bad nights exasperates me and I turn into a fiend, I suppose. And when you turn to me and say 'you *did* have a bag of herbs IF you remember' as though those words of yours came out of an absolute cavern of HATE I realise 'the change'. All the same, and knowing and realising this as I do I *still* ask you to come to Hampstead— until I am better. For the sake of all that *has* been I ask that of you. I know I shall get better there—quite well again—but see me through these next few months—will you?

I know exactly why you talk of what you are going to do after the war—'Carrie'—the 'big house'—'I may be in a factory'. That is because, untrue to my first talk about Hampstead I have never made you feel part of it, and every time you say 'our' I give you a vile look. This is wrong in me but at present I cant control it. Ill try and explain it a bit. You see out of all my external world only the house remains just now. Its all my little world & I want to make it *mine beyond words*—to express myself all I can in the small circle remaining. And so I am plagued with a wicked childish jealousy—lest my last doll shall be taken from me—dressed as I dont want it dressed— hugged by other arms. You wont understand this in me; there is no reason why you should. But you must believe that, as we live there, things will quite change, and if only you are 'careful for me' it will all be *quite* different & we shall [call] each other over the stairs.

Oh, it is (yes it is) incredible that one should have to explain all this. I always felt that the great high privilege, relief and comfort of friendship was that one had to explain nothing. But I have sinned against friendship, that's why.

Only I do think I am the last person on earth who has undying, unbroken faith. That will really seem to you *too* contradictory altogether. Nevertheless it is true.

If I dont see you before your weekend I hope you have a happy time, dearie, and take an old *well* Katie in a corner of your heart to think about if you have a moment.

In this imperfect, present world we have failed each other, scores of times, but in the real unchanging world we never have nor come down from our high place.

Yours ever
Katie.

If you buy a book for the journey the August English Review has a story by K.M.°

To Dorothy Brett

[47 Redcliffe Road, Fulham] Wednesday
[14 August 1918]

My dearest Brett

I was so glad of your letter today. Yes, it is an *immense* blow.° She was the most precious, lovely little being; ever so far away, you know, and writing me these long long letters about the garden and the house and her conversations in bed with Father, and of how she loved sudden unexpected cups of tea— 'out of the air, brought by faithful ravens in aprons'—and letters beginning 'darling child it is the most exquisite day'— She *lived* every moment of Life more fully and completely than anyone Ive ever known—and her gaiety wasnt any less real for being *high courage*—courage to meet anything with.

Ever since I heard of her death my memories of her come flying back into my heart—and there are moments when its unbearable to receive them. But it has made me realise more fully than ever before that I love *courage—spirit—*poise (do you know what I mean? All these words are too little) more than anything. And I feel inclined to say (not to anybody in particular) 'let us love each other'. Let us be *kind* and rejoice in one another and leave all squabbles and ugliness to the dull dogs who can only become articulate when they bark and growl. The world is so dreadful in many ways. Do let us be tender with each other.

I dare say that to you because I know you understand.

With much love
Tig

To Ottoline Morrell

[2 Portland Villas, East Heath Road,
Hampstead] Tuesday. [8 October 1918]

Dearest Ottoline,

I have been thinking of you so much since you went back to Garsington, and *realising* over & over again how more than dear it was of you to have come so dreadfully far to see me & to have given me so much of your time. Oh, but I *loved* seeing you—& when ever I feel the biting cold beginning I wrap up warm in the memory of our last 'talk'.

Such strange actual things seem to have happened. Fancy Robbie Ross dying°—that was surely very odd in him. He must have been, poor fellow, greatly surprised himself—to be, so suddenly, *nipped* into Eternity on a Saturday night. I expect he still feels that it is a mistake, simply a mistake. He has gone behind the wrong curtain, found the Wrong Exit—is wandering down a passage for Artists Only—Death, how dreadful a thing is Death!! I have such a horror of it; it ought not to be. We should simply go from star to star——But no—even that is not good enough. Id arrive & find Frieda swooping down upon me, with meringue wings & a marzipan wand, a real German angel.

Speaking of Frieda. Gertler came to supper on Sunday night

& told us that the Lawrences are coming to live in London indefinitely—They *are* come, in fact, yesterday & are staying just round the corner in Well Walk.° This really horrifies me. I am sure they will turn up here, & though I have armed M. with every possible weapon & warned him against L. I have a terrible idea that they will fight—and it will be hideous and lacerating. L. has come up to look for work in an office—which of course he'll *never* do for more than three days.° But altogether, I feel they are better as many miles away as there *are* miles. Everytime the bell goes I hear Frieda's '*Well* Katherina—*here* we are!' and I turn cold with horror.

I had such a depressed, fish-out-of-water back-to-the-nursery little letter from poor Brett. Her father won't speak, her mother treats her as though she were a vase, the children are charming with vile nurses and mademoiselle has a well developed bosom and is fat. There is very little to eat and she is always hungry & bitterly cold. It sounds *too* forlorn. Julian Huxley° has been and impressed her as *throbbing* with fire, ambition and attainments. In fact it read like some unfinished novel by Turgenev, with Brett for the heroine & J.H. for a sort of Bazarov-Rudin.°

Oh—I *wish* we could find a new country. There is a vine outside my windows & all the little grapes are purple & down below in the yard a lady is pegging a pair of gents. woven underpants . . . Gissing in Italy—it looks to me . . .°

This letter is *too* dull—But I feel I must just write to you.

> With very much love dearest
> Katherine.

Mrs Hamilton° is coming to tea next week. I am jingling my political threepenny bit already!

To Ottoline Morrell

> 2 Portland Villas | East Heath Road | N.W.3.
> [22 October 1918]

Dearest Ottoline

I was so happy to hear from you today but I wish you had not a cold. Its such appaling ghastly weather to *fight*; one needs double strength and double health. I wish I were near. I wish I could tap at your door. I simply LONG for a talk—just with you—nobody else—a long talk—in which we can really *let fly*.

Oh, my dearest woman friend—how vivid you are to me—how I love the thought of you; you cannot know. And it is such a 'comfort' to feel that we are in the same world—not in this one. What has one to do with this one? I feel that winter, cruel forbidding winter is content to leave nothing unfrozen—not one heart or one bud of a soul to escape! If only one did not feel that it is all so wrong—so wrong. It would be much happier if one could feel—like Murry—mankind is born to suffer—But I do feel that is so wrong—so wrong. It is like saying: mankind is born to walk about in galoshes under an umbrella. Oh dear—I should like to put a great notice over England—*closed* during the winter months. Perhaps if everybody were shipped off to blue skies and big bright flowers they would change. But I don't know—The miracle is that one goes on hoping and believing *through it all* just as passionately as ever one did—

It is a grey grim, pavement of a day, with slow dropping rain. When the Mountain [Ida Baker] brought me my early morning tea this morning she whispered, tenderly: 'Do you think it would be a good idea to change one ton of coal for two of large anthracite? I don't think we require a special permit and even if we do I think it is worth it.' My bed turned into a railway truck, shuffled off to the pit head, and two tons of large anthracite were tumbled on it . . . A very lourd paquet [heavy parcel] to begin the day with . . .

Lawrence has been running in and out all this week. He is gone off to the Midlands today—still without Frieda. He seems to have quite forgotten her for the time—merely saying: 'she wants me to become a german and Im *not* a german'—and so dismisses her. But I wonder why he is taken in by the most impossible charlatans—I am afraid he will never be free of them. Perhaps his whole trouble is that he has not a real sense of humour—He takes himself dreadfully seriously now-a-days; I mean he sees himself as a symbolic figure—a prophet—the voice in the wilderness crying '*woe*'. And what is amusing is his opinion of Murry as a flipperty-gibbet—'play on, ye mayflower' kind of figure who never will take Life or himself seriously enough!

This is a dull letter—a rattling old withered leaf of a thing—
not what I want to send you—Forgive it and me — —

Do you think—one day—we might go abroad together?
That is always a dream of mine—

Forever | Your loving
Katherine.

To Anne Estelle Drey

[2 Portland Villas, East Heath Road,
Hampstead, 13 January 1919]

My darling Anne

After my Plan
For New Year's Day fell through
I gave up hope
Of catching a rope
Which would land me down near you.
Since then Ive been
(Pulse one sixteen
Temperature one o three)
Lying in bed
With a wandering head
And a weak, weak cup of tea.
Injections, chère
In my derrière
Driven into a muscular wad
With a needle thick
As a walking stick—
How *can* one believe in God!
Plus—pleurisy
And je vous dis [I tell you]
A head that went off on its own
Rode a circular race
That embraced every place
I ever shall know or have known.
I landed in Spain
Went to China by train

And rounded Cape Horn in a gale
Ate an ice in New York
Caught the boat for Majourke
And went up the Nile for a sail.

Light refreshments, bouillon raw eggs and orange juice were served on the journey. Jack M. came in, fell over the screen, went out again, came back, dropped a candle, groaned, said 'Oh God does my love for you matter tuppence?' and went again, & the Faithful One changed the hot water bottles so marvellously often that you never had a hot water bottle at all. It was always being taken or brought back. All this, Anne darling, is a new treatment that my new doctor has started—a treatment by injections.

Hes a wonderful man. He was a doorstep baby, left in Paris with nothing but a shawl on and a paper pinned on his poor little chest with SORAPURE written on it. That is what he calls himself. (It always sounds to me like a soap that does your washing for you while you sit in the kitchen all comfortable with your feet in the gas stove and read 'Freckles'.) In April he says I ought to go to a place like Corsica. Switzerland is impossible, tank de Lord. So I think I shall. I cant help wishing we were going to help you produce *Marigold et Cie*, ma chère. Anne, if there are more than two you must give me one. Ill carry it away in my heavenly bag and turn it into a Corsican baby° for you in a moment. I think twins would be perfect! They would be so self contained—such a pair—you could get such a good *balance* with one on either side of the fire. Also one could play the piano while the other played the violin, one could hold the basket while the other dropped the peaches into it, one could set the house on fire while the other turned the hose pipe on to it, one could always row to shore and tell you the other had fallen out of the boat, one could pull the communication cord if the other dropped out of the train, one could always hand around the coffee while the other poured. In fact, thinking it over why are children ever born singly? It seems just a waste of time. Do please have the most engaging adorable mischievous *two*. Just think of the DECORATION you could make with two? Enfin — — if one is a boy will you call him Valentine—because he is a February chile?°

Well, Anne dearest, Ill keep on thinking & thinking about you—and wishing you all the luck there is. I shall be no good after today until the end of this week for I have another consignment shipped in to me tomorrow. But Ill write again then. Quelle vie! [What a life!]

Yours with tenderest love & a big warm hug
Katherine.

To S. S. Koteliansky

[2 Portland Villas, East Heath Road,
Hampstead, 7 April 1919]

Murrys telephone number is 9712 central.

Dear Kotelianski

I was as much surprised as you to find we were nameless.° No reason was given. I shall ask M. on your behalf tonight; I shall also mention the question of a cheque. I do not know how they pay. I gave my letter to you with several others to the new maid to post. I presume she 'lost' the stamp money; there is really nothing that she has not lost.

I dislike IMMENSELY not going over the letters with you. I dont want you to rely on me and M. I have long ago finished all that you gave me—But I feel Tchekov would be the first to say we must go over them together. However, dear Kotelianski, I dont want to worry you.

And you are depressed. I am so sorry. I wish you would come in now, this moment, & let us have tea and talk. There is no one here except my cough. It is like a big wild dog who followed me home one day & has taken a most unpleasant fancy to me. If only he would be tame! But he has been this last week wilder than ever. It is raining but its not winter rain. — — This early spring weather is almost too much to bear. It wrings ones heart. I should like to work all day & all night. Everything one sees is a *revelation* in the writing sense.

Have you ever owned a cat who had kittens? Or have you ever watched them from the first moments of their life? On

April 5th Charlie was delivered of two—He was so terrified
that he insisted on my being there and ever since they have
lived in my room. Their eyes are open already. Already they
smile and smack the spectator in the face (the spectator being
their mother). One is like a minute tigress, VERY beautiful and
the other is like a prehistoric lizard in very little. Their tiny
paws are pink & soft like unripe raspberries. I am keeping a
journal of their first days. It is a pity that human beings live so
remote from all animals ...

Frieda writes me that there is a 'rumpus'° between me and—
them I suppose. I see this 'rumpus'—don't you? A very large
prancing, imaginary animal being led by Frieda—as Una led
the Lion.° It is evidently bearing down upon me with Frieda
for a Lady Godiva on its back. But I refuse to have anything to
do with it. I have not the room now-a-days for rumpuses. My
garden is too small and they eat up all ones plants—roots and
all.

Goodbye.
Katherine.

To Virginia Woolf

Portland | East Heath Road | N.W.3.
[c.10 April 1919]

My dear Virginia
I have burned to write to you ever since you were here last.°
The East Wind made my journey in the train an impossibility;
it set up ponds & pools in my Left Lung wherein the Germs &
the Toxins—two families I detest—bathed & refreshed themselves & flourished & multiplied. But since then so many
miracles have happened that I don't see how one will be able to
bear real, full spring. One is almost tired already—one wants
to swoon, like Charles Lamb, before the curtain rises.° Oh God!
To look up again & see the sun like a great silver spangle: big
bright buds on the trees, & the little bushes caught in a net of
green — — But what I chiefly love, Virginia, is to watch the
people. Will you laugh at me!—It wrings my heart to see the

people coming into the open again, timid, airing themselves;
they idle, their voices change & their gestures. A most unexpected old man passes with a paper of flowers (for whom?), a
solider lies on the grass hiding his face; a young girl *flies* down a
side street on the—positive—*wing* of a boy — —

On April 5th our one daffodil came into flower & our cat,
Charlie Chaplin, had a kitten.

Charlie Chaplin

Athenaeum   April

Athenaeum is like a prehistoric lizard, in very little. He
emerged very strangely—as though hurtling through space—
flung by the indignant Lord. I attended the birth. Charles
implored me. He behaved so strangely; he became a beautiful,
tragic figure with blue-green eyes, terrified and wild. He would
only lie still when I stroked his belly & said: 'it's all right, old
chap. Its bound to happen to a man sooner or later.' And, in
the middle of his pangs, his betrayer, a wretch of a cat with a
face like a penny bun & the cat-equivalent of a brown bowler
hat, rather rakish over one ear, began to *howl* from outside.
Fool that I have been! said Charles, grinding his claws against
my sleeve. The second kitten April was born during the night, a
sunny compact little girl. When she sucks she looks like a small
infant saying its prayers & *knowing* that Jesus loves her. She
always has her choice of the strawberry, the chocolate and the
pistacchio one; poor little Athenaeum has to put up with an
occasional grab at the lemon one ... They are both loves; their
paws inside are very soft, very pink, just like unripe raspberries.
Would a baby be more enchanting? I could get on without a
baby—but Murry? I should like to give him one—but then I
should like that he should be denied *nothing* ... Love's very
strange.

Virginia, I have read your article on Modern Novels.° You
write so *damned* well, so *devilish* well. There are these little
others, you know, dodging & stumbling along, taking a sniff
here and a stare there—& there is your mind so accustomed to
take the air in the 'grand manner' — — To tell you the truth—
I am *proud* of your writing. I read & I think '*How* she beats
them — — —'

But I positively must see you soon. I want to talk over so much. Your room with the two deep windows—I should love to be there now. Last time the rambler roses were nearly over & there was a sound of someone sawing wood—

I think of you often—with love

Katherine.

To Ottoline Morrell

2 Portland Villas [c.12 June 1919]

Dearest

The flowers! I came in from posting your book and the whole house had a sweet scent. What peonies! And the roses. I am saving the petals to dry. Oh, they are all so wonderfully beautiful. When M. came home we made a solemn journey & reviewed all the gay bouquets. He has such a longing to grow flowers—and when they really *do* set him alight he glows almost enough to satisfy me ... I *embrace* you for them. While I sit writing here I am conscious of them all the time—I wish I were a poet. I'd so much rather write about them than—the things these poets write about—pompes funèbres [funeral processions].

The sound of the wind is very loud in this house. The curtains fly—there are strange pointed shadows—full of meaning—and a glittering light upon the mirrors. Now it is dark—and one feels so pale—even ones hands feel pale—and now a wandering broken light is over everything. It is so exciting—so tiring, too—one is waiting for something to happen—One is not oneself at all in this weather—one is a being possessed—caught in the whirl of it—walking about very lightly—blowing about—and deeply, deeply excited ... Do you feel that, too? I feel one might say anything—do anything—wreck one's own life—wreck anothers. What does it matter. Everything is flying fast. Everything is on the wing.

On Bank Holiday, mingling with the crowd I saw a magnificent sailor outside a public house. He was a cripple; his legs were crushed, but his head was beautiful—youthful and proud. On his bare chest two seagulls fighting were tattooed in red and blue. And he seemed to lift himself—above the crowd—above the tumbling wave of people and he sang:

'Heart of mine—summer is waning.'

Oh! Heavens, I shall never forget how he looked and how he sang. I knew at the time this is one of the things one will always remember. It clutched my heart—It flies on the wind today— one of those voices, you know, crying above the talk and the laughter and the dust and the toys to sell. Life is wonderful— wonderful—bitter—sweet, an anguish and a joy—and oh! I do not want to be resigned—I want to drink deeply—deeply. Shall I *ever* be able to express it. It is always of *you* I think when I see & feel these things.

I have had such a tragic letter from Brett. Its made me feel a perfect wretch to have written as I did about her. I wrote to her, too, and said I really didn't like flings unless they were 'delicate' flings & drunken Chilis° I could not bear. And poor little Brettie said she agreed—she didn't really enjoy her Bolshies and hated the tittle-tattle of Nina Hamnet.° But what can one do for her? She sounded so helpless. *I do not know.*

Have you seen 'Mary Olivier'? By May Sinclair.° It is coming to me for review. It sounds from what I have read— most extraordinary—And the new Quarterly 'The Owl'° flew into the house the other day—What a forlorn old bird—what pickings for a nest!

My cat and kitten are fighting and loving on the couch. First the cat devours the kitten & then the kitten eats up the Mother. Lawrence would see an Unholy Meaning in them — —
Goodbye for now, dearest Ottoline

Ever your devoted
Katherine.

To Ottoline Morrell

[2 Portland Villas, East Heath Road,
Hampstead, *c.*13 July 1919]

My dearest Ottoline,

If I have not written before it is not my fault really not my fault—it is this confounded weather which puts me so out of tune. I hate to send such a Jangle—Here I sit, staring at the writing-table like some sea sick traveller who dares not lift his eyes to the waves outside but he will be quite undone—IF I do—there is the grey cloud chasing the black cloud and the trees in their dark ugly green tossing their branches like old crones at a weak-tea party telling how that Autumn has come back unexpected and has turned Summer into the Street and Summer has gone off dear knows where without even her flowery shawl poor lamb and Autumn has wired to winter to curtail his journey and start for home—*home*—This desperate news makes ones flesh creep again. I heard a coal man pass this morning and was half inclined to put a black cross on our door—

Do not think I am not grateful for the exquisite sweet scented basket, *dearest* of my friends—All my flowers this year have come from you—I never shall forget them—Its so strange. I feel that I have spent almost a whole summer at Garsington: each of these flowers is a remembrance. I love your garden: I often walk in it invisible. How long *is* it since we have really walked there together. Why does it seem so long? My heart aches at the thought.

I have seen nobody and have not been 'out'. Brett was my last guest. She is pitiful. I do not think she has any idea of what is to happen to her—she lifts with one wave and is thrown back upon another. I think her only salvation is the WILL to work. Do you think she has it? I have a horror of Nelson (whom Ive never seen.) I feel he is a type of the dog eternal—not *waiting* for the crumbs that fall from the table—but positively sitting up to them—and to those of the largest size. Does he intend to make a meal of Mrs Baker° who most certainly (if what Ive heard is true is no chicken among the chickens.) What upstarts these creatures are! How dare she sit on your lawn!!

These preparations for Festivity° are too odious. In addition to my money complex I have a food complex. When I read of the preparations that are being made in all the workhouses throughout the land—when I think of all these toothless old jaws guzzling for the day—and then of all that beautiful youth feeding the fields of France—Life is almost too ignoble to be borne. Truly one must hate humankind in the mass—hate them as passionately as one loves the few—the very few. Ticklers, squirts, portraits eight times as large as life of Lloyd George & Beatty blazing against the sky°—and drunkenness and brawling & destruction. I keep seeing all these horrors, bathing in them again & again (God knows I don't want to) and then my mind fills with the wretched little picture I have of my brother's grave°—What is the meaning of it all? One ought to harden one's heart until it is all over. But Oh—Life might be so wonderful—There's the unforgettable rub! And weve only one life and I cannot believe in immortality. I wish I could. To arrive at the gates of Heaven—to hear some grim old angel cry 'Consumptives to the right—up the airy mountain, past the flower fields and the boronia trees—sufferers from gravel, stone & fatty degeneration to the left to the Eternal Restaurant smelling of Beef Eternal.' How one would skip through! But I see nothing but black men, black boxes, black holes, and poor darling Murry splitting a very expensive black kid glove his Mama had made him buy . . . One must get out of this country.

Did you read about Mrs Atherton.° It was a strange peep through the windows. I wanted very much to write to the Earl of March° & thank him for his evidence—How queer it all was. There were touches positively Shakespearean. When she said to her maid: 'this is the last time you will brush my hair' and 'please hold my hand a little' it was like Desdemona & Emilia° at 47 Curzon Street.

Oh God how Id love to talk to you now! Why cannot we just appear to each other without railway trains and hills & cold blasts—

Forgive my black mood. Don't forget me—And remember how *much* I love you—& am always your devoted

Katherine.

To Ottoline Morrell

[2 Portland Villas, East Heath Road,
Hampstead, 17 August 1919]

Dearest, wonderful Friend

Here's an absurd situation! My doctor strongly urges me *not* to put myself away—*not* to go into a sanatorium—he says I would be out of it in 24 hours and it would be a 'highly dangerous experiment'. 'You see,' he explained, 'there is your work which I know is your Life. If they kept it from you you'd die—and they *would* keep it from you. This would sound absurd to a german specialist but I have attended you for a year and I know.' After this, I with great difficulty restrained my impulse to tell the doctor what his words did for me. They were breath, life—healing, *everything.* So it is the Italian Riviera after all, a maid to travel with me and a little villa—Being ill, & bearing all the depression of those round me had I think almost made me insane. *I just gave up hope.* Now I am full of hope again—and I am 'off' the third week in September. M. is going across the first week in September to find me a villa and then I go. It is a blessed relief. And to think there will be the sun and another summer and unlimited time to write—It is next door to Heaven.

Your wonderful letter! I walked and talked with you & we were in the garden together and everything but the thrilling wonder of late summer was forgotten—Oh, how I cherish your friendship. It is there—for ever and I come to you so often—to talk—to know you understand just how *this* and *this* appears— Life is so strange—so full of extraordinary things ... Today, this afternoon, waiting for my Father to come to tea—I felt I could have made—but only of that waiting—a whole book—I began thinking of all the time one has 'waited' for so many and strange people and things—the special quality it has—the *agony* of it and the strange sense that there is a second you who is outside yourself & does nothing—nothing but just listen—the other complicated you goes on—& then there is this keen— unsleeping creature—waiting to leap—It is like a dark beast— and he who comes is its prey — — —

Yes, my Father is here; he arrived yesterday—just as I had imagined, but even fuller of life, enthusiasm, with his power of making all he says vivid, alive, and full of humour. I find him adorable; I could listen to him for hours—But Alas! I had so longed for him and M. to meet & like each other—*longed* for it to happen and M. was in one of his moods when he laughed & looked away—never spoke *once* to him—paid him not a moments attention. It could not have been more fatal. Why wouldn't he, just for my sake, make the effort—(You know how one feels?) But no. Though he confessed afterwards how amazing he thought Father was—he treated him as if he was not here—This is unimaginative—so tactless—Oh, my efforts to get M. into the conversation—I look back on them with dismay—and M. like a fish would not be caught—swam the dark waters and refused—Good good! It was again the *spontaneity* of father which fascinated me—and it was just that which made M. go dead. How tragic this is. It really does seem to me tragic that M. is (except in his work) so covered with a dark wing. But he is—& will be. I really don't think he wants anything else; anything else feels false to him—Oh, I long, I long for merriment—joy, excitement—Even though we *do* work—because we take our work seriously we MUST live. Not in stupid pleasures, nor in Clives way° nor in Chilis, but real warm thrilling life—with music—and light . . .

I do hope dearest I see you before you go to Ireland. I want to so tremendously. If you have sold Bedford Square° does that mean you will spend the winter in the country? Or does it mean you might, perhaps, *after all*—come out to me for as long as you wished?

I want to see the French pictures—M. liked some—I cant bear Roger's art criticism:° this patting on the head & chucking under the chin is so tiresome.

Everybody has deserted me—I don't hear from a soul—

But oh—I am tired of sorrow—The beautiful earth—your tobacco plants—the scent—dearest dearest Friend. I LOVE you
                                                    Katherine.

To J. M. Murry

[Casetta Deerholm, Ospedaletti] Sunday
[12 October 1919]

My own Bogey

I am sitting in the Bastick chair covered with the Jaegar rug as although the sun is hot the air is chilly (its about 4.45 p.m.). It has been a marvellous day here; Ive not moved except for meals. Ive been reading & writing & after lunch I fell asleep from the general *shipboard* atmosphere. Speaking of ships such a small jewel of a sailing ship passed the house today—riding close enough in to see the men on board. She had two small sails at the bows, one big one at the stern & a medium *very* movable one amidships. The sea is my favourite sea—bright bright blue but showing a glint of white as far as one can see—that lift of white seen far away—as far as the horizon moves me terribly. In fact it is *the very thing* I should like to express in writing—it has *the very quality*—Here comes another most interesting little steamboat—a very small trader, she looks, painted black & red with a most ridiculous amount of smoke coming out of the funnel. [*drawing*] No, I cant draw her. From where I sit I cannot see any ground below the balustrade—that is threaded through with sea. One would think it was a sheer drop from there into deep water. What a place—eh Bogey?

I had a nasty jar last night. As there was no water last week the laundry was put 'out' & it came home, exquisite, covered with white net with a rose on top, carried by the nicest old body on her head who seemed to take the greatest fancy to me as I did to her—*long* conversation—'comme vous êtes bien ici [how you are well here]' etc. etc. etc. etc., & under all this a bill for 37.85. This of course after the old un had gone & the rose had been smelled admired & Wig had thought how *much* better, after all, they order these things in Italy. L. M. did not really 'think it very heavy. I don't think you could have expected it to be less, Katie'—This with her overall *4.50* & an immense white petticoat *3.85*. As to serviettes at 1 lira a piece 'oh well, my dear thats not quite sixpence if the exchange is still at 41 for a £1— its about—let me see, *hardly* fivepence' and so on & so on and so

on. How I should beat her if I were married to her—its an
awful thought—She thinks Im made of money—thats the
worst of it. On her last but one journey to San Remo she
bought 1 hecto° of coffee for 4.50 from 'such a funny little
shop' & when I protested she 'though the parcel was small for
the money but the beans felt very tightly packed.' Could you
believe it—However, let her go. And I shall never shoot her
because the body would be so difficult to dispose of after. One
couldn't make it into a neat parcel or put it under a hearth-
stone & she would *never* burn—

Every day I love this house more for some new grace—&
every day I hold a minute review of the garden & there is
always something fresh & wonderful. Then there is the wild
hill never the same—*satisfying* ones deep love for what is living
and ancient in literature. I look at the hill, dearest Bogey, &
because I have not had a classical education it seems to me full
of the spirit of those old boys—the wild fig & olive, the low
growing berries and the tufts of sweet roots—

This is a place for lovers. (Hullo! there goes a swallow.) Yes,
it is made for lovers. You know, don't you, how even now I am
preparing it for you. I look at it & think I shall put net curtains
here & the baskets under the verandah shall be flower baskets
and — — It is enough to keep one busy until May—My very
own. Another Sunday, thats two gone—now there are only 26.

Yours for ever & ever amen.

[*No signature*]

To J. M. Murry

[Casetta Deerholm, Ospedaletti] October
13th. [1919]

My precious little Husband (this title is reserved for State
Occasions)

It is not only that the spoon is the most exquisite perfect little
spoon, a spoon that faeries might go to battle for—a spoon that
fascinates—that just to hold and turn & balance & feel is a
joy—it is over and above these things a sign between us—a

secret message from our real house. It is come from the tea table on the southern terrace, where we sit, idle, drinking tea & there it lies, winking bright in the late sun. And it shall be the spoon our own little boy shall eat his first strawberry and cream out of—standing by you, clutching your knees while you prepare the marvellous dish & make eyes at him. Ah the darling! Ah, *both my darlings*. All this & more the little spoon brings.

October 14th.

No 6 Wednesday
No 7 Birthday letter
Thursday, both here.

My Precious

You see that spoon came a day early even though it was registered, just to please us. It wont happen again. There are two Letters Extraordinary from you. Letters with icing, candles, marzipan, cupids & sugar Wingleys° on them with angelica eyes. They *are* my birthday. Next one—where shall we be? We shall be in our own home eating off Italian plates, drinking out of honey coloured fluted cups. But stop! You are nice enough. Don't be any sweeter, more adorable, more Bogey-like, more precious, more cherished than you are—or I shall fly off into a shower of stars.

I *note* the saucepans. It was high time we had them—I hope they were not 2 dear. Violet° will give them a mothers care I expect & not leave them to cook themselves away. Fancy Sydney being there.° May fortune favour the arrangement. See that you both eat enough. Do get home to tea as often as you can.

Fancy 2nd the Moults° to dinner on Wednesday—That thrills me. I see you at the top serving or *not* serving or serving with your own spoon & then licking it afterwards & Wing under the table playing a tune on Sydney's shoe laces—Oh dear.

I send what I have penned. But I cannot make up every week. Where are the novels?° How disgraceful it is. Conduct an enquiry. Have some menial burned.

You ask me how I am—

Oh, first, about my other birthday presents. Told you about

the 1d matchbox° didn't I? That curve over the 1d is a *fling* of disdain. Thank Heaven Ive scratched a bit off the Chinaman's hat already. Then L. M. gave me a bottil of Genêt Fleuri.° Wasn't it remarkable—the chemist had it *here*, same bottil and all. It must have cost an awful lot. Well, Ive given her her money for this month—& it is a heavenly scent. Thats all I got. Father sent me a communication not mentioning it—so all my fervour has gone to nothing so far. I thought my opinions on the Labour Crisis were good for a fiver—but *no*. He gave Marie £10 in hers. Isn't it *awful minge*. Never mind. We dont want them. They can go on eating their Wood Hay.° *Very* Wood Hay—

It is a brilliant glancing day. You should have seen after the rain was over yesterday little old men appeared from nowhere in peaked hats crawling over the wild hill looking for snails. They carried coloured handkerchiefs which *frothed*—Flowers are coming up everywhere on the hill. I just went for a glance today—not more than five steps high and there were 8 kinds there.

Caterina came yesterday (the pretty one from the laundry). She brought me vivid pink carnations & two eggs in cotton wool for a present. But I felt she could afford to. All the same, she was fearfully nice, laughing, gay, beautiful, *healthy* creature. She says May here is magnifique beyond anything—the whole place is covered with flowers—and all the little kinds pour les distillations [for distilling from] are out—tiny hyacinths—violets—small roses—

Well now Ill tell you about myself. I feel marvellously better. All that remains is my cough. It has bad moments still, but that terrible boiling sensation when I cant stop I have not had *once* since you left. Nor have I *once* had a temperature. I get short of puff if I cough but my lungs don't hurt at all. The pain in my joints is—well its not outwardly better yet I feel it is. So it is evidently on the mend. Think of last October 14th. Sydney Beauchamp° came & at night I had fever in that North room & felt I was going to die.

Here's Ida for my letter. Shes off to San Remo for supplies—Tram waiting.

Yours for ever.
Wig.

To J. M. Murry

[Casetta Deerholm, Ospedaletti,
20 October 1919]

198 received

(*no* 199).° Books received: Benson & Weyman.°
Oh Bogey why are people swindlers? My heart *bleeds* when they
swindle me, doesn't yours? This gardener—he promised to
come & put the garden in order for 10 francs & bring me some
little plants, too. It was to be 10 francs a day *with* the plants &
now his wife has come & explained the plants are *10 francs more.*
And he only came for ½ a day yesterday but she says he spent
the other half looking for the plants—so they between them
charged me 30 francs. It isn't the money that matters—though
I felt ashamed as I gave it to them & could not look at their
eyes—it is that *they are dishonest.* That hurts so! Yes, put the wall
round the house. Why will people do such things? Id rather
they turned & beat me. The sun streams through the folded
clouds on to the sea in long beams of light—such beams as you
see in picture books when the Lord appears. It is a silent day
except for the sound of this *false* pick as he digs up the little
beds. L. M. is in San Remo. I have to hide from this old man
now. I wish he'd go. His wife was all in grey, with big black
hollow places where her teeth had been & she said *firmly* 'c'est
moi qui vient tous les soirs arroser votre jardin pour vous [I'm
the one coming every evening to water your garden for you]'.
When I said no—her 'c'est bien [all right then]' was like *steel
spittle.* Well, Ive cried my cry to you. But my dear love—this
vileness—this snail on the underside of the leaf—always there!

199 is lost—is roaring in the wilderness. Perhaps I shall still
get it. Its awful to miss letters—This today—Mrs W. seems
established° in the house. Oh I hope not. Its what I had feared.
Can't you send her away. She mustn't be there long. No, thats
childish. You know what is best from where you are & you will
do it. But *another woman*—it *hurts.* Still, be sensible, Katherine.
Don't mind. What does it matter—she goes & comes on the
stairs. She waits in the hall & I expect she has a key—I *knew* it
would happen, I *knew* it. She pulls the chairs forward. It makes

me feel exactly as if I were dead. I see it all. She talks to Violet & would Violet mind doing this instead of that. Oh, curse my heart—curse it!! Why am I not a calm indifferent grown up woman ... and this great cold indifferent world like a silent malignant river & these creatures rolling over one like great logs—crashing into one—I try to keep to one side, to slip down unnoticed among the trembling rainbow coloured bubbles of foam & the faint reeds—I try to turn & turn in a tiny quiet pool but its no good—sooner or later one is pushed out into the middle of it all. Oh, my enchanted boy I am really sadder than you, I believe. At any rate if they weighed us in the scales we'd both dip as deep—

Two books have come. Stanley Weyman & Stella Benson. Good. Ill do them. Stella Benson seems to me just to miss it; she reminds me of Colette in a way. But Ive only *dipped* into her book. A very attractive creature—

Father wrote to me: he is only coming as far as Nice or Cannes. Guaranteed no infection, I suppose. I shall go on writing away to him so as to be sure of my portion. L. M. is at San Remo buying butter—This week I hope to work more— My hands are still poisoned by the bites & my eyes are not Dorothy Wordsworth eyes.° Its a bore. Shall I send this letter? Or write another one—a gay one? No, youll understand. There is a little boat—far out—moving along, *inevitable*, it looks & *dead silent*—a little black spot like the spot on a lung—

Dont mind me: I am very foolish and ought to be punished. Even as I wrote that the little boat is far away & there have come out of the sea great gold streamers of light such as I never before saw.

Your own
Wig.

To J. M. Murry

[Casetta Deerholm, Ospedaletti] Monday.
[27 October 1919]

My darling
    I am sending 3 novels together this week so as to be ready for

the new ones. As Madeleine & Virginia° are evidently on a like
tack (from what V. told me of her book) Ill do them together.
No letter came today, but the paper did. We had the devil of a
great storm last night, lasting for hours, thunder, lightning,
rain & I had appalling nightmares! I think it must be the noise
of the sea which makes me dream so: it excites ones nerves at
night & one longs for it to 'lie down' ... Old age, I expect.
After the thunder the day is very lovely, cool but so *definite* and
on a *big scale*. I began to write an article for the paper yesterday
called Eternity;° I hope it will be finished today. If you dont
care for it, please just keep it: it will go in some book sometime
or other. Its so nice to walk in this little garden. After tea
yesterday I went up and down, up and down, thinking out
things. It was then I hit on the subject for the article. Ive been
out of doors all day. I still am, in fact, under a sunshade on the
verandy; I feel quite alright, Bogey, not a suspicion of anything
is wrong with me but Im FLAT. Its the albatross round my
neck. Never mind she will be cut off in April & fly back to
Rhodesia. But its weary living with her—and never seeing
another person. I come up out of my pool & there she is on the
side staring down into the water, glassy eyed to find me. Oh, I
do *hate* her so. Theres nothing to be done, a maid would not
help matters in the least. Of course nearly all the time I am
working but to come out of work to a person, the person whom
you really *hate*—this is very horrible. No-one can ever know
what it is like, for the form it takes is so strange. Her passion for
me feeds on my hate. I wont talk about it, Bogey. I have only
mentioned it because it accounts for my *flatness*. Awful isnt it?
However let us put a penny in the box—Let us have a tune. Let
us nod and grin while the others get up and do our dancing for
us as we sit over here in the corner—waiting waiting, for the
bead curtain to jingle to be pushed aside for La Santé [Health]
to come laughing laughing in, running over to our corner,
putting her arms round our neck & saying my friend—my
darling friend. The garçon [waiter] hovers by, biting his nails
& shooting me a glance or two. Ive read *all* the illustrated
papers—*all* the comics. Suddenly he swoops forward & piles
two chairs on the table next to mine. Good heavens its nearly
closing time! Why doesn't she come—why doesn't she! ... I
don't know why I am writing this—please forgive it, my angel.

And forgive me for not being gay—forgive me for that. I always want to be like a little bell, ringing in our happiness when I write to you—but then at the same time I cant be insincere. Its such a predicament! And oh my Bogey, *dont worry about me.* Ill get out of this—See in your minds eye Wig under an umbrella much too large—thinking its still raining—& open the window & tell her how silly she looks and how that policeman with his scythe is laughing at her—

Your life is so dreadfully hard I feel—I ought to give you all thats fair—L. M. has gone off to 'look' at 'Bawdygerra' as she calls it & wont be back till evening, so Im quite alone. Now Ive come in to get out of the glare and am sitting in my room—Your spectacle case is on the mantelpiece. On the table with the russian bottle & Ottolines book & the green paper knife is your spoon. I don't use it. I cant have it washed and polished here. I only eat fairy soup out of it. There's a strong eager wind blowing—very cool—Ill write about the Athenaeum tomorrow, dearest for I am giving this letter to Caterina when she comes up for the laundry and here she is. Otherwise it will miss the post.

'Bonjour Madame.'
'Bonjour Caterina. Que vous êtes jolie aujourd'hui [Good morning Caterina. You're pretty today].'
'Ah, c'est mon nouveau golfe! [Ah, it's my new pullover!]'
Goodbye my precious—I am for ever

Your own
Wig.

To J. M. Murry

[Casetta Deerholm, Ospedaletti] Wednesday.
[29 October 1919]

My own love
No letter today so far. I may get one this evening. I have heard from Father at Menton. Poor darling! he was robbed at Boulogne of his wallet—all his money, addresses, papers, £50 in Bank Notes, a letter of credit for £500. This really wrings

my heart. I cant help it. If he does mind so terribly about money it must have been so *ghastly* to be *alone* among foreigners having to keep up & be a man of the world and look out of the railway windows as tho' it hadn't happened—I really literally nearly fainted when this swept over me—and I 'saw' him with a very high colour 'putting on' a smile—I do hope to God people don't suffer quite as I think they do: its not to be borne if they do.

I am writing this in a hurry. I seem to have such acres to plough & the horse is going so slow. I wish I could change the horse, Boge. He just sits on his hind legs & scratches his ear & looks round at me when we're ½ way through a furrow. Its icy cold, thundering—blue grey with a flash of steel. I should think it was going to snow—I will write to you again later, my precious when this review is done, but I wanted to catch the post with this. Would you send me the Times review° of Virginia? Id *very* much like to see it or any other. I want to read the book but dare not so much as put my nose in till Ive cleared off this accumulation.

Take care of yourself, my *very own* Bogey. Love me: I love you.

Wig.

To J. M Murry

[Casetta Deerholm, Ospedaletti] Thursday.
[30 October 1919]

My darling
I am sending a review today and I shall send another tomorrow. Things have not gone as fast as I wished (as usual) but from now onward they will improve. I expect you wonder why with such unlimited opportunity I do not just waltz through with things. Alas! Up till now it has been—not so much my health, indeed, except for that chill and mal à la tête [headache] not my health at all—but my 'domestic' arrangements. Now I have discovered how I can live with L. M. It is by not speaking more than is necessary for the service of the house.

Two nights ago we had a 'crise' which made me realise it must
be the very last, that if it occurred again Id have to ask her to
go & to make other arrangements. This, of course, I dont at all
want to do, so the other plan is adopted. I don't know what she
thinks. I imagine she is furious but I don't care. Its *such a rest*—
you cant imagine. No shouting, no quarrelling, no violence,
just quiet: I am basking in it. I can keep it up, too, by an effort
of Will; I am *sure* I can. Otherwise there would have been no
work done—nothing done—nothing written—for our hate had
got to such a pitch that I couldn't take a plate from her hand
without shuddering. This *awful relationship* living on in its secret
corrupt way beside my relationship with you is very extraordinary; no-one would believe it. I am two selves—one my true
self—the other that she created in me to destroy my true self.
Still Ill write no more about it & try & think about it less and
less so that the fire gets more & more covered. But thats what
makes my work so hard, what *paralyses my mind*. Its just like a
terrible fog; Im lost in it and I go mad—just like L. [D. H.
Lawrence] used to. Here I have thrown things at her—yes,
even that—called her a murderer, cursed her—Her three
standing remarks 'give me time', 'Ill learn by degrees, Katie'
and 'you must just teach me, thats all' are to me too sinister. I
haven't the time to give—However, its over. And I shall live in
silence with her now and put it away. Better a thousand times
be lonely than speak to her. But that is *the real reason* why I
cannot work as I could—L. M. L. M. and L. M. So after this
Ill do better—see?

No letters came today, none yesterday. I am longing for the
post. There'll be two tomorrow I expect. Its fine today though
still bitter cold: Ive been lying still in the sun all morning—
haven't moved. The sea is wonderfully beautiful, so deep and
dark—yet with the light on it, moving and glittering.

I heard from Chaddie & Jeanne, yesterday, both full of
Wood Hay. 'How I wish I could send you a great hamper from
the orchard of nuts and apples' ... Its a safe wish at this
distance. One page was devoted—this is *dead true*—to the
matchbox. She knew it would appeal to me—so delighted it
had fetched up safe. J & she both said '*K*' when they saw it,
etc. It made me violently jealous that they should have a house
and nuts & apples. I *yearn* to beat them—I feel I shall buy all

the china I can get here to beat their china & oh if we had more money you could be looking out for oddmints too. We must have our house Bogey, next year. Is there any star on the horizon? Chaddie also sent me a photograph of myself at three months old. It was a *dreadful shock*. I had always imagined it—a sweet little laughing thing, rather french, with wistful eyes under a fringe, firmly gripping a spade, showing even then a longing to dig for treasure with her own hands—But this little solemn monster with a wisp of hair looked as though she were just about to fall backwards head over heels. On her feet she wears as far as I can make out a pair of ordinary workmen's boots which the photographer, from astonishment or malice, has photographed so close up that each tootsie is the size of her head. The only feature about her is her ears which are neatly buttonholed on to the sides of her head & not just safety-pinned on as most babies' are—Even the spade she clasps with the greatest reluctance . . .

Now I must work. The hot water runs at last, for the first time yesterday. Vince° is not going to London until the end of *November*. I thought Id let you know. Oh, I do hope there is a letter tomorrow darling with news of you in it. I am anxious about this ghastly press of work. Otherwise all goes well here and under my new regime it can only go better. Goodbye my own precious Bogey. When you get this it will be November—2 months to the New Year.

Your own Wig.

To J. M. Murry

[Casetta Deerholm, Ospedaletti] A blank day |
Saturday [1 November 1919]

My darling Bogey

I had thought to have your Monday letter yesterday—but no: it wouldn't come. You must throw them more quickly down the letterboxes, darling, *hurl* them, send them *flying*: tell them that if they come quickly there is nothing—nothing she wont give them. They can take whatever they please, pull off her rings & put them on their thumbs, peacock in her flowery shawl, eat all the honey jar at once ... Oh *no* they are not children. I won't have them children. Little children must never travel. How could I have written so! It breaks my heart only to think of them. No, they are just—birds to whom the journey is no labour—up they fly, out of sight with one beat of a delicate wing ... But birds are so heartless, alas!

It is a fearful day, long cold rain, a homeless wind crying at the windows, the sea like ashes. I am sitting in my little room in a corner, wrapped up with a hot brick at my feet. I must work hard today—Thank God for definite work—work that must be done. Bogey darling, precious, do tell me when my reviews are not up to the mark—criticise them & *please* let me see the Lit. Sup. I really am a bit lost without it over here—If you cant send it to me then Ill write direct. Just let me know. Couldn't I have the office copy?

November 1st. Six months to May. After that don't leave me alone. I am not made to live alone, not with an enemy. Hating L. M. as I do I should have gone to a place like Mentone where I could sometimes go for a small walk without a climb *and lift the shutter* that I live behind. But work work work—simply to thy cross I cling° (why must it be a cross. Ah why! What a question to ask at 31!) ((But I *do* still ask it.)) Six months. Bogey. Let us look across them and sign to each other. Only six months to cross—a mountain a month—six mountains & then a soft still quiet valley where no wind blows—not even enough to fray the one o clock dandelions—And we are there and hidden—*Love* me. You <u>must</u> love me—as much as I love you. Send me a very brave piece of love to pin in my bosom.

Wig.

To J. M. Murry

[Casetta Deerholm, Ospedaletti] Sunday in bed
[2 November 1919]

Darling of darlings

I have heard from you twice this week—du reste [for the

rest]—silence. If I do not get a letter today it will be *too* dreadful. My mind is paralysed with dismay and apprehension, and I am in bed with this terrible storm raging day & night outside—No-one to speak to—Like Robinson Crusoe— <u>he</u> lived alone—Worse—oh much, much worse—

I have just seen the Hochwohlgeborene [his esteemed worship] Doktor Bobone. I did not want to wait any longer for Ansaldi.° Yesterday was so terrible, Bogey, in my darkish room—like a cave—unable to write or think—no news—no letters—I sent her to San Remo: because I felt I must at least have some one in touch with me—He stayed about an hour and most thoroughly examined me. I think he is a very good doctor indeed—scientific—dry—*german*, and as frank with me as if Id been a student examining the case—with him. He says the fact I have so little fever is good—all on my side. 'So long as you have not the fevers you do not die. It is de fevers which kills.' I don't think he had at all a *great* opinion of me. On the other hand he said he thought I might go in to see him once a fortnight—go into San Remo! He says the apex of the right lung only is affected; the left is infiltrated to the third rib. He is giving me a medicine *for* tuberculosis. This I don't like. Sorapure said they were so often dangerous. This man said himself it is not one of the dangerous ones. 'It do nothing or it do well.' I suppose I must trust him, then. This villa he approves of for fine weather but when the weather is not fine he says I must stay in bed to be out of draughts & to be warm— Air, to lie out in the sun, food, and no worry, no fever, 'and you will not die. It is the fever kills the patient.' This was his one cry. But when I tried to tell him of my appalling *mental* state of depression he didn't even listen. No-one *listens* to a patient except Sorapure.

Now listen. <u>Try</u> to send me letters often or cards or papers from the office—anything. If I were there you'd spend 10 minutes with me. Give me those 10 minutes here. <u>Help me help me!</u> If I veep I getta de fever and I am veeping strong!! I have no negative tonic. I am tired—I cant always write or work or read—Then I have nothing but darkness—I live on this desolate hillside with L. M. munching by me. *But I can fight through all this* if I am in touch with you. If you are ill *Arthur must let me know immediately*—Reality Bogey is ALWAYS less than my dreams and apprehensions. If you will bear that in mind you will make Life easier. SILENCE is the ULTIMATE BLACKNESS—I must stop crying & send this to post. Oh God—what an end of all my fine hopes—to be rewriting my S. of France letters because of these cursed posts. The weather is perfect hell, the sea roars: its never never quiet—it eats away the air. The room is half dark and Im alone all day all day all day every day every day—Mrs Jones° can do up a paper can't she? But you are so pitiful have pity on me & <u>write</u>.

Wig.

Nothing is hopeless. Nothing is lost. No new terror has been added no new fear really. But this loneliness is what opens the gates of my soul & lets the wild beasts stream howling through. I shall get over it. Let us keep firm—But write me <u>AT LENGTH</u>.

To J. M. Murry

[Casetta Deerholm, Ospedaletti] Monday.
[3 November 1919]

186 Monday &
185 Tuesday received.

My darling Bogey

I got your Monday & Tuesday letters yesterday and they reassured me that nothing was wrong. In fact everything seemed alright: Sydney there for tumpany & Eliot's poetry lecture° . . . It sounds Gaierty.° The storm at present is hanging over: it has withdrawn to await re-inforcements—a horrible lowering violet sky, a boiling sea like porridge—snow on the mountains. Fancy, with that—to get more air I had one side of the net up last night & I am bitten frightfully by mosquitoes. This is almost laughable . . . Everything about this Côte d'Azur is lies. Why does one believe it. One might as well believe that London is a rich magnificent city—or that the Midland Hotel Manchester is the most comfortable place in the world. Why believe *liars*: everybody lies. I don't know—but there you are. Dostoievsky at least understands through & through . . .

I feel a bit like the outside elements—at least I feel they've
had their way with me for the moment & Im now high &
dry—on a rocky ledge looking up at the sky and simply vaguely
wondering. <u>Im not ill</u>. No temperature today. Ive taken it &
written it down in my book. But I shall get up & go downstairs
& lie in my little room—My joints wont stand any more bed. I
hope to get work done today. I long to—ah! so much!!! If that
were possible Id get back my *spirit*. When that goes (the power
to work) then Im nothing.—Just a straw before the wind and I
feel *one must hurry*. There are you & the paper, so important so
enormously important—Your big number Nov 12th nearly
there. Believe that I try ALL I can, every single bit I can.
Nothing less than La Faiblesse [physical weakness] (who is
really the toughest old hag of them all) keeps me from the
performance of my promises.

I had 2 letters from Father yesterday. He is ill too with the
cold and of course terribly disappointed with the climate.
Thinks it a 'perfect farce' ... Cant keep warm even in bed with
a hot water bottle and a Kaiapoi rug.° Very anxious to know if
my villa is adequately heated. I only pray he doesn't come here
while this cold spell is on: he'd be so cross & want to make other
arrangements & I could NOT stand that.

Good God! Theres a little wavering gleam of sun on the
wall—white, still: it makes everything look shabby & dirty. Its
gone again.

Perhaps now I have encountered the whole troupe of fiends
so early on I shall get better of them & be at peace. I suppose
any one who has lived my life of the last two years is bound to
have these moments. That is what I hope. When I am with you
I am furious because you will not see 'happiness' in the future.
Well, still if we're together in our own house, living our own
life *I do see it*—Apart from that there is nothing: I mean there is
just a living death or a dead one: it really dont signify (yes, it
does.)

But to walk, kiss the earth, run, laugh, go in and out of
houses & rooms, if I could do any of these things—'You are
always an invalid—hein?' says Bobone, looking at me with
absolutely inexpressive *red* eyes like an ox—no whites to them
at all. 'Vot is your age—dirty-five?'

'No,' I said—'dirty-one.'

'*Zo.*'

Well, well, well. Why do I feel ever new about Dostoievsky—*my* Dostoievsky—no-one elses—A being who loved in spite of everything—adored—LIFE even while he knew the dark dark places.

Arthur wrote me a little letter—so awfully nice. He is a very fine lad indeed. 'Jack seems happy in his quiet way & very keen on his paper.' He positively worships you. All his fineness is come from loving you. He is so young. You are in time to save him from so much that you suffered. There is no reason why he should not just go straight ahead & grow into a *real man*. He put at the end—'oceans of love'—Wasn't that sweet? Fancy *oceans* of love—aren't they *boys* words—such a fling about them.

Tell Wing Ganma has been a very pore girl & would love to see him climb on to her bed now and would make him a whole cake for himself with Wing written on it in mouse tails of icing—

Well, my beloved Boy, goodbye for now. Perhaps this is partly due to the terrific shock of the cold and rain and dark— when one thought all was going to be so fair. It is well to look for reasons. I am always looking for reasons *why* my courage goes. But after all, here it is. I am not WELL. No good pretending I am. Im bound to get these fits of depression, I suppose. The only thing that helps is to feel you are there, to know about your life which is my *real* life—not my sick life, and to WORK. We must stick to our six months. Last night I felt in the middle of the night L. M. must not turn us away from our month here: one must conquer that & not let her win. I shall try. Remember always how long Ive been ill and don't think hardly of me. I have been ill for 200 years—

Love me. I am your true love

Wig.

To J. M. Murry

[Casetta Deerholm, Ospedaletti] Friday.
[7 November 1919]

My dearest Love

I heard the front door bell—Its just after 8 a.m. and [I] knew it was a telegram. L. M. has gone off to wire you. I am frightfully worried that you should have felt compelled to send it. Ever since I had that crise of depression I have bitterly reproached myself for letting you know. Madness—madness! I shall never do so again if I am in my right mind. Let me try and be very plain with you. *All is alright* here. I thought in those first weeks it was going to be 'happy', & its not. But I have lost my capacity for happiness for the time. I am sure, even counting the climate, it is right to be here and to stick it out. I am lonely, very lonely. I somehow hadnt counted on that. Its like imprisonment. And I find it inconceivably difficult to work. Work is an immense effort of will such as I had never dreamed of. Now I know what *your* will is like. Nevertheless work is all I have. If I am not working I want to run up and down, just that—And I am fearful that my reviews are not what you want. It would greatly help if you would tell me. Would you? I am seem to be nothing but a great great drag on you—no comfort, no blessing—no help or rest. I just put out my hands & say 'please'. Its not really so. *Ill make it otherwise.* Tell me though if you feel a grudge against me or if you want to shut the door in my face—enfant trop gâté [an over-spoiled child], am I? Do you think like that?

It won't go on—my mental state I mean. It will change. And physically I am really and truly much stronger. That's genuine. Id like to see Sorapure & find out from him whether it 'showed'. That would be immensely comforting and a great spur. No other doctor is of the slightest use; he knows nothing. I *ought* not to be so unhappy. After all I am able to—and there I want to make a line—able to—what? You see its like a kind of *blindness*. I only thought of Mentone because I thought there might be concerts there & music would help. I simply hate the sea. But *please* think and believe that physically I am better.

Then you have your paper and winter campaign. Oh to think I should bind you. It cannot be. Will you please, after this letter trust me not to do it again? And just plant your feet on a rock and say Tigs alright and so forget me—I mean forget me as a worry. Think of me as on a sea voyage or something like that—not much use (no use) to you while she's there but when she steps on dry land again all will be as it was before the blow fell. Nothing can take away from the fact that the blow did fall you know. But I want to put myself away and think of you. For you are not to be worried. Do you _feel_ that?

Forgive me. Can you forgive me? If someone was being attacked in a wood youd not be angry with them for interrupting would you? It was like that. Its sunny, today. No, only forgive me—forgive me.

Wig.

To J. M. Murry

[Casetta Deerholm, Ospedaletti]—181,
180.|Friday [7 November 1919]

My darling

She came back with your Saturday night & Sunday letter (inclu. Butler.°) They heap coals of fire on my head. But I must tell you your Saturday letter when you spoke of us being lovers—was like a credo I believe to me. It seemed to bring the future near and warm and _human_ for a minute. At sight of it— of so much life, the birds drew back—flew up and away. And then you seemed to tell me so much of what you were doing and it was home like. Our tiny Wing, clean in patches!

Early summer morning—think of it—a day before us—in the garden and the house. Peace—Holding each other, kissing each other until we are one world. It is all memories now— radiant, marvellous far away memories of happiness. Ah, how terrible life can be. I sometimes see an immense wall of black rock, shining, in a place—just after death perhaps—and _smil-_

ing, the *adamant* of *desire*. Let us live on memories, then and when the time comes—let us live so fully that the memories are no nearer than far away mountains — —

Arthur sent me another of his letters: you & he eating sausages & mash. *Hug* the old boy for me—tell him hes my brother. My 'Eternity' seemed perfect rubbish: Ill send it if you like. It seemed to go out as I wrote & I raked ashes. Ill send Butler back tomorrow. Ill send Dosty tomorrow. This isn't a letter: its just a word again with you, my precious lover.

Ive paid Porter.° Its alright. I wish youd go, though—Think of me as your own

Mouse.

To J. M. Murry

The Athenaeum for Ever!!!!! | [Casetta
Deerholm, Ospedaletti] Saturday afternoon.
[8 November 1919]

My own Bogey

I will give this letter to L. M. to post in San Remo. I went out today and weighed myself & found in a fortnight I had gained over 2 lbs. I weigh *46 kilos 70* and last time it was just on *45*. This is as you can see extraordinary. Now you will believe that I rest. I went then to the P.O. and found your Monday letter written after three awful ones of mine. What could I do? I could only send that p.c. *Now* I want to say—I would really count it almost as fearful if you gave up the A.° and came out here as if all were lost. It would in a way mean all were lost; it would mean scrapping our future. Never think of it; never do it. I can imagine nothing more horrible for us both than that. It would mean—looked at from whatever angle—that this thing had beaten us and it would mean—oh, it is not possible to contemplate such a thing. I had rather live here the 2 years than that. That is the solemn truth. You see I *am* getting better; my body is getting better. I have a theory that perhaps the creaking and pain I had were caused by the moist spot drying up in my bad lung. Its quite possible. Old Bobone of course would not know a thing like that. But then he, good as I think he is, does not believe tuberculosis is curable; its evidently a craze of his. I saw it & he said as much. 'Quick or soon coma de fever—' But never come to me or give up a thing or send me money or bind yourself whatever I say *now or in the Future.* Please my own precious, <u>never</u> do. We must see this through *successfully*, not otherwise. If you will just accept the fact that I am not gay—see? I will try not to talk of my loneliness & depression nor of L. M.

It is a bright sunny day today and I am not in the least tired after my walk—only hungry. As usual I thought I was going to have it all my own way—get well—be happy—the horror of my disease (it *is* a horror) over—peace with L. M., and ease to work in. What a fat head I am! Out of those—I'll get well— and thats all and enough. Let the others wait. *Work* of course— work is second breath. When you spoke [of] planting a tree of hope I felt oh—it was *you* to speak so. Plant it—plant it darling—I will not shake it. Let me sit under it & look up at it—spread it over me and meet me there often and let us hold each other close and look up into the boughs for buds and flowers. No, theres no God. That is queer. This morning I wanted to say 'God keep you' or Heaven guard us—Then I thought of *The Gods* but they are marble statues with broken noses. There is no God or Heaven or help of any kind but love. Perhaps Love can do everything. Lo! I have made of Love all my religion.°—Who said that? Its simply marvellous.

L. M. is ready to go. I shall have the place to myself. Its nice. Then I turn into a real Mouse and make as tiny a noise as possible—so as not to disturb the life round me.

We shall not get another sou out of Father, darling, not on any account. I wish you would send him a farewell note to the Hotel Westminster—just for 'the firm'—would you? It *does* please me enormously that he goes back to N.Z. enthusiastic about us, and he is. The worst of it is he keeps writing about us going there. 'Pray God the day be not far off.' It *is*, its very far. I want Sussex and you and Arthur & the cats but only <u>YOU</u>.

[*No signature*]

To J. M. Murry

[Casetta Deerholm, Ospedaletti] Monday
morning. [10 November 1919]

My own dear Love

Here is another Monday. They do seem to come round so
fast—like the horses we saw at the fair—no, the *roosters*—that
was our one, wasn't it? Do you remember those little Princesses
who went round for ever? They wore cotton frocks & tiny
leather belts. Its a chill strange day. I breakfasted in Val-
halla—cracks of lightning, thunder, tearing rain. Now Im on
the verandy & the clouds are immensely near and distinct like
mountains. Will you please say if my Dosty is alright?° I sent it
rather in fear and trembling, but I meant it. I am doing
Virginia for this week's novel. I don't like it, Boge. My private
opinion is that it is a lie in the soul. The war never has been,
that is what its message is. I dont want G. forbid mobilisation
and the violation of Belgium—but the novel cant just leave the
war out. There *must* have been a change of heart. It is really
fearful to me the 'settling down' of human beings. I feel in the
profoundest sense that nothing can ever be the same that as
artists we are traitors if we feel otherwise: we have to take it
into account and find new expressions new moulds for our new
thoughts & feelings. Is this exaggeration? What *has* been—
stands—but Jane Austen could not write Northanger Abbey
now—or if she did Id have none of her. There is a trifling scene
in Virginias book where a charming young creature in a bright
fantastic attitude plays the flute:° it positively frightens me—to
realise this *utter coldness* & indifference. But I will be very
careful and do my best to be dignified and sober. Inwardly I
despise them all for a set of *cowards*. We have to face our war—
they wont. I believe Bogey, our whole strength depends upon
our facing things. I mean facing them without any reservations
or restraints. I fail because I don't face things. I feel almost I
have been ill so long for that reason: we *fear* for that reason: I
mean fear can get through our defences for that reason. Weve
got to stand by our opinions & risk falling by them. Oh, my
own Bogey, you are the only one in the world for me. We are

really absolutely alone: we're a *queer couple* you know, but we ought to be together—in every sense really. *We* just because we are 'like this' ought not to be parted. We shall not be after May. Ill come home then.

Do you want to know how I am? Yesterday upstairs in my room I suddenly wanted to give a small jump—I have not given a small jump for two years—you know the kind—a jump-for-joy—I was frightened. I went over to the window & held on to the sill to be safer—then I went into the middle of the room and *did* jump. And this seemed such a miracle I felt I must tell somebody—There was nobody to tell—so I went over to the mirror—and when I saw my excited face I had to laugh. It was a marvellous experience.

Blessed little Wing! Kiss his nose for me—& whistle in his ear & say your gan'ma loves you—She does—I wish he would have *one* kitten in May—Has he grown very big? And how is Athy? And how does the house look? Does it shine? And do you have nice food? Why cant we meet in dreams & answer all each others questions—Our nights are wasted. The sea is up to the brim of the world today—

Your own
Wig.

To J. M. Murry

[Casetta Deerholm, Ospedaletti] Wednesday.
[12 November 1919]

My precious own

I got a telegram from you today. It was an extra luxury, a *great* joy but it is not to happen again. A nice little boy literally *blew* in with it.

Strange strange day! My party has just gone. Connie, Jinnie (admirable person) and Papa. They arrived at about 10.30 (I expected them 2 hours later) but it didnt matter. The Casetta seemed to turn into a dolls house. Pa couldnt even find room for his glasses. The womens furs & coats & silk wraps & bags were scattered everywhere—Father suggested a run into San

Remo which we took. I was I am just a little corrupted Bogey
darling. That big soft purring motor, the rugs & cushions—the
warmth the delicacy all the uglies so far away. We 'ran' long
past San Remo. It was *thrilling* for me. I didn't dare to speak
hardly because it was so wonderful & people laughing & silly
Pa talking Maori down the whistle to the chauffeur. Very
silly—but very nice, somehow. It carried me away. Then we
got up & bought a cake & were as they say the cynosure of all
eyes & it was nice, too. I was glad the chemist saw me. (See
what a snob you married!) & then while Connie & Jinnie were
at Morandis Pa & I talked & the sun streamed into the car &
he said we were like a couple of hothouse plants ripening. They
have just gone. Jinnie left me a pair of *horn* spegglechiks
[spectacles] of her grandfathers (the kind on a long black
ribbon, which suit me admirably.) She took photos of the
Casetta, too, & said 'theyll do to send your husband'. I don't
know what happened. They seemed to me so many. Father at
the last, was wonderfully dear to me. I mean—to be held &
kissed & called my precious child was almost too much. To feel
someones arms round me & someone saying 'get better you
little wonder. You're your mother over again.' Its not being
called a wonder—its having *love* present close warm to be felt
and returned. And then both these women had been desperately homesick for their dogs so they understood Wing. That
was nice too.

Pa did not like this place, neither did they. They were
horrified by the cold. Pa said at Menton they have had *none* of
this bitter wind—that it has never been cold like today. He
seemed to think I had made a great mistake to be in such a thin
house & so exposed. So, alas! did they. They said Menton was
warm, still, with really exquisite walks, sheltered. I said Id
consider going there in the spring. But I wont. When the bad
weather is over here will be warm too & I dont want a town. I
don't want to uproot. At the same time I was a bit sorry it was
so much warmer. I *fed* them & Pa left me five 3 Castles
cigarettes!!! He made the running, talking french—telling
stories—producing spectacles (he had *four* pairs of them—
Connie had three & Jinnie had three. At one moment they
were all trying each others on—in this little room—it was like a
dream). And here on the table are five daisies & an orchid that

Pa picked for me & tied with a bit of grass & handed me. If I had much to forgive him I would forgive him much for this little bunch of flowers. What have they to do with it all?

Wig.

To J. M. Murry

[Casetta Deerholm, Ospedaletti] Sunday
8 a.m. [16 November 1919]

My own Bogey

It was a fearful *blow* to get no letters yesterday again. I shall never understand it. When L. M. came back after the last chance I *hid* for a moment or two upstairs just to delay the 'no letters—nothing'. Perhaps my luck will turn today and the sea have a pearl.

Such a night! Immense wind and sea and cold. This is certainly no 'pensive citadel'.° This morning the storm still rages. Its a blow. I long to go out and have a walk but I darent face the wind.

What is this about the novel.° Tell me thou little eye among the blind° (its easy to see whom my bedfellow has been). But seriously Bogey, the more I read the more I feel all these novels will not do. After them Im a swollen sheep looking up who is not fed.° And yet I feel one can lay down no rules: Its not in the least a question of material or style or plot. I can only think in terms like 'a change of heart'. I cant imagine how after the war these men can pick up the old threads as tho' it never had been. Speaking to *you* Id say we have died and live again. How can that be the same life? It doesn't mean that Life is the less precious or that the 'common things of light and day'° are gone. They are not gone, they are intensified, they are illumined. Now we know ourselves for what we are. In a way its a tragic knowledge. Its as though, even while we live again we face death. But *through Life*: thats the point. We see death in life as we see death in a flower that is fresh unfolded. Our hymn is to the flower's beauty—we would make that beauty immortal because we *know*. Do you feel like this—or otherwise—or how?

But of course you dont imagine I mean by this knowledge 'let us eat and drink-ism'. No, I mean 'deserts of vast eternity'.° But the difference between you and me is (perhaps Im wrong) I couldn't tell anybody *bang out* about those deserts. They are my secret. I might write about a boy eating strawberries or a woman combing her hair on a windy morning & that is the only way I can ever mention them. But they *must* be there. Nothing less will do. They can advance & retreat, curtsey, caper to the most delicate airs they like but I am bored to Hell by it all. Virginia—par exemple.

Here is the sun. Ill get up. My knees are cold and my feet swim between the sheets like fishes.

Si tu savais com-me je t'ai ... me [If you knew how I love you].

Oh Bogey darling Heart, I shall never reconcile myself to absence from you—never. Its waste of life. But be happy, my precious.

Wig.

To J. M. Murry

[Casetta Deerholm, Ospedaletti] Thursday
[20 November 1919]

Dearest of All

Your Saturday letter has come when you are just off for the weekend & you tell me O. has invited you there° for Xmas. I strongly advise you to go. Its so comfortable and one always gets ideas for the house—from just being among those Spanish chests.

Its a very dull day here with wild ragged clouds and a cold halting miserable wind. My black fit is on me—not caused by the day altogether. Christ! to *hate* like I do. Its upon me today. You don't know what hatred is because I know you have never hated anyone—not as you have loved—equally. Thats what I do. My deadly deadly enemy has got me today and Im simply a blind force of hatred. Hate is the *other* passion. It has all the opposite effects of Love. It fills you with death and corruption. It makes you feel hideous degraded and old—it makes you long to <u>destroy</u>. Just as the other is light so this is darkness. I hate like that—a million times multiplied. Its like being under a curse. When L. M. goes I dont know what I shall do. I can only think of breathing—lying quite still and breathing. Her great fat arms, her tiny blind breasts, her baby mouth, the underlip always wet and a crumb or two or a chocolate stain at the corners—her eyes fixed on me—fixed—waiting for what I shall do that she may copy it. Think what you would feel if you had consumption and lived with a deadly enemy! Thats one thing I shall grudge Virginia all her days—that she & Leonard were together. We cant be: weve got to wait our six months but when they are up I WILL not have L. M. near—I shall rather commit suicide. That is dead earnest. In fact, I have made up my mind I shall commit suicide if I dont tear her up by the roots then. It would be kinder for us both—for you and for me of course I mean. We'd have no love otherwise—you'd only slowly grow to think I was first wicked and then mad. Youd be quite right. Im both with her—mad—really mad like Lawrence was only worse. I leaned over the gate today and dreamed she'd die of heart failure and I heard myself cry out 'oh what heaven what heaven.'

Should I *not* send this? I must. I want you to know so that when the time comes for her to go you will remember. The worst thing about hate is that it never spends itself—is never exhausted and in this case isn't even shared. So you come up against something which says hit me hit me hate me hate *feel strongly* about me—one way or the other—it doesn't matter which way as long as I make you <u>feel</u>. The man who murders from sheer hate is right to murder: he does it in self-defence. Worst of all is that I cant write a book while I live with her. I tried now for two months. It wont go. Its no good.

Does this seem to you just absurd? Can you imagine in the least what it is like? I feel I must let you know even though you wave the knowledge aside & think it just 'Tigs tearing off at a tangent'. Its not. It is a curse like the curses in old tales.

Well thats enough 'in all conscience' as Mr Salteena would say.° I shall recover darling, as I did before. Ill get over the positive imperative overwhelming suffocating mood of it and

pass into the other. But oh! 'let this cup pass from me'° in April.
Its <u>too</u> <u>much</u>.

> Your (in a black cloud hidden away)
> Wig-wife.

To J. M. Murry

166 received.| Friday Morning 8.30 after
déjeuner. [Casetta Deerholm, Ospedaletti]
[21 November 1919]

My own

It happened rather luckily yesterday that L. M. and I
reached a crise at teatime and after that the frightful urgency
of our feelings died down a bit. So Ill not say more about it. It
ruined yesterday and made me so tired that I felt I could have
slept days and nights away.

Here is your letter from Oare, about the Waterlows house.°
They are lucky—arent they. Shall we really have such a house?
Its not too late? We don't just make up dreams—precious
dreams—it's not 'all over'? I get overwhelmed at times that it *is*
all over, that we've seen each other for the last time (imagine
it!) ((no, don't imagine it)) and that these letters will one day
be published and people will read something in them—in their
queer finality—that 'ought to have told us.' This feeling runs
exactly parallel with the other—the feeling of hope. They are
two roads I cant *keep* to either. Now I find myself on one, now
on the other. Even when you tell me about the table° I think
how perfect but at the very same moment I think 'will he sell
it—of course not. He must have a table, after all.' Its all part of
what Ive said before—haven't I. I say it so many thousand
times over in my mind that I forget whether Ive written it.
Once the defences are fallen between you and Death they are
not built up again. It needs such a little push—hardly that—
just a false step—just not looking—and you are over. Mother,
of course, lived in this state for years. Ah, but she lived
surrounded. She had her husband her children, her home, her
friends—physical presences—darling treasures to be cher-

ished—and Ive not one of these things. I have only my work. That might be enough for you in like case—for the fine intelligence capable of detachment—but God! God! Im *rooted* in Life. Even if I hate Life I cant deny it. I spring from it and feed on it. What an egoist the woman is!

And now Love, just supposing by a miracle the blissful thing should happen — — — I dont remember where it was I stayed with the Waterlows. It was near Marlboro' and the country was beautiful. There were forest glades—a beautiful forest. They took me for a walk that was miles too long I remember that. I remember standing in a rank smelling field and seeing them far ahead and waving very gaily when they looked round — — — But the country does not really matter a great deal does it? As long as it *is* country and one can grow things (oh MAKE it happen!). But the money question is pretty dreadful. As to furniture that we can always accumulate Eric-or-little-by-little° but I should think an anthracite range cost at least £30 or more and alterations—we know what they run one into. I think we might do it by not paying down. We overdo the paying down—I believe. Other people never have their money in bags—but first we ought to find the house—take it and then consider. That is my idea. The house (like the Jew)° first. ((I never understood that text.)) Oh God! When you say well have to get a builder in I suddenly dimly see—a hall—a staircase with shavings—a man with a rule and a flat pencil measuring for a cupboard. I hear a saw and the piece of sawn wood creaks and tumbles (such a *final* sound). I hear the squee-quee of a plane—and the back door of the house is open and the smell of the uncared garden—so different to the smell of the cared one—floats through—and I put my hand on your sleeve and rest a little against you—and you say 'do you agree' and I nod 'yes'. But these dreams are so dear that they feel unearthly— they are dreams of Heaven. How could they become reality? *This* is reality—bed, medicine bottle, medicine glass marked with tea and table spoons, guiacol tablets, balimanate of zinc. Come—tell me—tell me *exactly* what I am to do to recover my faith. I was always the one who had a kind of overplus of it: you hated it in me—it seemed to deny you so many of your more subtle emotions. You made me feel it was so crude a thing—my belief that wouldn't be shaken.

Take this all *coolly*: its all—what? Just add to my diseases a touch of melancholia, let us say. And remember how I adore you for as long as I live.

                                                                        Wig.

To J. M. Murry

[Casetta Deerholm, Ospedaletti] 5 p.m.
                    Thursday. [4 December 1919]

My darling

Your Saturday letter telling me of your cold and your Sunday letter are come. I do hope the journey to Penge° didn't make the cold worse; it seemed a bit like madness to go and risk waiting at the railway stations—but—what could you do? Wing° ought to be trained to balance the paperweight on his nose, like Dora's Gyp did the pencil° you remember? I have been wondering whether you marked the new linen and how: it *is* so important to have it plainly marked & to see it comes back from the wash. I expect Violet is careful, though. Would you put an *ad* of my story in the T.L.S.° Ill pay. I feel we must sell it now its been such a labour & thats the only way it will sell. But it ought to be in before Xmas.

Dont overwork, Boge. I wish I could see your Georgian poetry review:° I tremble a little for you when you go 'eyes out' for or against a thing. I always feel you dont quite get the measure of your opponent—you expose yourself in your enthusiasm and he takes a mean underhand advantage. But perhaps that is nonsense. Its sunset, with a wide, wide pale yellow sky and a blue sea gilded over. I feel horribly weak after this fever attack but calmer—just now—thank the Lord. My heart is so hateful. It you had such a heart. It *bangs throbs beats* out 'tramp tramp tramp the boys are marching'° double quick time with very fine double rolls for the kettle drum. How it keeps it up I dont know. I always feel its going to give out. I think every day I shall die of heart failure. I expect its an inherited feeling from Mother. Oh—*envied* Mother—lucky lucky Mother—so surrounded—so held—so secure. Cant I hear her 'child you mustnt be left here <u>one</u> <u>instant</u>' and then shed make miracles happen and by tomorrow shed have wrapped me up and defied everybody.

But we are firmly held in the web of circumstance. Weve got to risk it—to see it through. If you were to leave there our future is wrecked. If I came there Id die. No, once I am better I go to Menton and Ill return here later in the spring when Im stronger with a maid so as to be ready for you in May.

L. M. is out to tea with some people in Ospedaletti—gone off with a big bunch of roses for them. The wind sighs in the house and the fire goes chik-chik—very small. My fever makes everything 100 times more vivid—like a nightmare is vivid. But it will be over in a day or two, I expect. A bad business! Brett sent me some photographs.° Will you thank her for me. I can't lash myself into any kind of a friendly cackle. I thought the photographs very weak, thats all, but she sent me a nice letter.

Can you get Lawrences address° for me? I should like to have it.

Goodbye darling | I am ever your own
Wig-wife.

I am sure Menton will do wonders for my old depression—Ive great hopes of it. Bogey forgive me. All you tell me about the house I cant help feeling is all part of the hideous vile joke thats being played on us for les autres [other people] to read about in days to come. I *cant* see it except like this. I sometimes even get to the pitch of believing that subconsciously you are aware of this, too, and with colossal artistry are piling on delicate agony after delicate agony—so that *when* the joke is explained all will be quite perfect even to a silver teapot for her.

P.S. Darling please keep all these verses for me in the file—will you? Ill polish them up one day & have them published. But Ive no copies—so don't leave 'em about—will you. Just thrust them into the old file or into my cupboard.

Wig.

The New Husband.

Some one came to me and said
Forget, forget that you've been wed
Who's your man to leave you be
Ill and cold in a far country

Whos the husband—who's the stone
Could leave a child like you alone.

You're like a leaf caught in the wind
You're like a lamb thats left behind.
When all the flock has pattered away
Youre like a pitiful little stray
Kitten that Id put in my vest
Youre like a bird that's fallen from nest

We've none of us too long to live
Then take me for your man and give
Me all the Keys to all your fears
And let me kiss away these tears
Creep close to me. I mean no harm
My darling. Let me make you warm

I had received that very day
A letter from the Other to say
That in six months—he hoped—no longer
I would be so much better and stronger
That he would close his books and come
With radiant looks to bear me home.

Ha! Ha! Six months, six weeks, six hours
Among these glittering palms and flowers
With Melancholy at my side
For my old nurse and for my guide
Despair—and for my footman Pain—
Ill never see my home again

Said my new husband: Little dear
Its time we were away from here
In the road below there waits my carriage
Ready to drive us to our marriage
Within my home the feast is spread
And the maids are baking the bridal bread.

I thought with grief upon that other
But then why should he aught discover
Save that I pined away and died?
So I became the stranger's bride
And every moment however fast
It flies—we live as 'twere our last!

                        Elizabeth Stanley.°

To J. M. Murry

[Casetta Deerholm, Ospedaletti] *In the night.*
[12 December 1919]

I am awake and I have reread your letter.° It is stranger than ever. It is half an account of what I have done to you and the other half is all money. And you say I dont appreciate the seriousness of these your views about money. You do me great wrong. But I must not be kept in the dark. Have your creditors come down on you? But if they have—it is since Ottoline's sale? For were the burden of your debts so imperative & terrible you could not have spent any money there. What are these terrible debts? I must be told them. You cannot hint at them and then say I lack sympathy. You are not a pauper. You have £800 a year and you only contribute to my keep—not more than £50 a year at most now. You write as though there were me to be provided for—yourself, and all to be done on something like £300. I know you have paid my doctors bills and that my illness has cost you a great deal. It will cost you no more. I cannot take any more money from you ever and as soon as I am well I shall work to make a good deal more so that you have to pay less. But your letter frightens me for you—I think you have allowed this idea of money to take too great a hold on your brain. Either we must do nothing but pay off your debts or you must not care so greatly. Its madness to write like this to your wife & then to buy furniture. Its unworthy of our love surely to taunt me with my lack of understanding. How *could* I understand? I had no idea you still felt these crying claims: I thought all was going fairly smoothly. You must stick to the paper. I have never had another thought. Your being here is impossible from every point of view. I do not want to at all. I thought I had made that plain and about the paper—many many times. You say money is 'fundamental to any decision you make'. Yes of course it is. But I do not need to be told, and truly you should know that. I feel ashamed when I read that.

What I do beg you to do is to stay there, to live quietly and get the paper really going. *Live quietly.* I suppose you laugh. I have made that so impossible in the past. Youll have no cause

to blame me in the future for it. I leaned on you—and *broke you*.
The truth is that until I was ill you were never called upon to
'play the man' to this extent—and its <u>not</u> your role. When you
said you ought to be kept you spoke the truth. I feel it. Ever
since my illness this crisis I suppose has been impending when
suddenly in an agony I should turn all woman and lean on you.
Now it has happened. The crisis is over. You must feel that. It
won't return. Its over for good.

And I dont ask you to 'cut off with nothing' or to sacrifice
anything. All I do ask of each of us is to keep very steady and
calm now and by May we shall have recovered. But please be
calm. You are not asked to do anything quickly—theres *no*
decision for you to make.

However ill I am you are more ill. However weak I am you
are weaker—less able to bear things. Have I really put on the
last straw? You imply in this letter I have. You make me out so
cruel that — — — I feel you cant love me in the least—a
vampire—I am not. That is all.

I am not so hurried now—I want to talk more with you. God
knows if I have managed to stop you. I can do no more.

Granted (and I grant absolutely) that I have sent you this
'snake' (though now Im not talking of the verses but of my
depression in general), granted that—are you fair in punishing
me so horribly? I know when I write happy letters they make
you happy. You ask me to write more and you say if you want
to keep me happy thats the way to do it. Listen. When I was in
Hampstead with you were you always able to put all else aside
and make me happy? Did you never come to me depressed,
fearful, uneasy, fatigued and say 'you cant expect me to
dance—or act up to what you want'? Did I ask you to make
such an effort that your whole nature should change and you
should be *really* happy, *believing* in happiness. You have even
denied you *wanted* happiness—on the Heath by a broken tree. I
did not think I had to make the effort. I thought you alone—
you, the secret, secret you would understand. The effort to keep
perpetually radiant was too great. But you asked it of me. I did
not *only* write to make you and keep you happy. That was
important but not of first importance. Of first importance was
my desire to be truthful before you. Love, I thought, could
stand *even that*. Love could penetrate the isolation surrounding

another and lovers did not suffer alone. Not that I required of you that you should suffer with me. Never. Never. From the bottom of my heart I can say that. But I took you at your word: it seemed to me almost my duty to tell you all in the greatest possible honesty—anything less would not be *our love*.

When you wrote thats the stuff to keep me happy I was full of despair. I knew that I could not go on giving it you. It was not as though you were ill and turned to me, strong and well, as a flower would turn to the sun, crying: 'I am in the shadow, shine on me.' Alas, I was no sun. I was in the shadow—and when at times I came into a bright beam & sent it to you it was only *at times*.

I keep thinking of Wing as I write this and of our love. Will it all come back or have I the snake laid everything waste. Peace! Peace! It could not be helped. If I have done this it was a snake in my bosom—yea in my bosom and not I. I will not receive your dreadful accusations into my soul for they would kill me.

But here is your letter and you tell me I have driven you nearly insane—ruined you—it seems—quenched your hopes even of getting your money affairs straight. You tell me again that you are a bankrupt.° It cant be helped. No protestations now. Remember how weve loved—remember it all and let us not talk of *money*. It is not necessary to tell me to hint that they will come after you & perhaps put you in jail for debt if you run away. I dont ask these things. I never asked them. I believed that the human being did not suffer alone. I showed you my sufferings. I have learned the truth. Do not let us talk of it again. Let us just go on. Let us bury the past and go on and *recover*. We shall. Our only chance now is not to lose Hope but to go on and not give each other up.

Your devoted—yours eternally | Your

Wife.

To S. S. Koteliansky

[Casetta Deerholm, Ospedaletti]
Saturday Evening [13 December 1919]

Koteliansky

Your letter has made me very happy. Thank you for it. You know, it is still here, in my room, sounding like music that has been played. 'Be well'. And I am ashamed that I broke down in my last letter. That night I went to bed with pneumonia. That was why I was so depressed. Of course I am still in bed but it does not matter. *All is well.*

We are quite alone here tonight. It is so far away and still. Everything is full of silent life—complete with its shadow. From the sea there comes a soft *ruffled* sound and its beat is regular and soft like the beat of mowers cutting through a deep meadow. Yes, one day when we have the money we shall meet somewhere and talk quietly for as long as we wish. It will happen, I think. Your loneliness is precious to you, I know. Does it disturb it to know you are dear to me. Do not let it. It is such a quiet feeling. It is like the light coming in to a room— moonlight—where you are sitting.

I shall try and get well here. If I *do* die perhaps there will be a small private heaven for consumptives only. In that case I shall see Tchekov. He will be walking down his garden paths with fruit trees on either side and tulips in flower in the garden beds. His dog will be sitting on the path, panting and slightly smiling as dogs do who have been running about a great deal.

Only to think of this makes my heart feel as though it were *dissolving*—a strange feeling. But the Knipper° ... You know Koteliansky, I cannot like her. There is a kind of false brightness about her. Perhaps I am very wrong.

Lawrence wrote from Florence. Frieda had arrived—*thinner*—but very well. This thinness will not last. He said Florence was lovely° and full of 'extremly nice people'. He is able to bear people so easily. Often I long to be more *in life*—to know people—even now the desire comes. But immediately the opportunity comes I think of nothing but how to escape. And people have come to see me here. *What* are they? They are not

human beings; they are never children—they are *absolutely
unreal*—mechanisms.

And those people in England—when one goes away the
memory of them is like the memory of clothes hanging in a
cupboard. And yet the beauty of life—Koteliansky—the
haunting beauty of 'the question'.° Sometimes when I am
awake here, very early in the morning, I hear, far down on the
road below, the market carts going by. And at the sound I live
through this getting up before dawn, the blue light in the
window—the cold solemn look of the people—the woman
opening the door and going for sticks, the smell of smoke—the
feather of smoke rising from their chimney. I hear the man as
he slaps the little horse and leads it into the clattering yard.
And the fowls are still asleep—big balls of feather. But the
early morning air and hush ... And after the man and wife
have driven away some little children scurry out of bed across
the floor and find a piece of bread and get back into the warm
bed and divide it. But this is all *the surface*. Hundreds of things
happen down to minute, minute details. But it is all so full of
beauty—and you know the voices of people before sunrise—
how different they are? I lie here, thinking of these things and
hearing those little carts ... It is too much. One must weep.

Forgive a long letter. I shall send you the letters.°

I do not know if Murry is coming. I have sent him several
wires asking him not to come. It is not at all a good idea.

Goodnight. When you think of me call me by my other
name—°

[*No signature*]

To J. M. Murry

[Casetta Deerholm, Ospedaletti] Tuesday
Night. [13 January 1920]

My dearest Bogey

Thank you for your letter today and for letting me see the
two poems; I think they are exquisite and could not be
improved on. I return you them.

I return also Nevinson's letter.° It is an outrage; it made me feel quite sick and faint—the spirit of it seemed to get into the room . . . and to go on and go on. It is a really revolting letter.

I am enclosing a letter to Marie Dahlerup° which I want you please to read before you send it to her. I am very much afraid that the contents will surprise and anger you. Will you please try to be patient with me while I explain. Bogey I am so sorry—when I have anything to explain to you now I have a kind of premonitory shiver—I see you turn away so quick and sharp . . . but you *really must* please be patient with me now.

I do not want Marie any more. Ever since you left here this time—since this last 'illness' of mine—(what the doctor calls acute nervous exhaustion acting on the heart) my feelings towards Lesley are absolutely changed. It is not only that the hatred is gone—Something positive is there which is very like love for her. She has convinced me at last, against all my opposition that she is trying to do all in her power for me—and that she is devoted to the one idea which is (please forgive my egoism) to see me well again. This time she has fed me, helped me, got up in the middle of the night to make me hot milk and rub my feet, brought me flowers, *served* me as one could not be served if one were not loved. All silently and gently too, even after all my bitter ravings at her and railing against her. She has simply shown me that she *understands* and I feel that she does.

Am I right in feeling you never would have disliked her had it not been for me? How could you have! I look back and think how she tried to run the house for us. She failed—but <u>how</u> she tried! I think of her unceasing devotion to us—her patience with me—her trying to help you and to efface herself when we were together. Who else would have done it? Nobody on earth. I know she loves <u>us</u> as no one ever will. She thinks (<u>still</u> thinks) it would be the ideal life to be near us and to serve us. In Hampstead she was in a false position. She cannot be a servant—a nurse—a companion—all these things. But to over-look—to help—to keep an eye on <u>our</u> possessions (precious to her because she knows what we feel about them) there is no one like her. My hate is quite lifted—quite gone; it is like a curse removed. Lesley has been through the storm with us. I want her now to share in the calm—to act Marie's part for us in our country house. Do you agree? I feel I cannot do without her now. Here is someone *tried trusted*—who understands who is really bound to me now because of what she has done here for me. I think I would have died without Lesley these last terrible times. You know she has such an affection for you, too, deep and true: 'Jack is Jack'. I know she is not perfect. I know she sometimes will annoy us. God—who wont? And who will leave us so utterly free and yet be *there* in *charge* when we want her. I confess that now I do lean on her. She looks after me; she has become (or I see her now in her true colours) the person who looks after all I cannot attend to. It was only when I refused to acknowledge this—to acknowledge her importance to me that I hated her. Now that I do I can be sincere and trust her and of course she, feeling the difference, is a different person. Her self respect has all come back. She thinks *for* me and seems to know my ways as nobody who had not been with me for years ever could.

This great change will I am sure astonish and I am afraid anger you. I think my hatred must have been connected with my illness in some way. I cannot explain it—only tell you and though I am afraid I must trust that you will believe me. Will you please tell me what you think? You must realise that now that we are at peace I am never exasperated and she does not annoy me. I only feel 'free' for work and everything.

My dearest, I am still waiting to hear from Menton. It is still early to expect an answer. Foster° comes again tomorrow. I got up for an hour or two today but now I am in bed again. Did I tell you we have had an alarm here at night. Some men very late, ringing and ringing the bell until finally Lesley shot out of the window. It was so queer—like a siege—very dreadful, really. Lesley did not take off her clothes all night.

Thank you for sending me the Tchekhov.° I will do my very best. It is awfully good of you to let me do it. Tell me about *yourself*—will you? My darling, remember how I love you—If you knew what your letters mean to me!

Be happy. Fare well. I am your devoted

Wig.

To J. M. Murry

My own precious Husband

I have escaped. Do you know what that means? There has been a postal strike in Italy—no letters, no wires. *Nothing* comes through or goes out—a strike of the railways—and now from today a strike of automobiles. We just got through by taking a round about route & escaping the police.

All all my thoughts, hopes, longings were for an answer to my telegram, here. I managed to get a telegram telephoned to you at Menton—at what pains I cant describe—and I knew there was time for an answer. I simple tore the telegram from these people & read *story arrived safely*° not even a signature. Was that from you? Could it have been. I have sent Ida out with another—thats all I can do. For about a moment I nearly broke down but I must steel myself & wait wait wait again.

Bogey I have got away from that hell of isolation—from the awful ringing at night—from the loneliness & fright. To tell you the truth I think I have been *mad*, but really, medically mad. A great awful cloud has been on me & now if I hear from you & all is well it will lift & you will see your own Wig under it—the *old true loving* Wig—your own wife who adores you. Its nearly killed me. Yes. When Jinnie took me in her arms today & she cried as well as I. I felt as though Id been through some awful deathly strain—and just survived—been rescued from drowning or something like that. You cant understand love— its not possible you should know what that isolation was when you left again and I again was ill—

Forgive me forgive me completely for ever will you. I ought never to have done it. Of course it was all an awful mistake but now at last it is over—& wont happen again. If I dont get well here Ill never get well. Here—after the journey—was this room waiting for me—exquisite—large with four windows overlooking great gardens & mountains—wonderful flowers—tea with *toast* & honey & butter, a charming maid—and these two dear sweet women to welcome me with papers books etc. This is really a superb place in every way. Two doctors live here. They

are coming to examine me tomorrow. They 'called' after tea &
just chatted & ordered my extra milk and dinner in my room &
so on—awfully nice men. The cleanliness is almost superna-
tural. One feels like a butterfly—one only wants to fan ones
wings on the couch the chairs. I have a big writing table with a
cut glass inkstand—a waste paper basket—a great bowl of
violets & *your* own anemones & wallflowers on it. The directress
is a very nice french woman only too anxious to look after me
& see that there is no change in anything. She will give me a
litre of milk & butter as much as I want. There is also a sort of
Swiss nurse in white who has just been in & says she answers the
bell at night. She is so good to look at that I shall *have* to ring.

Boge Boge Boge. Ive got away from under that ghastly
cloud. All is absolutely changed. Im here with people with
care. I feel a different creature *really*—different eyes, different
hair. The garden is gorgeous: there is a big shelter, chauffé
[heated]. What do you think of that.

Precious I have to catch the post—& heres my dinner in my
room—all lovely. This is just on the spot to let you know I am
here and all goes marvellously well. Only you you you now
thats all I want. A new-old Wig will come back in May. Ill
write tomorrow & every day.

Your own wife.

To J. M. Murry

[L'Hermitage, Menton] Friday.
[23 January 1920]

Dearest

I thought when I had sent my letter yesterday that you don't
really know where we stand. The last letter I had from you was
on a Wednesday and you contemplated spending the following
weekend with the Waterlows to see *the Lacket*.° Did you go?
What happened? I know nothing after that until I received
your letter about Wells yesterday. And what was the last you
received from me I wonder? It is all terribly confusing. Have
you got my cards of this place? Do you know how we

stand? Oh, a hundred curses on the italian post. It is too distracting. . . .

Reviews of course—Chinese Poetry, Sir Limpidus, Coggin°
all have been sent, & four parcels of books. Two I imagine arrived before the strike. If they did will you please let me have the money? I need every single penny I can get. You see in addition to my room I have *wine* & *medicine* & laundry & odd expenses and L. M. to not only keep but to give pocket money to and provide for. I don't care two figs. I feel perfectly reckless. Until Kay° says the Bank will summons me Ill just *go on*. Its worth it. One day here makes me feel better—and only to have escaped that TRAP is such a triumph.

Connie came yesterday to see me carrying a baby Pekinese. Have you ever seen a really *baby* one about the size of a fur glove—covered with pale gold down with paws like minute seal flappers—very large impudent eyes & ears like fried potatoes? Good God! What creatures they are. This one is a perfect complement to Wing. We <u>must</u> have one. They are not in the least pampered or fussy or spoilt. They are like fairy animals. This one sat on my lap, cleaned both my hands really very carefully, polished the nails then bit off carefully each finger & thumb & then exhausted & blown with 8 fingers & two thumbs inside him gave a great sigh & crossed his front paws & listened to the conversation. He lives on beef steaks and loaf sugar. His partner in life when he is at home is a pale blue satin bedroom slipper. Please let us have one at the Heron.

I had a long talk with Connie yesterday. She and Jinnie are really—no joking—superb women. Its a queer queer relationship. C. obviously adores J. and refers everything to her but she is not in the least a parasite or overshadowed. She is a complete creature who yet *leans* on J. as a woman may do on a man. One feels her happiness to an extraordinary degree. That is what is so restful about both these women. They are deeply *secure*—and they are well *bred*—they are *english ladies*—which means a great deal.

I went downstairs yesterday for lunch & dinner. Dear love I am here on false pretences. I am the only healthy creature here. When I entered the salle a manger [dining room] I felt that all the heads were raised all the noses sniffed a frampold rampant lion entering. Its not that these people are *ill*. They look exactly as though they were risen from the dead—stepped out of coffins & eating again pour la première fois [for the first time]. Their hair is thin & weak and poor—the eyes are cold & startled —their hands are still waxen—& THIN! They are walking sticks. All the little arts & allurements they have shed & not yet picked up again. They are still sexless & blow their noses in a *neuter* fashion—neither male nor female blows. At the tables there are the signs & tokens of their illnesses—bottles, boxes. *One* woman gave me a nasty knock. She had a réchaud beside [her]—a lamp & stand & she reheated everything even the plates. There but for the grace of God went Wig. The waitresses of course thrive in this atmosphere. They are two pretty full-bosomed girls—with spider web stockings, shoes laced up their legs—little delicate wispy aprons—powdered necks—red lips—scent—& they move like ballet dancers—sliding & gliding in the fullness of their youth and strength over the polished floors. All this amuses me very much.

Later. The masseuse has just been and ironed me from top to toe. I am all tingling as though I had been a 10 mile walk. BOGE. See how <u>very</u> silly I am getting. You just wait until we meet again and you find a brand new girl.

But never never shall I cut myself off from Life again. I haven't any illusions darling; I know all about it and am not really a baby saying 'agoo-a-gah!' but in spite of everything I know *il y a quelque chose* [*There is something* . . .] . . . that I feed on, exult in, and adore. One must be, if one is a Wig, continually giving & receiving, and shedding & renewing, & examining & trying to place. According to you I suppose my thinking is an infant affair with bead frames and coloured blocks. Well its not important. What is important is that I adore you & I shall go up in flame if I do not show you these cornflowers & jonquils.

The day is cloudy—but it doesn't matter. Landscape is lovely in this light—its not like the sea. The mimosa great puffs of mimosa & great trees of red roses & oranges bright and flashing. Some boys are being drilled outside. The sergeant major keeps on saying '*T'ois cinquante, n'est-ce pas* [*Three fifty, right?*]' & there is a most for*lorn* bugle.

Here is a story my little femme de chambre [maid] told me. Please read it.

Do you know Madame que les fleurs sont trop fortes to be left dans la chambre pendant la nuit & surtout les joncs. If I put them sur le balcon—n'est-ce pas & bring them in early in the morning. Vous sa-vez quand ma petite mère etait tres jeune elle etait la maitresse d'une petite école pour les tous petits enfants, et sur son jour de fête les bébes elle a apporté un bouquet énorme grand comme un chou—rond comme ça Madame de ces joncs. Elle les a mis dans sa chambre à coucher. C'êtait un Vendredi. Le soir elle est endormie, et, puis, tout le samedi, le dimanche—jusqu'a le lundi matin elle dort pro*fond*ement. Quand les petites eleves ont arrivés le lundi la porte etait fermée. Ils ont frappés—pas de reponse. Enfin mon père qui n'etait pas mon père à ce temps-la, alors est venu du village et il a forcé la porte et voila ma mère qui n'etait pas ma mère ni même marié a ce temps-la—toujours dans un sommeil *profond*, et l'air etait chargée de la parfum de ces joncs—qu'elle a mis sur une petite table pres du lit — —

[Do you know Madame that flowers are too strong to be left in your room all night, jonquils especially. It's all right if I put them on the balcony, isn't it, and bring them in early in the morning? Let me tell you when my dear mother was very young she was the headmistress of a small school for very young children, and on her birthday the little ones brought her a bouqet as big as a cabbage—enormous, like this Madame— of jonquils. She put them in her bedroom. It was a Friday. That evening she went to sleep and then, all through Saturday, all Sunday—right up till Monday morning she slept *heavily*. When the children arrived for school on Monday the door was shut. They knocked but there was no answer. In the end my father—who wasn't my father then—came up from the village and forced open the door, and there was my mother—who wasn't my mother, nor even married at that time—still in a deep sleep and the air was full of the scent of the jonquils that she'd put on a little table beside the bed ...]

Don't you like that story? Do you see the infants looking in with their fingers in their mouths & the young man finding her blanc comme une bougie [white as a candle] & the room & the flowers. Its a bit sentimental, praps, but I love it. I see such funny little worms with sachets and socks & large tam o'shanters.

Post has been. Your Thursday letter is arrived & here is only Friday. Isn't it a <u>comfort</u> to be out of that awful silence? But here you talk of farmhouses. Does that mean the Lacket is off? Oh, shall I ever catch up?

Why did not Sydney tell you—or why didn't you enquire at the post office about Italy? Sydney <u>must</u> have known at the F.O. Yesterday tho' I saw a copy of the D. T. [*Daily Telegraph*] which said the strike was over on the 20th. What a lie! It is really only beginning—San Remo you know was guarded by the military. I feel this place is so near—so *easy* to get at. Its like being out in the garden with you in the house. It really is. But its so beautiful, darling, what I see of it at least—*superb*. The one brick is the expense. I wrote to Rutter° yesterday. If *he* pays me it will make a difference. Did you see the story? Did you like it? What did you think? I must get up—& open the windows.

Goodbye my precious. Give my love to the pussies & to Violet & keep it all down to the last crumb for yourself. Did Arthur get a long letter from me? And a lovely inkpot posted in a diplomatic cardboard box? I shall be so thankful when you have heard from me. Perhaps you'll get a letter tomorrow or praps you'll be in Sussex ... Goodbye my own. Do write as long a letter as you can and tell me <u>all</u>.

Your own wife
Wig.

To J. M. Murry

[L'Hermitage, Menton] In reply to your
Tuesday letter. [7 February 1920]

My dear Bogey
I have your Tuesday evening letter. That you took my letter as being primarily concerned with money is horrible. However Ill answer that first. I send you back the cheque for £20. As you have paid £20 into my bank I shall use that at the rate of

£10 a month and by the time it is finished that is at the end of
March I hope that my book will be paid for and I shant have to
ask you for any more money. You ask me if we havent known
each other long enough for me to wire for £20. But Bogey
haven't we known each other long enough for you to have said
to me: *I realise* you must need money. But Im cleaned out this
month. Ill send some next? If only you'd thought for me—or
imagined for me: it was *that* that hurt.

You say I ought to have guessed you misunderstood. Curse
money! Its not really a question of money. It was the question
of sympathy, of understanding, of being in the least *interested* of
asking just once how I was—what I thought about & felt—
what I did—if I was 'alright'? I cant get over the fact that it
never occurred to you and it makes me feel you don't want my
Love—not my living love—you only want an 'idea'. When that
strike was on—fool that I was—my first thoughts always were
'what *I* feel doesn't matter so much. Jack must be in such
agony. When he doesn't hear he'll try & wire and the P.O. will
tell him no wires are delivered & he knows Im ill . . .' But your
letter came 'drunk with the magnificence of the downs', a day's
'sheer joy',° the 'note of hysteria would go out of my work',
'very fit'. And when you *did* hear—good—your anxiety was
over & you never referred to me again. So I *must* face the fact
that you have put *me* away for the time. You are withdrawn—
self-contained and you don't want in the deepest widest sense
of the word to be disturbed. As long as Im on a suitable shelf—
and ∴ you're not worried—ça va! [So that's alright!] Of
course I still love you. I love you as much as ever. But to know
this is torture until I get it in hand.

'A love that might break through *if she would let it*, the ghastly
terror of her loneliness!' Does not that show it up? Who could
write such unspeakably cruel words if he loved? (at the
moment). You suggest that my suffering was self-imposed, in so
far as it was really a failure to love enough. If I had loved you
enough I need not have suffered as I did. Bogey, you must
believe me that is a deadly false view. A living, loving warm
being could not believe that or say it. Its a vile intellectual
idea—and it simply appals me. I can't wire the word Love
because of it. (Of course I can of course I will.° You do *love* me:
its only you dont love me just now.) To make out my agony was

my failure to love—oh that is really too much. You have stabbed me to the heart with these words.

I want to mention something else. Lawrence sent me a letter today: he spat in my face & threw filth at me and said 'I loathe you. You revolt me stewing in your consumption. The Italians were quite right to have nothing to do with you' and a great deal more.° Now I do beseech you if you are my man to stop defending him after that & never to crack him up in the paper. *Be proud.* In the same letter he said his final opinion of you was that you were a 'dirty little worm'. Well, *be proud.* Dont forgive him for that, please.

Goodbye. I am utterly disappointed with the answer to my letter but I *must* bear it. You say you are not ashamed: I dont want you to be ashamed. And then you say you sent the £20 the moment you had it. February 1 came too late. *Damn* the £20. I suppose from that you look upon yourself as a man who is being bled—*you* did all in your power but FATE and your wife would not wait. Its <u>utterly</u> false. I wanted love & sympathy and understanding—were you cleaned out of those until February 1st? It is nightmare that you wont understand.

Your own
Wig.

[*Across top of letter*]
Of course you love me of course you do. Its only since Ive been away you have withdrawn yourself from me & ever since I broke down at the Casetta and appealed to you things have never been the same. Its only that you don't love me <u>now</u>. Oh, darling—do do break through. <u>Do</u> care. Its so hard—wait till Im strong before you run away for a bit. Its so awful. Bogey you must love me. Fancy writing so coolly to me & asking me to wire if I think you do. Would I be *here* if I thought you didn't—somewhere—deep down love me?

To Sydney and Violet Schiff

[2 Portland Villas, East Heath Road,
Hampstead, 4 May 1920]

My dear friends,

Art and Letters° came today reminding me of the day we talked it over. It *looks* very well.

Still the sun lingers. Still, one walks up and down up and down waiting, staring out of the windows—waiting for that moment—that marvellous moment—when you step out of the shadow into the embrace which is like a blessing. It is very cold; do not come back too soon.

Yesterday I drove down to the city to my Bank. It is almost terrifying to see such blank, strained faces moving in the fog. I drove to the office of the Athenaeum & thought there at least there would be men I knew who responded who—were alive and cared about life and the paper and work and—The untidiness of John's desk (laugh, Violet dear!) was my first crushing blow. There was over all the office a smell of stone and dust. Unthinkable disorder and ugliness. Old Massingham° like a cat dipped in dough blinking in the doorway & asking whether the French were furious with [Lloyd] 'George'— Huxley wavering like a candle who expected to go out with the next open door, poor silly old men with pins in their coat lapels, Tomlinson harking back to the mud in Flanders, Sullivan and E. M. Forster° very vague, very frightened. I heard myself speaking of lemon trees & then I said that in one valley I knew there was a torrent. Nobody cared, nobody wanted to know. I ran downstairs back into the car with Murry (we were going to buy a coffee pot because it was the anniversary of our wedding.) He was sure the shop would be shut because I'd talked instead of coming away so he looked out of his window and I looked out of mine and I listened to that lovely swift rushing sound & remembered how blue the lavender was the day we sat in that part of the garden.

One must live alone and work & put away one's passion— ones passion for Life. It must all go into work. Queer—isn't it—how one realises it and yet there persists this longing not to take part in, but to see, to feel, to absorb, to find out. But perhaps, by accident, it will be fed occasionally—and for the rest—travailler—travailler [to work—to work] — — —

Goodbye
K.M.

To Sydney and Violet Schiff

[2 Portland Villas, East Heath Road,
Hampstead] Friday. [14 May 1920]

I have had your note; I have had your postcard and am wondering every day if you are home. The Elliots have dined with us tonight. They are just gone—and the whole room is *quivering*. John has gone downstairs to see them off. Mrs E's° voice rises 'Oh dont commiserate Tom; he's *quite* happy.' I know its extravagant; I know, Violet, I ought to have seen more—but I dislike her so *immensely*. She really repels me. She makes me shiver with apprehension . . . I don't dare to think of what she is 'seeing'. From the moment that John dropped a spoon & she cried: 'I say you are noisy tonight—whats wrong'—to the moment when she came into my room & lay on the sofa offering idly: 'This room's changed since the last time I was here.' To think she had been here *before*. I handed her the cigarettes saying to myself: 'well you won't find it changed again'. Isn't that extravagant. And Elliot, leaning towards her, admiring, listening, making the most of her—really minding whether she disliked the country or not . . .

I am so fond of Elliot and as he talked of you both tonight I felt a deep sympathy with him. You are *in* his life like you are in mine. Don't think that is impertinent. Oh, I could explain and explain that. But this teashop creature.

M. comes up after they are gone, and he defends her. He tells me of a party he gave here & how she came & was friends with him & how he drank to get over the state of nerves she had thrown him into. 'I like her; I would do the same again.' I feel as tho' Ive been stabbed.

Now its dead still—except for the far-off noise of the trains drumming round the hollow world.

Where are you both? You are *somewhere*. I am in the middle of a long long new story. I must push further out to sea.

Let us meet soon.

Yours ever
K.M.

To J. M. Murry

Villa Isola Bella.|Sunday afternoon|
September 19th [and 21 September] 1920

My darling little Follower,

It is true—isn't it—that we are going to walk out together every single Sunday? All through the week we are hard at work—you, in that horrible black town that I hate, me, on my beautiful island but when Sunday comes (it was my first thought this morning) we adorn ourselves and soon after midi [midday] I hear that longed for but rather peculiar, rather funny whistle. I run to the window and there below is a lovely vision in a faded very much-washed creamy linen shirt, linen trousers, a scarlet bellyband—a wide silver-grey hat just a little on one side. I kiss my hand to it, spin down the stairs, and away we go. But for this week at least we'll not go far—only out of sight of the world—that's far enough. For your Wig is still so weak that she can't walk straight—sometimes I fling myself at the doors or take a great high step in the air. But I *am* really on the mend, dear darling and as to my cough—fancy—I've been here five days & I cough hardly at all. This morning in fact I didn't cough *at all* and cant remember if I have until now *6 p.m.* I only have to get my strength back after this 'attack'. That is all about me, dear darling.

(There is so much to tell you. I tell you in my mind and then the effort of writing is too much. Forgive for this week an infernally dull girl.)

My feeling for this little house is that somehow it ought to be

ours. It is I think a perfect house in its way and just our size.
The position—up a side road *off* a side road—standing high—
all alone—the chief rooms facing South & West—the garden,
the terrace all South is ideal. You could do all the garden.
Theres a small vegetable plot outside the kitchen & scullery—
there is a largish piece in the front—*full* of plants & trees—with
a garden tap and at the side another bed—a walk—a stone
terrace overlooking the sea—a great magnolia tree—a palm
that looks as tho dates must ripen. You shall have photographs
of all this. And then its so solid inside and so somehow—
spacious. And all on two floors and as well all the kitchen
premises away—shut away and again perfectly equipped. I
shall of course keep the strictest accounts and see exactly what
it would cost us to live here.

Marie, the maid, is an excellent cook—as good as Annette
was. She does all the marketing, and as far as I can discover
she's a very good manager. A *marvel* really. Of course she cooks
with butter but then one doesn't eat butter with ones meals so it
comes to the same thing. The food is far better than any
possible house we go to in England. I don't know to whom to
compare it—and all her simple dishes like vegetables or salads
are so good. Its a great pleasure to go into the kitchen for my
morning milk & see this blithe soul back from market in the
spotless kitchen with a bunch of lemon leaves drying for tisane
& a bunch of camomile hanging for the same. All is in exquisite
order. There are pots on the stove, cooking away—mysterious
pots—the vegetables are in a great crock—in bundles—and she
tells me of her marvellous bargains as I sip the milk. She is the
kind of cook Anatole France° might have.

As to the weather it is really heavenly weather. It is too hot
for any exertion, but a breeze lifts at night—and I can't tell
you what scents it brings—the smell of a full summer sea and
the bay tree in the garden and the smell of lemons. After lunch
today we had a sudden tremendous thunder storm, the drops of
rain were as big as marguerite daisies—the whole sky was
violet. I went out the very moment it was over—the sky was all
glittering with broken light—the sun a huge splash of silver.
The drops were like silver *fishes* hanging from the trees. I drank
the rain from the peach leaves & then pulled a shower bath
over my head. Every violet leaf was full. I thought of you—

these are the things I want you to have. Already one is conscious of the whole sky again & the light on the water. Already one listens for the grasshoppers' fiddle, one looks for the tiny frogs on the path—one watches the lizards . . . I feel so strangely as though I were the one who is home & you are away. I long for you here.

Tuesday. I dropped this letter and only today I pick it up again. Your cards came & your treasure of a letter, *my own boy* and I long to answer—I keep on answering, as it were. There is so much to tell you & apart from that there's the paper—your Stendhal°—so *first chop*—the books you've sent me. And I still haven't told you about this house or the life or the view or what your room is like. It all waits. Will you—my wise comprehending boy—just take me and it for granted for about a week? In a week Ill be a giant refreshed—but Ive simply got to get back my strength after the last blow.

But you know how soon I come to the surface. It did pull me down. Its only a few days. Its over. Im on the *up grade* but there you are—just for the moment. Each day the house finds its order more fixed and just (thats not English). Marie does every single thing. I am having an awning made so that I can lie out all day. The weather is absolute exquisite radiance—day after day just variegated by these vivid storms. Its *very* hot & the insects are a trouble—but its perfect weather for you & me here. Im doing all wise things.

Dear Darling. I'll just have to ask you to take a wave of a lily white hand to mean *all* for the moment. Yes, Im sending a review this week. I note the novels are coming across quickly. Im going to do three together. Can you bring Wing at Xmas? If not Ida says she will go across & fetch them both when you give up the house. They'd be happy here.

I *wish* I were stronger. Im so *much* better. My cough is nearly gone. Its nothing but de la faiblesse [weakness] & I know it will pass. But not to be able to give you all this when I so want to— that's hard to bear. The papers come, thank you dearest.

Your own loving
Wig.

To J. M. Murry

[Villa Isola Bella, Menton, 4 October 1920]
My darling Bogey

Its Monday—and the sun has come back—its fine and warm. I had 2 cards from you today—but you didn't tell me how your cold was. Does that mean it is better?

Yesterday the paper came. *I* thought it a very good number. You felt rather 'faint' about it didn't you & Miss Brett found it 'dull'. But I thought it was full of meat, somehow. I read it, and I thought of you and of what an amount of work it means and of how you labour at it—and I sent you that wire. *Whatever* my feelings are I am *not* justified in giving way to them before you or in letting you see even the shadow of the border of that shadowy country that we exiles from health inhabit. It is not fair. So Im resolute that you shant be plagued again, my dearest darling and determined to keep my resolution. Help me to.

Im sending you and Milne° a dozen kāhki (I don't know how to spell it thats phonetic) to eat for your breakfasts. They are very good & very healthy. I send them unripe. You must wait until they are soft, then cut off the top, squeeze a *lot* of lemon juice inside & eat with a teaspoon. Perhaps they won't be a treat, after all. I always long to *send* you things. Please give my love to Milne. He sounds so nice in the house. I wonder what Wing thinks of the clarinet.

Walpoles novel° which I mean to do for next week (1 col.) ought to be a very good prop to hang those very ideas on that I tried to communicate to you. I want to take it seriously and really say why it fails—for of course it does fail. But his 'intention' was serious. I hope Ill be able to say what I do mean. I am *no* critic of the homely kind. 'If you would only explain quietly in simple language' as L. M. said to me yesterday. Good Heavens that is out of my power.

The garden menagerie includes snakes—a big chap as thick as my wrist, as long as my arm, slithered along the path this morning and melted into the bushes. It wasn't horrid or fearful, however. As to the mice—Marie's piege [trap] seems to

snap in the most revolting way. A fat one was offered to a
marauding cat at the back door yesterday—but it *refused* it.
'Polisson! Tu veux un morceau de sucre avec? [Do you expect
sugar with it, wretch?]' I heard Marie scold. She is very down
on the cats here; she says they are malgracieux [ill-natured].
Yes, she is a most *remarkable* type. Yesterday afternoon—it was
terribly gloomy & triste [sad] outside & she came in for the
coffee tray—& said how she *hated* Menton. She had lived here 8
years with her pauvre mari [poor husband] and then they'd
lived 2 years in Nice where he died & was buried. She said she
could *bear* Nice because il se repose là bas mais ici—Madame—
il se promenait avec moi—partout partout [he lies there, but
here, Madame, he walks about with me—everywhere every-
where]—and then she beat her little black crepe bodice & cried
'trop de souvenirs—Madame—trop de souvenirs [too many
memories Madame—too many memories]'. Oh, how I love
people who feel deeply. How restful it is to live with them even
in their 'excitement'. I think for writers, people like you and
me, it *is* right to be with them—but the feeling must be true—
not a hair breadth assumed—or I hate it as much as I love the
other. As I write that I don't believe it any more. I could live
with you and not care 2 pins if people 'felt' anything at all—in
fact I could draw away and be very aloof and cold if they did. *I*
don't know. Its too difficult.

More reams from Brett. Tennis and Gertler's threatened
tuberculosis° are the themes. How he mustn't be told and will
crumple up if he *is* told and Dr Sorapure says and she dreams
tennis. But I wish she would keep her pen off tuberculosis—she
doesn't know what she is writing about & its desperately
tactless to 'tee-hee' at the idea of it. Heavens what irony! I have
no doubt Gertlers friends will subscribe £1000 and send him to
Egypt for the winter. Oh, Brett does make me loathe London.
She seems to sweep a gutterful of it into an envelope and then
she *goads* me—on purpose. *Shes* not ill *she* can run, *she* can play
tennis with Murry. No, I can't write to her. 'You must get
better & you & I & Murry will go streaming away.' <u>Oh Bogey!!</u>
But people with spots on their lungs are not subjects for
merriment.

I feel this letter is cold and poor; the fruit is not good to eat.
Its rather like that withered fig tree. Do you know there is a

kind of fig tree which is supposed to be of the family of that unfortunate one—it is dark stemmed and its leaves are black. They flap on the blackened boughs—they are like leaves that a flame has passed over. *Terrible.* I saw one once in a valley, a beautiful valley with a river flowing through it. There was linen drying on the banks and the women were beating the water and calling to one another—gaily. And there was this *sad* tree. L. M. who was with me said 'of course the *explanation* is that one must never cease from giving.' The fig tree had no figs—so Christ cursed it.° *Did you ever*! There's such a story buried under the whole thing—isn't there if only one could dig it out.

Well darling Im going back to my chaise longue. I spend all day either lying on the terrace or in this salon with both windows open and I go to bed at 8 p.m. & get up at 10 a.m. Each day is the same.

How are you? Your poem? You—the very you? Do you feel we are near each other? I love you. I think of you at the yellow table. I miss you at night & in the early morning & when I am awake at night I think of you—lying asleep. I wonder what suit you are wearing. I see you in your jersey. 'Don't be afraid'. I do not ask you, my darling own, to come under my umbulella.°

But I have a deep, *pure* love for you in my heart.

Your Wig.

To J. M. Murry

[Villa Isola Bella, Menton, 18 October 1920]

My darling Bogue (yes that is right. Its your other name, you know)

I return DelaMare's letter.° I long to hear of your time with him. Its very queer; he haunts me here—not a persistent or substantial ghost but as one who shares my (our) joy in the *silent world.* Joy is not the word: I only used it because it conveys a stillness—a remoteness—because there is a faraway sound in it.

You know, darling, I have felt very often lately as though

the silence had some meaning beyond these signs—these intimations. Isn't it possible that if one yielded there is a whole
world into which one is received? It is so near and yet I am
conscious that I hold back from giving myself up to it. What is
this something mysterious that waits—that beckons?

And then suffering—bodily suffering such as Ive known for
three years. It has changed forever everything—even the
appearance of the world is not the same—there is something
added. *Everything has its shadow.* It is right to resist such
suffering? Do you know I feel it has been an immense privilege.
Yes, in spite of all. How blind we little creatures are! Darling,
its only the fairy tales we *really* live by. If we set out upon a
journey the more wonderful the treasure the greater the
temptations and perils to be overcome. And if someone rebels
and says Life isn't good enough on those terms one can only
say: 'It *is*'. Dont misunderstand me. I don't mean a 'thorn in
the flesh,° my dear'—its a million times more mysterious. It has
taken me three years to understand this—to come to see this.
We resist—we are terribly frightened. The little boat enters the
dark fearful gulf and our only cry is to escape—'put me on
land again'. But its useless. Nobody listens. The shadowy figure
rows on. One ought to sit still and uncover ones eyes.

I believe the greatest failing of all is *to be frightened*. Perfect
Love casteth out Fear.° When I look back on my life all my
mistakes have been because I was afraid ... Was that why I
had to look on death. Would nothing less cure me? You know,
one can't help wondering, sometimes ... No, not a personal
God or any such nonsense. Much more likely—the soul's
desperate choice ...

Am I right in thinking that you too have been ridden by Fear
(of quite a different kind). And now its gone from you—and
you are whole. I feel that only now you have *all* your
strength—a kind of *release*.

We are as different as can be but I do believe we have the
same devils as well as the same gods.

Here are your letters back again, love. They interested me
deeply. Your Stendhal article ... seemed to fetch the french
ducks off the water ... didn't it? Im sorry about Knopf and the
Yazpegs°—but cant be helped.

Take care of yourself—my beloved child with all these wild

men about throwing stones and striking. Make yourself small—fold yourself up. Im (privately—it doesn't do to tell you these things) terrified that in your lunch hour you'll take your bisticks [biscuits] into the street & get caught in a crowd & march away. *Eat*, don't catch cold whatever you do. I want to put my hands on you—to touch you—anxiously & lovingly. I *miss* you. Do you miss me? I miss your voice and your presence and all your darling ways.

Your
Wig.

Could you bring Ribni at Xmas? There is a shop in Nice which cures poupées cassées [broken dolls]. When I read of it I almost telegraphed for Ribni. I want him to be made good as new again. He haunts me. Ah, I can see a story in this idea ...

To J. M. Murry

[Villa Isola Bella, Menton, 1 November 1920]
Monday. Midi. Waiting for Lunch. 'En tirant
la langue comme un chien [drooling like a
dog]' as they say here.

My Own Precious
  Its simply heavenly here today—warm, still, with wisps of cloud just here & there & le ciel [the sky] deep blue. Everything is expanding & growing after the rain; the buds on the tea roses are so exquisite that one feels quite faint regarding them. A pink rose—'chinesy pink' in my mind—is out—there are multitudes of flowers and buds. And the freesias are up & the tangerines are turning. A painter whose ladder I see against the house across the valley has been singing ancient church music—awfully complicated stuff. But what a choice! How much more suited to the day and the hour than—and now, Im dished. For every song I wanted to find ridiculous seems somehow charming & appropriate & quite equally lovable.

I put more white wash on the old woman's face
Than I did on the gar-den wall!

For instance. That seems to me a thoroughly good song. You know the first two lines are

Up an' down up an' down in an' out the window
I did no good at all.

Sam Mayo used to sing it.° Things werent so bad in those days. I really believe everything was better. The tide of barbarism wasn't flowing in.

Oh, Bogey I want to ask you. Did you care about the Mayor of Cork?° It was a most terrible shock to me. Id been reading about his appaling suffering in the Eclaireur and you know I never thought he *would* die. I thought he simply couldnt. It was a ghastly tragedy. Again, I feel the people ought to have rushed out of the prison and made Lloyd George or whoever it was free him. My plan (this sounds heartless; yes, but I would have done it, Im not laughing at the Lord Mayor—God forbid) was to kidnap Megan Lloyd George° & inform the père [father] that as long as the Lord Mayor was imprisoned she went unfed. Why don't the Sinn Feiners do things like this. Murder Carson for instance,° instead of hunger strike.

After lunch
Ive read your Baudelaire.° I think its extremely fine—really *masterly*. It made me thirst after a book of such critical portraits. Youve made a most extraordinary leap forward in your *power of interpreting*. One used to feel with you a certainty that the knowledge was there but a kind of difficulty prevented you from sharing it. There was in spite of your desire to express yourself *almost an involuntary* withholding of something. Thats very difficult to explain. I felt it until quite recently, really. And now that its gone not only have I the readers deep 'relief' but I seem (am I fantastic) almost to rejoice in your consciousness of your liberation as well.

Goodbye dearest love. No letters today—as yet. <u>Next</u> month we meet! Oh, *Bogey*.

Your
Wig.

I was all wrong about the house painter!! Hes just come back from lunch in a grey flannel suit, put on his white overall & started singing in English! Elizabethan airs. He must be some sensible fellow who's taken the little house and is doing the job himself. He makes me think of you—but his singing is different—more difficult, darling.

'What is milk a *metre* now?' L. M.

Dream I.

I was living at home again in the room with the fire escape. It was night: Father & Mother in bed. Vile people came into my room. They were drunk. Beatrice Hastings led them. 'You dont take me in old dear' said she. 'Youve played the Lady once too often, Miss—coming it over me.' And she shouted, screamed *Femme marqué* [Scarlet woman] and banged the table. I rushed away. I was going away next morning so I decided to spend the night in dark streets and went to a theatre in Piccadilly Circus. The play a costume play of the Restoration had just begun. The theatre was small and packed. Suddenly the people began to speak too slowly, to mumble: they looked at each other stupidly. One by one they *drifted* off the stage & very slowly a black iron curtain was lowered. The people in the audience *looked* at one another. Very slowly, silently, they got up and moved towards the doors—stole away.

An enormous crowd filled the Circus: it was black with people. They were not speaking—a low murmur came from it—that was all. They were still. A whitefaced man looked over his shoulder & *trying to smile* he said: 'The Heavens are changed already; there are six moons!'

Then I realised that *our* earth had come to an end. I looked up. The sky was ashy-green; six livid quarters swam in it. A very fine soft ash began to fall. The crowd parted. A cart drawn by two small black horses appeared. Inside there were salvation army women doling tracts out of huge marked boxes. They gave me one. 'Are you Corrupted?' It got very dark and quiet and the ash fell faster. Nobody moved.

Dream II

In a café. Gertler met me. 'Katherine you must come to my table. Ive got Oscar Wilde there. Hes the most marvellous man I ever met. Hes splendid!' Gertler was flushed. When he spoke of Wilde he began to cry—tears hung on his lashes but he smiled.

Oscar Wilde was very shabby. He wore a green overcoat. He kept tossing & tossing back his long greasy hair with the whitest hand. When he met me he said: 'Oh *Katherine*!'—very affected.

But I did find him a fascinating talker. So much so I asked him
to come to my home. He said would 12.30 tonight do? When I
arrived home it seemed madness to have asked him. Father &
Mother were in bed. What if Father came down & found that
chap Wilde in one of the chintz armchairs? Too late now. I
waited by the door. He came with Lady Ottoline. I saw he was
disgustingly pleased to have brought her. Dear *Lady* Ottoline &
Ottoline in a red hat on her rust hair *'hounyhming'*° along. He
said 'Katherine's hand—the same gentle hand!' as he took
mine. But again when we sat down—I couldn't help it. He *was*
attractive—as a curiosity. He was fatuous & brilliant!

'You know Katherine when I was *in that dreadful place*° I was
haunted by the memory of a *cake*. It used to float in the air
before me—a little delicate thing *stuffed* with cream and with
the cream there was something *scarlet*. It was made of *pastry* and
I used to call it my little Arabian Nights cake. But I couldn't
remember the name. Oh, Katherine it was *torture*. It used to
hang in the air and *smile* at me, and every time I resolved that
next time *they let some one* come and see me I would ask them to
tell me what it was but every time, Katherine, I was *ashamed*.
Even now . . .'

I said 'mille feuilles à la creme? [cream puffs?]' At that he
turned round in the armchair and began to sob, and Ottoline
who carried a parasol opened it and put it over him . . .

To J. M. Murry

[Villa Isola Bella, Menton] Wednesday.
[10 November 1920]

Darling little Fellow,

Your long descriptive letter has come. Dont observe too
much. I feel at the end you were <u>gasping</u>. I dont want you to
see more than its easy to see. Yes, I do admire your observations
of course & I am ashamed to say a wave of pure disgusting
female relief went over me at your description of Rose Macaulay.° I was lying on my bed, dressed in a peach coloured
handkerberchief having my bang de soleil [sun bath] and I

kicked up my toes at their dinner. Oh, how it does *bore* me—the Naomi type° & that kind of conversation. If I were there & you were there we should do something desperate. Youd make yourself a ladder & Id climb on to your head & turn there on one toe. (Perhaps). All that you said about Elizabeth [Russell] is extremely interesting. And the queer thing is that she only wants a *male appearance*. Theres her essential falsity. Forgive my frankness: she has no use for a physical lover. I mean to go to bed with. Anything but that. That she cant stand—she'd be frightened of. Her very life, her very being, her gift, her vitality, all that makes her depends upon her *not surrendering*. I sometimes wonder whether the act of surrender is not one of the greatest of all—the highest. It is one of the [most] difficult of all. Can it be accomplished or even apprehended except by the *aristocrats* of this world? You see its so immensely complicated. It 'needs' real humility and at the same time an absolute belief in ones own essential freedom. It is an act of faith. At the last moments like all great acts it is *pure risk*. This is true for me as a human being and as a writer. Dear Heaven how hard it is to let go—to step into the blue. And yet ones creative life depends on it and one *desires* to do nothing else. I shouldn't have begun on this in the corner of a letter, darling. Its not the place.

> Forgive
> Wig.

Darling Bogey

Kissing is a queer thing. I was standing under a tree just now—a tree that is shedding exquisite golden yellow leaves all over my garden path. And suddenly one leaf made the most ethereal advances to me and in another moment we were kissing each other. Through the silvery branches one can see the deep blue sky . . . lapis lazuli.

I think the time has come it really has come for us to do a little courting. Have we ever had time to stand under trees and tell our love? Or to sit down by the sea and make fragrant zones for each other? The tea roses are in flower. Do you know the peculiar exquisite scent of a tea rose? Do you know how the bud opens—so unlike other roses and how deep red the thorns are and almost purple the leaves?

I think it must be the orange flower which Marie has

brought home from market. I have been arranging branches of
it in jars and little slips of it in shallow glass bowls. And the
house has a perfume as tho the Sultan were expecting the
première visite [initiating visit] of his youngest bride. Marie,
standing over me chanted the while—almost sang a hymn to
the cyclamen sauvage qu'on trouve dans les montagnes [wild
cyclamen one finds in the mountains] and the little violettes de
mon pays [local violets] which grow so thick that one trempe
ses pieds dedans [drenches one's feet in them].

If I live here much longer I shall become a bush of daphne
or you'll find no one to welcome you but a jasmine. Perhaps its
the effect of receiving the Sun every morning—très intime
[very intimate]—the lady clad only in a black paper fan. But
you must come here, you must live here in the South and forget
greyness. It is *divine* here—no less.

Wig.

To J. M. Murry

[Villa Isola Bella, Menton,
10 November 1920]

My precious Bogey
I am awfully excited today. Its for this reason. I have made
an offer to Jinnie for this villa for one year from May 1st next
and tho' the offer has not been accepted it has also not been
refused. Chances are even. *Oh dear what torture.* Perhaps you
don't know that my feelings towards this villa are so fearfully
intense that I think I shall have to be evicted if she doesn't give
it to me. Its the first real home of my own I have ever loved.
Pauline—yes, it wasn't home tho', neither was Runcton, not
even Hampstead. Not really—not with this thrill. This little
place is and always will be for me the one and only place, I feel.
My heart beats for it like it beats for Karori. Isn't it awful. And
for us it is made in every single particular. True theres no salle
de bain [bathroom]. But theres a huge saucer bath and a spung
as big as me. So what matters! The divine incomparable
situation is the trick, I suppose. Heaven from dawn to dawn.

Walking on the terrace by starlight looking up through my vieux palmier [old palm tree] I could weep for joy. Running into the garden to see how many more buds are out in the morning is to run straight at—into—a blessing. The fires all burn—but not frightfully. The doors shut. The kitchen is big & the larder is down 10 steps that send a chill to ones knees. The garde-linge [linen-cupboard] is immense, all fitted with cupboards & shelves. The luggage is kept there & the umbrellas & the flags that flew at my gate on the 11th. One gets ones parasol from the garde-linge. Your feltie would be there, too. There's enough garden for you to bien gratter [scratch about] in. At the back we could grow veg. In fack it is the dearest most ideal little corner. And private—just the next thing to an island.

If Jinnie accepts I thought we'd stay on here until le grand chaleur [the great heat]. Then take the funicular to Annunciata for those weeks & leave Marie here. She could come up & take away our laundry & bring it back & generally keep our things in order while we were there. I mean shed come by the day. It only takes 40 minutes to the hotel. Wed be back here in September & plant a *terrific* garden. Do you like the plan? You see we'd know just where we were for that first year. No worry. No moving. You'd <u>rest</u>. No responsibility. Youd just I pray get rested & happy & loaf about & garden & play with me & whistle on the stairs. There are 3 bedrooms not counting Maries room so you could have a guest if you liked.

Bogey—hold thumbs for me. Truly this is a great turning point. Im trying to be calm but its not easy with such bliss in the balance. I had to offer an immense sum—6000 francs. That means your share of the rent is 3000 for the year and the franc is at present at 57.

Am I a little bit mad? You will find ISOLA BELLA in poker work on my heart. The baths are only 10 minutes away for you in the summer—sea baths with splash boards—no springboard for you to plop off. I wait outside with a bun for you with big currant eyes (the bun I mean).

Je t'aime [I love you]. But *do* wish it will come true!!!

Wig.

Do you love me as I love you? Its getting frightfully urgent. I mean a kind of sweet blissful longing excitment & joy—always <u>joy</u>.

To J. M. Murry

[Villa Isola Bella, Menton,
c.8 December 1920]

I have sent back the books today.

My dear Bogey

It is with the most extreme reluctance that I am writing to tell you K. M. cant go on.° The fact is she ought to have given up months ago but money was so urgent that she dared not. I know you suggested a months holiday—but a months holiday doesn't fit the case. She wont be well in a month. The strain will begin all over again, and I think she has told you fairly often *what* a strain it is.

She would not, however, have taken this step if Doctor Bouchage° had not made her realise it was *absolutely necessary*. He has. It is not that her health is worse than it was in London. But its no better. She has good days she didn't have then; but she has BAD ones she didn't, either. And she is not improving, as they say.

In two words—& plain ones: its a question of shortening her life, to keep on. And that she cant do.

But you must realise how deeply she 'appreciates' the awkwardness of this for you. She knows it all: feels it all.

One thing must be perfectly clear. She wants NO money from you and no sacrifice. She hates even discussing money affairs with you. She knows you have paid debts of hers; she hopes they are the last you'll ever pay. *This is final*. You may smile at this and say: 'I haven't any money to give her, at any rate'—Right-o. But she just had to tell you.

And now Ill be personal, darling. Look here you ought to have sent me that Corona! You really ought to have. Can't you possibly imagine what all this writing out has been to a person as weak as I *damnably* am? You can't or a stone would have sent it. You knew what a help it was to me in London.

But oh dear I don't mean to accuse you—because I cant bear, as you know, to make you feel unhappy. But what you would have saved me—I cant *say*! Isn't it awful that I have not dared to *add to your burdens* by reminding you before? Thats Mother in me. And you rather count on it, my darling.

But don't feel sad—or knocked over—or don't take any of this too seriously. Easy to say—isn't it. Yes, all the same its not RIGHT to <u>live</u> among mountains of gloom—or to sweat blood as one climbs them. One must just run on top and be careless. I don't now mean that in putting you in this hole Im laughing at the hole. But think of the hole that I might so easily trip into!! Its far bigger—far blacker—but I <u>wont</u> moan.

This is a very mixed letter. You ought just to love me—thats all the best—and you *must* understand.

Your own
Tig

Darling

I open this letter to say Ive just got yours of the 5th. The Morning Post is very 'whiskery'—isn't it. But oh, I wish I didn't have to send my letter! Your letter makes it so hard.

My chill is a bit better today but always there. 'C'est pas gran' chose mais enfin [it's not a big deal but enough]' is the feeling.

Ive had a letter from Squire° saying my story is at the printers & asking for another as soon as & whenever I have one. Ill give you one to take back.

Now about things you ought to bring. Do you mean—for me? I have no commissions for you. Bring warm clothes for yourself. Its v. cold here & the last leaves are gone. We are very exposed—all our lovely trees are bare. I fear you will not think it is very pretty at all. The lemons shine on bare boughs, & the freckled tangerines have two little leaves left to fly with.

I feel so queer—so *abnormal*—shorn of my job that I can scarcely write to you until I have heard. And it pains me to think I shant be there in the paper. Im shut out. But it cant be helped. No complaining!

Farewell my darling
Wig.

To J. M. Murry

[Villa Isola Bella, Menton,
12 December 1920]

Bogey

A letter has come from you in which you say you are 'annihilated' & tell me of Madame la Princesse° because you think your — — — what shall I call it—meeting her may have had something to do with my illness. Well, Bogey—please let me speak.

I told you to be free—because I meant it. What happens in your personal life does <u>not</u> affect me. I have of you what I want—a relationship which is unique but it is not what the world understands by *marriage*. That is to say I do not in any way *depend* on you, neither can you shake me.

Nobody can. I do not know how it is but I live *withdrawn* from my personal life. (This is hard to say.) I am a writer first. In the past, it is true, when I worked less, my writing self was merged in my personal self. I felt conscious of you—to the exclusion of almost everything, at times. (All this is just outline.)

But now I do not. You are dearer than anyone in the world to me—but more than anything else—more even than talking or laughing or being happy I want to write. This sounds so ugly; I wish I didn't have to say it. But your letter makes me feel you would be relieved if it were said.

Cant we stop this *horrible drama*! I hate explaining myself: its so unnatural to me. It makes me feel indecent.

Let us quit ourselves like men.°

Tig.

This is much harsher than I feel, but you compel me to speak out. It isn't even *as* I feel; its so crude. But I simply CANT — — — bear your lack of a sense of proportion. It *will* be the ruin of us both.

To Anne Drey

Villa Isola Bella, | Garavan | Menton | A/M. |
26 xii 1920

My Precious Friend,

The parcel arrived on Xmas morning but it was a separate fête by itself—just your letter & the two enchanting sketches. I love them, Anne. They remind me of our spring together & the laburnum seems hung with little laughs. If you knew how often I think of that time at Looe—our pic-nic, the white-eyed Kaffir, the midget infant hurling large pieces of Cornwall into the sea on the beach that afternoon! Its all as clear as today.

But you know—dont you?—that all the times we have ever spent together are clear like that. And here—I am always sending you greetings—always sharing things with you. I salute you in tangerines and the curved petals of roses thé [tea-roses] and the crocus colour of the sea & in the moonlight on the poire sauvage [wild pear]. Many many other things. It will *always* be so with me however seldom I see you. I shall just go on rejoicing in the fact of you and loving you and feeling in that family where Monsieur le Beau Soleil est notre père nous sommes des soeurs [the warm sun is our father, we are sisters]. But all that's jolly fine. I shan't be content, darling, unless we do have a real summer together one day with the blessed enfant pouring sand down our necks . . . . .

Murry tells me you are working. I hope it goes very well. I hope there are a whole flock of masterpieces with canvas wings flying towards you from shadowy 1921. Whenever I *examine* things here—the lovely springing line of flowers & peach leaves, par exemple, I realise what a marvellous painter you are—the beauty of your line—the *life* behind it.

I am still hard at the story writing and still feeling that only now do I begin to see what I want to do. Im sending you my book.° Its not a good one. I promise the next will be better but I just wanted you to have a copy. Living solitary these last months with a servant who is a born artist & says 'un ou deux bananes faisent plus *intrigantes* le compotier [one or two bana-

nas make the fruit-bowl more *intriguing*]' & who returns from
market with a basket which just to see on the kitchen table is
food for the day—makes work a great deal easier to get at. The
strain is removed. At last one doesn't worry any more. And
fancy ones domestique having an idea of what work is! She
won't even let a person talk at the front door if Im working.
She whispers to them to go to la porte de la cuisine [the kitchen
door] ... parce que c'est tres enervant pour Madame d'en-
tendre causer quelqu'un pendant qu'elle travaille [because it's
very disturbing for Madame to hear someone talking while she
works]! Its like being in Heaven with an ange gardienne
[guardian angel].

Murry is here for Christmas. The weather is superb &
champagne is only 30 francs a bottle. There is always un feu
d'enfer in my chambre à coucher [a raging fire in my bed-
room]. The result is, chère (oh I can only say these things to
you!) we are continually suggesting to Marie she should go to
Vespers, Bénediction, la messe [Mass]. The poor old creature
can't understand this mania de la pousser vers l'église [to push
her to church]. Its a mystery! But what is one to do? The house
is so small. I send her to market, to the poste, out to see her
friends—anywhere .... and when she comes back she cries
Dieu me garde! Que Madame et Monsieur ont bonne mine!
[God help me! Madame and Monsieur look on top of the
world!] Champagne in this air & this sun is unsafe for all
people under—say ninety-nine! Queer it is. I believe if I lived
in England I could be a eunuch quite cheerfully, but .....
there's something in the air of France — — — which is very
restorative, lets say.

To turn to more serious subjects. How awfully well Drey
writes in The Athenaeum. I do so immensely enjoy his articles.
He's the only man who seems to write about painting as though
it wasn't first put through the intellectual mincing machine.
Will you tell him how awfully I like his work & serre lui la main
pour moi [press his hand for me]?

I hear that he has been to MY Sorapure. There's a doctor—
and a very fine honest man.

Darling—its lunch time—I tremble de faim [tremble with
hunger]. Bless you for Ever. Take care of your self. Come to

France soon. Let us meet one day soon—and until then know you have my deep love & devotion.

Toujours

Your
Katherine

To Richard Murry

VILLA ISOLA BELLA | GARAVAN | MENTON
A/M. | 17.I.1921.

My dear Richard,

If you knew how I love hearing from you and how honoured I am by your confidence! I want you to feel I am a *real* sister to you. Will you? Remember that here is your sister Katherine who is not only interested in everything that you do but who wants to be made use of. Treat me as a person you have the right to ask things of. Look here—if you want anything & you haven't the dibs—come to me *bang* off and if I have the money you're welcome to it—without a single hesitation. Ill always be truthful with you, that's a promise. Ill be dead straight with you in everything.

Why I am saying all this is (I see your eyes rolling and your hair rising in festoons of amazement and I dont care!) Well, why I am saying it is that we 'artists' are not like ordinary people and there are times when to know we have a fellow workman who's ready to do all in his power, because he loves you and believes in you, is a nice comfortable feeling. I adore *Life* but my experience of the world is that its pretty terrible. I hope yours will be a very different one dear old boy, but just in case . . . [if] you'd like to shout Katherine at any moment— here she is—See?

Having got that off my ches' (which is at this moment more like a chest of super-sharp-edged cutlery) let me say how I appreciate all you feel about *craft*. Yes, I think youre absolutely right. I see your *approach* to painting as very individual. Emotion for you seems to grow out of deliberation—looking long at a thing. Am I getting at anything right? In the way a thing is made—it may be a tree or a woman or a gazelle or a dish of fruit—you get your inspiration. This sounds a bit too simple when it is written down & rather like 'Professor Leonard The Indian Palmist'. I mean something though. Its a very queer thing how *craft* comes into writing. I mean down to details. Par exemple. In Miss Brill° I chose not only the length of every sentence, but even the sound of every sentence—I chose the rise and fall of every paragraph to fit her—and to fit her on that day at that very moment. After Id written it I read it aloud—numbers of times—just as one would *play over* a musical composition, trying to get it nearer and nearer to the expression of Miss Brill—until it fitted her.

Don't think Im vain about the little sketch. Its only the method I wanted to explain. I often wonder whether other writers do the same. If a thing has really come off it seems to me there mustn't be one single word out of place or one word that could be taken out. Thats how I AIM at writing. It will take some time to get anywhere near there.

But you know Richard, I was only thinking last night people have hardly begun to write yet. Put poetry out of it for a moment & leave out Shakespeare—now I mean prose. Take the very best of it. Aren't they still cutting up sections rather than tackling the whole of a mind? I had a moment of absolute terror in the night. I suddenly thought of *a living mind*—a whole mind—with absolutely nothing left out. With *all* that one knows how much does one *not* know? I used to fancy one knew all but some kind of mysterious core (or one could). But now I believe just the opposite. The unknown is far far greater than the known. The known is only a mere shadow. This is a fearful thing and terribly hard to face. But it must be faced.

Well, thats enough at a time for you. I hope you're not bored. I long to see the landscape. Am I to be allowed to hang it on my walls to bear me company?

With my love to you
Ever
Katherine.

To Richard Murry

VILLA ISOLA BELLA | GARAVAN | MENTON
A/M | February 3rd 1921

My dear Richard,

I dont suppose you really realise what your two last letters to me have been like. Well, I must say Ive *never* had any letters to beat them, and when you are in Paradise I hope the Lord will present you with two brushes of comets hair in token of appreciation for same. Paint brushes, of course I mean. In the meantime je vous serre le main bien fort [I press your hand very warmly] as they say, for them ... I'll take em in order.

The first, I must say, was what the French newspapers call un espèce de bowl-over! [a kind of bowl-over!] Your interview with Fate (not forgetting his Secretary) written on that beautiful leming coloured paper was simply a proof of what you could do at this imaginative short story writing if you really got going. Richard Murry enters the ring & shows Kid Mansfield How to Do it. I leave the drawing of the scene to you—me, in black welvet shorts with a crochet lace collar and you in a kind of zebra tights costume ... Well, dear old boy you wiped the ring with me. Not only that I do really think that things have taken a Turn and that Jack and I have seen our worst days. Hope so, at any rate.

I think your Easter plan is a first rate one. Its down in my diary as a certainty. Do lets bring it off! Dont worry about the fare. When the time comes just put your toospeg brush, pyjamas and a collar (for Sundays & fête days) into a handkerchief & Ill send along the ticket & a dotted line for you to follow. Seriously a rucksack is all you'll need. My grandpa said a man could travel all over the world with a clean pair of socks and a rook rifle. At the age of 70 odd he started for England thus equipped but Mother took fright & added a handkerchief or two. When he returned he was shorn of everything but a large watering can which he'd bought in London for his young marrows. I don't suggest him as a Man to be Followed, however. Already, just with the idea of you coming Ive seen you on the terrace—the three of us, talking. Ive packed the picnic basket & weve gone off for the day.

Lunch under the olive trees ... and so on ... Richard dear, it will be awful if it doesn't come true! We must make it. Jack has a scheme to meet you in Paris & convey you to and from The Louvre on your way.

Well, I now come to your Letter II containing your photograph. I love having it. You have, as Koteliansky used to say, an 'extremely nice face', Richard. Being fond of you as I am I read into it all sorts of signs of the future painter ... I believe they are all there.

My honest opinion is that if there is a person going on the right lines—you are he. I can't tell you how right I feel you are. It seems to me like this. Here is painting, and here is life. We can't separate them. Both of them have suffered an upheaval extraordinary in the last few years. There is a kind of tremendous agitation going on still, but so far anything that has come to the surface seems to have been experimental or a fluke—a lucky accident. I believe the only way to *live* as artists under these new conditions in art and life is to put everything to the test for ourselves. We've got, in the long run, to be our own teachers. There's no getting away from that. We've got to win through by ourselves. Well, as I see it, the only way to do that honestly, dead truthfully, shirking nothing and leaving nothing out, is to put everything to the test. (Your desire for technical knowledge is a kind of profound *symbol*.) Not only to face things, but really to find out of what they are composed. How can we know where we are, otherwise? How can we prevent ourselves being weak in certain places? To be *thorough*, to be *honest*, I think if artists were really thorough & honest they would save the world. Its the lack of those things & the reverse of them that [are] putting a deadly blight on life. Good work takes upon itself a Life—bad work has death in it.

Well, (forgive me if Im dull, old boy) your longing for technical knowledge seems to me profoundly what an artist ought to feel today. Its a kind if deep sign of the times—rather the Zeitgeist [spirit of the time]—thats the better word. Your generation & mine too has been 'put off' with imitations of the real thing and we're bound to react violently if we're sincere. This takes so long to write & it sounds so heavy. Have I conveyed what I mean to even? You see I too have a passion for technique. I have a passion making the thing into a *whole* if you know what I mean. Out of technique is born real style, I believe. There are no short cuts.

Look out! I mustn't get off the lines. Ive just read your last pages again. An aesthetic emotion is what we feel in front of *a work of art*—one doesn't feel an aesthetic emotion about a thing, but about its artistic representation. Example: Richard Murry in front of Portrait of Madame Manet.

Oh Richard! Believe me! I think you're terribly right to feel as you do and not to pretend. Only, dear old boy, the price you pay for your honesty is you don't have any false thrills about the pose & the form & the vision. I don't mean the chaps in your class are insincere, but evidently you are coming to it in a different way. Don't forget that intellectually you are stages beyond the men you draw with. That makes you critical in a way its very rare to be when one is starting out.

But I wish you were not so far away. I wish the garden gate flew open for you often & that you came in & out & we talked—not as in London—more easily and more happily. I shall pin the sun into the sky for every day of your holiday and at night I shall arrange for a constant supply of the best moonlight.

Well, my fellow worker—lets get on with the job. If its any help to you to know theres someone who believes in you . . . here she is. The House Flag is always flying.
Goodbye for now.

With a whole mountain of love
Katherine

Jack will be in London on Bunday [*sic*].

To Sydney Waterlow

VILLA ISOLA BELLA | GARAVAN | MENTON
A/M. | 9 II 1921

My dear Sydney,

Don't feel bound to answer this, but I can't *enjoy* a letter as I did yours without saying thank you . . . And I want to tell you a queer thing. You know where you speak of your 'superiority of apprehension' ... God knows we have seen little enough of each other, & I hadn't (to be frank) the faintest idea that you thought of me other than as a 'cold aloof little creature'—that you shared the general opinion, in fact. And yet, just before Christmas I wrote a very long story & y<u>ou</u> were my reader. I hope that doesn't sound impertinent. I confess the impression was that you enjoyed the story, *saw* it, *felt* it, as I did—in a quite special way that outsiders wouldn't appreciate. I even had a mental picture of you sitting in an armchair, reading it. It is called, in case you should ever see it 'The Daughters of the Late Colonel' ... and Squire is going to publish it in The Mercury.

Let me salute you, Sydney, through my story; let us be friends because of it. Good Heavens if you knew how pleasant it is to know there is someone who cares to tell you he makes his fire first arranging the twigs in a pyramid, & that the logs are 'self cut'. I share that delicious first moment & while I warm my fingers I forget these nasty foreign palms ... Your room sounds lovely.

I shall never live in England again. I recognise Englands admirable qualities, but we simply don't get on. We have nothing to say to each other; we are always meeting as strangers. Murry, on the other hand is *made* for England and I am certain he will not remain abroad for long. I understand that very well in him. No, Ill go finally to some place like Yalta & build a little house at Oreanda°—if I *do* succeed in keeping the coffin from the door for so long.

What are you going to do in the immediate future, I wonder. Where are you going to live. And I wonder if you are happy and what you really think about Life & if you have friends— real friends.

I am sitting up in bed in an ugly little room with a huge dead clock in it & a pink screen worked with a needlework picture. *Scène*: Game of billiards *sur l'herbe fraiche* [on the cool grass]. Lady with die-away look being kissed by military party & very impertinent dog looking on. At moments it seems to me that <u>all</u> France, <u>all</u> French literature is in that picture. The wind is blowing. Strange shadows fly over the walls & ceiling from the palm outside, and these quick shadows are awfully beautiful ...

Lebe wohl [Goodbye]|With love from
Katherine.

To S. S. Koteliansky

VILLA ISOLA BELLA | GARAVAN | MENTON
A/M. [19 February 1921]

What has happened to the inkstand with the elephants on it—mother-of-pearl, inlay—or was it ivory. Some of the inlay had begun to come off; I fancy one of the elephants had lost one eye. And that dim little picture of a snowy landscape hanging on the wall in your room. Where is it now? And where are the kittens and the children and Christ, who looked awfully like a kitten, too, who used to hang in the dining room. And that leather furniture with the tufts of horsehair stuffing coming out.

Where are all the hats from the hatstand. And do you remember for how long the bell was broken. Then there was the statue on the stairs, smiling, the fair caretaker, always washing up, the little children always falling through her door.

And your little room with the tiny mirror and the broken window & the piano sounding from outside. Those were very nice teacups—thin—a nice shape, and the tea was awfully good—so hot. 'At the Vienna Café° there is good bread.' And the cigarettes. The packet done up in writing paper you take from your pocket. It is folded so neatly at the ends like a parcel from the chemist's.

And then Slatkovsky°—his *beard*, his 'glad eye', his sister, who sat in front of the fire and took off her boot. The two girls who came to see him the Classic Day his Father died.

And the view from your window—you remember? The typist sits there & her hat & coat hang in the hall. Now an Indian in a turban walks up that street opposite to the British Museum *quartier*.

It begins to rain. The streets are very crowded. It is dusky. Now people are running downstairs. That heavy outer door slams. And now the umbrellas go up in the street and it is much darker, suddenly. Dear friend—do not think evil of me—forgive me.

Kissienka.

To Dorothy Brett

VILLA ISOLA BELLA | GARAVAN | MENTON
A/M. [1 March 1921]

Dear Brett

You sound so rich in plans, determinations, adventures and
'*Revelations*' that I feel my ambling nag can scarce keep pace
with such a swift charger. And then—what do you mean
exactly by revelations? And how do they beget other revelations? I don't know—I feel mystified ...

Im sure its an awfully good plan to go into the country for
the summer, and what luck to have Sylvia Sullivan° to paint.
She would be a lovely little creature under a tree, I should
think. I feel I have been awfully wanting in kindness to Sylvia
Sullivan: Im sure she's simple and very lovable really. But
you'll find out in the summer.

Don't blame your parents too much! We *all* had parents.
There is only one way of escaping from their influence and that
is by going into the matter with yourself—examining yourself
& making perfectly sure of their share.

It can be done. One is *NEVER* free until one has done
blaming somebody or praising somebody for what is bad &
good in one. Don't you feel that? By that I dont mean we ought
to live each of us on an island. On the contrary—Life is
relationship—its giving & taking—but thats not quite the same
as making others *responsible*, is it? There lies the danger. Dont
think I underestimate the enormous power that parents can
have. I dont. Its staggering—its titanic. After all they are real
giants when we are only table high & they act according. But
like everything else in Life—I mean all suffering, however
great—we have to get over it, to cease from harking back to it,
to grin & bear it & to hide our wounds. More than that and far
more true is we have to find the *gift* in it. We cant afford to
waste such an expenditure of feeling; we have to learn from
it—and we <u>do</u>, I most deeply believe come to be thankful for it.
By saying we cant afford to waste — — feeling I sound odious
& cynical. I don't feel it. What I mean is—*everything must be
accepted.*

But I run on—and Im dull. How lovely your Down country sounded. Larks, too!

I am only on nodding acquaintance with Spring. We talk from the window. But she looks from this distance fairer than ever, more radiant, more exquisite. It is marvellous to know the earth is turned to the light. Murry is very well. He looks and sounds happy. I don't see a great deal of him as Im finishing a book & he's terribly busy. I wonder what you think of the fat Nation or the thin Athenaeum—like Jack Spratt & his wife. Fare well. Be happy!

K.M.

To Ida Baker

Tuesday. [Villa Isola Bella, Menton,
8 March 1921]

This is just a note to let you know that tout va bien à la maison [everything at the house is fine]. It is the late afternoon of an exquisite day. That heavy evening rain that made water spouts of Jack's trousers fell like a blessing upon the garden. When I went out today the air smelt like moss, and there was a bee to every wallflower. The peach leaves are like linnet wings; the branches of the fig are touched with green, the bush of may is just not in flower. I had to lift up the daffodils & set them on their legs again and to give a finger to the reclining freezias. But nothing had come to harm. As to that white rose bush over the gate & the gas meter it is sprinkled with thousands of tiny satin fine clusters. This is a darling little garden when one can get out of ones shell & look at it. But what does it profit a man to look at anything if he is not *free*? Unless one is free to offer oneself up wholly and solely to the pansy—one receives nothing. Its promiscuous love instead of a living relationship— a dead thing. But there it is—And my gland is a great deal more swollen for some reason. The blood goes on tapping squeezing through like a continual small hammering and all that side of my head is numb. Its a vile thing.

I hope you had a good journey. Will you please wire me

immediately if you want any money & Ill wire it to you. I am now v. serious. Don't go to other people first. I can so easily over draw for now: I dont care a button. But you must feed properly in London, eat nourishing food—not scones & coffee, and you must take taxis. Dont buy things in bags & eat them. Make Violet cook you porridge, bacon & eggs & toast for breakfast. That climate is the devil. And wear a thick scarf when you go out & change your shoes & stockings when you come in. And burn the anthracite. And get people to come & see you if you want to see them & make Violet cook for them. I feel you will never be sensible enough to keep warm, dry shod and fed. I have no confidence in you.

I wish I were back in that Hampstead house, wafted to the top landing, allowed to linger on the stairs to look out of the windows to see if the lemon verbena is still alive. It should have been a perfect little house: it never came to flower. And the view of the willows—bare now, and the room that was mine— so lovely. The light was always like the light in a pale shell.

Tell me what happens. Take things easy. I beg you to wire me for money without hesitating. Dont work too hard.

Try and be happy; be sure to keep well

Katherine.

To Ida Baker

(Confidential) | Sunday. [Villa Isola Bella,
Menton, 13 March 1921]

I really must tell you this or jump out of bed or out of the window. You'll appreciate it so. I paid the surgeon on the nail yesterday. That was all right. I expected to. Only 100. But Jack came down & paid the cocher [driver]. When I said Id paid the surgeon he replied 'The cocher is mine. I agreed on the price 20 francs beforehand'. Just now—making out the weeks bills he asked me for 11 francs for the carriage—half, plus a 2 franc tip! I think its awful to have to say it. But fancy not paying for your wifes carriage to & from the surgery! Is that simply extraordinary or am I? I really am staggered. I think it is the meanest thing I ever heard of. Its not the fact which is so queer but the lack of fine feeling. I suppose if one fainted he would make one pay 3d for a 6d glass of sal volatile and 1d on the glass. That really does beat Father.

Things are serene otherwise. My head hurts but not more than is to be expected. Cousin Lou° has been in today. Shes infinitely kind and affectionate. In fact she lavishes kindness on me in an old fashioned family way.

The old villain° is being as sweet as sugar. Hangs up my dresses, puts away my hats, brings up supper for 2 into this room without a murmur. I feel like Koteliansky when he says: 'Let her be beaten—simply—but to death!' I hope to hear from you tomorrow.

Dont rush things. Keep well & be happy!

ALL IS WELL
Katherine.

To Sydney Waterlow

VILLA ISOLA BELLA | GARAVAN | MENTON
A/M. | 16. III. 1921

Dear Sydney

Since receiving your letter Life has driven me through dark little doorways, down underground passages which ended this week in one of those white tiled rooms, with glass shelves, a fine display of delicate steel, too many wash basins, a frosted windy glass & a narrow little black sofa with steel grips for the patient to cling to. Here the surgeon & my doctor decided to risk it and plunged about $2\frac{1}{2}$ inches of hollow knitting needle into my neck & withdrew it. Success triumphant. This process, repeated twice or thrice will, they hope, in time, relieve the accumulation ... And so on and so on and so on ...

Brett sends me a silly letter: I return a tart reply. But really to emerge, to be above ground long enough, peacefully enough to take my friend by the hand & beg him not to talk of 'boring me' and not to imagine Ill accept 'obvious explanations'—thats been awfully difficult. In fact its not been possible. So Ive had to risk your cursing me and turning away from me and thinking your very worst.

All the same, *I* shall risk coming back to my small place by the fire. I shall even pretend (until I know) that you understand and are not at all fierce . . . I loved your letter. Life is so very short. Let me say again, quickly, nothing you can tell me *bores* me. The only thing in the world that bores me is falsity, insincerity. I cannot tell you how I value, how I appreciate, anything you may ever care to tell me. But I wish you may soon know me well enough to feel I do not misunderstand you — — —

Yes, I feel you are going to write. Its in your letters. They have that curious deliberate quality of one who is revolving something in his mind. What is it? I feel that you can afford to, and you do, see Life as you see it at present because you are absorbed in something else.

And heres a queer idea for which I've no justification. I feel certain that one day you'll write a play. But a very fine play. Or is that wide of the mark.

You see, as I 'see' you (forgive me if I ever sound impertinent. Its so hard to speak from a distance) you have been moving hidden through Life. You have been a hidden, secret spectator when *les autres* [*the others*] did not even know that YOU were by. You have lived by apprehensions far far more than most people, I imagine. But I am timid of talking to you about yourself—even though I want to so much. You may dislike it extremely.

Is your new room your real *writing room*? Will you be working late there at the weekends? And what do your windows look out on. It will be lovely as the spring advances. I love a room that is a fortress and I love to work at night. To be free to get up and lean out of [the] window into that dark, airy stillness— is happiness. Dear Heaven! How little has been written about the extraordinary charm of <u>not</u> going to bed at night! Only to think of it and one passes into a whole strange world where to be awake is enough. As long as one isn't at a London party, or taking dinner with the Hutchinsons.°

But I remember, I expect you do, too, walks, drives, walking over wet lawns and down dark garden paths, finding oneself on the wharf or the station at a quarter to two in the morning, exploring empty kitchens long after midnight, watching the light change while you lie on the divan smoking and listening— one could go on for ever. And thats all too trivial—I mean something more—which makes every breath one takes, as it were—an emotion.

It is very mysterious how, in spite of everything, we find ourselves at the last *praising Life.*

But this disjointed letter must end. Big green stars glitter in the deep sky; the frogs are shrilling and the sea beats 'A-Ah'. It is like summer.

Goodnight. I ought to give you news of Murry, tho'. Let me see ... As far as I know he is quite unchanged. He is working but not too hard. And in the intervals he smokes his pipe, sews, and irons his trousers.

Salute your New Baby° for me and her fortunate mother. I hope they are both well.

Je vous serre le main [I press your hand]

Ever
Katherine.

To Ida Baker

Sunday. [Villa Isola Bella, Menton,
20 March 1921]

D. I.

Your telegram about Wingley came late last night. It was very thrilling. I long to know how he was found, and even more, if possible, what was the meeting like between Athy and him. I envy you seeing that. I hope you really saw it and can tell me what happened. It is a great triumph to have found him. But now the question is—what to do with them? If we were not leaving for Switzerland I wouldn't hesitate. But all these train journeys—arriving at hotels, and so on? Would it be torture for cats? I feel the cats' first need is a settled home; a home that never changeth. And I know that is just what I am not going to have. At the same time the idea that they should be destroyed is *horrible*! You see, just suppose you and I hear, when we are in Switzerland, of another place & decide to try it. Or decide to make a sea voyage. Or . . . so much is possible. We couldn't ever leave the cats with Jack, & to take cats where they are not wanted is cruelty. I confess I don't see a way out. If Richard were older Id suggest asking him to mind them. Id better leave it like this. If when you have thought it over you decide it would be an unhappy life for them or impractical for you—have them destroyed.

Elizabeth Bibesco has shown signs of life again. A letter yesterday begging him to resist Katherine. 'You have withstood her so gallantly so far how can you give way now'. And 'you swore nothing on earth should ever come between us'. From the letter I feel they are wonderfully suited and I hope he will go on with the affair. He *wants to*. 'How can I exist without your literary advice', she asks. That is a very fascinating question. I shall write to the silly little creature & tell her I have no desire to come between them only she must not make love to him while he is living with me, because that is undignified. He'll never break off these affairs, tho', and I dont see why he should. I wish hed take one *on* really seriously—and leave me. Every day I long more to be alone.

My life is the same. I get up at about 11, go downstairs until 2, come up & lie on my bed until five when I get back into it again. So I am infinitely worse than when I left England. There's no comparison. I wish I could consult Sorapure. Its all a great bother. I 'note' what you say about your Thursday letter. I'll destroy it.

I find it possible to speak to you today. I am not in despair about my health. But I must make every effort to get it better *soon*, very *soon*. You see Jack 'accepts' it; it even suits him that I should be so subdued & helpless. And it is deadly to know he NEVER tries to help. But I was not born an invalid and I want to get well—I long for—Do you understand? I feel every day must be the last day of such a life—but I have now felt that for years. Ida—let us both try. Will you? Bouchage has failed. Help me to escape!

Later.

Your Wednesday letter has come re the furniture. I'd take what they will offer. Perhaps £8 is rather too little, tho.

I have decided to give up this villa for good & to really try Switzerland. I shall try & find that man *Spahlinger*° & see if his treatment suits me. Jack goes to England in the first week in May. I have arranged with him not to return abroad, at any rate until the winter. But to spend the summer in the English country, with a bicycle. It would be *impossible* to have him in Switzerland while one was 'looking round' & deciding. I can imagine it too well. He is v. willing not to come. So we'll burn our French boats & go off together. I wish you could get Spahlingers address or an address where the treatment is followed. But how can you? I don't know . . . I must now make a real effort to make money for this. Somehow, it *must* be done.

Take things easy—& look after yourself. I hope the little boy is better.

Yours
Katherine.

To Princess Bibesco

[Villa Isola Bella, Menton] 24. III. 1921.

Dear Princess Bibesco,

I am afraid you must stop writing these little love letters to my husband while he and I live together. It is one of the things which is not done in our world.

You are very young. Won't you ask your husband to explain to you the impossibility of such a situation.

Please do not make me have to write to you again. I do not like scolding people and I simply hate having to teach them manners.

Yours sincerely,
Katherine Mansfield.

To J. M. Murry

[Hôtel Beau Site, Clarens-Montreux]
Saturday. [7 May 1921]

My darling Bogey,

I have been walking round and round this letter, treading on my toes & waving my tail and wondering where to settle. There's *too* much to say! Also, the least postcard or letter penned in view of these mountains is like presenting ones true account to ones Maker. Perhaps their effect will wear off. But at present, Boge ... one keeps on murmuring that about cats looking at Kings but one feels a very small cat, sneezing, licking one's paw, making a dab or two at ones tail in the eye of Solemn Immensities. However the peasants don't mind, so why should I? They are cutting the long brilliant grass; they are wading waist high through the fields with silver stars—their scythes winking-bright in the sun—over their shoulders. A cart drawn by a *cow* (Im sure it is a cow) drags over a little bridge & the boy driver, lying like a drunken bee in his fresh green bed doesn't even *try* to drive. Its a perfect, windless day. Im, as you have gathered, sitting on the balcony outside my room. The sun is wonderfully warm, but the air is just a little too clean not to be chill. The cleanliness of Switzerland! Darling it is frightening. The chastity of my lily-white bed! The waxy-fine floors! The huge bouquet of white lilac, fresh, crisp from the laundry in my little salon! Every daisy in the grass below has a starched frill—the very bird droppings are dazzling.

Bogey: But Wig—this is all jolly fine but why dont you tell me things.

Get down to it!

I'm sorry, my precious. Ill have another try. You got my telegram. The journey was excellent. The lits salons [sleeping carriages] were horrid—when they unfolded they were covered thickly with buttons so that one felt like a very sensitive bun having its currants put in. But it was soon morning & my mountains appeared as of yore with snow, like silver light on their tops, and beautiful clouds above, rolling solid white masses. We passed little watery villages clinging to the banks of rivers, it was raining, the trees dripped, and everybody carried a gleaming umbrella. Even the fishers fished under umbrellas, their line looked like the huge feeler of a large water beetle. And then the rain stopped, the cows began to fatten, the houses had broad eaves, the women at the bookstalls got broader & broader & it was Switzerland. I sat on a neat green velvet chair in Geneva for 3 hours. L. M. brought tea on a tray—do you see her, coming from afar, holding the tray high, her head bent, a kind of reverent beam on her face, & the smoke of the teapot mounting like the smoke of sacrifiges? Then we mounted an omnibus train & *bummelt*ed [*dawdled*] round the lake. The carriage was full of germans; I was imbedded in huge ones. When they saw a lilac bush, Vater und die Mamma [Father and Mother] and even little Hänsl all cried *Schön* [Beautiful]. It was very old world. Also they each & all read aloud the notice in the carriage that a cabinet was provided for the convenience of the passengers! (What other earthly reason would it have been there for?) We reached Clarens at 7. The station clock was chiming. It was a cuckoo clock. Touching—don't you think, darling? I was *v.* touched. But I didn't cry. And then a motorcar, like a coffee mill, flew round & round the fields to Baugy. The manager, who is very like a goldfish, flashed through the glass doors and our journey was over . . . This hotel is admirable. The food is prodigious. At breakfast one eats little white rolls with butter & fresh plum jam & cream. At lunch one eats—but no, I can't describe it. It could not be better though. I suppose, in the fullness of time I shall take soup at midday, too. But at present I can only watch and listen. My rooms are like a small appartement. They are quite cut off & the balcony is as big as another room. The sun rises in the morning vers les sept heures [around seven o'clock] & it sets or it begins to set, for it takes its setting immensely seriously here, at seven in the evening. It has no connection whatever with the S. of France sun. This is le soleil père [the father sun]—and shes a wanton daughter whose name is never mentioned here. The air, darling, is all they say. I am posing here as a lady with a weak heart & lungs of Spanish leather-o. And so far, I confess, I hardly cough except in the morning. One mustn't be too enthusiastic though. Perhaps its the hypnotic effect of *knowing* one is so high up. But the air is amazing!

Its all very German. Early German. Fat little birds, tame as can be—they look as though their heads unscrewed & revealed marzipan tummies—fat little children, peasants, and—I regret to say—ugly women. In fact everybody seems to me awfully ugly. Young men with red noses & stuffy check suits & feathers in their hats ogling young females in mackintoshes with hats tied with ribbons under the chin! Oh weh, oh weh! [Alas! alas!] And if they try to be 'chic'—to be French—its worse still. Legs—but legs of mutton, Boge, in silk stockings & powder which one feels sure is die Mamma's icing sugar.

Of course I quite see the difficulty of being chic in this landscape. I can't quite see . . . yet. Perhaps a white woolen dress, a Saint Bernard, a woolen viking helmet with snowy wings. And for you . . . more wool, with your knees bare, dearest, and boots with fringèd tongues . . . But I don't know—I don't know . . .

I am sure you will like Switzerland. I want to tell you nicer things. What shall I tell you? I should like to dangle some very fascinating & compelling young carrots before your eminent nose. The furniture of my salon is green velvet inlaid with flesh pink satin, & the picture on the wall is Jugendidylle [young lovers]. There is also an immense copper jug with lovely hearts of imitation verdigris.

Goodbye, my darling. I love you v. much & Im fond of you and I long to hear from you.

Wig.

To Anne Drey

Hotel Beau Site, | Clarens-Montreux | La Suisse
Suisse Suisse. [12 May 1921]

My Precious Darling Anne,

If I were in Paris wouldn't I fly to where you were! Its so perfect of you even to think Im there. I feel as though I was. Or at least that for two quite inferior pins I could pack up and go. But, chère, at the moment I can only walk from the kerridge to the door and from the door to the kerridge. Cant

mount a stair, cant do *anything* but lie in a chaise longue looking
at mountains that make one feel one is living in the Eye of the
Lord. Its all temporary—I am full of beans and full of fight,
but unfortunately darling Im full of Bacilli too. Which is a
bother. If you came here Id simply have such a laugh about it
that this rotten old chaise longue would break its Swiss legs.
Instead Im waiting for docteur Figli (good name that!) and Ive
got a very nice little booklet of information to give him about 2
little guineas which have just died for my sake. The number of
guinea pigs Anne that Ive murdered! So that, my precious
dear, is *that*. Paris might be—might very *well* be la pleine lune
[the full moon] for me.

I left my dear little Isola Bella last week. The South of
France is fever to the feverish. Thats my experience. Adorable
pays [country]—Ill go back there one day but sans un thermo-
metre [without a thermometer]. Switzerland, which I have
always managed to avoid is the very devil I knew it would be. I
mean the people are so UGLY; they are simply hideous. They
have no shape. All the women have pear shaped derrières, ugly
heads, awful feet. All the men wear ready made check flannel-
ette suits, six sizes too small and felt hats another six sizes too
small with a little pre-war feather sticking up behind. Curse
them. And the <u>food</u>. Its got no nerves. You know what I mean?
It seems to lie down and wait for you; the very steaks are meek.
Theres no contact between you and it. You're not attracted.
You don't feel that keeness to meet it and know more of it and
get on very intimate terms. The asparagus is always stone dead.
As to the puree de pommes de terre [potatoes] you feel inclined
to call it 'uncle'. Now I had food in the South that made me
feel—should there be a Paradis you and I shall have one lunch
cooked by my old Marie which will atone for years of not
meeting. And then Anne, Switzerland is revoltingly clean. My
bed! Its enough to unmake any man—the sight of it. Dead
white—tucked in so tight that you have to insert yourself like a
knife into an oyster. I got up the first night and almost
whimpering like Stepan in The Possessed° I put my old wild
jackal skin over the counterpane. But this cleanliness persists in
everything. Even the bird droppings on the terrasse are imma-
culate and every inch of lilac is crisp home from the laundry.
Its a cursed country. And added to this there are these terrific

mountains. I keep saying that about cats looking at Kings but one feels a very small cat, licking ones paw, making a dab or two at ones tail in the face of Immensities.

However, darling, I believe it is the only place where they do give one back ones wings and I cant go on crawling any longer. Its beyond a joke.

I hope you have a perfect time in Paris. Murry has been there. He was very happy. He's at present lecturing in Oxford on Style.° I had a very long story in The Mercury this month° which I rather hoped you'd see because you'd see the point of it. I hope you do. Tell me about your work when you have time. The precious babe's little picture follows me everywhere. The one in the pram—looking out.

I shant stay here at this hotel long so my London address is best. The sight of distant Montreux is altogether too powerful. As to the people in this hotel—it is like a living cemetery. I never saw such deadness. I mean belonging to a by gone period. Collar supports (do you remember them?) are the height of fashion here & hair nets and silver belt buckles and buttonboots. Face powder hasn't been *invented* yet.

Its a queer world, but in spite of everything, darling, its a rare rare joy to be alive—and I salute you and it & kiss you both together—but you I kiss more warmly. Love please to Drey.

Goodbye for now.

Toujours, ma bien-chère [Always, my dear one]

Ta [your]
Katherine.

To J. M. Murry

[Hôtel Beau Site, Clarens-Montreux]
Monday night. [23 May? 1921]

Dearest Bogey darling

I have been trying to write out a long explanation of the reasons why I have felt out of touch with you. But I don't think such explanations are of the smallest good. If you were here I could tell you what I feel in a minute—but at a distance—its different—I dont think its good.

Do you know, darling, what I think Love is? It is drawing out all that is finest and noblest in the soul of the other. Perhaps the other isn't conscious this is what is happening & yet he feels at peace—and that is why. That is I think the *relationship* between lovers, and it is in this way that, because they give each other their freedom (for evil is slavery) they 'ought' (not in the moral sense) to *serve* each other. By service I mean what Chaucer means when he makes his true Knights wonder what they can do that will give joy to their love. (But the lady must, of course, serve equally.) And of course I dont mean anything in the least 'superficial'. Indeed I mean just what there was between us in the last months at the Isola Bella—that—more and more perfect.

You ask me how I am, darling. I am much the same. This chill has been the worst I have ever had since I was ill, and so I feel weak and rather shadowy, physically. My heart is the trouble. But otherwise I feel . . . well, Bogey, its difficult to say. No, one can't believe in *God*. But I must believe in something more *nearly* than I do. As I was lying here today I suddenly remembered that: 'O ye of little faith!'° Not faith in a God. No, thats impossible. But do I live as though I believed in *anything*? Dont I live *in glimpses* only? There is something wrong; there is something small in such a life. One must live more fully and one must have more <u>power</u> of living and feeling. One must be true to ones vision of life—in every single particular. And I am not. The only thing to do is to try again from tonight to be stronger and better—to be *whole*.

Thats *how I am*, dear Love. Goodnight.

Tig.

To Ottoline Morrell

Hotel Chateau Belle Vue | Sierre | (Valais)
[*c*.23 June 1921]

Dearest Ottoline,

I have been hoping to hear from you; I am so glad to know

how you are, though the news isn't at all satisfactory. How horrible to have to undergo another operation! It is simply devastating. The only consolation is you have your lovely home to go to after & will not be in a Swiss hotel. I only hope THEY will do you some real good.

I am leaving here tomorrow. If I look down upon Montreux another day I shall fly into pieces with rage at the ugliness of it all. Its like a painting on a mineral water bottle—*batiment des Eaux* [the bottling factory]. And then along the road that winds through (I must say lovely) vines go these awful, ugly people, & one can't help looking at them. Never have I seen such ugliness. Father, with a straw hat on the back of his head, coat off, waistcoat unbuttoned & stiff shirt showing, marches ahead & Mother follows—with her enormous highly respectable derrière & after them tag the little Swisses—Oh! Oh!! Oh!!! Matters have reached a crisis too, as these last 2 days there has been the Fête des Narcisses. Hoards of uglies rushing by on bicycles with prodigious bunches of these murdered flowers on the handlebars, all ready for the fray. Happily, it rained & became a Fete des Ombrelles instead. I think from the expressions of the company homeward bound the umbrellas had been thrown as well!

To me, though, the symbol of Switzerland is that large middle class female *behind*. It is the most respectable thing in the world. It is deathless. Everyone has one in this hotel; some of the elderly ladies have two.

I think Sierre may be better & there one is at least in reach of forests and tumbling rivers. The man from Montana who is going to keep an Eye on me is near too, but thinking him over (as one does) I believe he's no better than the rest of them and he overcharged me *horribly*. I shall pin my faith on forests. Bother all doctors!

I was so interested in what you told me about Gertler—and Brett. I know I *ought* to love Brett and she is such a 'brick', they say. But when that brick comes flying in my direction—oh, I do so want to dodge it! Why will she [be] so jocose? And why does she have a kind of *pet name* for everyone? And why does she talk of 'streaming into pubs' or 'tickle and run'? This last phrase is really *too* awful. And I think she makes such a dreadful mistake in being on *her* terms with all these men. Its too undignified. I ought not to say a word of this, but ... you know the feeling? And I feel she has such an awful idea of me. Im not that person at all. I don't want to smile when she tells me she has been 'sick'; I want to hang my head.

How lovely Garsington must be! The grass, the shadows of the trees, the lemon verbena in the flower garden. I can see it all. And always coming into the house from the garden—the still, delicate beauty of the house ... It is a memory to keep for ever. I really cannot imagine a house more beautiful. I wish Chaucer had stayed there ...

I hope you do see Murry but when he gets to England he simply disappears. I *never* know where he is. I only hear from him that his pursuit of pleasure is very wearying & painful. But once M. is out of sight he is swallowed up. However, other people tell me he is full of gaiety whereas he tells me how he is *suffering* from the Coal Strike!! Isn't that like Murry!

I have just read his review of the Tchekhov notebooks.° Did you see the book? It was a dreadful *ice bath*, & now the last book of stories 'The Horse Stealers' is a cold douche to follow. I thought the notebooks were in a way almost funny—but its cruel to laugh. Its not fair to glean a man's buttons & pins & hawk them after his death. But the lack of humour on the part of the *translators*! Poor Leonard Woolf typing out all those Russian names! How absurd it is!

Have you read Virginia's stories?° I havent—yet. And I haven't read Queen Victoria° either. Its so dear to buy, & one cant borrow at this distance. But I mean to read it. I saw a quotation from the death of the Queen & that sounded very good. But from all the reviews it seemed to me that Lytton hadn't really spread his wings. It sounded, all, just a little *cramped*.

I read less and less, or fewer and fewer books. Not because I don't want to read them. I do—but they seem so high up on the tree. Its so hard to get at them & there is nobody near to help ... On my bed at night there is a copy of Shakespeare, a copy of Chaucer, an automatic pistol & a black muslin fan. This is my whole little world.

Forgive this 'scrappy' letter. And the torn page with the great pin in it. I have just finished a new story° which Im going

to send on spec. to The Mercury. I hope someone will like it.
Oh, I *have* enjoyed writing it.

With my sincerest good wishes for your *health*, dearest
Ottoline and my warm love

Ever yours
Katherine.

To Ottoline Morrell

Chalet des Sapins | Montana-sur-Sierre |
(Valais) | Switzerland |
24. VII. 1921

Dearest Ottoline,

Will you write to me one day & tell me how you are? I should
love to know. I think of you so often and wonder how you are
passing this lovely summer. It *is* lovely in England, too—isn't
it? The papers groan and gasp but thats only in London. Surely
its not too hot under the ilex tree—or *in* the pond.

Here it is simply exquisite weather. We are so high up (5000
feet above the sea) that a cool breeze filters through from
Heaven, and the forests are always airy ... I cant imagine
anything lovelier than this end of Switzerland. Once one loses
sight of that hideous Lac Leman & *Co.* everything is different.
Sierre, a little warm, sunripe town in the valley was so perfect
that I felt I would like to live there. It has all the flowers of the
South and its gay and 'queynt' and full of nightingales. But
since we have come up the mountains it seems lovelier still. We
have taken a small not very small chalet here for two years. It is
quite remote—in a forest clearing. The windows look over
treetops across a valley to snowy peaks the other side. The air
feels wonderful but smells more wonderful still. I have never
lived *in* a forest before. One steps out of the house & in a
moment one is hidden among the trees. And there are little
glades and groves full of flowers, with small ice-cold streams
twinkling through. It is my joy to sit there on a tree trunk; if

only one could make some small grasshoppery sound of praise to *someone*—thanks to *someone*. But who?

M. and I live like two small timetables. We work all the morning & from tea to supper. After supper we read aloud and smoke; in the afternoon he goes walking & I crawling. The days seem to go by faster and faster. One beaming servant who wears peasant 'bodies' & full skirts striped with velvet looks after everything. & though the chalet is so arcadian it *has* got a bathroom with hot water & central heating for the winter & a piano & thick carpets & sun blinds. I am too old not to rejoice in these creature comforts as well.

The only person whom we see is my Cousin Elizabeth who lives ½ an hours scramble away.° We exchange Chateaubriand and baskets of apricots and have occasional long talks which are rather like what talks in the afterlife will be like, I imagine ... ruminative, and reminiscent—although dear knows what it is really all about. How strange talking is—what mists rise and fall—how one loses the other & then thinks to have found the other—then down comes another soft final curtain ... But it is incredible, don't you feel, how mysterious and isolated we each of us are—at the last. I suppose one ought to make this discovery once & for all but I seem to be always making it again.

It seems to me that writers dont acknowledge it half enough. They pretend to know all there is in the parcel. But how *is* one to do it without seeming vague?

Some novels have been flung up our mountainside lately. Among them Lawrence's Women in Love. Really! Really!! Really!!! But it is so *absurd* that one cant say anything; it after all is almost purely pathological, as they say. But its sad to think what might have been. Wasn't it Santyana° who said: Every artist holds a lunatic in leash. That explains L. to me. You know I am Gudrun? Oh, what rubbish it all is, tho'. Secker is a little fool to publish such STUFF.° I wish a writer would rise up—a new one—a really good one—

M. is engaged in a fat novel.° He is quite wrapt away in it. I keep on with my short stories. I have been doing a series for *The Sphere*,° because it pays better than any other paper I know. But now they are done I don't believe they are much good. Too simple. It is always the next story which is going to contain everything, and that next story is always just out of reach. One seems to be saving up for it. I have been reading Shakespeare *as usual*. The Winters Tale again. All the beginning is very dull—isn't it. That Leontes is an intolerable man and I *hate* gentle Hermione. Her strength of mind, too, in hiding just round the corner from him for 15 years is terrifying! But oh—the Shepherd scene is too perfect. Now I am embedded in Measure for Measure. I had no idea it was so good. M. reads aloud in the evening & we *make notes*. There are moments when our life is rather like a school for two! I see us walking out [in] crocodile for two and correcting each others exercises. But no—not really.

Dearest Ottoline. Is this a Fearfully dull letter? Im afraid it is. Im afraid 'Katherine has become so boring nowadays'.

But I send it with much love, very *very* much.

Katherine.

To Ida Baker

[Chalet des Sapins, Montana-sur-Sierre]
Monday 29. VIII. 1921

Dear Ida,

I shall destroy the other letter I have written. Perhaps Jack is right; I *am* a tyrant. But . . . look here.

(a) Will you please either date your letters or put the day on the top.

(b) Do you mind cutting out the descriptions as much as you *can*?

That kind of yearning sentimental writing about a virginia creeper & the small haigh voices of tainy children is more than I can stick. It makes me hang my head; it makes Jack play the mouth organ whenever we meet it in females. But I shall say no more. This is where the tyrant comes in. Its so much worse when the spelling is wrong, too. Brett is just exactly the same in this respect . . . Its very queer . . .

I don't like any of the stuffs. Will you go to *Lewis Evans* & *Selfridge* or *Debenham*. Number the patterns & Ill wire a reply.

Miss Read won't get them done, of course, but arrange with her to send them over. Try for ROYAL blue instead of cornflower. These are either 2 dark or 2 light. As for tartans—try for soft smoky checks on any coloured ground instead—like the red & black check we saw in Menton. You remember? Thats the kind of stuff I meant, too. They had both better be lined with v. fine silver grey *viyella* or cashmere, I think. And tell Miss Read to cut them on the big side so that I can wear my woolen jumpers underneath if necessary. Id rather have nothing than these ugly dull stuffs. I am a very MODERN woman. I like Life in my clothes. Its no good going to Liberty for plain colours—ever. Try & think of a picture in a French pattern book or a figure on the stage, cant you?

Sorry to give you so much trouble. Id no idea it would be all so *very* difficult. My advice is to 'concentrate more' & not worry about the golden leaves so much. Fall they will! I am up. I am better and at work again. Cheer up!

Katherine.

To Dorothy Brett

[Chalet des Sapins, Montana-sur-Sierre,
29 August 1921]

Dearest Brett,

I would have written before but the Furies have had me until today. Something quite new for a change—high fever, deadly sickness and weakness. I haven't been able to lift my head from the pillow. I think it has been a breakdown from too much work. I have felt exhausted with all those stories lately & yet—couldn't stop. Well, there has been a stop now & I am just putting forth my horns again & thinking of climbing up the hill . . . How I do abominate any kind of illness! Oh God, what it is to live in such a body! Well, it doesn't bear thinking about . . . As soon as I can get well enough to go downstairs I shall engage our one original cab & go for a long drive behind the old carthorse with his jingle-bells. The driver—as a great honour—throws the foot mat over the seat when one goes for a party of pleasure. He seems to think that is *very* chic! But this is such a beautiful country. Oh! It is so marvellous. Never the same—the air like old, still wine—sounds of bells & birds and grasshoppers playing their fiddles & the wind shaking the trees. It rains & the drops in the fir trees afterwards are so flashing-bright & burning that one feels all is enchanted. It is cloudy—we live in fine white clouds for days & then suddenly at night all is crystal clear & the moon has gold wings. They have just taken the new honey from the hives. I wish I could send you a jar. All the summer is shut up in a little pot. But summer is on the wane—the wane. Now Murry brings back autumn crocuses and his handkerchief is full of mushrooms. I love the satiny colour of mushrooms, & their *smell* & the soft stalk. The autumn crocuses push above short, mossy grass. Big red pears—monsters jostle in Ernestine's° apron. Yes, ça commence, ma chere [it begins, my dear]. And I feel as I always do that autumn is loveliest of all. There is such a sharpness with the sweetness—there is the sound of cold water running fast in the stream in the forest. Murry says the squirrels are tamer already. But Heavens Brett—Life is so marvellous, it is so rich—such a store of marvels that one cant say which one prefers.

I feel with you, most deeply and truly, that its not good to be 'permanent'. Its the old cry: 'Better be impermanent move-ables'. Now here for instance—we are only 4 hours from Italy. One can run into Italy for tea. Murry went down to see Elizabeth last week & she had so done. She had waked with a feeling for Italy that morning & behold she was flown. And that night she sat in the Opera House in Milan ... That is *right*—I am sure. Thats why I hate England. I can't help it, Miss, downs or no downs. There is that Channel which lies like a great cold sword between you and your dear love Adventure. And by Adventure I mean—yes—the wonderful feeling that one can lean out of heaven knows what window tonight—one can wander under heaven knows what flowery trees. Strange songs sound at the windows, the wine bottle is a new shape, a perfectly new moon shines outside ... No, don't settle. Dont ever have a convenient little gentleman's residence. Hot baths in ones own bathroom are fearfully nice—but they are too *dear*. I prefer to bath in a flower pot as I go on my way ...

I absolutely agree with you, too, about Manet & Renoir.
Renoir—at the last—bores me. His feeling for flesh is a kind of
super butchers feeling about a lovely little cut of lamb. I am
always fascinated by lovely bosoms but not without the heads
& hands as well—and I want in fact the feeling that all this
beauty is in the deepest sense attached to Life. Real Life! In
fact I must confess it is the spirit which fascinates me in flesh.
That does for me as far as modern painters are concerned, I
suppose. But I feel bored to my last groan by all these pattern
mongers. Ah, how wearying it is! I would die of it if I thought.
And the writers are just the same. But they are worse than the
painters because they are so many of them dirty minded as
well. I don't deny—I even can admire a dung hill. But Virginia
Woolf tittering over some little mechanical contrivance to
'relieve virgins' that I abhor & abominate & am ashamed of!

What makes Lawrence a *real* writer is his passion. Without
passion one writes in the air or on the sands of the seashore. But
L. has got it all wrong, I believe. He is right, I imagine or how
shall I put it . . .? Its my belief too, that nothing will save the
world but Love. But his tortured, satanic demon lover I think is
all wrong. The whole subject is so mysterious, tho'; one could
write about it for ever. But let me try & say something.

It seems to me that there is a great change come over the
world since people like us believed in God. God is now gone for
all of us. Yet we must believe and not only that we must carry
out weakness and our sin and our devilish-ness to somebody. I
don't mean in a bad, abasing way. But we must feel that we are
known that our hearts are known as God knew us. Therefore
Love today between 'lovers' has to be not only human, but
divine today. They love each other for everything and through
everything, and their love is their religion. It cant become
anything less—even affection—I mean it can't become less
supreme because it is an act of faith to believe! But oh, it is no
good. I can't write it all out. I should go into pages & pages.
But I think L. is a sign of the times—just as M's reply was, too.

How lovely your children sound. I *saw* them. Leonora's hair,
Angela's 'ways' the expression of the little boy & Marie Loo's
sort of *plunge* into Life. You made them simply lovely and so
real!!° I do wish I could appear behind a bush & see you
painting them. How I love little children & being with them! I

envy you them *fearfully*. What is your picture like? I *see* the little heads & the green leaves behind them, but what is it really like? Tell me, do, & the colours.

My stories for the Sphere are all done, thank the Lord. I have had copies with ILLUSTRATIONS! Oh Brett! Such fearful horrors!° All my dear people looking like—well—Harrods° 29/6 crepe de chine blouses and young tailors gents. And my old men—stuffy old wooly sheep. Its a sad trial. I am at present imbedded in a terrific story but it still frightens me. And now I have to emerge & write some special things for the old Daily Chronicle who [is] going to make a feature of 'em.°

The Mountain is in London buying sweaters & stockings for our winter outfit. She has become a very fierce Swiss patriot. Switzerland is her *home*; she's perfectly happy here & is getting awfully good looking. M. says he won't stir for 5 years from this spot. Then we *say* we will sail to New Zealing. But I don't know.

Goodbye for now, dear Brett.

I send you my love & my duties.

Yours
Tig.

To Ida Baker

[Chalet des Sapins, Montana-sur-Sierre]
7. IX. 1921

My dear I,

Its not possible to say all I wish to. Ill write it. Do you feel inclined to take this *job*—really? I mean to manage things for me as if I were a man. Its like this. I have gone to a new agent, he's got me work which will keep me busy until Christmas at earliest. Then the Daily N. has asked me to do some special articles for them and so has the Daily Chronicle. All this is *extra*. I cant devote myself to it if I have to look after the house & my clothes and so on. Its impossible. At the same time I *must* do it without delay. I can pay you between £10–12 a month. But tho' payment is important—its not the important thing. Can I rely on you? Can I ask you just simply to do what is necessary— i.e. what I should do if I hadn't a profession? In a word—can I feel, payment apart and *slavery* apart and false pride apart— that you are mine? That you will accept this situation as the outcome of our friendship? Does it satisfy you? May I consider you as permanently part of the scheme & will you consider me in the same light?

The truth is friendship is to me every bit as sacred and eternal as marriage. I want to know from you if you think the same.

Yours ever
K.M.

As for my *violence* and so on I could explain all that, too, but it takes too long. Try and accept it, while it lasts.

To Dorothy Brett

[Chalet des Sapins, Montana-sur-Sierre] In harbour. Monday. [12 September 1921]

Brett,

Take a long breath. Im going to write masses. First about your picture. I think the little girl in the front is amazingly good. She is beautifully felt. You have got the essential 'childishness' of her and you've got it by *painting*. I mean all is so firm, so compact, modelled and simple. And it remains warm. I think you ought to pride yourself no end on that little girl et je vous serre la main pour elle [I press your hand for her]. I have put the photograph on the top of this page so Im looking at it as I write. Please remember how Fearfully good I think that small child!

I don't think it comes off as a composition chiefly because of the big child. She seems to me too big, too pale (even tho' I realise you want to get her fairness over) too broad, too much an *expanse*. She [is] in a different world to the other child and therefore they cant be really related. Theres a kind of weakness, too, in the painting of the head. Its as though you haven't held it in your hands & felt it all over. While you were painting you were not touching her. Thats how it looks. And her size distracts one. The picture falls away in her corner. The boy seems to me just very nearly successful. But in his case your sympathies—your feeling for his disposition—seem to me to have interfered with your tranquility. You know how, whatever one feels in ones excitement, when one sits down to work that goes. All must be smooth. No *novelty*, no appearance of effort. Thats the secret. It must appear so natural, so without effort. I feel you have strained a bit to get across the fact of the boy's sensitiveness, and so you show him off a little instead of paint him. See what I mean?

Look here, Brett. Don't be angry with me for saying all this. If I am your friend you have the right to expect the truth from me. I cant, in these days, give less. Life is too important as well as too short. So forgive me, my girl, if I hurt you. Three heads—a group like that—are—is—hard to manage. One wants to roll them round softly, until they combine. They want to flow into each other a bit, especially if they are children. You want a kind of soft nudging if one of the children is your little girl. This doesn't upset their 'differences' but it *does* make one feel the artist has seen them as a THREE not as a 1, 2, and 3.

I expect after this youll never send me another photograph. Well, I shall be awfully sorry if you dont. Good luck! All success to you!

The Cezanne book, Miss, you won't get back until you send a policeman or an urgent request for it. It is fascinating, & you can't think how one enjoys such a book on our mountain tops. He is awfully sympathetic to me. I am absolutely uneducated about painting. I can only look at it as a writer, but it seems to me the real thing. Its what one is aiming at. One of his men gave me quite a shock. He is the *spit* of a man Ive just written about—one Jonathan Trout.° To the life. I wish I could cut him out & put him in my book. Ive finished my new book. Finished last night at 10.30. Laid down the pen after writing 'Thanks be to God'. I wish there was a God. I am longing to (1) praise him (2) thank him. The title is *At The Bay*. Thats the name of the very long story in it, a continuation of 'Prelude'. Its about 60 pages. Ive been at it all last night. My precious children have sat in here playing cards.° Ive wandered about all sorts of places—in and out. I hope it is good. It is as good as I can do and all my heart and soul is in it—every single bit. Oh God, I hope it gives pleasure to someone ... It is so strange to bring the dead to life again. Theres my grandmother, back in her chair with her pink knitting, there stalks my uncle over the grass. I feel as I write 'you are not dead, my darlings. All is remembered. I bow down to you. I efface myself so that you may live again through me in your richness and beauty.' And one feels *possessed*. And then the peace where it all happens. I have tried to make it as familiar to 'you' as it is to me. You know the marigolds? You know those pools in the rocks? You know the mousetrap on the wash house window sill? And, too, one tries to go deep—to speak to the secret self we all have—to acknowledge that. I mustn't say any more about it.

Im glad you have left Scotland. Its so bad to be with people who depress you. I felt that your wings, quivering and pressed together like a butterfly's opened wide & fanned with joy to breathe the air of your own room. When do you give up your house? I think its not good to be alone. You want people for many reasons, even for the sense of security a lodger gives you at night. Thats a very real thing! The point is to try to have a house with as little 'trouble' as possible. How do you manage? And certainly to be a moveable as often as you can. But don't you find housekeeping very difficult? I have had to give it up entirely. If one has a profession one has no more time for it than a man has. One cannot arrange food, do one's mending, see that there are flowers and that all is in order and work too. Murry and I have tried it and neither he nor I can bring it off. So we have engaged the 'mountain' quite finally to be a professional housekeeper—to be the 'mistress' of the house in fact as a servant understands that word. It works well. When the mountain feels that she is needed she is quite different. And what a joy it is to be free and not to know what there is for dinner? The only perquisite we retain is jam-making. Murry and I brew our jam on the electric toaster in a big saucepan. We have just made red plum & aspire towards quince. Its a thrilling job, especially taking 'specimens' in a saucer—one ends with a ring of saucers.

No, we certainly shan't be back in England for years. Sometimes, in bed at night, we plan one holiday a year but everywhere else feels nearer than England. If we can get the money we shall build here in two or three years time & we have already chosen the way to look—the way the house shall face. And it is christened *Chalet Content*. We are both most fearful dreamers, especially when its late & we lie staring at the ceiling. It begins with me. M. declares he won't talk. Its too late. Then I hear 'Certainly not more than two floors & a large open fireplace.' A long pause. K: 'What about *bees*?' J.M.M.: 'Most certainly bees and I aspire to a goat.' And it ends with us getting fearfully hungry & J.M.M. going off for two small whacks of cake while I heat two small milks on the spirit stove.

You know Wingley? The mountain brought him over. He arrayed with immense eyes after having flashed through all that landscape & it was several hours before the famous purr came into action. Now he [has] completely settled down & reads Shakespeare with us in the evening. I wonder what cat Shakespeare is like. We expect him to write his reminiscences shortly. They are to be bound in mouse's skin.

Goodbye dear Brett. Im taking a holiday today after my labours last week. I wrote for 9 solid hours yesterday. But it has been such a pleasure to talk to you. Id like to send my love to Kot, if he wasn't my enemy. Take care of yourself. Keep well. Eat nourishing food. But one can't say to another Be happy. One can only wish it.

Yours, dear little painter
Tig.

Who do you think turned up at the end of this letter? Mrs H. G. Wells & two young H. G. Wells.° *Very* nice boys. We feel full of gaierty.

To Ida Baker

Chalet des Sapins |
Montana-s-Sierre | Saturday.
[24 September 1921]

Dear ? [*sic*]
Thank you for your letter. I would have written a card before but the Furies have been busy. I have been—am—ill

ever since you left with what Doctor H.° calls acute enteritis. High fever, sickness, dysentery and so on. I decided yesterday to go to the Palace° but today makes me feel Ill try & see it through here. Jack is awfully kind in the menial offices of nurse & as I cant 'take' anything except a little warm milk E. cant do her worst! Is v. unfortunate because it holds up my work so. Just when I am busy. But cant be helped. If I were to tell you how Ive missed you even you might be satisfied! At the same time—this is serious—don't hurry back, will you? The worst is over. Dont rush. I shall manage. Dont come before you have arranged—i.e. the 6th. At the *same* time dont, just to oblige a Glasspool,° come later!

I am glad you are safely there. Not a word about your new neffy°—or haven't you seen him yet. Oh, I would *hate* to be in England. If only, in the next two years I can make enough money to build something here. But my soul revolts at your pension-talk° again. I suppose it gives you a trumpery sense of power to take on one job & pretend all the time you're perfectly free for any other that comes along. A pity you can't resist the female in you. You're the greatest *flirt* I ever have met—a real *flirt*. I do wish you weren't. With all my heart I do. It seems so utterly indecent at our age to be still all a-flutter at every possible glance. But—there—I still hope one day you will be yourself. I am not going to flirt back, Miss & say how I want you as part of my life and cant really imagine being without you. The ties that bind us! Heavens, they are so strong that youd bleed to death if you really cut away. But *don't*. Oh please don't make me have to protest. Accept! Take your place! Be my friend! Don't pay me out for what has been. But no more about this. Ive no doubt Ill get a card today saying your idea is to go out to Africa and so on and so on. I *really mean* it *is* detestable.

E. is as mad as a sober Swiss can be. I think she puts all the thick soups into my hot water bottils.

When you send papers—get a label the size of the paper! Otherwise the copy arrives *torn, black* & *disgusting*. Didn't you know that? And I cant help the illustrator.° It was so *like Clive* [Bell] to ask who he was—<u>so</u> tactful!

You can, in spite of my rages, read as much love as you like into this letter. You won't read more than is there.

Katherine.

What about money? Be frank!

To Jeanne Renshaw

Chalet des Sapins | Montana sur Sierre | Valais
Switzerland | 14 X 1921

My little sister,
   Your handkerchief is such a very gay one—it looks as though
it had dropped off the handky tree. Thank you for it, darling. I
remember the birthday when you bit me! It was the same one
when I got a dolls pram & in a rage let it go hurling by itself
down the grassy slope outside the conversatory [*sic*]. Father was
awfully angry & said no one was to speak to me. Also, the white
azalea bush was out. *And* Aunt Belle had brought from Sydney
a new receipt for icing. It was tried on my cake & wasn't a
great success because it was much too brittle. I can see & feel its
smoothness now. You make me long to have a talk with you, in
some place like the corner of the lily lawn. Ah, Jeanne, anyone
who says to me 'do you remember' simply has my heart . . . I
remember everything, and perhaps the great joy of Life to me
is in playing just that game, going back with someone into the
past—going back to the dining room at 75° to the proud and
rather angry looking selzogene on the sideboard, with the little
bucket under the spout. Do you remember that hiss it gave &
sometimes a kind of groan? And the smell inside the sideboard
of worcester sauce and corks from old claret bottles?
   But I must not begin such things. If we are ever together
down the Kenepuru Sounds° come off with me for a whole
day—will you? And lets just remember. How Chummie loved
it, too. Can't you hear his soft boyish laugh and the way he said
'oh—abso*lute*ly!'
   Im sending you a copy of The Mercury in case you didn't see
this story. Tell me if you like it. Just for once—will you? Im
also slipping inside it my new press photograph in case you'd
care for it. Haven't you got a photograph for me? I have such a
lovely one of Marie. Its excellent. But the last was you & uncle
Sid!°

Ever your sister
K.

To John Galsworthy

Chalet des Sapins | Montana sur Sierre |
Valais | Switzerland | 25 X 1921

Dear Mr Galsworthy

By an unfortunate mischance your letter only reached me today. My silence must have seemed very ungracious. Though, even now, I scarcely know how to thank you. Your noble generous praise is such precious encouragement that all I can do is try to deserve it. I want to promise you that I will never do less than my best, that I will try not to fail you. But this sounds superficial and far from my *feeling*. There the letters are, tied up in the silk handkerchief with my treasures. I shall never forget them. I wish, someday, I might press your hand for them. Thank you 'for ever'.

I ought to tell you—for after all, you have the key—I have been haunting the little house in the Bayswater Road last week—looking at the place where the humming birds stood, and standing where Soames stood in the hall by the hatstand. How I can hear Smithers word 'Bobbish'. But one must not begin. One would go on for ever. All the life of that house flickers up, trembles, glows again, is rich again, in these last moments. And then there is Soames with Fleur running out of his bosom, so swift, so careless—leaving him bare ... Thank you for these wonderful books° ...

You ask me about my work. I have just finished a new book which is to be published at the New Year. And now I am 'thinking out' a long story about a woman which has been in my mind for years. But it is difficult. I want her whole life to be in it—a sense of time—and the feeling of 'farewell'. For by the time the story is told her life is over. One tells it in taking leave of her ... Not one of these modern women but one of those old fashioned kind who seemed to have such a rich being, to live in such a living world. Is it fancy? Is it just that the harvest of the past is gathered? Who shall say!

In November or December the London Mercury is publishing a day in the life of the little family in Prelude.° If I may, I should very much like to send you a copy.

The mountains here are good to live with, but it doesn't do to look lower. The Swiss are a *poor lot*. Honesty and Sparsam Keit [thrift]—in themselves—don't warm one's heart.

But I must detain you no longer.

Fare well! May all good things attend you!
Katherine Mansfield.

To Harold Beauchamp

Confidential. | Chalet des Sapins |
Montana-sur-Sierre | (Valais) | Switzerland |
1 XI 1921

Father darling,

I must get over this fear of writing to you because I have not written for so long. I am ashamed to ask for your forgiveness and yet how can I approach you without it? Every single day I think and wonder how I can explain my silence. I cannot tell you how often I dream of you. Sometimes night after night I dream that I am back in New Zealand and sometimes you are angry with me and at other times this horrible behaviour of mine has not happened and all is well between us. It is simply agony *not* to write to you. My heart is full of you. But the past rises before me, when I have promised not to do this very thing that I have done and its like a wall that I cant see over.

The whole reason for my silence has been that, in the first weeks I was ill and waited until I was better. And then events conspired to throw me into a horrible depression that I could not shake off. Connie and Jinnie made me understand how very much you considered you were doing for me. They made me realise that for you to give me £300 a year was an extreme concession and that as a matter of fact my husband was the one who ought to provide for me. Of course I appreciate your great generosity in allowing me so much money. And I know it is only because I am ill in the way I am that you are doing so. But it is highly unlikely that I shall live very long and consumption is a terribly expensive illness. I thought that you did not mind looking after me to this extent. And to feel that you did—was like a blow to me—I couldn't get over it. I feel as though I didn't belong to you, really. If Chaddie or Jeanne had developed consumption husbands or no husbands they would surely have appealed to you. One does turn to ones father however old one is. Had I forfeited the right to do so? Perhaps ... There is no reason, Father dear, that you should go on loving me through thick and thin. I see that. And I have been an extraordinarily unsatisfactory and disappointing child.

But in spite of everything, one gets shot in the wing and one believes that 'home' will receive one and cherish one. When we were together in France I was happy with you as I had always longed to be but when I knew that you grudged me the money it was simply torture.° I did not know what to say about it. I waited until I saw if I could earn more myself at that time. But it was not possible. Then I had waited so long that it seemed impossible to write. Then I was so seriously ill that I was not in a state to write to anybody. And by the time that crisis was over it seemed to me my sin of silence was too great to beg forgiveness, and so it has gone on.

But I cannot bear it any longer. I must come to you and at least acknowledge my fault. I must at least tell you, even though the time has passed when you wish to listen, that never for a moment, in my folly and my fear, have I ceased to love you and to honour you. I have punished myself so cruelly that I couldn't suffer more.

Father don't turn away from me, darling. If you cannot take me back into your heart believe me when I say I am

Your devoted deeply sorrowing child
Kass

To Dorothy Brett

Chalet des Sapins | Montana-sur-Sierre | Valais
[5 December 1921]

Dearest Brett,

Forgive my delay in answering. I wanted to answer bang off, but these last few days have been rather bad ones—tired ones. I haven't been able to do anything but read. Its on these occasions that one begins to wish for queer things like gramophones. It wouldn't matter if one could just walk away. But thats out of the question at present. But no more of it.

If possible I will certainly meet you in Paris in the Spring near the Luxembourg Gardens. Lovely idea! It shall be done. I hope to have enough money by then to spend a month in Paris. Wouldn't it be thrilling for you to arrive? I love Paris at that time of year.

Wasn't that Van Gogh shown at the Goupil° ten years ago? Yellow flowers—brimming with sun in a pot? I wonder if it is the same. That picture seemed to reveal something that I hadn't realised before I saw it. It lived with me afterwards. It still does—that & another of a sea captain in a flat cap. They taught me something about writing, which was queer—a kind of freedom—or rather, a shaking free. When one has been working for a long stretch one begins to narrrow ones vision a bit, to fine things down too much. And its only when something else breaks through, a picture, or something seen out of doors that one realises it. It is—literally—years since I have been to a picture show. I can smell them as I write.

I am writing to you before breakfast. Its just sunrise and the sky is a hedge sparrow egg blue, the fir trees are quivering with light. This is simply a marvellous climate for sun. We have far more sun than at the South of France, and while it shines it is warmer. On the other hand—out of it—one might be in the Arctic Zone—and it freezes so hard at night that one dare not let the chauffage [heating] down, even. It is queer to be in the sun and to look *down* at the clouds. We are above them here. But yesterday for instance it was like the old original flood. Just Montana bobbed above the huge lakes of pale water. There wasn't a thing to be seen but cloud below. When are the photographs of your paintings to come? Send them soon! Are you working? Or resting after your last. Are people gay in London this winter? Those awful fogs—I feel I should have to fly to something to get over them, and yet—if one is well— perhaps they dont matter so much and even have their beauty, too.

Oh dear! I am sure by now you are gasping at the dullness of this letter. To tell you the truth—I am terribly unsettled for the moment. It will pass. But while it is here I seem to have no mind except for what is worrying me. I am making another effort to throw off my chains—i.e. to be well. And I am waiting for the answer to a letter—I'm half here—half away—its a bad businesss. But you see I have made up my mind to try the Russian doctor's treatment.° I have played my card. Will he answer? Will anything come of it? One dares not speak of these things. It is so boring for it is all speculation, and yet one *cannot* stop thinking . . . thinking . . . imagining what it would be like to run again or take a little jump.

Forgive me, dear Brett. In my next letter I shall be over this. Do please write if you can. It would be fearfully nice to get a long letter, especially as I don't deserve one. And tell me please what size you take in shoes. Don't forget! It will be too late if you do, and be sure to let me know where you will be at Christmas Time. I want (as I daresay you have guessed) to send you a small present.

Goodbye for now. My *love* to you

Ever
Tig

To S. S. Koteliansky

Chalet des Sapins | Montana sur Sierre | Valais
[c.20 December 1921]

Koteliansky,

I want to write to you at this time in memory of that other Christmas when Lawrence gave his party° in the top room of Elsie Murray's cottage. Thank you again for the Vienna Café chocolates and the cigarettes. I see the boxes now. But far more plainly I see *you*, as if I could put out my hand and touch your breast.

Wasn't Lawrence awfully nice that night. Ah, one must always *love* Lawrence for his 'being'. I could love Frieda too, tonight, in her Bavarian dress, with her face flushed as though she had been crying about the 'child*er*en'. It is a pity that all things must pass. And how strange it is, how in spite of everything, there are certain people, like Lawrence, who remain in one's life for ever, and others who are forever shadowy.

You, for instance, are part of my life like that. One might say 'immortal'. I mean, just supposing there were immortality it would not be at all strange if suddenly a door opened and we met and sat down to drink tea. Thus it will always be with me. It is no idle pretence. If it is in the least atom a comfort to you to know there is one who loves you and thinks of you (without a shadow of responsibility involved or of anything that is not perfectly 'simple') please remember you have

For ever
Katherine.

And no answer is required, dear friend. I *mean* that.

To Dorothy Brett

Chalet des Sapins | Montana-sur-Sierre | Valais
[21 January 1922]

Warning. Pages <u>all</u> wrong.

Darling Brettushka,

The jumper has jumped & the ribbons fluttered over today. And I can't thank you. It seems feeble just to thank a person for such loveliness. I rejoice in the garment & the exquisite colours beyond words but that is not all. Its your thought in sending them which makes them so precious. I dont see how I am going to keep up with your lovely ways. I shall lag behind & admire. Thank you from my heart. Isn't the jumper an exquisite creature. When I go to Paris I shall wear it to carry you with me in the interview with Manouhkin. It will be my mascot. As for the ribbons. My brother's greenstone looks exquisite hung from one or the other of them. If I had been the child of a conjuror I should have eaten ribbons instead of producing them from my hat.

I cant get off to Paris just yet for I am still in bed. Six weeks today with one days interval. I cant shake off this congestion

and ALL the machinery is out of order. Food is a horror. But I
won't go into it. I feel most frightfully inclined to hold your
hand, too, & just let this month & February & March stream
by like a movie picture. Then let it be April and all this dark
and cold over. Huge fringes of icicles hang from the windows. I
know one thing. I must never stay up here for another winter.
Evan had a heart of brass. That is why he could stand it. We
talked it over together over chops and cabbage in a Pullman
one night when he'd just got back. If I can get well enough to
go to Paris. Its all I ask. I am fighting for that now . . . I wish I
had got there before this last bout. I was so much stronger than
I am now. But this is a bad black month, darling. There is a
new moon on the 27th. Look at it & wish. I will look at it &
wish for you. I feel so in your mood—listless, tired, my energy
flares up & won't last. Im a wood fire. However, I swear to
finish my big story° by the end of this month. Its queer when I
am in this mood I always write as though I am laughing. I feel
it running along the pages. If only the reader could see the snail
in its shell with the black pen! Don't work too hard just now.
Let things be. Let things grow in the quiet. Think of your mind
as a winter garden—growing underneath, you know with all
the lovely shapes & colours of thrice blessed longed for spring.
I think it is good sometimes just to let things be. But what does
one *do* on those occasions? I can think of all kinds of plans but
they need you near. Tell me about your little house. A queer
strange feeling that I cannot explain away tells me I shall see it
& know it & stay there once. One is shy of saying these things
for some reason. But I feel there is a possibility of a much
deeper relationship between us than ever we dream of. I feel a
bit like a man about you. I mean by that Id like to make you
feel loved. There is something I don't like in most of the men you
know (I mean those that I know too). They lack delicacy and
perception and they do not *give*. I except of course Koteliansky
& Tomlinson,° both beautiful men. But I would like to try &
make you happy, my dear—make you feel *cherished*. I wonder if
you know what I mean. We grow in the bosoms of others; we
rest there; it is good sometimes to feel carried.

Your still life sounds lovely & I like to think of your bottils,
all in a row. They *are* lovely things, even those slender hock
bottles. But I see *them* from the 'literary' point of view. They

say summer & lunch out of doors and strawberries on a glass
plate with gold specks in it . . .

I have just heard from DelaMare about my little family in
The Mercury and from America where another story of the
same people is coming out in The Dial.° I feel like Lottie and
Kezias mother° after the letters I have got this month. It is
surprising and very lovely to know how people love little
children, the most unexpected people—

Heres the doctor stumping up the stairs. No, he has stopped
half way to talk to the Mountain.

Elizabeth is here again with a minute sledge on a string
wherever she goes. She herself in tiny black breeks & gaiters
looks like an infant bishop. Murry & she flew down thousands
of feet yesterday—right down into the valley. She is a radiant
little being whatever the weather. Born under a dancing
star°—

He comes. I must end this. Goodbye for now—You know
what I think of these gifts. But send me no more, my little
artist. You are too lavish. Keep your pennies now.

I embrace you—You must feel that there is in this letter
warm tender love. For its there.

                                                        Tig

To S. S. Koteliansky

Victoria Palace Hotel | 6 Rue Blaise Desgoffe |
Rue de Rennes | Paris |
III Fevrier 1922

Koteliansky

There is no answer to this letter. But I wanted to tell you
something very good that happened today. Yesterday I decided that I must take this treatment and I telephoned M
[Manoukhin]. I was sitting alone in the waiting room of the
clinique reading Goethes conversations with Eckermann° when
M. came in. He came quickly over to me, took my hand and
said simply 'Vous avez decidé de commencer avec la traitment.
C'est très bien. Bonne santé [You have decided to begin the
treatment. That's very good. Good health!]', and then he went

as quickly out of the room saying 'tout de suite' [immediately]
(pronounced '*toot sweet*' for he speaks very little French). But
this coming in so quickly and gently was a beautiful act, never
to be forgotten, the act of someone *very good*.

Oh, how I love gentleness, Koteliansky, dear friend. All
these people everywhere are like creatures at a railway
station—shouting, calling, rushing, with ugly looks and ways.
And the women's eyes—like false stones—hard, stupid—there
is only one word corrupt. I look at them and I think of the
words of Christ 'Be ye therefore perfect even as your Father in
Heaven is perfect.'° But what do they care? How shall they
listen? It is terribly sad. Of course, darling Koteliansky, I don't
want them to be all solemn or Sundayfied. God forbid. But it
seems there is so little of the spirit of love and gaiety and *warmth*
in the world just now. Why all this pretence? But it is true—it is
not easy to be simple, it is not just (as A.Ts friend used to say) a
sheep sneezing.°

It is raining. There is a little hyacinth on my table—a very
naive one.

Heaven bless you. May we meet soon.

Katherine.

To J. M. Murry

[Victoria Palace Hotel, 6 Rue Blaise Desgoffes,
Rue des Rennes, Paris] Friday.
[3 February 1922]

My precious Bogey

Your telegram came yesterday as a complete surprise—a
very very marvellous one—a kind of miracle. I shall never
forget it. I read it, scrunched it up, then carefully unscrunched
it and put it away 'for keeps'. It was a very wonderful thing to
receive. I agree absolutely it is best that I start now & I
telephoned the same moment to M. whose sole reply was 'deux
heures [two hours]'. (But before I speak of my time there I
want to say your two letters my dear one are simply such
perfect letters that one *feeds* on them. I don't know. You have

become such a wonderful person—well, you always were—but the beams are so awfully plain now—on se chauffe [one is warmed] at every word you write. And there is a kind of calmness which I feel, too. Indeed I feel we are both so changed since the days before Montana—different people. I do feel that I belong to you, that we live in our own world. This world simply passes by—it says nothing. I do not like it but thats no matter. It is not for long. Do you realise that if the miracle happens we May Go to England This Summer Together? Thats just an idea of what the future holds. May it make you a hundredth part as happy as it makes me!)

I went to the clinique today and there the French doctor with Manoukhine went over the battlefield. Really it was the first time I have ever been 'examined'. They agreed absolutely after a very prolonged examination that I had *no* cavities. Absolument pas de cavernes [Absolutely no cavities]. They tested & tested my lungs & always said the same. This means I am *absolutely curable*. My heart, rheumatism, everything was gone into and noted & finally I passed into another room & had a séance [session].

I want to ask you something. Do you really believe all this? There is something that pulls me back the whole time and which wont let me believe. I hear, I see. I feel a great confidence in Manoukhine—very great—and yet — — I am absolutely divided. You know how, to do anything well, even to make a little jump, one must gather oneself together. Well, I am not gathered together. A dark secret unbelief holds me back. I see myself after 15 goes apologising to them for being not cured, so to speak. This is very bad. You realise I am in the mood now when I confess to you because I want to tell you my bad self. But it may be its not me. For what is bad in me (i.e. to doubt) is not bad in you. Its your nature—If you do feel it— please tell me—please try and change. Try and believe. I know Manoukhine believes. I was sitting in the waiting room reading Eckermann when he came in, quickly, simply and took my hand and said 'vous avez décidé de commencer. C'est très bien. Bonne santé! [You have decided to begin. That's very good. Good health!]' But this was said beautifully, *gently*. (Oh, Bogey I do love *gentleness*.) Now I have told you this I will get over it. It has been a marvellous day here, very soft, sunny and windy, with women selling les violettes de Parme in the street. But I could not live in a city ever again. That's done—that's finished with. I read Shakespeare (I am with you as I read) and I am half way through a new story. I long for your letter which follows mine. Oh, those precious birds at the coconut. How I see and hear them! And E's fig pudding. You write the word fig in such a nice way that all your precious darling self walks in the world. Goodbye for now, my blessed one. I feel a bit mysterious, full of blue rays, rather like a deep sea fishchik.

Your
Wig.

To J. M. Murry

[Victoria Palace Hotel, 6 Rue Blaise Desgoffe,
Rue des Rennes, Paris] Tuesday.
[7 February 1922]

My darling Bogey

I have had no news from you today yet (3 p.m.). I expect it is the snow. Arctic conditions prevail in Switzerland, so the papers say. I hope you manage to keep warm and that Wingley's tail is not frozen.

Advise me—will you? I am looking for a tiny flat—very small—a mouse's hole just big enough to nibble a pen in. If I find anything suitable I shall take it until the end of May and Ida will look after it to save money on servants and so on. But (this is where I want your advice) to whom can I apply for a reference? They are sure to ask me for at least two—can you think of anybody? I wish you would answer this as soon as possible, Bogey. A card will suffice, as they say. Its rather urgent. Flats are so scarce here and I want to be settled as soon as possible once something is found. Of course it may all be a wild goose's chase. Ida has gone off to an agent this afternoon. But there it is!

I have started a new Shakespeare notebook. I hope you will let me see yours one day. I expect they will be legion by that time. And reading with the point of view of taking notes I begin to see those marvellous short stories asleep in an image as it were. For instance ...

> 'Like to a vagabond flag upon the stream
> Goes to and back, lackeying the varying tide
> To rot itself with motion.'°

That is terrible, and it contains such a terribly deep psychological truth. That '*rots* itself' ... And the idea of 'it' returning and returning, never swept out to sea finally. You may think you have done with it for ever but comes a change of tide and there is that dark streak reappeared, more sickeningly rotten still. I understand that better than I care to. I mean—alas!—I have proof of it in my own being.

There are awful good oranges to be had in Paris. But theres nothing else good that I know—nothing *fresh, sound,* or *sweet.* But mines a partial view, of course. I have done with cities for ever. I want flowers, rather sandy soil, green fields and a river not too deep to paddle in, also a large number of ancient books and a small but *very* pretty cow. In fact I should like the cow to be strikingly pretty. I shall put it in the advertisement. 'No plain cows may apply'. No, I cant do that. Its too cruel. But its an airy-fairy herd for a long time, Im afraid. How is your work going? If I am very dull for five weeks you must remember that for 5 weeks this treatment makes me rather worse. After that you will have to snatch my letters (like snapdragons) all blaging out of the postman's bag.

Your loving
Wig.

To J. M. Murry

[Victoria Palace Hotel, 6 Rue Blaise Desgoffes,
Rue des Rennes, Paris,
7 February 1922]

In reply to your telegram.°

My darling Bogey,

I do not 'understand' why you have sent this telegram, so my reply is rather in the dark. Still, I must send it. Please do not come here to me. That is what I wish to say, and I say it deliberately. It is not *easy* to write so to you. I will try and explain my reasons. I want you to have your freedom as an artist. You asked for it at Menton. I thought it was a mistake— that you did not mean it and only wrote under influence. But then after I left Montana you asked for it again. You were willing to join me *if I wanted you*—you were prepared, like a shot *to be of help to me*. (But that is exactly like saying to a person if you want to borrow money, borrow from me, or Fathers telling me I could count on him up to £50 if the necessity arose. It is not the gesture of people who deeply understand each other.) On the other hand your own personal feeling was not that at this most critical of all moments in her life I could not leave Wig. Golly—no! It was my work—May would be too late—my novel—and so on. Reverse the positions, darling. *Hear* me saying that to you!

It is no good. I now know that I must grow a shell away from you. I want, 'I ask for' my independence. At any moment in the future you may suddenly leave me in the lurch if it pleases you. It is a part of your nature. I thought that it was almost the condition of your working that we were together. Not a bit of it! Well, darling Boge, for various reasons I cant accept this. And now that I am making a bid for health—my *final bid*—I want to grow strong in another way, too. Ida is leaving here on Saturday. She will be with you on Sunday. Tell her what you want her to do, if you intend leaving Switzerland. And write to me about everything. But my very soul rebels against when its fine you prefer your work & your work is more urgent than this affair in Paris has been. When it snows you might as well be playing cribbage with me! And also that remark 'Moreover the rent is paid here!'

No, darling, *please*. Let me be alone here. This queer strain in you does not, for some extraordinary reason in the very least atom lessen my love for you. Id rather not discuss it. Let it be! And I must work now until May. These 'affairs' are 1000 times more disturbing than 1000 train journeys. Pax, darling. You will see Ida on Sunday. But for the last time I ask you not to join me. I cannot see you until May.

Your loving
Wig.

Please just accept this. Its awfully hard having '*it*' to fight as well as my other *not* dear Bogies!

Later.

Dearest Bogey

I have just opened my letter to say your Sunday & Monday ones have come—about the snow, about Elizabeth, about your staying there. If the weather is fine by now I dare say your doubts will have taken wings, too. But for my part—I would rather stay here alone. I have seen the worst of it by myself i.e. going alone to Manoukhin, having no one to talk it over and so on. I want now intensely to be alone until May. Then IF I am better we can talk things over and if I am not I shall make some other arrangement. There's no need to look ahead. But that is my very *calm collected* feeling. So if you do want to leave the chalet before May—let us still be independent of each other until then—shall we?

I hope that horrible weather is over. Dont we get dreadfully few letters! I am going to see a little flat tomorrow which I hope will be suitable. Here—I cant stay longer than necessary.

Your loving Wig.

P.S. We haven't read *The Schoolmaster*.° Have we? Are you certing? Dont bother to send the D.N. about Bibesco.°

To Elizabeth Russell

Victoria Palace Hotel | 6–8 Rue Blaise Desgoffe |
Rue de Rennes | Paris | 8.II.1922

My dear Elizabeth,

Thank you so much for your letter. But what horrid snow. There must be too much of it. I hope it now settles down and the sun shines warm. It seems impossible that I missed you at Randogne. You were in my thoughts as we waited at the station & I tried to catch a glimpse of your chalet. I hate to think I did not see you.

It served me right about John. After my agonies as to what would become of him—*relief* breathed in the poor boy's letter.

He was like a fish off a line, swimming in his own element again, and never dreaming really of coming here. He made me feel like a very stuffy old Prospero who had been harbouring a piping wild Ariel. I hope he does stay where he is. It would be much the best plan. Poor John! Its horrible to think how I have curtailed his freedom. In my silly innocence I felt certain he couldn't bear not to know what this Russian man said and so on. But not a bit of it. He is hand in hand with his new novel—I see them rather like the couple in Donne's Ecstasy.° But I *do* hope he wont change his ideas now. Bad weather and no posts are a trial which he hasn't experienced yet in solitude. He would repent of coming to Paris Im sure while he is seething with work which will out. Id much rather be alone until May, too, now that I know his sentiments.

Its literally years since I have been in a city. Hampstead was only my room—it wasn't any more of London. But in an hotel one is plunged into the very housemaid's pail of it, and odious it seems to me. There is nothing sweet sound fresh except the oranges. Paris looked at through a taxi window has its grave beauty. It *is* a lovely city! But the people. Did people always look so ... impudent? And I used to think *all* the women were pretty in a way. And now I think they are bold, stupid hussies and the men awfully like dogs. Is it because I do not leap and fly myself, Elizabeth? As to the flowers—I haven't had a flower yet. Tulips are 1.50 each. The F.O.° can't find anything sweet and reasonable. And it had been my plan to send you a basket the very first thing. Nothing but my horrid poverty stops that basket arriving. Manoukhin says that by the second week in May Ill feel perfectly well. Its exactly like being in prison and hearing somehow that there is a chance you may be let out. *Now* I know what a prisoner's dreams must be. I feel inclined to write a long story about a gaol bird. But I shouldn't know how to end it.

I wonder how your novel is going?° I am hard at Shakespeare again, tapping away at him like the birds tapped at my half coconut on the window sill.

The F.O. has been looking for *small flats*. Yesterday she found one—'*very* nice', where five girls with bobbed hair lived with their uncle. It was, she confessed rather full of beds at the moment. But when the girls, who were from the country had gone the beds would be whisked away. And the concierge was most agreeable. The house very quiet. It seemed to me rather a strange menage but I went to see over it today. Really the F.O. is like Una in the Fairy Queen.° She is too innocent for words to express. That flat! Those bobbed haired girls! 'Uncle' had departed but two cigars remained to *prove* as F.O. murmured to me 'that a man lived there'. And the BEDS. Merciful Powers! There was something horribly pathetic about it in the pale afternoon light, in its attempts at gaiety, at real flowering. But the whole place will haunt me for ever. I said to the F.O. as we left 'But its a bawdy-house.' And after a long pause she said 'Dear me! I had never imagined such a thing. But I quite see what you mean!'

This letter must end.

With *much* love dear Elizabeth

Yours ever
Katherine.

To Dorothy Brett

[Victoria Palace Hotel, 6 Rue Blaise Desgoffe,
Rue de Rennes, Paris] Sunday.
[26 February 1922]

Cherie,

I must answer your letter at once because I like it frightfully. What is it doing in London today? Here it is spring. For days past it has been warm, blue & gold, sunny, faint, languishing, soft, lovely weather. Isn't it the same over there? The reckless lift boy says 'dans un mois il serait plein été [In a month it will be full summer]'. Thats the kind of large remark I love the French for. They have very nearly hung out their sun blinds; they have quite turned the puddings into little ices in frills. But why cant I send some of this weather over to you? Can't it be done? Look in the glass. If there is a very bright gay sunbeam flittering over your hair I sent it from Paris, exprès. At any rate you *are* putting out new leaves, crepe de chine ones & baby ribbons ones. The craving for a new hat is fearful in the spring.

A light, crisp, fresh new curled hat after these winter dowdies. I suffer from it now. If I had one I should wear it in bed! But the barber is cheaper. He came yesterday and gave a coup de fer [touch with the tongs] to my wool. Now its all waves on top. (I have a *great* tendre [soft spot] for barbers.)

I not only know where your new house is. But I have been there & looked over one of three little houses in Pond Street. Three lambs they were—years and years ago before Anrep° was born even. I shall call you the little Queen B. when you are in yours, which is a kind of mixture of *you* & Queen Anne. Its much better to have a tiny wax bright hive. Everything will shine there. And then suppose you want to shut it up for a time you can just pop your thimble over the chimley and all's hidden. No good leaving those great barracks to stare house-breakers in the face and shout 'Look at *me*' ... (As you may realise I am walking through your letter as I write.)

About painting. I agree. Good as Gertler is I shall never forget seeing a ballet dancer of his—it was the last thing I saw of his—at his studio. A *ballet* dancer. A big big meaty female dressed in a cauliflower! I don't mean to be horrid; but I do not and cannot understand how one can paint such pictures. They are so dull they make me groan. Hang it all Brett—a picture must have *charm*—or why look at it? Its the quality I call *tenderness* in writing—its the tone one gets in a really first chop musician. Without it you can be as solid as a hill & I don't see whats the good. As to Ethel Sands° (isn't her name a master-piece—*wouldn't* it be Ethel) her painting is a kind of 'dainty' affair which it doesn't do to think about. You feel that ultimately where, of all places, she ought to be a woman she is only a very charming satin bow. Forgive my coarseness but there it is! Talking about feeling. I had a shock yesterday. I thought my new book would enrage people because it had too much feeling—& there comes a long review talking of the 'merciless analysis of the man of science'. Its a mystery. If you do see my book read a story called The Voyage°—will you? Keep it if you like it ...

So Elliot has been to your Thursdays. Yes he is an attractive creature; he is pathetic. He suffers from his feeling of power-lessness. He knows it. He feels weak. Hes all disguise. That slow manner, that hesitation, sidelong glance and so on are *painful*.

And the pity is he is too serious about himself, even a little bit absurd. But its natural; its the fault of London, that. He wants kindly laughing at and setting free.

Yes, I love Koteliansky—no less.

(Look here—darling—what can I give you? Tell me. What is the great difficulty? Show it to me. Or—can't you ... Don't you trust me? You *are* safe. You are wrong if you do not trust me. And why wait until we meet? Even this moment will not return. I have given up the idea of Time. There is no such person. There is the Past. Thats true. But the Present and the Future are all one—)

Once I settle down for a few months you must know DelaMare. He is a very wonderful man—beautiful. Now I have arrived at the word 'primroses' & I see them. Delicate pinkish stems, and the earthy feeling as one picks them so close to the damp soil. I love their leaves too, and I like to kiss buds of primroses. One could kiss them away. They feel so marvellous. But what about bluebells? Oh dear! Bluebells are just as good. White ones, faint blue ones that grow in shady hollows, very dark blue ones, pale ones. I had one whole spring full of bluebells one year with Lawrence.° I shall never forget it. And it was warm, not very sunny, the shadows raced over the silky grass & the cuckoos sang.

Later. I then got up had a big blue bath & rather a horrid lunch. Then played chess—rested for a couple of hours, had tea & foie gras sandwiches and a long discussion with M. on 'literature'. Now the light is lighted, outside theres a marvellous deep lilac sky and I shall work again until dinner. Its strange how nice it is here. One could scarcely be more free. The hotel servants are just a little bit impudent and thats nice, too. There is no servility. I meant to tell you the barber was in raptures with your still life. I think thats a great compliment, don't you? It's before ones eyes said he, 'il y a de la vie. Un mouvement dans les feuilles [it has life. A movement in the leaves].' Excellent criticism! He, good man, was small & fair & like all barbers smelt of a violet cachou and a hot iron. He begged, he implored me to go to the cinema near here. Downstairs it was a little mixed but upstairs on the balcon there were armchairs of such a size and beauty that one could sleep in them ... Oh Brett, how I like *simple* people—not all simple people, some are simple pigs—but on the whole—how much more sympathetic than the Clive Bells of this world! Whatever else they have— they are alive. What I cannot bear is this half existence, this life in the head alone. Its deadly boring.

I think my story for you will be about Canaries.° The large cage opposite has fascinated me completely. I think & think about them—their feelings, their *dreams*, the life they led before they were caught, the difference between the two little pale fluffy ones who were born in captivity & their grandfather & grandmother who knew the South American forests and have seen the immense perfumed sea ... Words cannot express the beauty of that high shrill little song rising out of the very stones. It seems one cannot escape Beauty—it is everywhere.

I must end this letter. I have just finished a queer story called *The Fly*° about a fly that fell into an ink pot and a Bank Manager. I think it will come out in The Nation. The trouble with writing is that one seethes with stories. One ought to write one a day at least—but it is so tiring. *When* I am well I shall still live always far away in distant spots where one can work and look undisturbed. No more literary society for me *ever*. As for London—the idea is too awful. I shall sneak up to Pond Street every now and again—very rarely indeed & Ill beg you not to let a soul know. Its no joke my dear to get the letters I do from people who want to meet one. Its frightening!

Dont leave me too long without letters. I have grown to look for you now and I cant do without you. I miss you. Youre my friend. See? Oh, one thing. When I *do* come will you ask the children to tea? I have had serious thoughts of adopting a little tiny Russian lately. In fact it is still in the back of my mind. Its a secret, though.

Easter this year is April 16th. That is March and a bit away. Blow quickly away March. Come April. Isn't it a divine word—and in all languages its so exquisite—Avril, Avrilo. What a name for a book—April!

Forgive my writing. My hand is always stiff with work. Can you read it? Yours ever, dear little artist

Tig.

To William Gerhardi

[Victoria Palace Hotel, 6 Rue Blaise Desgoffes,
Rue de Rennes, Paris]
March 13, 1922

Please do not think of me as a kind of boa-constrictor who
sits here gorged and silent after having devoured your two
delightful letters, without so much as a 'thank you.' If gratitude were the size and shape to go into a pillar box the postman
would have staggered to your door days ago. But I've not been
able to send anything more tangible. I have been—I am ill. In
two weeks I shall begin to get better. But for the moment I am
down below in the cabin, as it were, and the deck, where all the
wise and happy people are walking up and down and Mr.
Gerhardi drinks a hundred cups of tea with a hundred
schoolgirls, is far away . . . But I only tell you this to explain my
silence. I'm always very much ashamed of being ill; I hate to
plead illness. It's taking an unfair advantage. So please let us
forget about it . . .

I've been wanting to say—how strange, how delightful it is
you should feel as you do about *The Voyage*. No one has
mentioned it to me but Middleton Murry. But when I wrote
that little story I felt that I was on that very boat, going down
those stairs, smelling the smell of the saloon. And when the
stewardess came in and said, 'We're rather empty, we may
pitch a little,' I can't believe that my sofa did not pitch. And
one moment I had a little bun of silk-white hair and a bonnet
and the next I was Fenella hugging the swan neck umbrella. It
was so vivid—terribly vivid—especially as they drove away
and heard the sea as it slowly turned on the beach. Why—I
don't know. It wasn't a memory of a real experience. It was a
kind of *possession*. I might have remained the grandma for ever
after if the wind had changed that moment. And that would
have been a little embarrassing for Middleton Murry . . . But
don't you feel that when you write? I think one always feels it,
only sometimes it is a great deal more definite.

Yes, I agree with you the insulting references to Miss Brill would have been better in French. Also there is a printer's error, 'chère' for 'chérie.' 'Ma petite chère' sounds ridiculous ...

And yes, that is what I tried to convey in *The Garden Party*. The diversity of life and how we try to fit in everything, Death included. That is bewildering for a person of Laura's age. She feels things ought to happen differently. First one and then another. But life isn't like that. We haven't the ordering of it. Laura says, 'But all these things must not happen at once.' And Life answers, 'Why not? How are they divided from each other.' And they *do* all happen, it is inevitable. And it seems to me there is beauty in that inevitability.

I wonder if you happened to see a review of my book in *Time and Tide*. It was written by a very fierce lady indeed.° Beating in the face was nothing to it. It frightened me when I read it. I shall never dare to come to England. I am sure she would have my blood like the fish in Cock Robin.° But why is she so dreadfully violent? One would think I was a wife beater, at least, or that I wrote all my stories with a carving knife. It is a great mystery.

To Ida Baker

Please give this character to E. with mes mille remerciments [a thousand thanks] et mes meilleurs souvenirs [my fondest memories]. Better put it in an envelope, if you will.

> [Victoria Palace Hotel, 6 Rue Blaise Desgoffes,
> Rue de Rennes, Paris] Tuesday.
> [14 March 1922]

Dear Ida

I have just received your Sunday letter. Dont apologize for writing what you feel. Why should you? It only means I have to cry 'De rien de rien [It's nothing, nothing]' each time and thats silly. Heavens! What a journey it is to take one anywhere! I prove that to myself every day. I am always more or less marking out the distance, examining the map, and then failing to carry out my plans. Its rather nice to think of oneself as a sailor bending over the map of ones *mind* and deciding where to go and how to go. The great thing to remember is we can do whatever we wish to do provided our wish is strong enough. But the tremendous effort needed—one doesn't always want to make it, does one? And all that cutting down the jungle and bush clearing even after one has landed anywhere—its tiring. Yes, I agree. But what else can be done? What's the alternative? What do you want *most* to do? Thats what I have to keep asking myself, in face of difficulties.

But you are saying 'what has this to do with our relationship?' This. We cannot live together in any sense until we—*I*—are am stronger. It seems to me it is my job, my fault, and not yours. I am simply unworthy of friendship, as I am. I take advantage of you, demand perfection of you, crush you. And the devil of it is that even though that is true as I write it I want to laugh. A deeper self looks at you and a deeper self in you looks back and we laugh and say 'what nonsense'. Its very queer, Jones, isn't it? Can you believe it—that looking back upon our times in Italy and Garavan—even the afternoon when you were raking the garden and I was proving our purely evil effect on each other I keep on remembering that it was a lovely day or that the button daisies were ducks. How nice, how very nice it would be to bowl along in one of those open cabs with the wind ruffling off the sea & a smell of roasting coffee & fresh lemons from the land.

Oh dear! Oh dear! And do you remember standing at your window in your kimono one morning at five oclock while I sat up in bed behind the mosquito curtains and talked of decomposition? No, we can't simply live apart for all our lives from now on. We shall have to visit at least. How can we live? What is the best plan? The future is so wrapt in mystery. Until I am well its foolishness for us to be together. That we both know. If this treatment 'succeeds' I shall go to Germany for the summer, then to Elizabeth at Randogne and then come back here in September or October. If all goes well I shall then go back to Germany for the winter—or Austria or Italy. Then—I have not the remotest idea . . . Jack wants to take a little house in the English country in Sussex and put all our furniture in it and so on and have a married couple in charge. I feel it is my duty to spend 6 months of every year there with him. The other six

October to March I shall spend in either the South of France
or Italy and I hope and imagine that if he has his house,
Arthur, his books, his married couple, a little car, and friends
coming down, Jack will not want to come with me. They will
be my free months. Thats all I can see. Now my *idea* is that we
should spend the foreign months together, you and I. You
know by that I mean they will be my working months but
apart from work—walks, tea in a forest, cold chicken on a rock
by the sea and so on we could 'share'. Likewise concerts in
public gardens, sea bathing in Corsica and any other pretty
little kick-shaws we have a mind to. But here is a brick. Money.
If I can manage to pay for those months can you get a job for
the others? Thats the point. And of course the 'arrangement' is
only in case you care to, are not in Rhodesia, are not married or
living with some man. Tell me what you think. If you say 'what
the dickens could I do for six months?' I reply 'why not the
Universal Aunts.° Why not try them? See what kind of jobs
they have . . .' But don't fly off and cry 'this is very kind of you
to arrange for and dispense my life like this merci pour la
langouste [thanks for the lobster].' Im not doing it. Im only
talking in the dark—trying to keep you—yes, I will own to
that, and trying to make things easy, happy, good, delightful.
For we *must* be happy. No failures. No makeshifts. Blissful
happiness. Anything else is somehow disgusting. I must make
those six months with Jack as perfect as I can make them and
the other six ought to be fearfully nice. But I know any form of
life for Jack you & me is impossible & wrong. (There is all the:
if this treatment does not succeed but I pass it by.)

Now the immediate future for you. It seems you are not
going to get P.Gs.° Can you stay there until its time for the
chalet to be shut? Do you want to? And then—what do you
want to do? Will you go to the Palace° this winter? But this is all
far away and uncertain. And I must stop writing and begin to
work. The great point is—if you can—think of happiness, work
for happiness, look for it. I should like to ask you, every day
between sleeping and waking, i.e. before you go to sleep &
before you get up to practise this. Breathe *in* saying I am and
out saying hap-py. Your subconscious, Miss will then take note
of that fact and act according. However miserable you will be
that has a quite definite counteraction. I suggest you teach

Wing on the same principle to say 'I like—stopping at home
...'

Goodbye for now. You say don't write letters and you lead
me a terrific dance writing them. Thus it will always be—

Yours ever
K.M.

To Ida Baker

[Victoria Palace Hotel, 6 Rue Blaise Desgoffes,
Rue de Rennes, Paris] Wednesday.
[29 March 1922]

Dear Ida

Your As° have just been and gone. I thought they were nice
girls. What skin hair teeth the young one has! Youth itself is
beauty—*and* health. Theres no other beauty I feel after feast-
ing on that smiling creature in her white felt hat and big coat.
They delivered the parcel. I was v. thrilled by the oatmeal bags
& the honourable wounds in the stockings were miracles of fine
surgery. I feel *most* rich. I shall be able to change my stockings
once a fortnight now instead of once a month. And where did
the knickers come from? Such good quality too. The blue slip
looks very pretty & nice. I'll put it on when winter goes again.
The girls babbled away about that strange person called Miss
Baker. She'd been with them to the station, sat on their boxes,
packed them, got her P.Gs and was ever so pleased to have
them. They thought she might *stay* up there. She liked it so.
And spring had come & gone & they'd had to give away ½ pots
of jam and whole coat hangers at the last. It was a dear little
flat—it was indeed! But the mosquitoes in Venice were awful.
One saw nothing but woke a fright. And the Mystery was the
girl with us wasn't touched. Picnics in the summer were also
very nice but Edith wasn't there then. And it seemed from her
letters she had a little second hand shop. If you had a jumble
sale there was such a rush from miles around you had to have
the police. *Very* fond of Wingley. And the balcony was lovely,
too. Doctor Muralt had even asked what her age was. Well—

not *personally*, but he had asked. There was no room the first night but Miss Yates sent them to a quiet little hotel and it was cheap at all events ... I could go on with this indefinitely. I spent weeks & weeks with them in 20 minutes. They had just *had* tea thank you very much. And they didn't care in the least about carrying the big parcel. Paris wasn't Dublin, after all.

Yours ever
K.M.

To Dorothy Brett

[Victoria Palace Hotel, 6 Rue Blaise Desgoffe,
Rue de Rennes, Paris,
30 March 1922]

Darling Brett

I see your point about Easter. As regards *me* it wouldn't tire me at all for I feel we know each other too well now to tire each other. But its true the weather will be more settled in May and warmer. There is a chance still I may be able to get about and sit in the Gardens and so on and I shouldn't be able to do that in Easter. And then Ill know my plans more in May— everything is up in the air now ... Also I can't help thinking it would be a thousand times more satisfactory if you were already in your little house and no longer homeless. Oh you poor lamb! I think your friends are—to put it at its kindliest— terribly lacking in imagination. Why don't any of them give you a real room and a fire with trimmings. To think of you— frail little creature that you are—blowing along the streets like a leaf in this devilish East weather, and catching cold, and having to take a room in—of all depressing places—Padd-ington Green! It is all very wrong and horrid. Couldn't you afford a nice warm stuffy hotel like the Langham?° There at least one is tucked in and the bath water is hot and theres someone to run messages and so on. Will that nurse look after your cold properly? And I wish I didn't see your days dotted with buns. You need the Bes Food when youre moving. It takes such masses of energy and good humour out of one. The weather here is nothing short of horrible. Its almost dark all day, it rains and snows, drizzles with snow. I cant go out yet. I feel I shall soon come out in satin wallpaper stripes—after these eight weeks in one stuffy room. It has been terrible. Better not talk about it. The worst of it is I am not one atom better so far.—Theres no talking to Manoukhin. He either does not listen or does not understand but shouts across one about his other cases to his partner. So soothing! I get to the point of thinking he has no other cases & that they are both living on my 300 a week in the meantime. But it may turn out better than one imagines. Perhaps this is that famous 'darkness before dawn' . . .

And the big ray of light is I am fearfully lucky with my writing. In fact my agent wants far more than I can do. But the greatest pleasure is all the letters I get from strangers who know nothing whatever about technique but who go through all the stories and say how sorry they are for William and how they understood why Anne laughed at Reggie° and so on. I value these letters far more than any review. Its marvellous to feel these people care like that. And its amazing to find how generous they are. Fancy bothering to write all that! I had a wonderful letter from H. G. Wells yesterday, too. He is another incredibly generous man! I shall have to find a green place in the summer & just stay there fixed and work. Then if this has all been not successful I think Ill try and go to Nancy and have a go at the new psychotherapeutics. What confusion! Thats the result of hotels. AND poor Murrys excitement this morning. He lost his pocketbook. This to ordinary people doesn't matter much. I—at any rate—am so careless about money that even if I lose it and can't afford to I don't mind. I can't mind. There it is. One can always sell something to get along with. But for M. it is really the deepest most terrifying tragedy. He goes white as paper. He is hopeless at once. He drifted out of my room back into his, turned over everything, pulled everything out of the waste paper basket, made my writing table a haystack, banged the doors, smiled like a person on the stage, pulled the bed about, just didn't shake me by the heels. And his gloom is so dreadful that really one feels deadly sick—its as though one were hanging over a cliff. Finally after about half an hour in my room I got up, threw on my kimono and went off to his.

And *I* started while he declared 'No, it was no use. It was gone. Hed looked everywhere. The thing was hopeless.'

In about five minutes it was found. He looked like an angel as he clasped it or some saint visited by the Lord. Such is the effect of heredity! I suppose for years his family has felt like that, his mother suffered like that while she carried him and so passed it on. Devilish grind of life! But why do those people let themselves be ground. How I thank Heaven that there were a few rascals in my family. Its the rascals who save one from the peculiar tortures that M. suffers from.

I keep an eagle eye on the place where the parcels are put but no egg has arrived yet, darling. As for mine—don't scorn it. It will be the best I can do in the circumstances. Ill buy you a really good egg in May. Do you remember those rose buckles you gave me? They are really very lovely. I thought of having them mounted on a piece of black velvet & each of us wearing one for a bracelet. They are *so* charming. And the idea is nice, I think. How it would make peoples eyes pop if they had seen yours and then saw mine. Tell me if you agree . . .

No, I don't miss the Mountain for buttons. I miss her for tidying. I hate leaving my room in disorder or letting any of my personal things get out of place, and its tiring to do it oneself. Still Id far rather do it than have it done by the Mountain. It was always a false position.

How is your little house? And who is helping you with it. A very good moving firm is Popes Hammersmith. They clean and sweep one as well & they are cheap. Have you got a servant? If I were a well strong person I would come over & offer my services. I like to think youd accept them & we would make each other cups of tea and drink it sitting round a packing case. That is nice, too.

Goodbye for now, my precious little artist.

Always your
Tig.

Forgive writing. Am lying down & the book has no backbone.

To Sarah Gertrude Millin

[Victoria Palace Hotel,
6 Rue Blaise Desgoffes, Rue de Rennes, Paris]
permanent address | c/o The Nation and |
The Athenaeum | 10 Adelphi Terrace
W.C.2 | London | March. [1922]

Dear Mrs Sarah Gertrude Millin°

Your letter makes me want to begin mine with 'Do write again. Don't let this be your last letter. If ever you feel inclined for a talk with a fellow-writer summon me.' I cannot tell you how glad I am to hear from you, how interested I am to know about your work. Are you really going to send me a copy of Adam's Rest° when it comes out? It would give me great pleasure to read it.

Now I am walking through the third page of your letter. Yes I do think it is 'desolate' not to know another writer. One has a longing to talk about writing sometimes, to talk things over, to exchange impressions, to find out how other people work— what they find difficult, what they really aim at expressing— countless things like that. But there's another side to it. Let me tell you my experience. I am a 'Colonial'. I was born in New Zealand, I came to Europe to 'complete my education' and when my parents thought that tremendous task was over I went back to New Zealand. I hated it. It seemed to me a small petty world; I longed for 'my' kind of people and larger interests and so on. And after a struggle I did get out of the nest finally and came to London, at eighteen, *never* to return, said my disgusted heart. Since then Ive lived in England, France, Italy, Bavaria. Ive known literary society in plenty. But for the last four-five years I have been ill and have lived either in the S. of France or in a remote little chalet in Switzerland—always remote, always cut off, seeing hardly anybody, for months seeing really nobody except my husband and our servant and the cat and 'the people who come to the back door'. Its only in those years Ive really been able to work and always my thoughts and feelings go back to New Zealand—rediscovering it, finding beauty in it, re-living it. Its about my Aunt Fan who

lived up the road I really want to write, and the man who sold
goldfinches, and about a wet night on the wharf, and Tarana
Street in the Spring. Really, I am sure it does a writer no good
to be transplanted—it does harm. One reaps the glittering top
of the field but there are no sheaves to bind. And there's
something, disintegrating, false, *agitating* in that literary life. Its
petty and stupid like a fashion. I think the only way to live as a
writer is to draw upon one's real *familiar* life—to find the
treasure in that as Olive Schreiner° did. Our secret life, the life
we return to over and over again, the 'do you remember' life is
always the past. And the curious thing is that if we describe this
which seems to us so intensely personal, other people take it to
themselves and understand it as if it were their own.

Does this sound as though Im dogmatising? I don't mean to
be. But if you knew the numbers of writers who have begun full
of promise and who have succumbed to London! My husband
and I are determined never to live in cities, always to live
'remote'—to have our own life—where making jam and dis-
covering a new bird and sitting on the stairs and growing the
flowers we like best is—are—just as important as a new book.
If one lives in literary society (I dont know why it *is* so but it is)
it means giving up one's peace of mind, one's leisure—the best
of life.

But Im writing as if to beg you to unpack your trunk, as if
you were on the very point of leaving South Africa tomorrow.
And that's absurd. But I am so awfully glad you have Africa to
draw upon.

I am writing this letter in Paris where we are staying at [*i.e.*
till] May. I am trying a new Xray treatment which is supposed
to be very good for lungs. Its early spring, weather very lovely
and gentle, the chestnut trees in bud, the hawthorn coming into
flower in the Luxembourg Gardens. I can't go out, except to
the clinic once a week but my husband is a very faithful
messenger. He reports on it all for me, and goes to the
Luxembourg Gardens every afternoon. We work hard—we are
both very busy—and read a great deal. And both of us are
longing to be back in the country. If this treatment succeeds at
all we'll be gone in May. But its hard to write in a hotel. I can
only do short things and think out long stories. Do you have
anemones in South Africa. I have a big bowl of such beauties

in this room. I should like to put them into my letter, especially the blue ones and a very lovely pearly white kind—

It is late—I must end this letter. Thank you again for yours. I warmly press your hand—

Katherine Mansfield.

To Ida Baker

[Victoria Palace Hotel, 6 Rue Blaise Desgoffes, Rue de Rennes, Paris] Monday afternoon. [24 April 1922]

My dear Ida

The Flowers arrived in the most perfect condition—so fresh they might have been gathered $\frac{1}{2}$ an hour ago. I have made a most exquisite 'garden' of the moss, little violet roots, anemone roots & crocus blades. Its like a small world. The rest are in a jug. They are supremely lovely flowers. But please do something for me. I *beg* you. Tell me (1) where they grew (2) how they grew (3) was there snow near (4) what kind of a day was it (5) were they among other flowers or are they the first? Don't bother about description. I only want *fact*. In fact if you can send me a kind of weather & 'aspects' report as near as you can you would earn my deep deep gratitude. By aspects I mean the external face of nature.

If E. [Ernestine] had anything to do with the gathering mille remerciments [a thousand thanks]. If W. had a paw in the matter pull his tail for me.

K.M.

To Richard Murry

Address on and after June 1st: Hotel Angleterre|
Montana-sur-Sierre|Valais. Suisse|
Paree. Sunday. [28 May 1922]

Riccardo mio

I have just written as you sugges' to Arnoldo.° I do hope he
will send me some of his work. Id very much like to see it. It is
most awfully decent of him to have had the idea—don't you
think? I remember that story The Student of his very well. I
begin to believe you are as much a little ray of sunshine as I am.
Beams appear in your last two letters. It is a relief to think your
horrid old chilblains have gone and that you are looking your
beautiful self again. But seriously—isn't it almost frightening
the difference fine weather can make? I wish Einstein° could
find some way of shooting a giant safety-pin at the sun and
keeping it there. It has been tremendously hot in Paris. Like an
oven. Jack and I gave up writing altogether. We were overcome and could do nothing but fan ourselves, he with a volume
of Anthony Trollope (very cool) and me with my black penny
paper one. The strawberries and cherries came out in
swarms—very big cherries and little wild strawbugs. Finally we
found a spot in the Louvre among the sculpture which was cool
as a grotto. Jack had an idea of making himself a neat toga,
taking the Nation for a parchment roll and standing becalmed
upon a Roman pedestal until the weather changed. There are
glorious things in that first room in the Louvre—Greek statues,
portions of the Parthenon Frieze, a head of Alexander, wonderful draped female figures. Greek drapery is very strange.
One looks at it—the lines seem to be dead straight, and yet
there is movement—a kind of suppleness and though there is
no suggestion of the body beneath one is conscious of it as a
living, breathing thing. How on earth is that done? And they
seemed to have been able to draw a line with a chisel as if it
were a pencil—one line and there is an arm or a nose—perfect.
The Romans are deaders compared to them. We had a long
stare at the Venus de Milo, too. One can't get away from the
fact—she is marvellously beautiful. All the little people in

straw hats buzz softly round her. Such a comfort to see something they know. 'Our Maud has ever such a fine photograph of her over the piano.' But 'she' doesn't care.

About Rubens. I never can forget his paintings in Antwerp. They seemed to me far more brilliant than the London ones—I mean impressive. He must have enjoyed himself no end adoing of them. But I confess I like his small paintings best. One gets really too much for ones money in the big ones. There's rather a fat woman wading in a stream in the National Gallery°— quite a small one. Its very good, isn't it?

I shall have no time to look at pictures here till we get back from Switzerland. Its terrible how Jack and I seem to get engaged. We are pursued by dinners and lunches and telephone bells and dentists. Oh, Richard, do you FEAR the dentist? He reduces me to a real worm. Once I am established in that long green plush chair with my heels higher almost than my head all else fades. What a fiendish business it is! One day I shall write a story that you will have to tie up your face to read. I shall call it *Killing the Nerve*.

Since I last wrote to you a great deal seems to have happened. But that is the effect of living in a city. I long to get away and to work. We are spending June and July at a hotel about 750 feet below Montana. It is a very simple place and isolated, standing in one of those forest clearings. There are big grassy slopes almost like lawns between the clumps of trees and by the time we get there the flowers will all be out as they were last year. Paris is a fine city but one cant get hold of any big piece of work here; the day splits up into pieces and people play the piano below ones window or sing even if one sits with the door locked and the outside world put away.

There is just a vague idear that Jack may go to England this autumn for a few weeks. I hope he does. We both intend to come over next spring whatever happens and rescue our furniture and make one final tremenjous effort to catch a little house in the country.

Forgive this letter—all in bits, all scattered—Ill write a different one when I get to Switzerland. Richard, I wish—but no—things can wait. In the meantime we never see a painting without thinking of you, talking of you. In fact its hard to tell you how much of our life we share with you, the far away one.

Wingley, our small enchanted brother, passed through Paris last week on his way to England with Ida B. who is going to keep him until we can offer him a real home. It wrung my heart to see the poor little chap sitting in his bastick.

With love, dear Richard, a special summer line of love
Katherine.

To Elizabeth Russell

Hotel d'Angleterre | Montana-sur-Sierre
(Valais) | Suisse | Monday. [5 June 1922]

Dearest Elizabeth

I have been waiting until we got here before I answered your last letter. Rather a disappointing thing has happened. I suppose my enthusiasm was too much for the Furies.° At any rate I wish now I had waited before praising so loudly. For they have turned about their chariots and are here in full force again. It was 'silly' to be so happy and to say so much about it; I feel ashamed of my last letter. But I felt every word of it at the time and more—much more. However, perhaps the truth is some people live in cages and some are free. One had better accept one's cage and say no more about it. I *can*—I *will*. And I do think its simply unpardonable to bore one's friends with 'I can't get out'. Your precious sympathy, most dear Elizabeth I shall never forget. It made that glimpse of the open air twice as marvellous. But here I am with dry pleurisy, coughing away, and so on and so on. Please don't think I feel tragic or despairing. I don't. Ainsi soit-il [So be it]. What one cannot understand one must accept.

My only trouble is John. He ought to divorce me, marry a really gay young healthy creature, have childen and ask me to be godmother. He needs a wife beyond everything. I shall never be a wife and I feel such a fraud when he still believes that one day I shall turn into one. Poor John! Its hellish to live with a femme malade [ill woman]. But its also awfully hard to say to him 'you know darling I shall never be any good.'

But enough of this. I want to tell you what a perfect glimpse we had of the Chalet Soleil as we bumped here in the cold mountain rain. It was raining but the sun shone too, and all your lovely house is hidden in white blossom. Only *heavenly* blue shutters showed through. The little 'working' chalet is in an absolute nest of green. It looked awfully fairy; one felt there ought to have been a star on top of the slender chimney. But from the very first glimpse of your own road everything breathed of you. It was like enchantment.

We are alone in this big, very airy, silent hotel. The two ancient dames look after us and pursue me with 'tisanes' [infusions]. They are very anxious for me to try a poultice of mashed potatoes on my chest pour changer avec une feuille de moutarde [alternating with a layer of mustard]. But so far I have managed to wave the pommes de terre [potatoes] away. Its peaceful beyond words after that odious, grilling Paris. John goes out for walks and comes back with marvellous flowers. He says there are whole fields of wood violets still, and carpets of anemones. We are both working but I feel dull and stupid as though I have been living on a diet of chimney pots. I never want to see a city again.

We hope to stay here until the end of August. I am too much bother to have in a house, my dearest cousin. It would have been wonderful, but as it is I feel I should be a nuisance and Im frightened you would 'turn' against me. Fancy meeting me on the stairs, very short of puff, or seeing me always about. One can never get invalids out of one's eye—its the very worst of them. But it would be lovely if John might spend a few days with you ... It will be such a joy to see you! I do look forward to that.

With much, much love | Yours ever
Katherine.

To S. S. Koteliansky

Hotel d'Angleterre | Randogne-sur-Sierre |°
(Valais) Suisse. [17 June 1922]

Koteliansky

Would you care for a cat? I have a cat who is at present in England and I cannot have him with me. It is too cruel to make cats travel. He is a beautiful animal, except for a scratch on his nose, one ear badly bitten and a small hole in his head. From the back view however he is lovely for he has a superb tail. In all his ways he can be trusted to behave like a gentleman. He is extremely independent and, of course, understands everything that is said to him. Perhaps Mademoiselle Guita would like him?

But this is not urgent. At present he is with Ida Baker. She would hand him over to anyone in a basket. But I dont *want* you to have him. I mean I am not for one moment asking you to have him. Of course not. Simply, it occurred to me that you might find it a not unpleasant idea ... I must confess he will not catch mice. But mice do not know that and so the sight of him keeps them away. He has a fair knowledge of French.

It is very nice here, remote, peaceful, but not remote enough. It is difficult to manage one's external life as one would wish. I have been working towards one thing for years now. But it is still on the horizon. Because I cannot yet attain to it without 'misunderstanding' it cant be mine yet. But it comes nearer—much nearer. But I do not like to talk 'prudently'. In fact it is detestable.

To change the subject. I saw something awfully nice the day after I got here. Behind this hotel there is a big stretch of turf before one comes to the forest. And in the late afternoon as the herds were driven home when they came to this turf they went wild with delight. Staid, black cows began to dance and leap and cut capers, lowing softly. Meek, refined-looking little sheep who looked as though buttercups would not melt in their mouths could not resist it; they began to jump, to spin round, to bound forward like rocking horses. As for the goats they were extremely brilliant dancers of the highest order—the Russian

Ballet was nothing compared to them. But best of all were the cows. Cows do not *look* very good dancers, do they? Mine were as light as feathers and really gay, joyful. It made one laugh to see them. But it was so beautiful too. It was like the first chapter in Genesis over again. 'Fourfooted creatures created He them.'° One wanted to weep as well.

> Goodbye my precious friend
> Katherine.

To S. S. Koteliansky

Chateau Belle Vue° | Sierre (Valais) | Suisse |
17. VII. 1922

Dear precious Koteliansky,

After all, I shall not have the money to come to England for a week this autumn. I must be in Paris on August 20th and then for about 10 days I must attend to my Father who is coming to see me there on his way back to New Zealand. After that, I shall be alone for the autumn, and for 10–12 weeks I must go to the clinique once a week. But I tell you all these tedious details simply because, in spite of my Spartan feelings in my last letter, I wonder again if there is any possibility of your coming across during that time. I do—I *long* to see you and for us to talk. Do not think I am trying to interfere or to make demands. It is not that at all. But it would be so nice, so awfully nice to look forward to such happiness. I want to talk to you for hours about—Aaron's Rod,° for instance. Have you read it?

There are certain things in this new book of L's that I do not like. But they are not important or really part of it. They are trivial, encrusted, they cling to it as snails cling to the underside of a leaf. But apart from them there is the leaf, is the tree, firmly planted, deep thrusting, outspread, growing grandly, alive in every twig. It is a living book; it is warm, it breathes. And it is written by a living man with *conviction*. Oh, Koteliansky, what a relief it is to turn away from these little predigested books written by authors who have nothing to say.

It is like walking by the sea at high tide eating a crust of bread and looking over the water. I am so sick of all this modern seeking which ends in seeking. *Seek* by all means, but the text goes on 'that ye shall find'.° And although of course there can be no ultimate finding, there is a kind of finding by the way which is enough, is sufficient. But these seekers in the looking glass, these half-female, frightened writers-of-today—you know, darling, they remind me of the green-fly in roses—they are a kind of blight.

I do not want to be hard. I hope to God I am not unsympathetic. But it seems to me there comes a time in Life when one must realise one is grownup—a man. And when it is no longer decent to go on probing and probing. Life is so short. The world is rich. There are so many adventures possible. Why do we not gather our strength together and <u>live</u>. It all comes to much the same thing. In youth most of us are, for various reasons, slaves. And then, when we are able to throw off our chains, we prefer to keep them. Freedom is dangerous, is frightening.

If only I can be a good enough writer to strike a blow for freedom! It is the one axe I want to grind. Be free—and you can afford to give yourself to life! Even to believe in life.

I do not go all the way with Lawrence. His ideas of sex mean nothing to me. But I feel nearer L. than anyone else. All these last months I have thought as he does about many things. Does this sound nonsense to you? Laugh at me if you like or scold me. But remember what a disadvantage it is having to write such things. If we were talking one could say it all in a few words. It is so hard not to dress ones ideas up in their Sunday clothes and make them look all stiff and shining in a letter. My ideas look awful in their best dresses.

(Now I have made myself a glass of tea. Every time I drop a piece of lemon into a glass of tea I say 'Koteliansky'. Perhaps it is a kind of grace.) I went for such a lovely drive today behind a very intelligent horse who listened to every word the driver and I said and heartily agreed. One could tell from his ears that he was even extremely interested in the conversation. They are thinning the vines for the last time before harvest. One can almost smell the grapes. And in the orchards apples are reddening; it is going to be a wonderful year for pears. But one could write about the drive for as many pages as there are in Ulysses.

It is late. I must go to bed. Now the train going to Italy has flashed past. Now it is silent again except for the old toad who goes *ka*-ka—*ka*-ka—laying down the law.

> Goodnight.|Your
> Katherine.

To J. M. Murry

[Hôtel Chateau Belle Vue|Sierre (Valais),
7 August 1922]

Dearest Bogey,

I have been on the point of writing this letter for days. My heart has been behaving in such a curious fashion that I can't imagine it means nothing. So, as I should hate to leave you unprepared, I'll just try and jot down what comes into my mind. All my manuscripts I leave entirely to you to do what you like with. Go through them one day, dear love, and destroy all you do not use. Please destroy all letters you do not wish to keep and all papers. You know my love of tidiness. Have a clean sweep, Bogey, and leave all fair—will you?

Books are yours, of course .... Monies, of course, are all yours. In fact, my dearest dear, I leave everything to you—to the secret you whose lips I kissed this morning. In spite of everything how happy we have been! I feel no other lovers have walked the earth more joyfully—in spite of all.

Farewell°—my precious love,

> I am for ever and ever|Your WIG

To Sydney Schiff

6 Pond Street° | Hampstead N.W.3 | Monday
[26 August 1922]

My dear Sydney,

Your letter made me feel angry with myself & very ungracious at having refused your so kind invitation. Please forgive me! I look forward more than I can say to seeing you and Violet in London. By the time you come I hope to be *settled* in my new rooms (they are at this address). I already dream of *no end* of a talk before my fire.

I shall never be able to say a word to the intelligentsia, Sydney. They are too lofty, too far removed. No, that is unfair. Its simply that they are not in the least interested. Nor do they appear to know what one is driving at when one groans at the present state of English writing. As I see it the whole stream of English literature is trickling out in little innumerable marsh trickles. There is no gathering together, no force, no impetus, absolutely no passion! Why this is I don't know. But one feels a deathly cautiousness in everyone—a determination not to be caught out. Who wants to catch them out or give them away? I can't for the life of me see the need of this acute suspicion and narrowness. Perhaps the only thing to do is to ignore it all and go on with one's own job. But I confess that seems to me a poor conclusion to come to. If I, as a member of the orchestra think I am playing right, try my utmost to play right, I don't want to go on in the teeth of so many others—not playing at all or playing as I believe falsely. It is a problem. Let us talk it all over.

About Lawrence. Yes, I agree there is much triviality, much that is neither here nor there. And a great waste of energy that ought to be well spent. But I did feel there was growth in Aaron's Rod—there was no desire to please or placate the public. I did feel that Lorenzo was profoundly moved. Because of this perhaps I forgive him too much his faults.

Its vile weather here—a real fog. I am alone in the house—10.30 p.m. Murry & Brett are both at parties. Footsteps pass and repass. That is a marvellous sound—and the low voices—

talking on—dying away. It takes me back years, to the agony of *waiting* for one's love ... I am lunching with Orage° on Wednesday. What happiness! Goodnight dear friend. I press your hand.

Katherine.

To J. M. Murry

[Select Hôtel, 1 Place de la Sorbonne, Paris]
Wednesday. [11 October 1922]

Dearest Bogey

I have a letter and a card of yours to answer. How horrid your Father is—really horrid! I am so sorry for your Mother. Do you think your policy of keeping silent for her sake is a good one? I quite see quarrelling would be no use but I *do* feel a few *chosen words*, so that he can't preen himself upon having 'had the best of it', would be worth while. Give him something solid to think over. J.M.M. (quite quietly): 'You know Dad youre a horrid bully. Nobody loves you.' I am afraid hell live for ever, too. Why should he die? All his life is there coiled up, unused, in a horrid way *saved*. He is a very odd character. I feel you left your Mother, thinking of her with real, tender love, seeing her at Selsfield° even, helping her out of the car. Or am I wrong?

That lecture must have been a queer little aside—wasn't it? A sort of short loop line.

It has got very cold here. I feel it. I am adjusting myself to it and it makes me rather dull—distrait, you know. I have had to leave my dear little grenier au 6ieme [sixth floor attic] for something less lofty more expensive but warmer. However, its a very nice room 'et vous avez un beau pendule' [and you have a lovely clock] as the garçon said. *He* thoroughly approves of the change. All the same, you say 'tell me all about yourself'. Ill have a try. Here goes.

A new way of being is not an easy thing to *live*. Thinking about it preparing to meet the difficulties and so on is one thing, meeting those difficulties another. I have to die to so much; I have to make such *big* changes. I feel the only thing to do is to get the dying over—to court it, almost (Fearfully hard, that) and then all hands to the business of being reborn again. What do I mean exactly? Let me give you an instance. Looking back, my boat is almost swamped sometimes by seas of sentiment. 'Ah what I have missed. How sweet it was, how dear how warm, how simple, how precious.' And I think of the garden at the Isola Bella and the furry bees and the house wall so warm. But then I remember what we really felt there. The blanks, the silences, the anguish of continual misunderstanding. Were we positive, eager, real—alive? No, we were not. We were a nothingness shot with gleams of what might be. But no more. Well, I have to face everything as far as I can & see where I stand—what *remains*.

For with all my soul I do long for a real life, for truth, and for real strength. Its simply incredible, watching KM, to see how little causes a panic. Shes a perfect corker at toppling over.

I envy you Selsfield. How I should like to be there now, this morning. How beautiful it is—how gracious. I am so glad you are there, my darling Bogey. I feel it *is* the house of your dreams—isn't it? Do you have flowers on your writing table? Or only pipes in pots and feathers! *You wont forget the Tchekhov will you?* Id *like* the Lit. Sup. with your review° if it wasnt too much of a bore to send it.

Ever your
Wig.

To J. M. Murry

[Select Hôtel, 1 Place de la Sorbonne, Paris]
Sunday [15 October 1922]

I have opened my letter darling to add something. Its this. Darling Bogey in your spare time, however little that is, get nearer the growing earth than that wheelbarrow and spade. *Grow things*. Plant. Dig up. Garden. I feel with all the force of my being that 'happiness' is in these things. If its only cabbages let it be cabbages rather than chess. Sweep leaves. Make fires.

Do anything to work with your hands in contact with the earth.

You see chess only feeds your already over developed intellectual centre. And that regular spade-and-barrow becomes a habit too soon, and is likely only to feed your moving centre—to exercise your machine. Does that sound awful rot to you?

Why don't you get some animals? Im not joking. Two hours a day would be enough for them. Birds, rabbits, a goat—*anything* and live through it or them! I know you will say you haven't the time. But you'll find your work is a 100 times easier if you come to it refreshed, renewed, rich, happy. Does this sound like preaching. Dont let it. I am trying to tell you what I feel deep down is your way of escape. It is to really throw yourself into life, not desperately but with the love you even don't feel yet. People wont do. We know too well that unless one has a background of reality in oneself people can't endure in us. When we have a table spread we can afford to open our door to guests, but not before. But enough of this. I am afraid of boring you.

Did you ask L.E. [Locke-Ellis] about tulips? Has he got anemones in the garden? *You* ought to see to them; they are your flowers. Why don't you write to Suttons° and ask their advice.

Oh, if you knew how I believe in Life being the only cure for Life.

Ever your own
Wig.

About being like Tchekhov and his letters. Dont forget he *died* at 43. That he spent—how much?—of his life chasing about in a desperate search after health. And if one reads 'intuitively' the last letters they are terrible. What is left of him. 'The braid on German women's dresses—bad taste',° and all the rest is misery. Read the last! All hope is over for him. Letters are deceptive, at any rate. Its true he had occasional happy moments. But for the last 8 years he knew no *security* at all. We know he felt his stories were not half what they might be. It doesn't take much imagination to picture him on his death bed thinking 'I have never had a real chance. Something has been all wrong . . .'

To S. S. Koteliansky

[Le Prieuré, Fontainebleau, 19 October 1922]

My dear Koteliansky

I hope this letter will not surprise you too much. It has nothing to do with our business arrangements. Since I wrote I have gone through a kind of private revolution. It has been in the air for years with me. And now it has happened very very much is changed.

When we met in London and discussed 'ideas' I spoke as nearly as one can the deepest truth I knew to you. But even while I spoke it I felt a pretender—for my knowledge of this truth is negative, not positive, as it were cold, and not warm with life. For instance all we have said of 'individuality' and of being strong and single, and of growing—I believe it. I try to act up to it. But the reality is far far different. Circumstances still hypnotise me. I am a divided being with a bias towards what I wish to be, but no more. And this it seems I cannot improve. No, I cannot. I have tried. If you knew how many notebooks there are of these trials, but they never succeed. So I am always conscious of this secret disruption in me—and at last (thank Heaven!) it has ended in a complete revolution and I mean to change my whole way of life entirely. I mean to learn to work in every possible way with my hands, looking after animals and doing all kinds of manual labour. I do not want to write any stories until I am a less terribly poor human being. It seems to me that in life as it is lived today the catastrophe is *imminent*; I feel this catastrophe in me. I want to be prepared for it, at least.

The world as I know it is no joy to me and I am useless in it. People are almost nonexistent. This world to me is a dream and the people in it are sleepers. I have known just instances of waking but that is all. I want to find a world in which these instances are united. Shall I succeed? I do not know. I scarcely care. What is important is to try & learn to live—really live, and in relation to everything—not isolated (this isolation is death to me).

Does this sound fabulous? I cannot help it. I have to let you know for you mean much to me. I know you will never listen to whatever foolish things other people may say about me. Those other helpless people going round in their little whirlpool do not matter a straw to me.

I will send you my address this week. In the meantime all is forwarded from the Select Hotel by Ida Baker, with whom I must part company for a time.

I press your hands, dear dear friend

Katherine.

All this sounds much too serious and dramatic. As a matter of fact there is absolutely no tragedy in it, of course.

To J. M. Murry

Le Prieuré
Fontainebleau-Avon | Seine-et-Marne
[23 October 1922]

My darling Bogey

Ill tell you what this life is more like than anything; it is like Gulliver's Travellers. One has, all the time, the feeling of having been in a wreck & by the mercy of Providence, got ashore ... somewhere. Simply everything is different. Not only languages but food, ways, people, music, methods, hours—*all*. Its a real new life.

At present this is my day. I get up at 7.30, light the fire (with kindling drying overnight) wash in ice cold water (Id quite forgotten how good water is to wash in & to drink) & go down to breakfast—which is coffee, butter, bread, gorgonzola cheese & quince jam & eggs. After breakfast, make my bed, do my room, rest, & then go into the garden till dinner which is 11 A.M. Which is a very large meal with things like beans minced with raw onions, vermicelli with icing sugar & butter, veal wrapped in lettuce leaves & cooked in cream. After dinner, in the garden again till 3 o'clock teatime. After tea, any light job that is going until dark. When all knock off work, wash, dress & make ready for dinner again at 7. After dinner most of the people gather in the salon round an enormous fire and there is

music, tambourines, drums and piano, dancing & perhaps a
display of all kinds of queer dance exercises. At ten we go to
bed. Doctor Young,° a real friend of mine, comes up and makes
me up a good fire. In 'return' I am patching the knee of his
trousers today.

But its all 'stranger' than that. For instance. I was looking for
wood the other evening. All the boxes were empty. I found a
door at the end of the passage, went through & down some
stone steps. Presently steps came up & a woman appeared very
simply dressed with her head bound in a ⟨black⟩ white
handkerchief. She had her arms full of logs. I spoke in French,
but she didn't understand. English—no good. But her glance
was so lovely—laughing & gentle, absolutely unlike people as I
have known people. Then I patted a log & she gave it to me &
we went our ways ...

At present the entire Institute is devoted to manual work,
getting this place in order, out and inside. Its not, of course,
work for the sake of work. Every single thing one does has a
purpose, is part of a 'system'. Some of the English 'arty' &
theosophical people are very trying, too. But one can learn to
use them, I am sure. Though Im not much good at it yet. On
the other hand some of the advanced men and women are truly
wonderful. I am still on my fortnight's probation, simply
spending a fortnight here. Mr Gurdjieff hardly ever speaks a
word to me. He must know me pretty well.

But even if he won't let me stay here I am finished for the
time being with *old circumstances*. They have just not killed me,
and thats all there is to be said for them. All the people I have
known don't really matter to me. Only you matter—more and
more, if that is possible, for now that I am not so 'identified'
with you I can see the real tie that holds us.

Ida, of course was very tragic. She had got to the pitch of
looking after me when she gave me a handkerchief without my
asking for it. She *was* me. However, I am sure Ida will recover.
There is something rock-like in her under all that passion for
helplessness.

Jeanne's wedding° made me feel sad, Bogey. I too dislike
that man awfully. I think the fat purple fellow was Mac-
Gavin,° for some reason. Thank you for telling me about it. I

must write to Marie [Chaddie] in a day or two. Forgive this hasty writing. Do send Lit. Sups. They are so good for lighting fires. I wish you were here. Its such happiness. Ever my darling

Your

Wig Voyageuse.

To J. M. Murry

[Le Prieuré, Fontainebleu] Tuesday.
[25 October 1922]

My darling Bogey

I was so glad to get your second letter today. Don't feel we are silently & swiftly moving away from each other. Do you *really*? And what do you mean by us meeting 'on the othe side'? Where, Boge? You are much more mysterious than I!

I have managed this badly for this reason. Ive never let you know how much I have suffered in these five years. But that wasn't my fault. I could not. You would not receive it, either. And all I [am] doing now is trying to put into practice the 'ideas' I have had for so long of another, and a *far more truthful* existence. I want to learn something that no books can teach me, and I want to try & escape from my terrible illness. That again you cant be expected to understand. You think I am like other people—I mean—*normal*. I'm not. I don't know which is the ill me or the well me. I am simply one pretence after another—only now I recognise it.

I believe Mr Gurdjieff is the only person who can help me. It is great happiness to be here. Some people are stranger than ever but the strangers I am at last feeling near & they are my own people at last. So I feel. Such beautiful understanding & sympathy I have never known in the outside world.

As for writing stories & being true to one's gift. I couldn't write them if I were not here, even. I am at the end of my source for the time. Life has brought me no <u>flow.</u> I want to write but differently—far more steadily. I am writing this on a corner of the table against orders for the sun shines & I am supposed to be in the garden. Ill write again, my darling precious.

Ever your own
Wig.

To J. M. Murry

[Le Prieuré, Fontainebleau,
10 November 1922]

£5 note enclosed.

My darling Bogey

I had a letter from you today saying you had bought a pruning knife. I hope you succeed with the old trees. Here it is part of the 'work' to do a great many things, especially things which one does *not* like. I see the point of that. Its the same principle as facing people whom one shrinks from and so on. It is to develop a greater range in oneself. But what happens in practice is that no sooner do the people begin doing those things they don't like than the dislike changes. One feels it no longer. Its only that first step which is so terribly hard to take.

Are you having really divine weather? Its marvellous here— like late spring today, really *warm*. The leaves are still falling. The park belonging to this chateau is incredibly beautiful, and with our live stock roaming about it begins to look like a little piece of virgin creation.

I am fearfully busy. What do I do? Well, I learn Russian, which is a terrific job, have charge of the indoor carnations— no joke, & spend the rest of the day paying visits to places where people are working. Then every evening about 50 people meet in the salon and there is music and they are working at present at a tremendous ancient Assyrian Group Dance. I have no words with which to describe it. To see it seems to change ones whole being for the time.

Until I came here I did not realise with what a little bit of my mind, even, I lived. I was a little European with a liking for eastern carpets and music and for something that I vaguely called The East. But now I feel as though I am turned to that side far more than the other. The west seems so poor so scattered. I cannot believe knowledge or wisdom are there. I expect this is a phase. I tell it you because I said I would tell you my reactions ... In three weeks here I feel I have spent years in India, Arabia, Afghanistan, Persia. That is very odd, isn't it. And oh, how one wanted to voyage like this—how bound one felt. Only now I know!

There is another thing here. Friendship. The real thing that you and I have dreamed of. Here it exists between women & women & men & women & one feels it is unalterable, and living in a way it never can be anywhere else. I cant say I have friends yet. I am simply not fit for them. I don't know myself enough to be really trusted, and I am weak where these people are strong. But even the relationships I have are dear beyond any friendships I have known.

But I am giving the impression that we all live together in brotherly love & blissful happiness. Not at all. One suffers terribly. If you have been ill for 5 years you cant expect to be well in five weeks. If you have been ill for 20 years & according to Mr Gurdjieff we all of us have our 'illness' it takes very severe measures to put one right. But the point is there is hope. One can & does believe that one will escape from living in circles & will live a <u>conscious</u> life. One can, through work, escape from falsity & be true to ones own self—not to what anyone else on earth thinks one is.

I wish you could meet some of the men here. You would like them very very much, especially a Mr Salzmann,° who speaks very little. I must stop this letter. Is it a rigmarole?

I don't know what you mean darling by seeing me as an angel with a sword. I don't feel at all like one. There is another thing. You can't *really* be happy in my happiness. No one ever is. That phrase is only a kind of buffer—don't you think? Its like people living through their children. Well, they may do it. But its not life. Neither can I ever teach you how to live. How is it possible? You are you. I am I. We can only lead our own lives together.

But perhaps I am treating too seriously what you said.
Goodbye for now, my darling heart.

Ever your
Wig.

I enclose a £5 note. Will you pay Heals° bill & keep the rest for
any odd bills I may send you later. I know there are some. If
you know anyone coming to Paris *do* give them 2 pairs of grey
milanese stockings (for size 5 shoes) to post on to me. I need
them awfully. Merci en avance [Thank you in advance].

To J. M. Murry

[Le Prieuré, Fontainebleau,
17 December 1922]

My darling Bogey
  I am so delighted to hear of your ½ motorcar. I think it is a
most excellent idea. What fun you and Sullivan will have with
it. It is so pleasant to think of you two together and I like to
know that Sullivan will now understand you from a real
standpoint, after sharing your life & working with you in the
real sense. Do you teach him to cook and to sew and to knit.
The fairies in the keyholes must have a quiet laugh or two of a
gentle kind. As to those four little wood gatherers I love them. I
hope your tooth is better. Just the same thing has happened to
me. My biggest and brightest stopping has come out. But I
shall have to hang on until the spring when I can get to Paris.
So far all is well.
  My fortunes have changed again. I have been moved back
from my little bare servants bedroom on the general corridor to
my beautiful sumptuous first room overlooking the lovely park.
It seems almost incredible grandeur. I suppose—I feel I have
learnt the lesson that other room had to teach me. I have learnt
that I can rough it in a way you & I have never done, that I
can stand any amount of noise, that I can put up with
untidiness, disorder, queer smells, even, without losing my head
or *really* suffering more than superficially. But how did Mr.

Gurdjieff know how much I needed that experience? And another mystery is that last week when it was intensely cold I felt I had come to an end of all that room had to teach me. I was very depressed and longing beyond words for some real change and for beauty again. I almost decided to ask him to send me away until the weather got warmer. Then on Saturday afternoon when I was in the stable he came up to rest, too, and talked to me a little. First about cows and then about the monkey he has bought which is to be trained to clean the cows. Then he suddenly asked me how I was and said I looked better. 'Now,' he said 'you have two doctors you must obey. Doctor Stable and Doctor New Milk. Not to think, not to write ... Rest. Rest. Live in your body again.' I think he meant get back into your body. He speaks very little English but when one is with him one seems to understand all that he suggests. The next thing I heard was that I was to come into here for the rest of the winter. Sometimes I wonder if we 'make up' Mr Gurdjieff's wonderful understanding. But one is always getting a fresh example of it. And he always acts at precisely the moment one needs it. That is what is so strange ...

Dear Bogey darling I shall not have any Xmas present for you. But you know that £5 I sent you. How much did you spend. Would you buy a book each for Chaddie & Jeanne for me & keep the rest for yourself? Jeanne would like DeLaMares new poems Down-a-Down-Derry° I am sure (its 7/6, isn't it?) and Chaddie—hm—that is difficult! Some book that looks pretty and tastes sweet—some love poems. Is that too vague? And may I ask you to execute these commissions for me? I hope there will be something left over for you darling. Buy it with my love. I'll tell you what I want for a present. Your photograph. The proof of the drawing of course I should simply treasure, but why should you send me that. Keep it. Of course if you could have it copied. There is a man here who is going to take a photograph of me one day. I have changed. I have no longer a fringe—very odd. We had a fire here the other night. A real one. Two beautiful rooms burnt out & a real fear the whole place would go. Cries of 'Vode! Vode!' (water), people rushing past all black & snatching at jugs & basins, Mr Gurdjieff with a hammer knocking down the wall. The real thing, in fact.

What is the weather like with you. Its so soft & spring like here that actually primroses are out. So are the Christmas roses under the espalier pear trees. I *love* Christmas; I shall always feel it is a holy time. I wonder if dear old Hardy will write a poem this year.

God bless you my darling precious

Ever your
Wig.

To Ida Baker

Le Prieuré. [24 December 1922]

Dear Ida

This is to wish you a happy Xmas. I meant to have something for you. For the moment I have nothing & can't get anything. I can't give people commissions nor get to Fontainebleau myself. So take whatever you please that I happen to have and that you think you would like. What about the green cardigan par exemple? Especially as you probably paid for it yourself. In the course of a week or two I shall send you the sleeping vests you bought me. I cant wear them. That kind of wool next to my skin brings me out in a rash ... I presume of course, it doesn't you.

We are going to fêter le Noel [celebrate Christmas] in tremendous style here. Every sort of lavish generous hospitable thing has been done by Mr Gurdjieff. He wants a real old fashioned *English* Xmas—an extraordinary idea here!—& we shall sit down to table 60 persons to turkeys, geese, a whole sheep, a pig, puddings, heaven knows what in the way of dessert, & wines by the barrel. Theres to be a tree, too & Father Xmas. I am doing all I can for the little children so that they will be roped in for once. Ive just sent them over coloured paper & asked them to help to make flowers. Its pathetic the interest they are taking — —

Our pudding was made in a babys bath, stirred by everybody & Mr Gurdjieff put in a coin. Who gets the coin gets our darling new born calf for a present. The calf—1 day old—was

led into the salon to the beating of tambourines & to a special
melody composed for it. It took it very quietly. But two minute
baby pigs which were also brought in & allowed to play
squealed & shrieked terribly. I have been v. interested in the
calf. The cow didn't seem to mind the affair. She only lowed
faintly & when a leg appeared Madame Ovstrovsky° & Nina
put a rope round it & pulled & presently a tall weak feeble
creature emerged. The cows eyes as big as saucers reminded me
of Charles.° I wish we gave our cows apples. Some of the names
are Equivoqueveckwa, Baldaofim, Mitasha, Bridget. Our mule
is Drabfeet.

My existence here is not meagre or miserable. Nothing is
done by accident. I understand v. well why my room was
changed & so on, and to live among so many people knowing
something of them, sharing something, that is for me very great
change & ça donne beaucoup [it gives me much].

I shall be glad though when the spring comes. Winter is a
difficult time.

You know you must not worry about me or say you do or
dont. Its exactly as though you took a piece of my flesh and
gnawed it. It helps neither you nor me. *Worry is waste of energy*; it
is therefore sin. And to see you waste energy destroys energy in
me, so you sin in two ways. Thats surely easy to ⟨say⟩ see.

As to starting[?] gear why dont you begin taking photographs of yourself—take them all day. And look at them. Then
begin to decide which are 'good' and which are 'bad' ones.
Then try & sort the work bag in your mind before you begin to
learn to think & direct your thought. Open your mind & really
look into it. Perhaps you wont mind what you see. I mind.

I must end this letter. If youd like me for a friend as from
this Xmas Id like to be your friend. But not too awfully serious,
ma chère. The whole difficulty in life is to find the *way* between
extremes—to preserve ones poise in fact to get a hold of the
pendulum.

Jack said he would be delighted to have you whenever you
felt like it. He sounds different in his letters, much simpler.

Yours ever
K.M.

To J. M. Murry

[Le Prieuré, Fontainebleau] Boxing Day
[26 December 1922]

My darling Bogey

I think the drawing of you is quite extraordinarily good, and in a very subtle way. I had no idea Rothenstein was that kind of artist.° People will say it makes you look old. That is true. But you have that look. I am sure c'est juste [it's fair]. I am more than glad to have it & I shall keep it v. carefully. Thank you, my dearest. The photograph I don't like so well for some reason. But photographs always pale before good drawings. Its not fair on them.

How is the old Adam revived in you, I wonder? What aspect has he? There is nothing to be done when he rages except to remember that its bound to be—its the swing of the pendulum—ones only hope is when the bout is exhausted to get back to what you think you really care for aim for wish to live by as soon as possible. Its the intervals of exhaustion that seem to waste so much energy. You see, my love, the question is always '*Who am I*' and until that is discovered I don't see how one can really direct anything in ones self. '*Is there a Me*'. One must be certain of that before one has a real unshakeable leg to stand on. And I don't believe for one moment these questions can be settled by the head alone. It is this life of the *head*, this formative intellectual life at the expense of all the rest of us which has got us into this state. How can it get us out of it? I see no hope of escape except by learning to live in our emotional & instinctive being as well and to balance all three.

You see Bogey if I were allowed one single cry to God that cry would be *I want to be REAL*. Until I am that I don't see why I shouldn't be at the mercy of old Eve in her various manifestations for ever.

But this place has taught me so far how unreal I am. It has taken from me one thing after another (the things never were mine) until at this present moment all I know really really is that I am not annihilated and that I hope—more than hope—

believe. It is hard to explain and I am always a bit afraid of boring you in letters.

I heard from Brett yesterday. She gave a very horrid picture of the present Sullivan and his views on life and women. I don't know how much of it is even vaguely true but it corresponds to Sullivan the Exhibitionist. The pity of it is life is so short and we waste about 9/10 of it—simply throw it away. I always feel Sullivan refuses to face the fact of his wastefulness. And sometimes one feels he never will. All will pass like a dream, with mock comforts, mock consolations . . .

Our cowshed has become enriched with 2 goats and two love birds. The goats are very lovely as they lie in the straw or so delicately dance towards each other butting gently with their heads. When I was there yesterday Mr Gurdjieff came in and showed Lola and Nina who were milking the cows the way to milk a goat. He sat down on a stool seized the goat & swung its hind legs across his knees. So there the goat was on its two front legs, helpless. This is the way Arabs milk. He looked very like one. I had been talking before to a man here whose passion is astrology and he had just written the signs of the Zodiac on the whitewashed stable walls. Then we went up to the little gallery & drank koumiss.

Goodbye for now, my darling. I feel this letter is flat & dull. Forgive it. I am ever your own loving

Wig.

To Harold Beauchamp

Le Prieuré |
Fontainebleau-Avon | Seine-et-Marne |
31 XII 1922

My dearest Father

I am writing this letter when the old year is at his last gasp and in the very act of turning up his toes! May the New Year be full of happiness for you. I wish I could imagine we might meet in it but perhaps in the one after I shall be fortunate enough to turn towards home and to see you at the Grange. It is a dream I would love to realise.

Since I last wrote I have been leading a very tame semi-existence here. My heart, under this new treatment, which is one of graduated efforts and exercise, feels decidedly stronger, and my lungs in consequence feel quieter, too. Its a remarkable fact that since arriving here I have not had to spend one entire day in bed—an unprecedented record for me! I feel more and more confident that if I can give this treatment a fair trial—as I intend to do—and stay on for six months at least, I shall be infinitely stronger in every way. More I do not venture to say.

Did I tell you in my last letter that the people here have had built a little gallery in the cowshed with a very comfortable divan and cushions. And I lie there for several hours each day to inhale the smell of the cows. It is supposed to be a sovereign remedy for the lungs. I feel I must look a great pa-woman, perched up aloft. But the air is wonderfully light and sweet to breathe, and I enjoy the experience. I feel inclined to write a book called 'The Cowiness of the Cow' as a result of observing them at such close quarters.

We had a very quiet Christmas here, as the Russian Christmas is not until January 6th. Their New Year is on January 13th. What a frightful bother! Christmas, in any case, is no fun away from ones own people. I seldom want to make merry with strangers, and that particular feast is only enjoyable because of its childish associations. I remember us all going to St Paul's° and Mother's enjoyment of 'Hark the Herald Angels Sing'. And that makes me think of darling Leslie still a child, enjoying everything. Such memories do not make for gaiety.

I see by the papers I have received that my last book is nominated for the Vie Heureuse French Literary Prize° as the former one was. It has no chance of success, for the French never take short stories 'seriously'. However, it is a good advertisement and costs nothing.

Jack still sounds very happy and busy, dividing his time between the country and London, with a strong bias in favour of the country. I do wish the English climate were more temperate and that I could look forward to *settling down* there. But the idea of settling is to me what it seemed to be to grandpa Beauchamp. Only I am driven where he went willingly.

My new book° will not be out before the spring. I am still a little undecided about the title. I feel the choice of titles ought to be studied as a separate art.

Chaddie and Jeanne write very happily. I have no idea of what Charles does all day, though. Of course Jeanne will make the best of it and find happiness, but I don't think it can be much fun living in a hotel in South Kensington.

Chaddie sent me a handkerchief for Christmas (her invariable present) and little Wilfred [her sister Jeanne] a morsel of ribbon that looked like her doll's sash. I still cannot imagine her a married woman.

Well dearest Father this letter is very fragmentary. I so look forward to hearing from you. I expect you found everything in apple pie order and I am sure you had a very warm welcome. How I envy you summer weather, though there is little to complain of in the winter so far. If I began asking you questions about Wellington ways there would be no end to it.

Forgive this handwriting, dearest Father. My constant plea! But as usual my letter case is balanced on my knee & at a rather groggy angle.

The New Year is already here. I must leave the fire and go to bed. God bless you darling Father. May we meet again at not too distant a date.

Ever your devoted child
Kass.

NOTES

1 *The Retreat.* The home of Henry Herron Beauchamp (1825–1907), KM's great-uncle, and father of her novelist cousin 'Elizabeth'.

  Tom. Thomas Trowell (1889–1966), a young Wellington cellist then studying in Germany, with whom KM a little later would fall in love.

  Aunt Louie. Henry Beauchamp's wife.

2 *Gladys.* Gladys Williams, a friend from Queen's College who had gone up to Girton College, Cambridge. She later wrote fiction as 'John Presland'.

  German. Walter Rippmann (1869–1947), professor of German during KM's years at Queen's College; he was an important influence, introducing her to the work of Oscar Wilde and the 1890s.

  '*. . . white birds.*' Quoted from Maurice Maeterlinck's essay, 'The Deeper Life', in *The Treasure of the Humble,* trans. Alfred Sutro (1897), p. 183.

3 *Gwen Rouse.* A contemporary of KM's at Queen's College.

  Mudie's. A bookshop in New Oxford Street.

  Manchester Street W. Fripps Hotel, where the Beauchamp family was staying.

4 *writing.* During her time at Queen's College, KM took cello lessons at the London Academy of Music, and considered a musical career. But by Jan. 1907 she wrote: 'Definitely I have decided not to be a musician. It's not my forte, I can plainly see. The fact remains at that—I must be an authoress.' (*Journal of Katherine Mansfield,* Definitive Edition, ed. John Middleton Murry, 1954, p. 8.)

  '*cottage by the sea*'. At Downes Point, Days Bay, across the harbour from Wellington city.

  Louis Vintras. His *The Silver Net* was published in 1903.

  Dowson—Sherard—School. Ernest Dowson (1867–1900), poet and fiction-writer, became identified in the popular mind with 'decadence', and died at the home of Robert Harborough Sherard (1861–1943), novelist and critic. They did not, as KM suggests, form any kind of 'school'.

  the Bakers. The family of her friend Ida Baker lived in Welbeck Street.

5 *Cousin Ellie & Marjory.* Ellie was Sylvia Payne's mother; Marjory may have been Majorie Wilensky, a school friend.

  75 Tinakori Rd. The large wooden house in Thorndon, close to Wellington city, which Harold Beauchamp had bought in 1898 when the Prime Minister, Richard Seddon, appointed him a director of the Bank of New Zealand.

RLS. For a time Robert Louis Stevenson (1850–1894) was one of KM's favourite authors.

Whistler hour. Among the 'atmospheric' London paintings of James McNeill Whistler (1834–1903) was *The Last of Old Westminster*; however KM probably had in mind his *Nocturne in Blue and Gold: Old Battersea Bridge*.

the Swans. The Swanwick Society was the literary club at Queen's College.

6 *My Grandmother*. Margaret Isabella Dyer, née Mansfield (1840–1907).

'Vignettes'. Four pieces by KM were published in the Australian monthly, the *Native Companion*, under Brady's editorship: 'Vignettes' on 1 Oct. 1907, 'Silhouettes' on 1 Nov., and 'In a Café' and 'In the Botanical Gardens' on 1 Dec.

illustrious relatives. Brady felt that the pieces owed too much to Oscar Wilde.

7 *Waipunga Riverside*. Near the delicately spectacular waterfalls on the Waipunga river.

Pohui. Te Pohue, a settlement of fewer than half a dozen European families, 26 miles north-west of Napier.

'pahs'. Fortified Maori camps or villages.

Mr. Bodley. Henry Bodley was the owner of Whaka Station, a large sheep-run.

pa-man. A Beauchamp family expression for a typical *paterfamilias*, a person of strong personality and quirky individuality.

Millie, Mrs. Webber. Millie Parker, a young woman from Wellington whose relatives organized the expedition; the Webbers were a recently married couple also in the party.

biograph. Trade-name for an early form of cinema projector.

8 *Titi-o 'Kura*. Titiokura Saddle (2,289 ft.) and Turangakuma (2,625 ft.) were the two highest points in the mountain ranges crossed by the party.

konini. Maori name for *Fuchsia excortica*.

Tarawera. Another settlement, of about a dozen Europeans, fifty miles from Napier.

'agèd aged man'. Lewis Carroll's poem 'Upon the Lonely Moor' begins 'I met an aged aged man'.

Miss Wood's eggs. A memory of the Queen's College hostel run by Clara Wood.

9 *Solomon solution*. A cure-all distributed from Melbourne.

Rangitaiki. A settlement on the southern edge of the Kaiangaroa Plateau, at that time a vast tract of tussock and scrub.

10 *By the Sea*. At the 'ideal little cottage' referred to on p. 4.

Tudge. Ethel Tudge, a girl a year senior to KM at Queen's College.

New Barnet Station. After retiring from his medical practice, Sylvia's father Frank Payne moved from Wimpole Street to New Barnet.

Sylvia Gifford. Another fellow-student at Queen's College.

My First Book. A book of children's verses, to be illustrated by her Wellington friend Edith Bendall, which was never published.

11 *Marie Corelli.* Pen-name of the sensational and popular novelist, Mary Mackay (1855–1924).

12 *The Maori.* A ship on the Wellington–Lyttelton run. KM sailed to England from Lyttelton, a port near Christchurch, on 6 July.

The Technical School. KM had enrolled for 'Commercial Subjects' at the Wellington Technical School where she attended classes in typewriting and book-keeping.

Fan. Fanny Sealey, a music-teacher and friend who had been a resident at Beauchamp Lodge in Paddington, where KM would board.

Carennos Staccatto Etudes. The Étude in C Major, Op. 23, the 'Staccato Étude,' by Anton Rubinstein, was frequently performed by the Venezuelan pianist Teresa Carreño (1853–1911), who had toured New Zealand in 1907.

13 *Simpson Hayward.* G. H. Simpson-Hayward, a cricketer who toured New Zealand with the MCC in 1906–7; the team travelled from England on the *Corinthic* with the Beauchamp family.

eating very fast. A scene from chapter 3 of E. F. Benson's *Sheaves* (1908) in which Hugh Grainger carries on a conversation while 'eating fish very fast'.

Aunt Lil. Presumably an Australian relative, as Vera Beauchamp was now staying in Sydney.

Mac. James Mackintosh Bell (1877–1934), a Canadian appointed director of the geological survey of New Zealand, whom Vera married in 1909.

Giggleamus et Viandem— The 'Admiral's Broom'. Dog-Latin for something like 'Let's laugh our way to lunch': it may have been a family joke, or, like the 'Admiral's Broom', perhaps a parlour game.

14 *Ridge Cap.* One of the staff at Queen's College had a cottage at Ridge Cap, Haslemere, where Ida Baker and her sister May had been staying.

Aunt Belle and Uncle Harry. Belle Trinder, KM's mother's younger sister, had married Harry Trinder, a wealthy ship-owner.

Ralph's. Ralph (Rally) Beauchamp was the oldest of Henry Herron Beauchamp's children.

' . . . *blue china*'. The remark is usually attributed to Oscar Wilde.

Henry Wood. KM frequently attended the Promenade Concerts conducted at the Queen's Hall, London, by Henry J. Wood (1869–1944).

'. . . *set*'. Theodore Watts-Dunton (1832–1914), remembered mainly as Swinburne's 'guardian' at Putney during the last years of the poet's life, had applied the phrase 'the renascence of wonder' to Thomas Chatterton. He shared with the novelist George Borrow (1803–81) an avid interest in Romany and gypsies.

15 *Aunt Li.* Eliza Trapp, Annie Burnell Beauchamp's eldest sister.

Clara. Clara Palmer, a Wellington school-teacher and family friend.

tiki. A carved Maori pendant in the shape of a stylized human figure, often regarded as a good-luck charm.

W.F.C.A. Wairarapa Farmers' Co-op Association, a general merchant on Lambton Quay, Wellington.

16 *Maud Allen.* The Canadian dancer and actress (1883–1956) who was attempting to revive Greek classical dance.

the Victoria Hall. Garnet Trowell was then a violinist with the Moody-Manners Opera Company which toured England and Scotland with English-language productions of grand opera. KM is imagining meeting him at the Victoria Hall, Halifax, where they were playing that week.

Domestic Snoring. Cf. *Symphonia Domestica* of Richard Strauss (1864–1949).

18 *the unemployed.* There were up to 800,000 unemployed in England during the financial recession of 1908.

19 *Naval world.* HMS *Collingwood*, a battleship of the Dreadnought class, was launched at Devonport by the wife of the Prime Minister.

the fighting Temeraire. A famous battleship of Nelson's fleet.

20 *April 1909.* This letter was among papers left at George Bowden's flat. On either side of the paper wrapped round it she wrote 'Never to be read, on your honour as my friend, while I am still alive. K. Mansfield.'

his mental decay. KM's early notebooks and several early stories are heavily influenced by Wilde. In June 1907 she recorded her feelings for a female friend, and asked 'O Oscar, am I peculiarly susceptible to sexual impulse?' (*Journal*, 1954, p. 14.)

Kitty Mackenzie. A doctor's daughter in Wellington, who went to England in 1908.

21 *his face today.* 'Rudolf' was a friend of the Trowell twins whom KM met in Brussels at Easter 1906. He later committed suicide. 'Today' suggests that she had kept a photograph of him.

the Blue Review. Murry's periodical *Rhythm* appeared for its last three issues, May–July 1913, under the name of the *Blue Review*.

Secker. The bookseller and printer Martin Secker (1882–1978) was the magazine's publisher.

Boulestin. X. Marcel Boulestin (1873–1943), later famous as a restaurateur, discussed 'Recent French Novels' in the *Blue Review*, June 1913.

Tig. 'The Two Tigers' was a nickname given KM and Murry by the novelist Gilbert Cannan (1884–1955) because of an illustration by Margaret Thompson in the first number of *Rhythm* showing a tiger stepping on a monkey's tail. In the August 1912 number they signed a joint review 'The Two Tigers'. 'Tig', and more frequently 'Wig' for KM, became a common form of address between them.

22 *the Café Royale.* The café-restaurant in Regent Street, famous as a literary meeting-place.

23 *'57'.* Murry's flat at 57 Chancery Lane was also the editorial office for the *Blue Review*.

24 *le petit soldat.* KM had travelled to Gray, in the Zone des Armées, to spend time with Francis Carco, then serving in a postal unit.

25 *mysterious pains.* These recurring pains, which KM believed were rheumatic, were the result of a gonorrhoeal infection contracted several years before.

13 quai aux Fleurs. Francis Carco's flat near Notre-Dame on the Ile de la Cité, overlooking the Seine, which he made available to KM in his absence.

26 *Verlaine.* The bust of the poet by Auguste de Niederhäusern (1863–1913), called Niederhäusern-Rodo.

the raid last night. Two Zeppelins had flown over Paris dropping incendiary bombs on the rue Dulong and the rue des Dames, in the 17th arrondissement.

B. Beatrice Hastings (1879–1943), South African journalist, the mistress of A. R. Orage, editor of the *New Age*, in the years when she had strongly influenced KM, 1910–12. She now lived in Montmartre.

Lilas. The Closerie de Lilas, on the boulevard du Montparnasse.

Simple Contes des Collines. Rudyard Kipling's *Plain Tales from the Hills*, translated into French in 1906.

Bogey. Like 'Jaggle' a few lines above, one of KM's affectionate names for Murry.

The Critic in Judgment. Murry had completed a long poem with this name, published by the Hogarth Press in 1919. KM seems to be confusing its title with Byron's *The Vision of Judgment* (1822), and her memory of stanza LVII:

Upon the verge of space, about the size
   Of half-a-crown, a little speck appear'd
(I've seen a something like it in the skies
   In the Aegean, ere a squall); it near'd,
And, growing bigger, took another guise;
   Like an aerial ship it tack'd, and steer'd; ...

27 *Max Jacobs.* The modernist poet Max Jacob (1876–1944).

Dado. The Italian painter Amedeo Modigliani (1884–1920), whom she called 'Dedo', until recently had been Hastings's lover.

Picasso. KM is confusing Pablo Picasso with an Italian sculptor, Alfredo Pina.

Carco is going to Turkey. Carco avoided service in Turkey by training as an aviator.

28 *ripolin.* A proprietary name for a make of enamel paint.

the Botticelli Nativity roof. The *Mystic Nativity* by Sandro Botticelli in the National Gallery, London.

my first novel. KM had begun writing her long story *The Aloe,* which she eventually revised and altered to *Prelude.*

29 *Cooks.* The offices of Thos. Cook and Son, 69 Boulevard Hausmann.

30 *Kay.* Alexander Kay, the manager of the London branch of the Bank of New Zealand. A friend of her father's, he often acted as KM's adviser.

31 *that old beast.* Murry had told her of an old man upstairs who constantly bothered him.

Kot. As KM often referred to her friend S. S. Koteliansky.

Floryan. Floryan Sobieniowski (1881–1964), who translated forty of Shaw's plays into English, had hoped to marry KM soon after they met in Bad Wörishofen in 1909. He encouraged her interest in Slavic writing, but by this time had become a tiresome hanger-on.

32 *Orage is too ugly.* A. R. Orage had encouraged KM to write for his weekly the *New Age,* but after his malicious satires against her in May 1912 she broke with the paper. She resumed her contributions in 1917.

so far away. Ida Baker was with her family in Rhodesia between Apr. 1914 and Sept. 1916.

33 *your book.* Murry was then at work on his introspective novel, *Still Life.*

german chasing. Murry had sent a photograph from the *Daily News* showing the police looking on while a German's house was ransacked.

35 *our german professor.* Walter Rippmann, see p. 287, under 2.

... letzenmal. The lines quoted are from 'Erinnerung—an C. N. [Remembrance—to C. N.]' by the German poet Eduard Morike (1804–75).

36 *Barbara.* Koteliansky's friend Barbara Low (1877–1955), an early Freudian psychoanalyst in England.

37 *Farbmans.* The Russian journalist and political commentator Michael Farbman (?1880–1933), a friend of Koteliansky's from the Russian Law Bureau, and his wife Sophie took over the lease of 5 Acacia Road, KM's former address.

38 *after it happened.* The grenade accident that killed her brother near Armentières on 7 October.

39 *Death of Procris.* KM is comparing Shakespeare's poem *Venus and Adonis* with the painting by Piero di Cosimo in the National Gallery, London.

Frank Harris. Frank Harris (1856–1931), journalist, biographer and fiction writer, who had been something of a mentor to KM and Murry soon after they took up with one another.

Dan Ryder. KM frequently met Harris at Dan Rider's Bookshop in St. Martin's Court, off St Martin's Lane.

40 *that Englishman.* F. Newland-Pedley (1854–1944), one of the founders in 1889 of the dental school at Guy's Hospital. Murry describes his eccentricity and kindness in 'Portrait of a Pa-Man', in *Katherine Mansfield and other Literary Portraits* (1949).

41 *Rottingdean.* Where KM stayed with Ida Baker from Apr. to July 1910, after an appendectomy.

that quiet lady with the cast eye. Murry wrote on 9 Dec. (Alexander Turnbull Library) that when he announced his name to a landlady, she exclaimed 'Not Middleton Murry, the writer!'

exactly like me. KM must have heard the story—perhaps from X. Marcel Boulestin who records it in his *Myself, My Two Countries* (1936), p. 60,—that at one time the French author Colette Willy (1873–1954) appeared at first nights dressed identically with the music-hall star, Polaire.

43 *telegram.* AI REÇU LETTERS TOUT VA TRES BIEN ECRIT [have received letters everything splendid written] 21 Dec. 1915.

45 *your Dosty Book.* Martin Secker had commissioned a study of Dostoevsky from Murry, to cancel the £30 debt still owing from the collapse of *Rhythm*.

Hara. O Hara San, one of KM's dolls.

46 *this pa man.* See above, under 40.

your curdling effugion. Goodyear had written to her from the Front, declaring his warmth of feeling for her.

Henry James is dead. The novelist Henry James died on 28 Feb. 1916.

47 *The Kilner Idea.* Perhaps a hope for greater intimacy, or simply some personal plan.

Fire Whorls and *a Hedgehog.* On 28 Feb. Goodyear wrote, among other details of his sexual life, of '5 whores, 1 engagement, several interminable sentimental friendships. Like the hedgehog, I've never been buggered at all.' (Alexander Turnbull Library).

48 *bunkum.* Goodyear concluded that letter 'If love is only love when it is resistless, I don't love you. But if it is a relative emotion, I do. Personally, I think everything everywhere is bunkum.'

50 *to arrest Murry.* Rather, to ensure that he reported for military registration.

51 *Marjory's.* Marjory Elvery, Beatrice Campbell's younger sister.

S. F. The term Sinn Feiner was generally applied to those who supported political independence for Ireland, as well as specifically to members of Sinn Fein ('We Ourselves'), the political organization.

George-Out-of-Wells. KM thought the novels of W. L. George were derivative of H. G. Wells.

Gracie Gifford's story. Grace Gifford, the fiancée of Joseph Mary Plunkett, one of the signatories of the Proclamation of Independence in the Easter Rebellion in Dublin. They were married a few hours before his execution on 4 May.

On The Eve of Turgeniev. Ivan Turgenev's novel *On the Eve* (1860) depicts a young woman whose Bulgarian husband unreservedly works for his country's freedom.

Jack Squire and Willie Yeats. The poets John Collings Squire (1884-1958), and W. B. Yeats (1865–1939).

Orpen's drawing. The *Daily Mirror* for 9 May carried on its front page an oil portrait of Grace Gifford by the Irish painter William Orpen (1878–1931).

52 *inflamed by his youth.* Cf. especially Book One of the *Confessions,* where Rousseau writes of being inflamed by sexuality from an early age.

54 *Mary Hutch.* Mary Hutchinson (1889–1977) and her barrister husband St John Hutchinson were socially eminent in artistic circles.

Robby Ross, Roger Fry, Greaves, Eliot. The guests on this occasion at River House, Hammersmith, were Robert Ross (1869–1918), critic and connoisseur, the painter and critic Roger Fry (1866–1934), the poet and later novelist Robert Graves (1895–1985), and T. S. Eliot (1888–1965).

55 *... floated.* The novelist George Moore (1852–1933); essayist, novelist and artist Max Beerbohm (1872–1956); George Nathaniel Curzon, Marquess Curzon of Kedleston (1859–1925), then a member of the War Cabinet; Georges Duhamel (1884–1966), French poet and novelist, whose recent *Vie des Martyrs* was a realistic account of his own experiences as an army surgeon.

La Bassée. Graves had taken part in the offensive there in Sept. 1915, and records this incident in ch. 16 of *Goodbye to All That* (1929).

a battered old moon. KM is taking up the imagery of 'Rhapsody on a Windy Night' and 'Conversation Galante', poems in Eliot's *Prufrock and Other Observations* published that month.

Vanessa's. Virginia Woolf's sister, the painter Vanessa Bell (1879–1961).

56 *it had a cylinder.* Presumably a discussion of the hand press which the Woolfs had set up in their home, Hogarth House, Richmond.

Garnett. Murry was trying to find work for David Garnett (1892–1981), a conscientious objector then employed as a farm labourer. Or perhaps KM intended telling Virginia of Garnet Trowell.

Asheham. The farmhouse the Woolfs rented near Firle, Sussex.

57 *'Dixie'.* The American popular song (1859) by David Emmett.

Maison Lyons. One of a chain of Lyons coffee-houses in London.

the Lancers. A ballroom dance, a kind of quadrille.

Maggie Owen's. Margaret Owen was a girl in the same year as KM at Queen's College.

Augustus John. The painter and bohemian Augustus John (1878–1961) was at this time suffering from deep depression.

Margaret Morris's theatre. Margaret Morris (1891–1980), who lived with KM's friend, the painter J. D. Fergusson, was both dancer and choreographer. In 1914 she started The Club, a small theatre and social club for artists in Flood Street, Chelsea.

that man in Crime and Punishment. At the end of part VI, section 6, of Dostoevsky's *Crime and Punishment*, Svidrigailov dreams he meets a depraved child.

58 *your article on Leon Bloy.* Murry's 'The Loneliness of Leon Bloy', *Times Literary Supplement*, 19 July 1917.

a 'Signature' style of writing. Murry had contributed sections of an essay, 'There was a Little Man', to each of the three issues of his and Lawrence's magazine the *Signature*, confessing 'there remains always a little cloud of self-contempt hovering within my mind.' (*Signature* No. 1, 4 Oct. 1915, pp. 29–30.).

59 *the 'prelude'.* Cf. section IX of *Prelude*, where KM writes of ducks in a similar vein.

the instrument. Dorothy Brett was deaf, and frequently used an ear-trumpet.

the Brotherhood Church. Two months earlier Bertrand Russell had faced an angry crowd at the Brotherhood Church in Southgate, south London, when he spoke in favour of the Russian revolution.

60 *my darling to the wolves.* The Woolfs had just taken proofs of the opening pages of *Prelude*.

Chili. Alvaro ('Chili') Guevara (1894–1951) came from Valparaiso to England to study painting. He was associated with the New Art Club and became a close friend of Brett's.

bright umbrellas. Brett was working on 'Conversation Piece at Garsington', a painting of several of her friends under parasols.

61 *Bill Nobles.* An acquaintance of both Fergusson and Brett.

Fulham Road. Fergusson lived at 14 Redcliffe Road, off the Fulham Road.

62 *take me back to Blighty.* A song written by Jack Godfrey in 1916.

63 *Shelley died.* Percy Bysshe Shelley was drowned in a storm while sailing near Spezia, 30 June 1822.

65 *Rib.* A favourite doll, named after Colonel Ribnikov in a story of that name by Aleksandr Kuprin (1870–1938), translated by Koteliansky and Murry in *The River of Life and Other Stories* (1916).

une canne avec une frique. Clearly some sort of walking-stick. 'Une frique' is a local word for a sparrow, possibly referring to carving on the stick.

66 *le grand cerveau.* In fact, le Gros Cerveau, an eminent natural feature a little north of Bandol.

the studio is let. KM's flat at 141 Church Street.

the golden world, As You Like It, I. i. 124.

67 *your own person.' Othello,* III. iii. 78–81.

68 *Air Raid in London.* On the night of 28 Jan. the Germans made their first attack of the year on London, killing 47 and injuring 109.

69 *'pas de nougat pour le noël'.* KM is remembering the song by Jean-Henri Fabre, 'Ils sont pires que le chiendent [They are worse than weeds]', with its opening lines: 'Il y a des olives à Toussaint, et pour Pâques il y a des oeufs—pour Noël, du nougat, et des truffes s'il pleut [There are olives at All Saints, eggs at Easter, nougat at Christmas and truffles if it rains.]' *Poésies françaises et provençales de Jean-Henri Fabre,* ed. Pierre Julian (Paris, 1925), p. 69.

70 *another raid.* There was a less severe raid on the outskirts of London on the night of 29 Jan.

my old shoes. Murry was refused permission to send them through the post.

72 *Gertler.* Mark Gertler (1892–1939), the London Jewish painter KM had known since 1914.

Dick Harmon of course. KM had just sent Murry the first completed section of *Je ne parle pas français.* The character Dick Harmon is partly based on Murry himself.

74 *a 'perfeck bladge'.* i.e. a 'perfect blaze', an extension of KM's and Murry's hypocoristic exchanges.

76 *Cinnamon and Angelica.* Murry's verse play, published in 1920.

77 *hopping never never stopping.* Words from 'Moonstruck', a song in the musical *Our Miss Gibbs* by Ivan Caryll and Lionel Monkton (1909).

the Gs. Régine Geoffroi, an acquaintance of KM's from her earlier stay at Bandol, was married to a doctor who was now Mayor of Carpentras. Her earnest literary discussions were something of a trial to KM, and her visits unwelcome.

this violent battle. That is, her attempts to arrange an early return to England.

79 *Elle et Lui to read.* George Sand's novel, *Elle et lui* (1859).

80 *that Sunday afternoon.* 'Aunt Marthe' was KM's euphemism for menstruation. She is referring to the Sunday before she left for Bandol, back in January.

81 *this super Kanon.* The long-range 8.26 inch gun the Germans were then using for the shelling of Paris.

massacre in the church. During the Good Friday Tenebrae service, a shell from the 'super Kanon' had fallen on the church of Saint-Gervaise-Saint-Protais in the 4th arrondissement. Eighty people, mainly women and children, were killed, and 90 injured.

home for the 17th. The day KM and Murry planned to marry, although the ceremony was later postponed.

82 *the Heron.* Both the 'dream house' in the English countryside, and the 'dream life' KM and Murry frequently planned for after the war.

the cantine. As their funds diminished, Ida Baker began work at a services canteen at the Gare du Nord. KM also worked there for one day, but found it too exhausting.

Sydneys man. A contact of Sydney Waterlow, who was working in the Foreign Office.

84 *she must* never *know.* Murry's mother thought they were already married.

85 *Jones.* A name KM and Ida Baker used for each other.

Stella. Stella Drummond—later Lady Eustace Percy—worked with Ida Baker in a munitions factory in Chiswick.

Ainger. William Ainger, the doctor who had treated KM the previous year.

90 *J. D. F's show.* An exhibition of J. D. Fergusson's paintings at James Connell and Sons Galleries, 47 Old Bond Street.

91 *Dorothy Wordsworth's journals. The Journals of Dorothy Wordsworth* (1771–1855) were edited by William Knight (1896 and 1904).

92 *in the 13th. Corinth. manner 'winked at'.* Not Corinthians but Acts 17: 30: 'And the time of this ignorance God winked at'.

smiling at the flower woman. Murry had written on 20 May 'I could not be happier than I am', and mentioned 'I made the flower woman laugh.' (*The Letters of John Middleton Murry to Katherine Mansfield*, ed. C. A. Hankin (1983), p. 149.)

the Gwynne affair. Gwynne was Ida Baker's foreman at the Chiswick factory. It seems they had suggested KM enter some kind of institution.

93 *Mrs. Maufe's letter.* Gladys Prudence (later Lady) Maufe had been KM's neighbour at 139 Church Street, Chelsea.

96 *Eve's Ransom by Gissing.* The fiction of George Gissing (1857–1903) often drew on the poverty he had experienced himself. *Eve's Ransom* was published in 1895.

Harrison. Austin Harrison (1873–1928) was the editor of the *English Review,* to which KM had sent her story 'Bliss'.

97 *you suffered.* Murry's response to KM's letter of 23 May was amazement and hurt.

take you love away'. Murry wrote on 24 May 'It's comic how with one letter I am left shivering and naked. You say it all so beautifully that you must have meant it as it was written .... Shut up shop, Boge Murry, take your love away.' (*Letters of John Middleton Murry to Katherine Mansfield*, p. 152).

99 *the Elephant.* The name habitually used for the house at 2 Portland Villas. East Heath Road, Hampstead, for which Murry was then negotiating.

'*whiffing for pollocks*'. Pollocks are fish allied to cod; fishing for them with a handline is called whiffing.

Pagello. Her nickname for the young doctor who treated her in Looe, Christopher Costello.

100 *Chinese poems.* The *New Statesman*, 18 May 1918, published ten poems translated from the Chinese by Arthur Waley. His collection *A Hundred and Seventy Chinese Poems* came out the same year.

Thomas Hardy. The Well Beloved (1897).

101 *I hope Ottoline turns up trumps.* Murry had asked if his friend and colleague Sullivan might recuperate from a minor breakdown in one of Garsington's cottages.

Massingham. Henry William Massingham (1860–1924) was the editor of the *Nation*, in which KM's story 'Carnation' was published on 7 September 1918.

the review. Of Paul Margueritte's *Pour Toi, Patrie*, published in the *Times Literary Supplement*, 4 July 1918.

102 *Mr Pallisers.* Charles Palliser, a Wellington business friend of her father's who had retired to Cornwall.

Jimmy Wilde is more my size than Jack Johnson. Jack Johnson was world heavyweight boxing champion 1910–15; Jimmy Wilde the current flyweight champion.

poor Maud Allen. The danseuse, whom KM greatly admired, had lost a libel case against the jingoist Independent MP for East Herts., Noel Pemberton Billing, who claimed her performance of Wilde's *Salome* catered to sexual perverts and potential German spies. At the conclusion of the trial Billing and his key witness, Lord Alfred Douglas, were hailed by crowds outside the Old Bailey.

103 *the New Witness.* Nothing of KM's appeared in the *New Witness* edited by G. K. Chesterton.

that man Edwards. Tristyan Edwards, one of the few advance subscribers for *Prelude*.

Hugh W's cottage. The novelist Hugh Walpole lived at The Cobbles, Polperro.

104 [*9 June 1918*]. Murry found this letter sealed but unposted among KM's papers.

Gus Bofa. The pseudonym of Gustave Blanchot (d. 1968), a Parisian comic artist who during the war published a satirical weekly, *La Baïonette*. No article by KM appeared.

11500 miles. Roughly the distance to New Zealand.

105 *'will my candle last until it's light'*. Edna St Vincent Millay's 'First Fig' was published in *Poetry*, June 1918: 'My candle burns at both ends; It will not last the night; But ah, my foes, and oh, my friends, It gives a lovely light.'

Clovelly Mansions. KM was living at 69 Clovelly Mansions, Gray's Inn Road, when Murry became her lodger in 1912.

Johnny Keats anchovy. A month before he died in Rome on 23 Feb. 1821, Keats's diet was limited to a single anchovy and a morsel of bread a day.

106 *my stupid cry from Cornwall*. Her letter to Lady Ottoline of 24 May.

107 *when the russian music sounded*. A balalaika recital they attended at the Grafton Gallery, Picadilly.

you so beautifully say about my tiny book. Whatever she wrote to KM, Lady Ottoline told Bertrand Russell on 30 July: 'I quite agree with you really about *Prelude*. I hate such endless observation of trivialities . . . . . Why make such a damned fuss about it.' (McMaster University, Hamilton, Ontario).

in this weeks Nation. Murry had unfavourably reviewed Siegfried Sassoon's *Counter-attack, and other poems*, in the *Nation*, 13 July 1918, and set off a storm at Garsington. Philip Morrell in a letter to the *Nation*, 20 July, described the review as a 'detraction of a gallant and distinguished author'.

108 *Bill Sykes and Nancy*. A criminal and his mistress in Charles Dickens's *Oliver Twist* (1838).

come to Sassoon's rescue. Enid Bagnold (1889–1981), playwright and novelist, whose poem 'The Guns of Kent', dedicated to Sassoon, appeared in the *Nation*, 20 July.

Lyttons success. Lytton Strachey's *Eminent Victorians*, published in May 1918, was widely acclaimed.

measureless to man. 'Through caverns measureless to man', Coleridge, *Kubla Khan*.

the topmost leaf of the tallest tree. A memory of Sappho's verse on apple picking.

109 *Sassoon tucked up in bed with a wound in the head*. Lady Ottoline informed Murry that Sassoon had suffered a head wound, and that the review could cause his death.

110 *a teeny little study in the Nation*. 'Carnation' was not run until 7 Sept.

112 *a story by K.M.* 'Bliss'.

it is an immense blow. KM's mother died in Wellington on 8 Aug., aged 54.

113 *Robbie Ross dying.* Robert Ross (see p.294, under 54) died on 5 Oct.

114 *Well Walk.* The Lawrences were staying nearby, at 32 Well Walk, Hampstead.

more than three days. Lawrence was in London hoping to find employment that exempted him from war service.

Julian Huxley. The writer and scientist Julian Huxley (1884–1975) married Juliet Baillot ('mademoiselle' of two lines earlier) in 1919.

a sort of Bazarov-Rudin. Yevgeny Bazarov is a portrait of an emerging 'modern' mind in Ivan Turgenev's *Fathers and Sons* (1862); Dmitri Rudin is the gifted, idealistic, but ineffectual protagonist in *Rudin* (1856).

Gissing in Italy—it looks to me. KM had earlier used the novelist George Gissing as a touchstone for shabbiness. See p. 297, under 96.

Mrs Hamilton. Mary Agnes Hamilton (1884–1962), Cambridge graduate, journalist, novelist, ardent campaigner for the Labour Party.

117 *a Corsican baby.* KM is recalling the twins in *Les Frères Corses* (1845), by Alexandre Dumas *père*.

a February chile. David Drey was born in Feb.

118 *we were nameless.* The *Athenaeum*, 4 Apr. 1919, published 'Letters of Anton Tchehov', four letters translated by Koteliansky and stylistically polished by KM. Unlike similar later contributions, this was unsigned.

119 *a 'rumpus'.* The friendship between KM and Lawrence continued to be an uneasy one. The 'rumpus' may have had to do with her telling Frieda how she had been hurt by Lawrence, for he wrote to her on 27 Mar. 'Frieda said you were cross with me, that I repulsed you. I'm sure I didn't. The complications of getting Jack and you and F. and me into a square seems great—especially Jack.' (*The Letters of D. H. Lawrence,* ed. James T. Boulton and Andrew Robertson, vol. III (1984), p. 343.).

as Una led the Lion. Edmund Spenser, *The Faerie Queene,* I. iii. 9.

since you were here last. Virginia Woolf wrote after a visit to KM on 22 Mar., 'the inscrutable woman remains inscrutable I'm glad to say; no apologies, or sense of apologies due.' (*The Diary of Virginia Woolf,* ed. Anne Olivier Bell, vol. I (1977), p. 257.).

like Charles Lamb, before the curtain rises. Lamb described his feelings as a child at 'My First Play', *Elia* (1823): 'when we got in, and I beheld the green curtain that veiled a heaven to my imagination . . . . the breathless anticipations I endured!'

120 *your article on Modern Novels. Times Literary Supplement,* 10 Apr. 1919.

122 *Chilis.* See p. 295, under 60.

Nina Hamnet. Nina Hamnett (1890–1956), painter, writer, and one of the Brett–Gertler circle.

'Mary Olivier'? By May Sinclair. A novel KM reviewed in the *Athenaeum,* 20 June 1919.

'*The Owl*'. The first number of the *Owl*, edited by Robert Graves, included poetry by W. H. Davies, Graves, Hardy, Masefield, Sassoon, and J. C. Squire, as well as prose by Beerbohm and Galsworthy.

123 *Mrs Baker*. An acquaintance of Brett's friend since her days at the Slade School of Art, the painter Geoffrey Nelson.

124 *Festivity*. The Peace Treaty between the Allies and the German National Assembly was officially celebrated throuhout Britain on 19 July. *Lloyd George and Beatty blazing against the sky*. The fireworks display in Hyde Park was to include portraits of royalty, of the Prime Minister Lloyd George, and Sir David Beatty, Admiral of the Fleet.

My brother's grave. Leslie was buried at Ploegsteert Wood, where he died on 7 Oct. 1915.

Mrs Atherton. A society figure who shot herself at her home in Curzon Street.

the Earl of March. On 12 July the press reported evidence given at the inquest by her maid, and by the Earl of March, who spoke of her husband's affair with his step-daughter, and warmly of Mrs Atherton herself.

like Desdemona and Emilia. KM was reminded of *Othello*, IV. iii.

126 *Clives way*. Clive Bell (1881–1964), art critic and estranged husband of Vanessa Bell (see p. 294 under 55). KM disliked him for spreading gossip about her.

Bedford Square. The Morrells had owned 44 Bedford Square since 1906, and were about to sell it.

Roger's art criticism. Roger Fry discussed the French exhibition in a two-part article, 'Modern French Art at the Mansard Gallery', in the *Athenaeum*, 8 and 15 Aug.

128 *1 hecto*. Three and a half ounces.

129 *Wingleys*. Wingley was one of the cats at Portland Villas.

Violet. The maid at Portland Villas.

Fancy Sydney being there. Sydney Waterlow was then staying with Murry.

the Moults. Thomas Moult (b. 1895), minor poet, journalist, and sports writer, and his wife Bessie.

the novels. For her weekly fiction column in the *Athenaeum*.

130 *the 1ᵈ matchbox*. A cheap present from her sister Chaddie.

Genêt Fleuri. KM's favourite perfume.

Wood Hay. The house in the New Forest which Harold Beauchamp had bought for Chaddie and Jeanne.

Sydney Beauchamp. Sydney Beauchamp (1861–1921), the son of Henry Herron Beauchamp (see p. 287 under 1), an eminent physician, soon after knighted for his medical services at the Treaty of Versailles.

131 *198 received:* | (no *199*). Murry was numbering his letters by the days until they expected to see each other again, 1 May 1920.

Benson & Weyman. KM reviewed Stella Benson's *Living Alone* in the *Athenaeum*, 14 Nov., and Stanley Weyman's *The Great House*, 7 Nov.

Mrs W. seems established. Sydney Waterlow had brought his wife Helen to stay briefly at Portland Villas.

132 *Dorothy Wordworth's eyes.* From childhood Dorothy Wordsworth possessed fine sight and powers of close observation. In 'To a Butterfly' William complimented her: 'She gave me eyes, she gave me ears'.

133 *Madeleine & Virginia.* KM did not review Hope Mirrlees' recently published *Madeleine, One of Love's Jansenists*, but discussed Virginia Woolf's *Night and Day* in the *Athenaeum*, 21 Nov. 1919.

Eternity. The essay never appeared.

135 *the Times review.* A very favourable review of Virginia Woolf's *Night and Day* in the *Times Literary Supplement*, 30 Oct. 1919.

137 *Vince.* Thomas Vince, the English proprietor of the Villa Flora, San Remo.

138 *to thy cross I cling.* 'Nothing in my hand I bring, | Simply to thy Cross I cling', from the third stanza of A. M. Toplady's hymn, 'Rock of Ages'.

139 *Bobone . . . Ansaldi.* Two doctors she was then consulting.

140 *Mrs Jones.* Alice Jones was Murry's secretary at the *Athenaeum* office.

Eliot's poetry lecture. On 25 Oct. T. S. Eliot had lectured on modern tendencies in poetry for the Arts League of Service.

Gaierty. The erratic spelling she adopted from the then highly successful *The Young Visiters*, by Daisy Ashford (1919). See p. 303, under 152.

141 *a Kaiapoi rug.* A type of New Zealand rug named after Kaiapoi, north of Christchurch.

144 *Butler.* Murry sent her George Bernard Shaw's 'Samuel Butler: The New Life Reviewed', from the *Manchester Guardian*, 1 Nov.

145 *Porter.* KM's dentist in London.

If you gave up the A. Writing on 3 Nov., Murry proposed that he give up the editorship of the *Athenaeum*, borrow £200 from KM's father, and come out to look after her himself, thus ridding her of Ida Baker.

146 *all my religion.* KM is recalling 'Thou hast made of love all thy religion', a line from Murry's poem 'Supplication' . It was published in *Poems: 1917–18* (The Heron Press, 1919).

147 *say if my Dosty is alright.* KM reviewed Dostoevsky's *An Honest Thief: and Other Stories*, translated by Constance Garnett, in the *Athenaeum*, 28 Nov. 1919.

plays the flute. In her review of *Night and Day* KM remarked on a minor incident in chapter XXII where William Rodney, picking out melodies from *The Magic Flute* on his piano, briefly recalls his future fiancée playing the flute: 'The little picture suggested very happily her melodious and whimsical temperament.'

150 *'pensive citadel'*. 'And students with their pensive citadels', from Wordsworth's sonnet 'Nuns fret not at their convent's narrow room'.

What is this about the novel. In his letter of 13 Nov., Murry had told her that 'What I feel, and what a great many other people feel, is that as long as your novel page is there, there can't be a really bad number of the *Athenaeum*.' (*Letters of John Middleton Murry to Katherine Mansfield*, p. 210).

thou little eye among the blind. 'Thou best Philosopher, who yet dost keep | Thy heritage, thou Eye among the blind,' Wordsworth, *Ode: Intimations of Immortality*, 111–12.

who is not fed. 'The hungry sheep look up and are not fed, | But swoln with wind', John Milton, *Lycidas*, 125–6.

'common things of light and day'. 'And fade into the light of common day', Wordsworth, *Ode: Intimations of Immortality*, 77.

151 *'deserts of vast eternity'*. 'And yonder all before us lie | Deserts of vast eternity', Andrew Marvell, 'To His Coy Mistress'.

O. has invited you there. Lady Ottoline Morrell had invited Murry to stay at Garsington.

152 *'in all conscience', as Mr Salteena would say*. In ch. 5 of Daisy Ashford's *Young Visiters*, which KM reviewed in the *Athenaeum*, 30 May 1919, 'Mr Salteena crossed his legs in a lordly way and flung a fur rug over his knees though he was hot enough in all conscience.'

153 *'let this cup pass from me'*. 'O my Father, if it be possible, let this cup pass from me: nevertheless not as I will, but as thou wilt'. Matthew 24: 39.

The Waterlows house. Murry had spent the weekend with the Waterlows at Parsonage House, Oare, Pewsey, Wiltshire.

about the table. A retired friend from Murry's time at the War Office had offered to make them a table.

154 *Eric-or-little-by-little*. *Eric: or Little by Little* (1858), a popular schoolboy novel by the Revd Frederick William Farrar.

The house (like the Jew) first. 'For I am not ashamed of the Gospel of Christ; for it is the power of God unto salvation to everyone that believeth; to the Jew first, and also to the Greek.' Romans 1: 16.

155 *Penge*. Where Murry had visited Walter de la Mare (1873–1956).

Wing. i.e. Wingley, her cat at Portland Villas.

like Dora's Gyp did the pencil. KM is remembering the episode in *David Copperfield*, ch. 41, in which the dog stands on a cookery book while holding a pencil case in its mouth.

an ad of my story in the T.L.S. For *Je ne parle pas français*, which was then being collated and sewn. No advertisement appeared.

your Georgian poetry review. 'The Condition of English Poetry', Murry's devastating review of *Georgian Poetry, 1918–1919*, ed. Edward Marsh, and the periodical *Wheels*, Fourth Cycle, in the *Athenaeum*, 5 Dec.

'tramp tramp tramp the boys are marching'. The first line of the chorus from 'Tramp! Tramp! Tramp!', the well-known song of the Northern armies in the American Civil War, the words and music by G. F. Root.

156 *some photographs.* Brett had sent photographs of her recent paintings.

Lawrences address. D. H. Lawrence was then in Florence, later in the month moving on to Rome, Picinisco, and then Capri.

157 *Elizabeth Stanley.* A pseudonym KM took from the maiden name of her paternal grandmother, Mary Elizabeth Stanley.

158 *I have reread your letter.* Murry wrote on 8 Dec. that he had received her letter with the poem 'The New Husband'. 'I don't think that at any time I've had a bigger blow than that letter & those verses. Even now they hardly seem like a letter & verses—more like a snake with a terrible sting.' (*Letters of John Middleton Murry to Katherine Mansfield*, p. 239.)

KM wrote on the back of the envelope that brought Murry's letter: 'This letter killed the Mouse, made the Worm creep underground and banished the Dream Child forever. Before I had received it I had learned to live for Love and by Love. I had given myself up—and a kind of third creature US was what I lived by. After I had read it, quite apart from me, my own self returned and all my horror of death vanished. From this day I simply dont care about death! No question of heroics— or life not being worth living or anything like it. I simply feel alone again. Voilà.' (Alexander Turnbull Library.)

160 *you are a bankrupt.* Murry had been declared a bankrupt in Feb. 1914, following the financial collapse of *Rhythm* in 1912 when Charles Granville (the publisher 'Stephen Swift') fled the country and left Murry owing the printers.

161 *But the Knipper.* Olga Knipper, who played leading roles in several of Chekhov's plays, and married him in 1901.

He said Florence was lovely, Lawrence's letter does not survive.

162 *'the question'.* A letter to A. S. Souverin, 27 Oct. 1888, translated by Koteliansky and KM in 'Letters of Anton Tchehov, VI', in the *Athenaeum*, 6 June 1919, in which Chekhov wrote: 'You are right in asking from an artist a conscious attitude to his activity, but you are mixing up two things: the solving of the question and the correct putting of the question. It is the latter only which is obligatory upon the artist.'

I shall send you the letters. Other Chekhov letters they were translating together.

my other name. Koteliansky frequently called KM both Katerina and Kissienka.

163 *Nevinson's letter.* Presumably Murry had heard from Henry Woodd Nevinson (1856–1941), the eminent journalist and war correspondent.

Marie Dahlerup. A friend of KM's since her schooldays, whom she had invited to stay with her as helper-companion.

164 *Foster.* An English doctor in Menton.

the Tchekhov. KM's review was lost during the Italian postal strike, but Murry ran in the *Athenaeum*, 23 Jan. and 6 Feb., her unsigned 'Biographical Note (1860–1887)' on Chekhov.

165 story arrived safely. 'The Man without a Temperament'.

166 *the Lacket.* A house at Lockeridge, near Marlborough, Wiltshire, which Murry was thinking of leasing.

167 *Chinese Poetry, Sir Limpidus, Coggin.* KM's review of Arthur Waley's *More Translations from the Chinese* was not used; those of *Sir Limpidus*, by Marmaduke Pikthall, and *Coggin* by Ernest Oldmeadow, were published in the *Athenaeum*, 30 Jan. 1920.

Kay. See p. 292, under 30.

170 *Rutter.* Frank Rutter, the editor of *Arts and Letters*, which ran her story 'The Man without a Temperament' in the Spring 1920 issue.

171 *a day's 'sheer joy'.* KM is taking up phrases from a letter Murry sent her on 26 Jan. after looking for a house in the Sussex countryside, and another on 3 Feb., trying to explain his reaction to her own letter of 31 Jan.

Of course I can of course I will. KM sent a telegram on 7 Feb.: OF COURSE YOU LOVE ME. TIG.

172 *and a great deal more.* Lawrence's letter does not survive. His friendship with KM had been marked by great warmth as well as by malice and anger. But his feelings towards her were complicated by those towards Murry, which ranged from the erotic a few years before to the contemptuous now that his writings on several occasions were rejected by the *Athenaeum*. It was this assumed editorial condescension that fuelled his present rage against KM, although Lawrence often had been dismissive enough of *her* gifts, and any admiration they attracted.

173 *Art and Letters.* See p. 170, under 170.

Old Massingham. See p. 298, under 101.

Huxley ... Tomlinson ... Forster. Aldous Huxley (1894–1963), novelist and scholar, was one of Murry's assistant editors; Henry Major Tomlinson (1873–1958), one of Murry's close friends, was a journalist with the *Nation* in the same building as the *Athenaeum*; the novelist E. M. Forster (1879–1970) frequently wrote for Murry's paper.

174 *Mrs E's.* T. S. Eliot had married Vivienne Haigh-Wood in 1915, but by 1920 she was increasingly affected by mental illness.

176 *Anatole France.* Anatole France (1844–1924), French novelist, poet, editor and critic.

177 *your Stendhal.* Murry had reviewed Stendhal's *Rome, Paris et Florence* and *La jeunesse de Stendhal* by Paul Arbolet in the *Athenaeum*, 17 Sep. 1920.

178 *Milne.* Herbert Milne, a classics scholar who worked in the manuscripts

department at the British Museum, and frequently visited Murry at Hampstead.

Walpoles novel. Hugh Walpole's *The Captives*, reviewed in the *Athenaeum*, 15 Oct. 1920.

179 *Gertler's threatened tuberculosis.* Mark Gertler was suffering from advanced tuberculosis when he committed suicide in 1939.

180 *so Christ cursed it.* See Matthew 24: 32; Luke 21: 29.

　umbulella. KM is quoting from a favourite rhyme:
　　Come along Isabella
　　Under my umbellella
　　Don't be afraid
　　There's a good maid
　　Come along Isabella.

De la Mare's letter. The poet Walter de la Mare (1873–1956) had become a friend during the days of *Rhythm*.

181 *'thorn in the flesh'.* 'there was given to me a thorn in the flesh ... lest I should be exalted above measure.' 2 Corinthians, 12: 7.

Perfect love casteth out Fear. John 4: 18.

Yazpegs. KM's jokey spelling of 'aspects'. Murry's *Aspects of Literature*, published in England in 1920, had been turned down by the New York publishers Knopf.

183 *Sam Mayo used to sing it.* Sam Mayo (1884–1938), a popular music-hall artist and composer, known for his lugubrious delivery of comic songs.

Did you care about the Mayor of Cork? Terence MacSwiney, Mayor of Cork, dramatist, member of the Irish Parliament, and commander of the First Cork Brigade of the Irish Republican Army, was court-martialled and charged with possessing seditious documents. Refusing to recognize the courts, he began a hunger strike on 12 Aug., and died on 25 Oct.

Megan Lloyd George. The eighteen-year-old daughter of the British Prime Minister.

Murder Carson for instance. Sir Edward Carson (1854–1935), eminent barrister and MP for Balcairn, Belfast, was the strongest Unionist voice against home rule in Ireland.

your Baudelaire. Murry had reviewed Baudelaire's *Les fleurs du mal*, *Le Spleen de Paris*, and *Journaux intimes*, in the édition critique edited by A. van Bever, in two issues of the *Athenaeum*, 22 and 29 Oct. 1920.

185 *'hounyhming'.* From the Houyhnhnms, the speaking horses in bk IV of Jonathan Swift's *Gulliver's Travels* (1726).

in that dreadful place. Reading Gaol, where Oscar Wilde served much of his prison sentence 1896–8.

Rose Macaulay. The novelist Rose Macaulay (1881–1958). Murry's letter does not survive.

186 *the Naomi type.* Possibly a reference to their acquaintance Naomi Royde-Smith (d. 1964), novelist, playwright, and biographer, who was literary editor of the *Westminster Gazette* 1912–1922.

189 *KM cant go on.* The only letter from Murry at this period to survive was written around 10 Dec., when he spoke of several flirtations, and his 'agony of nerves' (*Letters of John Middleton Murry to Katherine Mansfield*, ed. C. A. Hankin, p. 319). Presumably other letters touched on similar occasions, and a notebook entry not used by Murry in his edition of KM's *Journal* recorded 'the fearful pain of these letters' (Antony Alpers, *The Life of Katherine Mansfield* (1982), p. 324). Murry's infatuation with Princess Bibesco (see next letter), KM's anger over a photograph she detested and that Murry had given the publishers, Constables, for publicity, as well as her illness and isolation, contributed to her decision to break off her weekly reviewing in the *Athenaeum*.

Doctor Bouchage. Dr. A. Bouchage, who treated KM during her time at Menton.

190 *a letter from Squire.* J. C. Squire published 'The Stranger' in the *London Mercury*, Jan. 1921.

191 *Madame la Princesse.* Princess Elizabeth Bibesco, with whom Murry was currently infatuated.

Let us quit ourselves like men. KM sent Murry a telegram on 12 Dec: STOP TORMENTING ME WITH THESE FALSE DEPRESSING LETTERS AT ONCE BE A MAN OR DONT WRITE ME. TIG. (Alexander Turnbull Library)

192 *Im sending you my book. Bliss and Other Stories* was published that month.

195 *Miss Brill.* 'Miss Brill', published in the *Athenaeum*, 26 Nov. 1920.

199 *some place like Yalta & build a little house at Oreanda.* KM is apparently thinking of the years Chekhov spent at Yalta, as well as either the house he had built in the Crimea, or the small house he bought at Kuchokoi in 1898. Oreanda was where he took Olga Knipper.

200 *the Vienna Café.* At 22–4 New Oxford Street, a favourite of KM's since her early years in London.

Slatkovsky. R. S. Slatkovsky, the proprietor of the Russian Law Bureau where Koteliansky had worked translating and certifying Russian documents.

201 *Sylvia Sullivan.* Murry's friend J. W. N. Sullivan had divorced his first wife, a schoolfriend of KM's, and remarried.

204 *Cousin Lou.* Connie Beauchamp's sister.

The old villain. Marie, the maid at Isola Bella, had turned out quite contrary to KM's first opinion of her.

205 *the Hutchinsons.* See p. 294, under 54.

206 *your New Baby.* Sydney and Helen Waterlow's first child, John.

208 *that man* Spahlinger. Henry Spahlinger, a Swiss doctor whose course of treatment she was thinking of taking.

212 *like Stepan in* The Possessed. Stepan Trofimovich Verkhovensky, a garrulous dandy and inept liberal in Dostoevsky's *The Possessed* (1871).

213 *lecturing in Oxford on Style.* The six lectures Murry delivered at the School of English during the Summer Term were published the following year in *The Problem of Style.*

a very long story in The Mercury *this month.* 'The Daughters of the Late Colonel'.

214 *'O ye of little faith!'.* Luke 12:28.

216 *the Tchekhov notebooks.* Murry had reviewed *Tchehov's Notebooks*, translated by S. S. Koteliansky and Leonard Woolf, and published by the Hogarth Press, in the *Nation and Athenaeum*, 4 June 1921.

Virginia's stories. Monday or Tuesday, also from the Hogarth Press, 1921.

Queen Victoria. Lytton Strachey's *Queen Victoria*, 1921.

a new story. KM finished 'An Ideal Family' on 22 July. It was published in the *Sphere* on 20 Aug. 1921.

218 ½ *an hours scramble away.* At the Chalet Soleil, Randogne-sur-Sierre.

Santyana. KM had met George Santayana (1863–1952), the Spanish-American philosopher and critic, when Murry invited him to write for the *Athenaeum.*

Secker is a little fool to publish such STUFF. Lady Ottoline had greatly resented Lawrence's depiction of her as Hermione Roddice when she read *Women in Love* in typescript at the end of 1916, and Philip Morrell had threatened libel action should it be published. After a small private edition in the United States, the novel was published in England by Martin Secker in 1921.

M. is engaged in a fat novel. The Things We Are, published in 1922.

I have been doing a series for The Sphere. At a time when her medical bills were considerable, KM accepted the offer of Clement Shorter, editor of the weekly *Sphere*, to write six stories at ten guineas each. These all appeared before the end of the year: 'Sixpence', 6 Aug.; 'Mr and Mrs Dove', 13 Aug.; 'An Ideal Family', 20 Aug.; 'Her First Ball', 28 Nov.; 'The Voyage', 24 Dec.; 'Marriage à la Mode', 31 Dec.

221 *Ernestine's.* Ernestine Rey, a local woman who cooked their meals.

222 *You made them simply lovely and so real!!* Brett's group portrait of her brother Maurice's children.

223 *Such fearful horrors!* Several of KM's recent stories in the *Sphere* were crudely illustrated by W. Smithson Broadhead.

Harrods. A department store in Knightsbridge.

make a feature of 'em. This did not happen.

225 *Jonathan Trout.* The romantic and disappointed uncle in 'At the Bay',

based on Val Waters, the husband of her mother's sister, Agnes. What KM has in mind is probably the figure on the right in Cezanne's painting of two men, *The Card Players* (1892). The story was published in the *London Mercury*, Jan. 1922.

226 *playing cards*. The scene in section IX of 'At the Bay'.

227 *Wells*. The H. G. Wells family were staying with KM's cousin Elizabeth.

228 *Doctor H.* Dr Hudson, whose mother was the owner of the Chalet des Sapins.

the Palace. The Palace was a large clinic for invalids which Dr Hudson had encouraged KM to enter.

Glasspool. An English girl Ida Baker accompanied back to Montana.

your new neffy. Ida Baker had crossed to England for a week in August, to get winter clothes for KM, and to fetch Wingley the cat from Portland Villas. She returned to England in September to see her sister, who had come from Rhodesia to have her second child.

your pension-talk. Before leaving for England, Ida Baker considered taking a job nursing in a clinic in Montana, and boarding in the village. KM objected to this plan, hence the accusation of 'flirting' with her friendship.

I cant help the illustrator. See p. 308, under 223.

229 *at 75*. 75 Tinakori Road, close to the centre of Wellington, where KM lived between the ages of 10 and 14.

the Kenepuru Sounds. Kenepuru Sound, a long walking-distance from Anikiwa in Queen Charlotte Sound, where the Beauchamp girls spent holidays with relatives.

uncle Sid! Sydney Dyer, her mother's brother.

230 *these wonderful books*. KM is complimenting Galsworthy on episodes in *The Forsyte Saga* series of novels, the most recent of which, *In Chancery*, was discussed in her last review for the *Athenaeum*, 10 Dec. 1920.

a day in the life of the little family in Prelude. At the Bay appeared in the *London Mercury* in Jan. 1922.

232 *simply torture*. Beauchamp wrote across the top of the letter: 'R. 7/1/22. A. Idem. I can emphatically say that in *thought, word* & *deed* I have never begrudged any of my children the amounts I have paid them by way of allowances. On the contrary, I have always considered it a *pleasure* and a *privilege* to do everything possible for their comfort, happiness & worldly advancement. HB. 9/1/22.' He underlined from 'Connie and Jinnie' in the second paragraph down to 'simply torture'. In the margin beside the first few of these lines he wrote 'Quite untrue. HB.' and beside the sentence ending in 'simply torture' he wrote 'Quite untrue—I never made such a statement at any rate. HB.' (Alexander Turnbull Library.)

233 *Van Gogh shown at the Goupil*. KM had seen the *Sunflowers* painting at the First Post-Impressionist Exhibition at the Grafton Galleries (not the Goupil) in 1912.

234 *the Russian doctor's treatment.* KM had decided, almost as a last resort, to undergo an expensive and in fact medically useless treatment with Ivan Manoukhin, who claimed to cure tuberculosis by submitting the spleen to X-rays.

when Lawrence gave his party. When KM and Murry lived at Rose Tree Cottage, Great Missenden, at the end of 1914, and the Lawrences a few miles away at Chesham.

236 *to finish my big story.* 'The Dove's Nest', which she had begun on 1 Jan., and was intended to be much longer than what survives.

Tomlinson. See p. 305, under 173.

237 *comin out in the Dial.* The *Dial* had accepted 'The Doll's House' but withdrew publication when the story appeared in the *Nation and Athenaeum*, 4 Feb. 1922.

I feel like Lottie and Kezia's mother. Linda Burnell and two of her children in 'At the Bay'.

Born under a dancing star. 'There was a star danced, and under that was I born.' *Much Ado About Nothing*, ii I 349.

Goethes conversations with Eckermann. KM was reading Johann Eckermann's *Gespräche mit Goethe* (1836).

238 *even as your Father in Heaven is perfect.* Matthew 5: 48.

it is not just (as A. T's friend used to say) a sheep sneezing. Perhaps an anecdote she had heard from Koteliansky.

241 *... To rot itself with motion.* Antony and Cleopatra, I. iv, 45–8.

In reply to your telegram. Murry's telegram, presumably saying he would come if needed, does not survive. He joined her in Paris a few days later.

243 *We haven't read* The Schoolmaster. Murry had received Chekhov's *The Schoolmaster and other stories*, translated by Constance Garnett, which he reviewed in the *Nation and Athenaeum*, 8 Apr. 1922.

Dont bother to send the D.N. about Bibesco. Murry had offered to send her Rose Macaulay's review of Princess Bibesco's *I have only myself to blame* in the *Daily News* on 2 Feb. 1922, which described the stories as inferior Mansfield.

244 *like the couple in Donne's Ecstasy.* A glancing jibe at Murry's 'intellectual' fiction, the thought (as in John Donne's poem) standing in for the deed.

The F.O. The Faithful One, a name KM gave to Ida Baker.

I wonder how your novel is going. Elizabeth's *The Enchanted April* was then in press.

245 *like Una in the Fairy Queen.* Una represents fidelity and true religion in Book I of Spenser's *The Faerie Queen*.

246 *Anrep.* Brett was shortly to move to 6 Pond Street, Hampstead, next door to the Russian artist Boris Anrep.

As to Ethel Sands. Ethel Sands (1873–1962), a wealthy American painter, one of the founders of the London Group.

The Voyage. In *The Garden Party*, published that week by Constable.

247 *one year with Lawrence.* Apr.–June 1916, when she and Murry lived at Higher Tregerthen in Cornwall, with the Lawrences in the adjoining cottage.

248 *I think my story for you will be about Canaries.* KM's last completed story, 'The Canary', was written in July 1922, to fulfil this promise to Brett.

The Fly. Published in the *Nation and Athenaeum*, 29 Apr. 1922.

250 *a very fierce lady indeed.* Mary Agnes Hamilton (see p. 300, under 114) in *Time and Tide*, 3 Mar. 1922.

she would have my blood like the fish in Cock Robin. See the second stanza of the anonymous 'Who Killed Cock Robin': 'Who caught his blood? | I, said the fish, | With my little dish, | I caught his blood.'

252 *the Universal Aunts.* An employment agency in London.

P.Gs. Paying guests.

Will you go to the Palace. Ida Baker had experience in nursing, and may have intended getting work at the clinic in Montana mentioned on p. 309, under 228.

253 *Your As.* The Aylesburys, sisters Ida Baker had met in Sierre, who delivered a parcel to KM in Paris.

254 *the Langham.* The Langham Hotel, Langham Place, where KM's father usually stayed.

255 *William ... Reggie.* The devoted but mocked husband in 'Marriage à la Mode', and the young couple in 'Mr and Mrs Dove', both stories in *The Garden Party*.

257 *Millin.* KM had reviewed Sarah Gertrude Millin's novel *The Dark River* in the *Athenaeum*, 20 Feb. 1920, praising it as a 'sudden view of a country and of an experience'. They had first exchanged letters at that time.

Adam's Rest. Millin's third novel, published in 1922.

258 *Olive Schreiner.* Olive Schreiner (1855–1920) went from South Africa to England in 1881, and as 'Ralph Iron' published the most famous of her books, *The Story of an African Farm*, in 1883.

260 *Arnoldo.* Arnold Gibbons, a young friend of Richard Murry's who later became an engineer, but at that time was trying his hand at short stories.

Einstein. Albert Einstein (1879–1955) had received the Nobel Prize for physics in 1921, for his work on light quanta.

261 *rather a fat woman wading in a stream in the National Gallery.* KM seems to be thinking of 'Woman Bathing', a painting not by Rubens but by Rembrandt.

262 *my enthusiasm was too much for the Furies.* On 23 Apr. KM had written

optimistically to Elizabeth about her progress, and concluded: 'I still hope to be well by May. But it only wakens the Furies to speak of one's health until one is out of their reach.'

264 *Randogne-sur-Sierre*. The Hôtel d'Angleterre stood more or less halfway between the adjacent villages of Montana and Randogne, hence KM's variant addresses.

265 *'Fourfooted creatures created He them'*. KM's misquotation of Genesis 1: 24–5, perhaps crossed with Romans 1: 23.

Chateau Belle Vue. After a disagreement with Murry at the end of June KM and Ida Baker moved to another hotel, where Dorothy Brett came to stay with her in early July.

Aaron's Rod. D. H. Lawrence's most recently published novel.

266 *'that ye shall find'*. Luke 11: 10.

267 *Farewell*. This letter was not sent immediately to Murry, but left for him at her bank where he received it after her death.

268 *6 Pond Street*. During her last visit to London KM stayed with her friend Dorothy Brett.

269 *lunching with Orage*. A. R. Orage encouraged her interest in Gurdjieff, and himself joined the Institute at Fontainebleau.

Selsfield. Selsfield House, East Grinstead, where Murry was staying with his friend Vivian Locke-Ellis, a minor poet.

270 *the Lit. Sup. with your review*. Murry reviewed Chekhov's *Love, and Other Stories*, translated by Constance Garnett, in the *Times Literary Supplement*, 19 Oct. 1922.

271 *Suttons*. A firm of garden suppliers in Reading.

bad taste. Writing to his sister Marie from Berlin on 8 June 1904, Chekhov observed: 'Fearfully bad taste. . . . I have not seen one beautiful woman, nor one who was not trimmed with some kind of absurd braid.' (*Letters of Anton Tchehov to his Family and Friends*, translated by Constance Garnett, 1920.)

274 *Doctor Young*. The psychiatrist James Young recalled this time in 'An Experiment at Fontainebleau', *New Adelphi*, Sep. 1927.

Jeanne's wedding. KM's youngest sister had recently married Captain Charles Renshaw in London.

MacGavin. A Beauchamp relative and surgeon, Laurie MacGavin.

277 *Mr Salzmann*. Alexander de Salzmann, painter and stage-designer, who, with his wife Jeanne, taught eurhythmics at the Institute.

278 *Heals*. A large department store in Tottenham Court Road.

279 *Down-a-Down Derry*. 'A Book of Fairy Poems' by Walter de la Mare, with illustrations by Dorothy P. Lathrop (1922).

281 *Madame Ovstrovsky*. The Polish Countess Ostrovsky, Gurdjieff's wife.

Charles. Charles Chaplin, one of the Murrys' cats.

282 *I had no idea Rothenstein was that kind of artist.* A drawing William Rothenstein (1873–1945) used in his *Contemporary Portraits* (1923).

284 *all going to St. Paul's.* The Anglican Cathedral in Wellington.

the *Vie Heureuse French Literary Prize.* The Femina–Vie Heureuse prize already had been awarded on 13 Dec. to Jacques de Lacretelle's *Silbermann.*

285 *My new book.* KM had not yet completed *The Doves' Nest, and Other Stories.* When Murry published the volume in 1923 it contained only six completed and fifteen unfinished stories.

INDEX

Text subjects which are cued to endnotes are indexed by text page numbers only.

Ainger, William 85, 86
alcohol 27
Allen, Maud 16, 102, 290, 298
Alpers, Antony xii, xiii
Anrep, Boris 246
art/artists, discussion of 197–8, 222, 265–6, 268
Arts and Letters 173
Ashford, Daisy 152, 303
Asquith, Margot 19
Athenaeum xxiii, 145, 150, 155, 167, 173, 178, 183, 190, 193, 300, 302, 303, 305, 307
Atherton, Mrs Thomas (Mrs Arthur Eliot) 124
Austen, Jane 147
Aylesbury sisters 253–4

Bagnold, Enid 108
Baker, Ida Constance ('L. M.') xi, xxi, xxii, xxiii, xxv, 4–5, 11, 14, 22, 32, 71, 73, 75–8, 81, 82, 84, 98, 104, 105, 115, 127–8, 130–6, 138, 139, 142, 143, 146, 150–3, 156, 163–4, 167, 177, 178, 180, 210, 223, 226, 240, 242, 244–5, 256, 273, 274
   letters to 20–1, 23–4, 85–7, 111–12, 202–4, 206–8, 219–20, 223–4, 227–8, 250–4, 259, 280–1
battleship, launching of 18–19
Baudelaire, Charles 183
Beauchamp, Annie Burnell xxv, 112–13, 153–4, 155–6, 284, 299
   letter to 7–9
Beauchamp, Charlotte Mary ('Chaddie') xxv, 11, 13, 87, 136, 137, 232, 275, 279, 285
Beauchamp, Connie xxv, 148, 149, 167, 231
Beauchamp, Harold xi, xxv–xxvi, 4, 11, 41, 125–6, 130, 132, 134–5, 141, 146, 148–50, 185, 229, 265, 287, 309
   letters to 231–2, 283–5
Beauchamp, Jeanne Worthington xxvi, 136, 232, 274, 279, 285
   letter to 229

Beauchamp, Leslie Heron ('Chummie') xxvi, 11, 38, 95–6, 229, 284
   letter to 36–7
Beauchamp, Lou 204
Beauchamp, Louie 1
Beauchamp, Ralph 14
Beauchamp, Sydney 130, 301
Beauchamp, Vera Margaret xxvi, 1
   letter to 12–15
Beerbohm, Max 55, 294
Bell, Clive 126, 228, 248, 301
Bell, James Mackintosh ('Mac') xxvi, 13, 289
Bell, Vanessa 55
Benson, E. F. 13
Benson, Stella 132
Bibesco, Elizabeth, Princess 191, 207, 243, 307, 310; letter to 208
Billing, Noel Pemberton 102, 298
Blanchot, Gustave (Gus Bofa) 104, 298
Bobone, Dr 139, 141–2, 146
Bodley, Henry 7, 288
Borrow, George 14
Bouchage, Dr A. 189, 207
Boulestin, X. Marcel 21, 293
Bowden, George xxi, xxvi, 290
Brady, Edward James xxvi, 6
Brett, Hon. Dorothy xi, xxvi, 106, 114, 122, 123, 156, 178, 179, 215–16, 219, 283
   letters to 59–60, 89–91, 109–10, 112–13, 201–2, 220–3, 224–7, 232–4, 235–7, 245–8, 254–6
Broadhead, W. Smithson 223, 228
Brotherhood Church 59, 295

Campbell, Beatrice (Lady Glenavy) xxvi–xxvii; letter to 51–2
Campbell, Henry Gordon (Lord Glenavy) xxvii, 22, 51, 52
Carco, Francis xxvii, 23, 27, 72, 291, 292
Carson, Sir Edward 183, 306
cats 118–19, 120, 122, 142, 148, 206–7, 227, 262, 264
Cézanne, Paul 225
Chaucer, Geoffrey 214

Chekhov, Anton 105, 118, 161, 164, 216, 243, 270, 271, 304, 307, 312
children 82–3, 222–3, 224–5
Christmas 44–6, 279, 280–1, 284
clothes 12–13, 219–20, 235
Colette Willy 41, 293
Corelli, Marie 11
Costello, Dr Christopher ('Pagello') 90, 99, 102, 104
cows 264–5
craft, concept of 194–5
Curzon, George, Marquess 55, 294

Dahlerup, Marie 163
Daily Chronicle 223
de la Mare, Walter 180, 237, 247, 279
Dial 237, 310
doctors 73, 78, 86, 90, 117, 125, 139, 141–2, 144, 146, 165–6, 189, 204, 207, 208, 237–8, 239, 244, 255
dogs 167
dolls 45, 65, 77, 85, 182
Donne, John 244, 310
Dostoevsky, Fyodor 57, 58, 105, 108, 140, 142, 145, 212
Douglas, Lord Alfred 102, 298
Dowson, Ernest 4, 287
dreams 10, 20, 38–9, 70, 95–6, 184–5
Drey, Anne Estelle xxvii, 43, 89, 95, 100, 103
    letters to 116–18, 192–4, 211–13
Drey, O. Raymond 89, 193
Drummond, Stella 85, 297
Duhamel, Georges 55, 294
Dyer, Margaret Isabella 6, 38–9
Dyer, Sidney 229

Eckermann, Johann 237, 239
Edwards, Tristyan 103, 298
Einstein, Albert 260
Eliot, T. S. 54–5, 140, 174, 246–7
Eliot, Vivienne 174
'Elizabeth' (Mary Annette Beauchamp) xxvii, 186, 218, 221, 237, 243, 251, 259, 312
    letters to 243–5, 262–3
Elvery, Marjory 51
English Review 112

Farbman, Michael 37, 292
fear, concept of 181
feminism 22

Fergusson, John Duncan xxvii, 85, 87, 89, 90, 104
    letter to 61–3
Figli, Dr 212
First World War 26, 33, 38, 50, 55, 61–3, 68, 70, 79, 80–1, 84, 91–2, 124, 147, 297
flowers 121, 123, 169, 186–7, 247, 259
food 13, 47, 176, 210, 212
Forster, E. M. 173
Foster, Dr 164
France 23–4, 25–36, 38, 39–40, 42, 43–6, 47, 61–4, 65–6, 67–8, 74, 77–84, 165, 175–7, 178–9, 193
France, Anatole 176
friendship 112, 115, 125, 224, 228, 236, 251, 277
Fry, Roger 54–5, 126, 301
Fullerton, Jinnie xxv, 148, 149, 165, 167, 187, 188, 231

Galsworthy, John xxvii, 309
    letter to 230–1
Geoffroi, Régine 77, 296
George, W. L. 51, 294
Gerhardi, William xxviii
    letter to 249–50
Gertler, Mark 72, 113–14, 179, 184, 215, 246, 306
Gibbons, Arnold 260, 311
Gifford, Grace 51, 294
Gifford, Sylvia 10
Gissing, George 96, 114, 297
God, concept of 146, 214
Goethe, Johann Wolfgang von 237
Goodyear, Frederick xxviii, 72, 293
    letter to 46–8
Graves, Robert 54–5
Greek statues 260–1
Guevara, Alvaro ('Chili') 60, 295
Gurdjieff, George Ivanovich x, xi–xii, xxiii, xxviii, 274, 275, 277, 279, 280, 283

Hamilton, Mary Agnes 114, 250, 300
Hamnett, Nina 122
Hardy, Thomas 100–1
Harris, Frank 39, 108, 293
Harrison, Austin 96, 297
Hastings, Beatrice xxviii, 26–7, 184, 291
honesty, concept of 159–60
hotels 90, 94, 167–8, 209, 210, 247
houses 136–7, 154, 187–8, 203, 227

housework 22, 226
Hudson, Dr 228
Hutchinson, Mary 54–5
Hutchinson, St John 54, 55
Huxley, Aldous 173, 305
Huxley, Julian 114, 300

Institute for the Harmonious Development of Man, *see* Prieuré, Le
Ireland 51, 183
Italy 127–8, 130, 131, 133, 135, 140, 162

Jacob, Max 27
James, Henry 46
jealousy 43, 131–2
John, Augustus 57–8, 295
Jones, Alice 140

Kay, Alexander 30, 167, 292
Keats, John 105, 299
Kenepuru Sound 229, 309
Kipling, Rudyard 26
Knipper, Olga 161
Koteliansky, Samuel Solomonovitch xi, xii, xxviii, 31, 93, 109, 197, 204, 227, 236, 247
    letters to 25, 34–6, 37–8, 48–50, 118–19, 161–2, 200, 234–5, 237–8, 264–7, 272–3

Lamb, Charles 119, 300
Lawrence, D. H. vii–viii, xi, xxii, xxix, 24, 25, 43, 48–50, 73, 100, 114, 115, 119, 136, 156, 161, 172, 218, 222, 234–5, 247, 265, 266, 268, 300, 305, 308
Lawrence, Frieda xxix, 28, 48–50, 70, 113–14, 115, 119, 161, 234, 300
    letter to 24
Lloyd-George, David 173, 183
Lloyd-George, Megan 183
Locke-Ellis, Vivian 271
London Mercury 199, 213, 229, 230
Looe 88–90, 93–4, 103
Low, Barbara 36

Macaulay, Rose 185, 310
MacGavin, Laurie 274
Mackenzie, Kitty 20
MacSwiney, Terence, Mayor of Cork 183, 306
Maeterlinck, Maurice 2–3

maids/household helps 64, 66, 74–6, 127, 130, 131, 134, 169, 176, 179, 192–3, 204
Manet, Edouard 222
Manoukhin, Ivan xxix, 234, 237–8, 239, 243, 244, 255, 310
Mansfield, Katherine:
    Aloe, The 28–9
    and cats 118–19, 120, 122, 142, 148, 206–7, 227, 262, 264
    and dolls 45, 65, 77, 85, 182
    and jealousy 43, 131–2
    and maids/household helps 64, 66, 74–6, 127, 130, 131, 134, 169, 176, 179, 192–3, 204
    and music 1, 4, 52, 287
    at Le Prieuré xi–xii, 272–85
    'At the Bay' 225–6, 230, 237, 308
    'Bliss' 112
    'Canary', The' 248
    'Carnation' 101
    character of vii–ix
    'Daughters of the Late Colonel, The' 199, 213
    'Doll's House, The' 237
    dreams of 10, 20, 38–9, 70, 95–6, 184–5
    'Fly, The' 248
    Garden Party, The xxiii, 246, 250, 255, 311
    girlhood friendships of 1–6, 10–11
    health of xi–xii, 25, 40–1, 42, 72–3, 78, 85, 86, 88, 90, 97, 105, 106, 111, 116, 119, 125, 130, 139, 141, 142, 143, 145–6, 155, 175, 177, 181, 189, 202, 204, 207, 211–12, 214, 220, 228, 234, 235–6, 239, 244, 255, 262
    'Ideal Family, An' 216–17
    'In the Botanical Gardens' 6
    '*Je ne parle pas français*' 155
    love affairs of xxi, 15–20
    'Miss Brill' 195
    money problems of 22, 23, 29–30, 66, 127–8, 131, 158–9, 160, 167, 170–1, 172, 189, 203–4, 231–2
    'New Husband, The' 156–7
    Prelude xxii, 59, 60, 107, 109, 225, 292, 295, 299
    relationship with brother 11, 36–7, 38
    relationship with father xi, 4, 11, 21, 125–6, 130, 132, 134–5, 141, 148–50, 231–2, 283–5

Mansfield, Katherine (*cont.*)
  relationship with Ida Baker ('L. M.')
    xi, 11, 20–1, 23–4, 32, 73, 84, 98,
    111–12, 115, 127–8, 133, 135–6,
    138, 146, 151–2, 153, 163–4, 180,
    202–4, 206–8, 219–20, 223–4, 226,
    227–8, 244–5, 250–4, 256, 259, 274,
    280–1
  relationship with mother 7–9, 112–13
  relationship with Murry ix–x, xi, xxi–
    xxii, xxiii, 21–3, 25–33, 38–46, 58,
    63–84, 88–9, 91–3, 95–106, 121,
    126, 127–60, 162–72, 175–91, 193,
    203–4, 207, 209–11, 213–14, 218,
    226–7, 238–44, 251–2, 255–6, 262,
    267, 269–71, 273–80, 282–3, 304,
    307
  relationship with sisters 12–15, 229
  verse by 116–17, 156–7
  views on art/artists 197–8, 222, 265–
    6, 268
  views on craft 194–5
  views on fear 181
  views on friendship 112, 115, 125,
    224, 228, 236, 251, 277
  views on God 146, 214
  views on housework 22, 226
  views on love 16, 42–3, 60, 97, 98,
    159, 171–2, 214, 222
  views on painting 194–5, 197–8, 222,
    224–5, 233, 246, 261
  views on parental influence 201
  'Voyage, The' 246, 249
  writing experiences of 25, 28–9, 32,
    59, 60, 69–70, 71–2, 133, 138, 144,
    189, 195, 218–19, 225–6, 248
Maoris 7–9
March, Earl of 124, 301
Marseilles 37–8, 61–2, 77–9
Massingham, Henry William 101, 173
Maufe, Gladys Prudence 93
Mayo, Sam 183, 306
Menton 149, 165–6, 167–8, 175–7, 178–
  9, 182, 186–8, 193
Millay, Edna St Vincent 299
Millin, Sarah Gertrude xi, xxix, 311
  letter to 257–9
Milne, Herbert 178, 305
Modigliani, Amedeo 27
money problems 22, 23, 29–30, 66,
  127–8, 131, 158–9, 160, 167, 170–1,
  172, 189, 203–4, 231–2
Montreux 209, 210–11, 215

Moore, George 55, 294
Morrell, Lady Ottoline xi, xxii, xxix,
  76, 90–1, 101, 151, 158, 185, 299,
  308
  letters to 54–5, 56–8, 87–8, 93–4,
    106–7, 113–16, 121–6, 214–19
Morrell, Philip xxix, 90–1, 107, 108,
  299, 308
Morris, Margaret 57
Morris, William 14
Moult, Thomas 129
Murray, Elsie 234
Murry, Emily (mother) 84, 269, 297
Murry, John (father) 269
Murry, John Middleton ix–x, xi, xxi–
  xxiii, xxix–xxx, 50, 56, 107–8, 109–
  10, 115, 117, 121, 126, 193, 202,
  203–4, 206, 213, 216, 218, 221,
  226–7, 243–4, 249, 251–2, 255–6,
  260, 261, 262, 263, 284, 298, 304,
  307
  letters to 21–3, 25–33, 38–46, 58, 63–
    84, 88–9, 91–3, 95–106, 127–60,
    162–72, 175–91, 209–11, 213–14,
    238–43, 267, 269–71, 273–80, 282–
    3
Murry, Richard (Arthur) xi, xxx, 76,
  84, 142, 145, 146, 170, 252
  letters to 194–8, 260–2
music 1, 4, 52, 287

Nation, The 107, 110, 248
Nelson, Geoffrey 123
Nevinson, Henry Woodd 163
New Witness 103
New Zealand 7–9, 229, 257
Newland-Pedley, F. 40–1
Noble, Bill 61, 110

Orage, A. R. xxviii, 32, 269, 292, 312
Orpen, William 51, 294
Ostrovsky, Countess 281
Owen, Margaret 57
Owl, The 122, 301

painting 194–5, 197–8, 222, 224–5, 233,
  246, 261
Palliser, Charles 102
Palmer, Clara 15
parental influence 201
Paris 25–36, 80, 82–4, 239–40, 241,
  244–5, 255, 258
Parker, Millie 7, 288

Pater, Walter viii
Payne, Sylvia xxx
   letters to 1–6, 10–11
Peace Treaty 124, 301
Polperro 103
Porter (dentist) 145
Prieuré, Le xi–xii, xxiii, xxviii, 272–85

Rangitaiki 9
Renoir, Pierre Auguste 222
Renshaw, Capt. Charles xxvi, 274, 285
Rey, Ernestine 221
Rice, Anne 90, 93
Rippmann, Walter 2, 35, 287
Ross, Robert 54–5, 113
Rothenstein, William 282
Rouse, Gwen 3
Rousseau, Jean Jacques 52, 294
Rubens, Peter Paul 261
Russell, Elizabeth, see 'Elizabeth' (Mary Annette Beauchamp)
Russell, Hon. Bertrand xxii, xxx, 299
   letters to 53–4
Rutter, Frank 170
Ryder, Dan 39

Salzmann, Alexander de 277, 312
Sand, George 79, 90
Sands, Ethel 246, 311
Santayana, George 218, 308
Sassoon, Siegfried 108, 109, 110, 299
Schiff, Sydney xi, xxx
   letters to 173–5, 268–9
Schiff, Violet xi, xxx, 268
   letters to 173–5
Schreiner, Olive 258, 311
Scott, Margaret xii
Sealey, Fanny 12, 289
Secker, Martin 21, 218, 308
Shakespeare, William 39, 67, 195, 219, 240–1
Shelley, Percy Bysshe 49, 63
Sherard, Robert Harborough 4
Sierre 217–18
Signature 58, 295
Simpson-Hayward, G. H. 13, 289
Sinclair, May 122
Sinn Fein 51, 183, 293
Slatkovsky, R. S. 200
Sobieniowski, Floryan 31, 292
Sorapure, Dr Victor 117, 139, 143, 179, 193, 207
Spahlinger, Dr Henry 208

Spenser, Edmund 245
Sphere 218, 223, 308
Squire, John Collings 51, 190
Stendhal 29, 177, 181
Stevenson, Robert Louis 5
Strachey, Lytton 108, 216
strikes 165, 170
Sullivan, John William Navin xxx, 76, 278, 283
Sullivan, Sylvia 201
Sundays 51–2
surrender, idea of 186
Swanwick Society 5
Swinburne, Algernon 14
Switzerland 209–11, 212–13, 215, 217–18, 220–1, 233, 240, 261, 263, 264–5

Tarawera 8
Tchekhov, Anton, see Chekhov, Anton
Te Pohue 7
Time and Tide 250
Times Literary Supplement 135, 138, 155, 270
Tomlinson, Henry Major 173, 236
Trapp, Eliza 15
travelling 61–2
Trinder, Belle 14, 73, 87, 229
Trinder, Harry 14
Trollope, Anthony 260
Trowell, Garnet xxi, xxxi
   letters to 15–20
Trowell, Thomas 1, 2, 287
Tudge, Ethel 10
Turgenev, Ivan 51, 114, 300

unemployment 18, 290
Universal Aunts agency 252

Van Gogh, Vincent 233
Verlaine, Paul 26
Vince, Thomas 137
Vintras, Louis 4

Waipunga Falls 9
Walpole, Hugh 103, 178
Waterlow, Helen 131–2
Waterlow, Sydney xi, xxxi, 129, 140, 153, 154, 166, 170
   letters to 198–9, 204–6
Watts-Dunton, Theodore 14, 290
Wells, H. G. 47, 227, 255
Weyman, Stanley 132

Wilde, Oscar viii, 20, 184–5, 290
Wilensky, Marjory 10
Williams, Gladys 2, 287
Wood, Henry 14
Woolf, Leonard xxxi, 152, 216
Woolf, Virginia ix, xxii, xxxi, 103, 133, 135, 147, 151, 152, 216, 222, 300
    letters to 55–6, 107–8, 119–21

Wordsworth, Dorothy 88, 91, 96, 132, 302
Wordsworth, William 78, 150

Yeats, W. B. 51
Young, James 274, 312

Index compiled by Peva Keane